ROUTLEDGE LIBRARY EDITIONS: ETHNOSCAPES

Volume 7

PLACEMAKING

PLACEMAKING

Production of Built Environment in Two Cultures

DAVID STEA AND METE TURAN

with a Foreword by
ANTHONY KING

LONDON AND NEW YORK

First published in 1993 by Avebury (Ashgate Publishing Limited)

This edition first published in 2025
by Routledge
4 Park Square, Milton Park, Abingdon, Oxon OX14 4RN

and by Routledge
605 Third Avenue, New York, NY 10158

Routledge is an imprint of the Taylor & Francis Group, an informa business

© 1993 David Stea and Mete Turan

All rights reserved. No part of this book may be reprinted or reproduced or utilised in any form or by any electronic, mechanical, or other means, now known or hereafter invented, including photocopying and recording, or in any information storage or retrieval system, without permission in writing from the publishers.

Trademark notice: Product or corporate names may be trademarks or registered trademarks, and are used only for identification and explanation without intent to infringe.

British Library Cataloguing in Publication Data
A catalogue record for this book is available from the British Library

ISBN: 978-1-032-86590-4 (Set)
ISBN: 978-1-032-86434-1 (Volume 7) (hbk)
ISBN: 978-1-032-86440-2 (Volume 7) (pbk)
ISBN: 978-1-003-52754-1 (Volume 7) (ebk)

DOI: 10.4324/9781003527541

Publisher's Note
The publisher has gone to great lengths to ensure the quality of this reprint but points out that some imperfections in the original copies may be apparent.

Disclaimer
The publisher has made every effort to trace copyright holders and would welcome correspondence from those they have been unable to trace.

New Series Introduction to
RLE: Ethnoscapes

The neologism *Ethnoscapes*[1] was created by David Canter and David Stea in 1987 when they happened both to be in Yogjakarta at the same time. They wanted a term to cover the rapidly emerging multidisciplinary field of research into many aspects of how individuals, groups and cultures interact and transact with their surroundings. It was derived as follows:

Ethno (combining form) indicating race, people or culture.

Scape (suffix-forming nouns) indicating a scene or view of something.

Ethnoscapes (plural noun) Scholarly and/or scientific explorations of the relationships people and their activities, have with the places they create and/or inhabit; historical, psychological, anthropological, sociological, and related disciplines that study the experiences of places, attitudes towards them, or the processes of shaping, managing, or designing them. The term was subsequently used to provide an umbrella for a series of books. These cover topics that are so multidisciplinary that they do not sit comfortably in any of the constrained silos of academic and scholarly research. As indicated on the opening page of the first book in the series, many disciplines "have developed marauding sub-groups who move freely across each others' borders, carrying ideas almost like contraband, without declaring that they have crossed any disciplinary boundaries."

They include domains labelled as Behavioural or Perceptual Geography, Environmental/Architectural Psychology, Urban History, Social Ecology, Behavioural Archaeology, Urban Planning, Behavioural Architecture, and Landscape Architecture. There are also many other areas of research and practice that, whilst not being overtly psychological, social, or cultural, do explore and act on the built and natural environment in a way that recognises the importance of the human transactions with those settings. These professions include interior and product design, comparative linguistics, and even aspects of criminology and mental health providers.

Like all such implicit and explicit transactions between different domains, a community of interest and support has emerged in which those who cross the boundaries often find they have more in common with other transgressors than with their mother disciplines. This has given rise to common means and forms of communication, with a shared understanding of the issues and approaches that are of value. Although, of course, these are not always understood in the same way by all those involved,

The *Ethnoscapes* series of books provides a forum for these multifarious, cross-disciplinary, determinedly international, studies and practices. Each of the books takes on board one or more of the environmental challenges that that individuals, societies and cultures are facing. Emphasising a social perspective, rather than the dominant 'hard' science viewpoints embedded in physical, geological and climate changes.

It may now be regarded as rather prescient that it was over three decades ago that the need and importance was recognised of bringing together the many strands of environmental social research and practice. But there is no doubt that there were academics and professionals exploring Ethnoscape topics, going back to the 1960s, often in isolation and with little recognition, that are today front-page, and podcast, news. The challenges in the environmental social sciences that Ethnoscapes explores are just as pertinent now as they were when initially identified.

The series, in essence, deals with four challenges the environmental social sciences embrace.

> 1. Addressing "the awareness of governments and public alike of the problems of environmental degradation and pollution."

This includes the challenge of providing acceptable housing and related environmental conditions that also encompassed the support for environmental and related cultural heritage. It also requires detailed consideration of the assessment and evaluation of designs and design proposals as well as background research on policy related issues.

> 2. Developing ways of conceptualising human interactions with the physical surroundings.

This may seem somewhat abstract but has practical implications. The dominant view that people are passively controlled by their surroundings supports a paternalistic, management of what it is assumed people need. That ignores the active way in which people make sense of their environment, drawing on cultural and historical influences. This recognises the importance of user participation in decisions about built and natural settings. That, in turn, requires a much richer understanding of how people interact with where they are or want to be.

3. A much wider range of ways of exploring people's transactions with the environment is needed to contribute to policy and practice as well as developing richer insights into human experiences.

The stock in trade of surveys, or the inevitably artificial laboratory-based experiments, whilst of value for some explorations, need to be augmented by methodologies that enrich an understanding of what the experiences are of being in, acting on, and developing places. They need to connect not just with the endeavours of individuals but also with how cultures and societies express these transactions.

4. Finding ways to enable practitioners and researchers to express their own encounters with the contexts they are influencing or studying.

Much of the research that is carried out in what are curiously called 'Ivory Towers', even when it is studying the big wide world, allows the pretence of distancing from the direct experiences of the issues being studied. Yet the challenges of moving across disciplinary boundaries are as much personal challenges of finding new ways of thinking, communicating, and acting, as an academic demand to develop more effective intellectual systems. The Ethnoscapes series recognises the value of exploring these challenges by hosting a variety of formats. Many of these go beyond the staid and limited formulations that academic discourse assumes to be the norms.

The Ethnoscapes series brings together a vibrant mix of cutting-edge explorations, from all over the world, of human transactions with the built and natural environments. This includes, for example, consideration of vernacular architecture that contrasts with the architecture and urbanism of the colonial enterprise, the meaning of home, aesthetics, well-being and health, and consideration of how environmental psychology has become 'green'. All of these topics, and more, provide an exciting basis for dealing with current challenges in the environmental social sciences.

Note

[1] Not to be confused by the term *Ethnoscape* later concocted by Arun Appadurai in 1990, to refer to **human migration**, the flow of people across boundaries. This includes migrants, refugees, exiles, and tourists, among other moving individuals and groups, all of whom appear to affect the politics of (and between) nations to a considerable degree. Ignorant of the lexicographical origins of the term 'scape' he rather confusingly added it to many ideas of flow, such as the flow of technology – technoscapes and the flow of ideas ideoscapes. Appadurai, A. (1990). "Disjuncture and difference in the global cultural economy." *Theory, Culture and Society* 7(2–3): 295–310.

Routledge Library Editions: Ethnoscapes

1. *Environmental Perspectives* David Canter, Martin Krampen & David Stea (Eds) (1988) ISBN 978-1-032-81616-6

2. *Environmental Policy, Assessment, and Communication* David Canter, Martin Krampen & David Stea (Eds) (1988) ISBN 978-1-032-81635-7

3. *New Directions in Environmental Participation* David Canter, Martin Krampen & David Stea (Eds) (1988) ISBN 978-1-032-81646-3

4. *Vernacular Architecture: Paradigms of Environmental Response* Mete Turan (Ed.) (1990) ISBN 978-1-032-82023-1

5. *Forms of Dominance: On the Architecture and Urbanism of the Colonial Enterprise* Nezar AlSayyad (Ed.) (1992) ISBN 978-1-032-84164-9

6. *The Meaning and Use of Housing: International Perspectives, Approaches and Their Applications* Ernesto G. Arias (Ed.) (1993) ISBN 978-1-032-84781-8

7. *Placemaking: Production of Built Environment in Two Cultures* David Stea & Mete Turan (1993) ISBN 978-1-032-86434-1

8. *Environmental Psychology in Europe: From Architectural Psychology to Green Psychology* Enric Pol (1993) ISBN 978-1-032-83324-8

9. *Housing: Design, Research, Education* Marjorie Bulos & Necdet Teymur (Eds) (1993) ISBN 978-1-032-86388-7

10. *Architecture, Ritual Practice and Co-determination in the Swedish Office* Dennis Doxtater (1994) ISBN 978-1-032-81774-3

11. *On the Aesthetics of Architecture: A Psychological Approach to the Structure and the Order of Perceived Architectural Space* Ralf Weber (1995) ISBN 978-1-032-82034-7

12. *The Home: Words, Interpretations, Meanings and Environments* by David N. Benjamin (Ed.) (1995) ISBN 978-1-032-86411-2

13. *Tradition, Location and Community: Place-making and Development* Adenrele Awotona & Necdet Teymur (Eds) (1997) ISBN 978-1-032-84608-8

14. *Aesthetics, Well-being and Health: Essays within Architecture and Environmental Aesthetics* Birgit Cold (Ed.) (2001) ISBN 978-1-032-86577-5

Other Ethnoscapes series titles also available:

Integrating Programming, Evaluation and Participation in Design: A Theory Z Approach Henry Sanoff (1992) HBK 978-1-138-20338-9; EBK 978-1-315-47173-0; PBK 978-1-138-20339-6

Directions in Person-Environment Research and Practice Jack Nasar & Wolfgang F. E. Preiser (Eds) (1999) HBK 978-1-138-68674-8; EBK 978-1-315-54255-3; PBK 978-1-138-68677-9

Psychological Theories for Environmental Issues Mirilia Bonnes, Terence Lee & Marino Bonaiuto (Eds) (2003) HBK 978-0-75461-888-1; EBK 978-1-315-24572-0; PBK 978-1-138-27742-7

Housing Space and Quality of Life David L. Uzzell, Ricardo Garcia Mira, J. Eulogio Real & Joe Romay (Eds) (2005) HBK 978-0-81538-952-1; EBK 978-1-351-15636-3; PBK 978-1-138-35596-5

Doing Things with Things: The Design and Use of Everyday Objects Alan Costall & Ole Dreier (Eds) (2006) HBK 978-0-75464-656-3; EBK 978-1-315-57792-0; PBK 978-1-138-25314-8

Rethinking the Meaning of Place: Conceiving Place in Architecture-Urbanism Lineu Castello (2010) HBK 978-0-75467-814-4; EBK 978-1-315-60616-3; PBK 978-1-138-25745-0

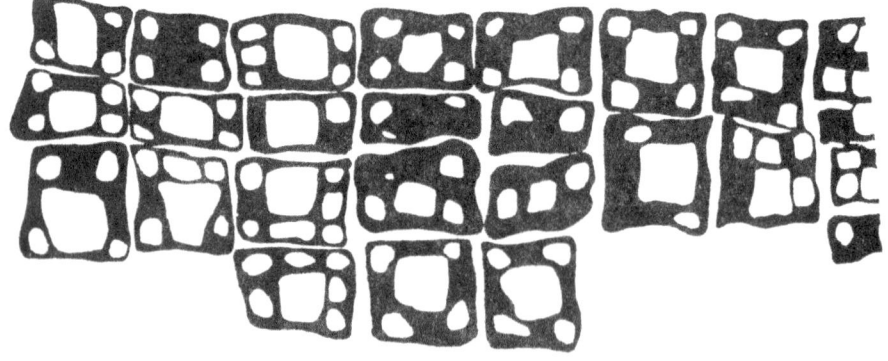

PLACEMAKING

for
Jeremy Anderson and **Tarik Okyay**
who, with their deep concern
for human-environment relations, were true "ethnoscapers"
and
to
Nilgun and Silvia
for their unflagging patience and support

Placemaking

Production of built environment in two cultures

DAVID STEA
METE TURAN

with a Foreword by
ANTHONY KING

Avebury

Aldershot · Brookfield USA · Hong Kong · Singapore · Sydney

© David Stea and Mete Turan 1993

All rights reserved. No part of this publication may be reproduced, stored in a retrieval system, or transmitted in any form or by any means, electronic, mechanical, photocopying, recording or otherwise without the prior permission of the publisher.

Published by
Avebury
Ashgate Publishing Limited
Gower House
Croft Road
Aldershot
Hants GU11 3HR
England

Ashgate Publishing Company
Old Post Road
Brookfield
Vermont 05036
USA

A CIP catalogue record for this book is available from the British Library.

ISBN 1 85628 460 3

Printed in Great Britain by
Ipswich Book Co. Ltd., Ipswich, Suffolk

Contents

Foreword by Anthony King — vii
Preface — ix
Acknowledgments — xi
List of Illustrations — xiii
Introduction: A Critical Overview — 1

Chapter One
Breaking Ground for Placemaking — 6
On the nature of placemaking — 10
On placemaking in dialectical perspective — 15
On the meaning of production — 17
Notes on the organization of the volume — 24

Chapter Two
Sheltering Landscapes and Vicarious Housing — 28
Setting the context — 29
Vicissitudes of the landscapes — 34
Crossroads of many peoples — 38
Comparative context — 50

Chapter Three
From Shelter to Settlement — 69
From subsistence to surplus — 70
Caves and cavates — 72
Places for all seasons — 79
Crossroads: A comparison — 96

Chapter Four
Urbanization in the Neolithic 101
A town among volcanoes 102
Anasazi urban systems 114
Anatolian fortified cities 126
Anasazi unfortified cities and their fortified southern neighbors 140
Retrospect and prospect 142

Chapter Five
Cliff Hangers and Troglodytes 164
Carving and building 165
Building down, building up, moving out 189
Research biases and vexing questions 199
Moving out: Anasazi abandonments 203
Complexity, hierarchy and placemaking 215
Bridging the gap 219

Chapter Six
Beyond Impressions: Structuring an Explanation 259
Establishing the framework 260
A typology of relationships in placemaking 262

Chapter Seven
Understanding Placemaking: The Anatolians and the Anasazi 277
Recapitulation 277
Reconstitution 280

Chapter Eight
Reconstruction: Toward New Foundations 302
A critique of inquiry concerning placemaking 305
Recapitulation 310
Reconstruction 312

Appendix One
Anasazi Abandonments and the "Mesoamerican Connection" 315

Appendix Two
Transitions in Modes of Production: Alternative Models of Social Change 321

Bibliography 324
Index 363

Foreword

By Anthony King

One of the many ironies and contradictions of contemporary scientific work, indeed, intellectual work in general, must be that, whereas knowledge continuously accumulates in different areas of disciplinary inquiry, knowledge put to an impressive range of uses in modern life, there has simultaneously been an immense fragmentation of understanding. Nowhere is this more apparent than in those myriad disciplines whose practitioners take it upon themselves to provide methodologically sound and theoretically viable explanations for the production, transformation, and social meaning of environments; and especially the way in which these both result from and help to constitute all forms of economic, social, cultural, and political life.

As the two authors of this innovative study refer to some of these problems in the early pages of this book, I shall not repeat them here. Nevertheless, the assumption, which both they and I share—that (to put it in the simplest terms) environments are socially produced—has established common ground between us.

More that this, however, it is their creative application of other theoretical tools which each of us has found, quite independently, to be of value in offering explanations for the production and transformation, over time, of particular environments and building forms.

The task to which Mete Turan and David Stea set themselves in this book, however, is a formidable one. They examine what they innovatively term placemaking, "the conception and realization of the built environment," and its relation to cultural change in two locations spatially separated by half the globe and, in terms of time, by millennia. In comparing settlement systems in two geologically similar yet culturally distinct places, they address the question of how and why people build and live the way they do. And as these are both prehistoric, preliterate societies—the one in the Cappadocian region of Anatolian Turkey flourishing some 8000 years ago, the other on the Pajarito Plateau of northern New Mexico in the American Southwest in more recent, though preconquest times—the authors are obliged to rely on a combination of current social theory (including recent work in urban political economy), the insights of archaeology, culture and environmental studies, and their own ingenuity.

In this respect, their flexible interpretation of basic Marxist concepts inherent in the mode of production paradigm, (which they usefully develop in Chapter One, both for their own, as well as for others' use), proves as valuable for interpreting their work as I myself have found it in the past, even without the more extensive theoretical elaboration and explication which the authors provide here. Their claim to methodological innovation is, to my mind, certainly valid, adopting as they do a diachronic, ecological, and comparative approach to the research object they identify. Yet they are also neither doctrinaire in their use of these theoretical paradigms nor dogmatic in their approach; rather, they "follow a line of reasoning to see where it leads, to indicate a new and interesting interpretation of inquiry." For them placemaking is a process "to which the producers contribute, containing social relations that affect all parties involved. Therefore, through production relations, placemaking is simultaneously economic, cultural, and political, and an integral part of one or more modes of production."

Their investigation of placemaking in these two strikingly similar yet historically and culturally unique environments concerns itself with an extremely wide range of questions, from regional connections and patterns of trade to the careful exposition of social structure and stratification, drawing on a very wide range of historical and theoretical literature to discuss them.

In conclusion, however, there is one question readers may have which I cannot fail to address. It concerns not the research object the two authors have chosen to address but, rather, the conditions which have constructed the authorial subjects themselves. It is characteristic of contemporary scholarship that the insights derived from a comparative study of two such widely separated phenomena emanate from a collaborative project undertaken by two scholars who, though having similar interests, nevertheless originate in very different, and at one time (though no longer) widely separated parts of the world.

Readers will make their own readings of the authors' account, no doubt choosing, at some times, to reflect on the historical narrative, and at others, the theoretical infrastructure or the archeological data on which they draw. Whichever is the case, they will certainly derive much intellectual stimulation from the authors' endeavors.

Anthony King
State University of New York at Binghamton

Preface

Between 1981 and early 1984, the two authors of this volume were impressed by the resemblance, both in geological terms and in terms of human adaptation of the environment of certain parts of Anatolia — the Greek name for Asiatic Turkey, (meaning "rising" referring to sunrise), — to an area of the American Southwest covering parts of four states — northwestern New Mexico, northeastern Arizona, southwestern Colorado, and southeastern Utah. In prehistoric times, this was the realm of a large group of people now called "Anasazi," a Navajo word meaning "the ancient enemy." At specific locations within these two regions separated by half the globe, volcanic eruptions covered many hundreds of square kilometers of surrounding territory with debris millennia in the past, producing bizarre geological "tent rock" formations of "tuff," or "tufa": the Cappadocian region of Anatolian Turkey and the Pajarito Plateau of northern New Mexico. Various observers have remarked on the nearly identical appearance of the two locations, in both of which erosion and other natural forces gradually perforated the geological formations left by these ancient volcanic eruptions.

In both locations, but at different geologic times, various groups of people also created homes within these perforations. While caves had provided temporary or permanent shelter in both places for ages, substantial alterations to the form of these caves — their influence on true cavate dwellings — was most prominent in Cappadocia beginning in the fourth century A.D. The

Christian refugees, who arrived from the south and first settled in the tent rocks, later, perhaps for reasons of superior defense, built subterranean "cities." The Anasazi, having abandoned early settlements during the twelfth century in the "four corners" area where Utah, Colorado, Arizona, and New Mexico now come together, moved east to the area of the Pajarito Plateau. They, like the people of the Cappadocia region some eight centuries earlier, moved into the perforated tent rock and carved the interiors into dwellings and ceremonial places. The Anasazi subsequently built outward from the faces of the tent rocks, establishing villages along cliff ledges.

While doing field work in these two locations, we also thought about and discussed the various ways in which scholars and researchers have tried to explain why people build the way they do. Many of these are among the so-called "determinisms" — environmental, cultural and so forth — and seemed inadequate and even barren to us. Our comparative study of two geologically very similar but culturally distinct areas allowed us to begin to weigh environmental and cultural determinisms against each other, and against alternative modes of explanation. We hypothesized that environmental determinism would predict convergent movements with increasing similarities, over time, in ways of life, while cultural determinism might predict the opposite. In fact, neither determinism — rather, a lack of determinism — seems to explain what has happened over centuries in the two locations. It seemed much more fruitful to explore other explanatory avenues.

In addition, we have had to expand the geographical areas of concern beyond Cappadocia and the Pajarito Plateau to include much of Central Anatolia and the geologically and climatically similar U.S. Southwest. We also extended the time frame of our concern into the past, beyond the specific periods during which Cappadocia and the Pajarito Plateau were settled and occupied.

This is a book about the context of placemaking — the production of vernacular architecture and settlement. It is an attempt at prototheory, the formation of a perspective with which to view built environment produced by traditional societies. We will be focusing upon two examples: carved dwellings and other masonry structures of Anatolian Turkey and pre- and post-conquest Southwestern pueblos in the U.S. Architectural and settlement phenomena will be analyzed primarily in terms of the social forces that gave rise to them, rather than their formal properties. This has been a challenging and rewarding enterprise.

David Stea and Mete Turan

Acknowledgments

Completion of this intricate comparative study without the assistance of much productive force and labor power—people, organizations, institutions, and money—would have been impossible. We used, cruised, and perused a number of libraries, many of which were especially cooperative, including Carnegie Mellon University; the History Library at the Palace of the Governors and the Laboratory of Anthropology (both in Santa Fe); the Library of Congress; Middle East Technical University in Ankara; New Mexico State Library; The Santa Fe Public Library; the Turkish Historical Society; the University of New Mexico; and the University of Wisconsin-Milwaukee.

A number of people, through their discussions with us and other interactions, direct and indirect, provided information, insights, and inspiration — some even joined us on field trips — we are in their intellectual debt. These include Mehmet Adam, Ayda Arel, Omur Bakirer, Tom Chavez, Bilgi Denel, Susana Devalle, Dennis Doxtater, Silvia Elguea, Laura Holt, Steve Lekson, Emre Madran, Russell Maeth, Joan Mathien, Selahattin Onur, Alfonso Ortiz, Alpay Ozdural, Suha Ozkan, Stewart Peckham, Henry Pisciotta, Mustafa Pultar, Amos Rapoport, Orlando Romero, David Saile, Joe Sando, Jan Schnorr, Albert Schroeder, Okan Ustunkok, Dave Warren, and Yildirim Yavuz.

Other institutions provided invaluable information, including el Colegio de Mexico, the Museum of Northern Arizona, the Museum of Turkish Civilizations in Ankara, the New Mexico State Office of Historic Preservation, the National Park Service, the Headquarters of the Chaco World Historic Site, the Chaco Research Center, Museo Nacional de Antropología and Museo del Templo Mayor in Mexico. The study was funded in part by a Fulbright Grant (1984), a Mellon Foundation Research Grant (1985), a Faculty Development Grant from Carnegie Mellon University (1986), and Research Allocations Committee Grant from the University of New Mexico (1992).

Students of the Department of Architecture at Middle East Technical University contributed to survey and measurement activities in Cappadocia, which were later rendered into drawings by Mark Donohue, Heidi Douden, and Alper Ünlu. Word processing was accomplished by Darlene Covington-Davis, Alpaslan Guler and Julie Marnell of the Department of Architecture at Carnegie Mellon University, and by Kathy Lelinski at the Urban Research Center, University of Wisconsin-Milwaukee. The assistance of Carnegie Mellon personnel was facilitated by Omer Akin, Akram Midani, and Judy Kampert. We also wish to thank Danna Strech for her editing and editorial assistance, and for all the help at the final stage of completion, which was at times "painful."

Very special thanks is due to Nilgun Turan, without whose extensive and dedicated work on survey, measurement, and drawings, this book would have been much more difficult to complete.

It is impossible to thank all those who helped individually, but the major actors are mentioned above. Naturally, while we cannot claim all credit for the contents of the book, we do assume all responsibility for errors of fact and interpretation, which we hope, of course, are very few indeed.

List of Illustrations

Figure	2.1:	Map of neolithic sites in Anatolian Turkey and adjacent areas.	52
Figure	2.2:	Distribution of major prehistoric cultures in the U.S. Southwest.	53
Figure	2.3:	Cappadocia, with locations of major ancient sites and natural features.	54
Figure	2.4:	Cappadocia: landscapes of "cones" not yet seperated from the main body of the rock.	55
Figure	2.5:	Cappadocia: detail of gradual formation of free-standing "fairy chimneys" by erosion.	56
Figure	2.6:	Cappadocia: Zelve Valley.	57
Figure	2.7:	Cappadocia: rock carved dwellings in Zelve Valley.	58
Figure	2.8:	Cappadocia: detail of rock-carved dwellings showing recent shearing of cliff face.	59
Figure	2.9:	Landscape of tent rock formations, Pajarito Plateau, New Mexico.	60
Figure	2.10:	Tent rocks along southern face of Pajarito Plateau.	60
Figure	2.11:	Tent rock with cap.	61
Figure	2.12:	Cave dwelling, southern face of Pajarito Plateau.	62
Figure	2.13:	Rock carved dwellings, Frijoles Canyon, New Mexico. (Photograph by Jesse Nusbaum.)	63
Figure	2.14:	Obsidian trade zones in Anatolia and adjacent areas about 4000 B.C.	64
Figure	2.15:	Ancient trade routes, used especially during the Hittite period.	65
Figure	2.16:	Probable major trade routes between Mesoamerica and "Oasis America" to A.D. 1400, prior to Spanish conquest.	66
Figure	2.17:	Major Anasazi sites in New Mexico.	67
Figure	2.18:	Major sites of Anasazi and adjacent cultures in Arizona.	68

xiv   List of Illustrations

Figure	3.1:	Anasazi pithouse (cutaway axonometric, oblique view).	97
Figure	3.2:	Anasazi early Pueblo I, reconstruction.	98
Figure	3.3:	Anasazi early Pueblo II, reconstruction of part of village.	99
Figure	3.4:	Portion of Anasazi village, early Pueblo III, reconstruction.	100

Figure	4.1:	Plan of portion of Catal Huyuk.	144
Figure	4.2:	Axonometric (oblique) view of Catal Huyuk about 5900 B.C.	145
Figure	4.3:	Anasazi sites in central Chaco Canyon beginning of second millennium A.D.	146
Figure	4.4:	Axonometric view of Pueblo Alto.	147
Figure	4.5:	Major arteries of Chacoan road system.	148
Figure	4.6:	Plan of Hacilar.	149
Figure	4.7:	Axonometric view of Hacilar about 5600 B.C.	150
Figure	4.8:	Fortress of Hacilar ca. 5250 B.C.	151
Figure	4.9:	Plan of part of Can Hasan, Level II, ca. 5000 B.C.	152
Figure	4.10:	Plan of a portion of Mersin, ca. 4400 B.C.	153
Figure	4.11:	Axonometric view of Mersin.	154
Figure	4.12:	A private house in Bogazkoy (Hattus).	155
Figure	4.13:	Courtyard houses from the Great Kingdom Period, Bogazkoy.	156
Figure	4.14:	Courtyard houses in Bogazkoy (lower city).	157
Figure	4.15:	Megaron type house in Kultepe.	158
Figure	4.16:	Courtyard houses in Kultepe, Level II.	159
Figure	4.17:	Courtyard houses in Kultepe, Level IB.	160
Figure	4.18:	A courtyard house in Kultepe, Level IA.	161
Figure	4.19:	Individual family courtyard houses in Karum-Kanes, Level II.	162
Figure	4.20:	House in Alisar, ca. 2500 B.C.	163

Figure	5.1:	Cappadocian dwellings in cones.	220
Figure	5.2:	Cappadocian cave and constructed cave dwellings.	221
Figure	5.3:	Presently occupied cavate dwellings in town of Urgup.	222
Figure	5.4:	Ruins of cavate dwelling and church.	223
Figure	5.5:	Contemporary cavate dwellings in town of Mustafapasa.	224
Figure	5.6:	Contemporary carved structure in free-standing cone.	225
Figure	5.7:	Contemporary structure, a combination of carving and building.	226
Figure	5.8:	Plan of carved dwelling, Urgup.	227
Figure	5.9:	Section of carved dwelling, shown in Fig. 5.8.	228
Figure	5.10:	Plan of carved dwelling, Urgup.	229
Figure	5.11:	Section of carved dwelling, shown in Fig. 5.10.	230
Figure	5.12:	Plan of carved dwelling, Urgup.	231
Figure	5.13:	Section of carved dwelling, shown in Fig. 5.12.	232
Figure	5.14:	First floor plan of carved dwelling, Urgup.	233
Figure	5.15:	Second floor plan of carved dwelling, shown in Fig.5.14.	234
Figure	5.16:	Section of carved dwelling, shown in Figs. 5.14 and 5.15.	235
Figure	5.17:	Cappadocian underground settlement.	236
Figure	5.18:	Interior carving detail, showing the rolling "millstone" to block the passage from inside.	237
Figure	5.19:	Axonometric view of Cliff Palace, Mesa Verde.	238
Figure	5.20:	Axonometric view of Kiet Siel, Kayenta area, latter part of 13th century.	239

List of Illustrations

Figure	5.21:	Plan and axonometric reconstruction of part of surface ruin above Puye Cliff, Pajarito Plateau, New Mexico.	240
Figure	5.22:	Axonometric reconstruction of Tyounyi, Frijoles Canyon, Pajarito Plateau, New Mexico.	241
Figure	5.23:	Talus House, a Frijoles Canyon cliff dwelling.	242
Figure	5.24:	Contemporary carved and built dwellings, Cappadocia.	243
Figure	5.25:	Contemporary carved and built dwellings, Cappadocia.	244
Figure	5.26:	Masonry reinforcement of carved structure, Cappadocia.	245
Figure	5.27:	Masonry reinforcement of carved structure, Cappadocia.	246
Figure	5.28:	Contemporary *eyvan* facade, Cappadocia.	247
Figure	5.29:	*Eyvan* and courtyard combination, Cappadocia.	248
Figure	5.30:	Plan of courtyard house, Urgup.	249
Figure	5.31:	Section of courtyard house, shown in Fig. 5.30.	250
Figure	5.32:	Facade masonry detail.	251
Figure	5.33:	Facade masonry detail.	252
Figure	5.34:	Facade masonry detail.	253
Figure	5.35:	Carved interior detail.	254
Figure	5.36:	Carved ceiling detail.	255
Figure	5.37:	Schematic progression of carving and building.	256
Figure	5.38:	Pre-columbian sites and trade routes between Mesoamerica and the American Southwest.	257
Figure	5.39:	Axonometric and partial plan of a portion of contemporary Acomo Pueblo, New Mexico.	258
Figure	8.1:	Typology of placemaking relationships.	314
Figure	AII:	Models of transition in modes of production.	323

All photographs are by the authors, except where acknowledged.

INTRODUCTION:
A CRITICAL OVERVIEW

> ...reflection and enquiry should satisfy us that to our predecessors we are indebted for much of what we thought most our own, and that their errors were not wilful extravagances or the ravings of insanity, but simply hypotheses, justifiable as such at the time when they were propounded, but which a fuller experience has proved to be inadequate... After all, what we call truth is only the hypothesis which is found to work best.
>
> Sir J. G. Frazer, *The golden bough.*

This is a book about placemaking—the conception and realization of built environment—and its relation to cultural change. Its authors, formally schooled in engineering, planning, architecture, and psychology, make no claim to extraordinary expertise in anthropology, political science, or archaeology: while we have taught in and written about these areas, our experience with them is primarily "in the field."

The project that yeilded this book was often a labor of love, and at other times simply labor; more than ten years have passed from initial conception to conclusion. In part its creation has been an (occasionally expensive) odyssey: our field work has involved some 15,000 miles of travel, and our scholarly efforts involved readings in five languages. The writing has spanned nearly nine years and two continents, having taken place in the U.S.A. (Wisconsin, Pennsylvania, and New Mexico), Mexico, Turkey, Indonesia, and points in-between, largely on the ground but in planes, trains, and even buses on occasion. During this period, scientific and scholarly perspectives have changed: particularly in the case of the Anasazi and their Mesoamerican connections, interpretation of available data has varied markedly from 1981 to the present, one reason why this manuscript was re-written three times.

For all this effort, we claim no final authority on the subject of our discourse; what we are attempting to present is a new interdisciplinary theoretical perspective with many antecedents, derived in part from certain Marxist concepts but not from doctrinaire application of Marxist theory. At the time we began this work, interdisciplinary efforts were still in vogue in some North American academic settings, and Marxist viewpoints enjoyed limited (ephemeral) popularity; since then, conservative trends in American academia have encouraged a retreat into the confines of traditional disciplines, if not entirely, then certainly considerably. At the same time, recent events in eastern Europe have served to discredit not just the credibility of the Soviet model of "Marxist" social and political development but Marxist philosophy itself.

What was originally intented to be an intellectually acceptable liberal view, therefore, ended in some circles as unacceptably radical. While trying to remain faithful to our core ideas, we have had to recognize that academic fashions change, as do audiences, and that those who read this book in its published form may come from a somewhat different context than its earliest reviewers. This is an expansion upon our original introduction, written in 1988, to clarify the origin of our ideas, changes in our direction, and consequent modification of our perspective since that time.

Our "jumping-off point" was a simultaneous observation of a striking resemblance, both in geology and ancient settlement forms, between Anatolian Cappadocia and the Pajarito Plateau of New Mexico. Both areas, semi-arid and characterized by fairly extreme temperatures, have extensive volcanic action, creating tent-like rock formations which later became sites for caves or cave-like habitations. We do not presume to have been the first investigators to note the above similarity, although our research turned up nothing previously published: we did, however, propose to develop a comparative study, and began to investigate further, both in libraries and in the field.

The first result was that we uncovered as many differences between the two widely seperated sites as similarities (environmental determinism failed once again; superficial similarities did not stand up to deeper scrutiny). The second was that we had to take into account much larger cultural, environmental, and historical contexts to provide a coherent comparative picture of the relationship of preliterate cultures to early settlement in the two areas. A study that was to have taken just months, then, expanded to fill a decade.

As we proceeded, our approach to the material we encountered in and on the two areas began to diverge more and more from that which has characterized studies performed by many investigators on the relation between built form and culture during the 1970s and 1980s. Much of the earlier work had emphasized (1) a rejection of environmental determinism, (2) visual and symbolic aspects of the products of building activity, (3) observations of behavior and its traces, and (4) a view of culture which regards certain factors, termed "cultural," as primary, and others (e.g., political and economic factors) as secondary in the generation of built form. To a lesser (but still considerable) extent, ethnographic-like accounts of specific case studies have tended to characterize both the form-culture literature and presentations at conferences on built form and culture which began in the 1980s; typological frameworks were in evidence, but genuinely comparative studies were rare indeed.

We are obviously adopting a critical pespective here, but not simply "behavior bashing." Earlier versions of this manuscript were criticized for neglecting latent functions of built environment—*meaning, ritual, ceremony, symbolism*, etc.— an for stressing needs rather than wants, downplaying the role of choice, and so forth. To all of these we plead "guilty—with reasons:" (1) such latent functions as *meaning* and *visual symbolism,* and many of the usual environment-behavior issues have been the focus of much of the vernacular/ traditional settlement literature excluding the kind of material we present here; (2) distinctions between "needs" and "wants" are, in general, not well drawn and difficult to apply to prehistoric/preliterate societies; perhaps, because (3) they are based too much in the jargon of mainstream North American housing markets, which are also the generators of much that we mean by "choice." People in general prefer place-consumption to placemaking (or, in other words, participation in consumption over production), and other ideas that may be difficult to sustain outside the contemporary context of the industrialized nations.

Fortunately, more recent research, while still informed primarily by the above perspectives, has gone beyond formalist approaches which engage in pseudo-analysis of a product in isolation and tend to reveal little about either vernacular architecture or culture. We have no quarrel with visual documentation which leads to beautiful pictorial presentations of vernacular architecture, often in the form of "coffee-table" books; it is only when such (often casual) documentation is presented as an end itself, without serious analysis or synthesis, that "architecture is culture" becomes "culture is architecture," usually generating spurious generalizations and misleading conclusions. There is thus some danger that the current trend toward the generation of abstract, reified jargon, and the treatment of compartmentalized built form, currently so popular in "mainstream" architectural education, may spill over into the interpretation of vernacular building, reducing its inherent richness.

"Placemaking," therefore, goes beyond the products of building per se to an examination of products within the context of historical processes. We question whether "cultural determinism" is an effective replacement for the discredited "environmental determinism," "historical determinism," or other Procrustean beds for either of the preceding; our position proposes the rejection of all "determinisms." We also question the simplistic cause-and-effect reasoning characterizing those aspects of North American (environmental) behavioral science that passively and uncritically accept "raw data," which often turn out to be appearances.

But the rejection of "determinisms" carries its own apparent contradiction. If "everything is related to everything else" and if "it's all relative, anyway," how can "positive results" in the manner of research models derived from experimental psychology be obtained? Our answer, as indicated in the opening chapter of this book, is "they cannot." Our proposal is not to attempt such answers, within the limitations of currently available material, but rather to provide windows into other possible interpretations of (Platonic) reality. The book begins with an initial set of concepts (windows), examines two different cases in light of these concepts, then uses the resulting insights to generate a new theoretical framework (one indebted, however, to a number of older theories).

One window provides a view; a number of windows provide a vista. Thus, rather than carpentering one more Procrustean bed in which to further distort reality, our use of Marxist concepts constitutes an attempt to create a window which, in the above sense and in combination with other windows, will provide an alternative vista. This is the basis of the (hopefully) constructive theoretical perspective proposed in this book's later chapters, a perspective intended to provide a self-critical basis for constructing and evaluating alternative explanations (and predictions) in the built form and culture arena.

Karl Marx's historical materialism is characterized by developmental stages, not unlike those proposed by another structuralist, Jean Piaget. In Piaget's system, children progress from one stage to the next within a range of ages rather than at specific ages. Similarly, transitions from one historical stage, from one mode of production, to another are not presumed to have occurred at the same time in markedly different societies. The accepted perspective, however, has been that such changes, whether Piagetian or Marxist, occur in one direction only, from "less developed" to "more developed," from "less differentiated" to "more differentiated," from "less complex" to "more complex." Thus, it might fallaciously appear that our point is to demonstrate a one-to-one correspondence between transitions from camps to villages to towns to cities — an increase in settlement size and physical complexity— and an ordered progression of modes of production. This is in no sense our goal, for if it were, and if we "succeeded," the correspondence so established would be demonstrably false.

Our purpose in writing this book has been neither to accept the unidirectional development of Marxist stages as revealed truth, nor to "test" them in a hypothetical-deductive manner. Rather, we have explored new ideas concerning form-culture relationships by viewing such relationships from a different

Introduction 5

perspective or, so to speak, through a different set of lenses. We are neither postulating nor testing "progressions" of any kind but simply examining the possibility of their existence; "if this, then what?"

To take one example, in the case of ancient Anasazi settlements in what are now New Mexico and Arizona, many more questions have been raised than answers found. One of these concerns is whether the Anasazi, whose architecture may have been the most advanced for a presumably kin-ordered mode of production, had at their height actually moved in the direction of the tributary mode of production, or followed a very different path. But the window of unilinear development cuts off certain views to production and sociopolitical organization; thus, if the Anasazi simply became the modern pueblos, either no change in (a kin-ordered) mode of production ever occurred, or conventional views of pre-contact (and perhaps even contemporary) modes of production are incorrect, or something else happened.

The possibility of that "something else," provided by an oblique glance through this one window, impelled us to look through other windows as well, to expand our vista to include possible connections between the Anasazi and Mesoamerica across the so-called "Chichimec Sea," just one of the exciting episodes in the intellectual voyage on which we embarked.

Chapter One
BREAKING GROUND FOR PLACEMAKING

> All social life is essentially *practical*. All the mysteries which urge theory into mysticism find their rational solution in human practice and in the comprehension of this practice.
>
> K. Marx, *Theses on Feuerbach.*

In this opening chapter, the concept of *placemaking* is introduced, defined, and described. Placemaking is an action, a process, literally "making places" (from the infinitive "to make places," presumably); it is what people do and have done historically, and were doing long before written history, an act that soon transcended mere settling to the formation of settlements themselves.

Settlements are part of the material culture of a society; they, together with other material products, incorporate in one form or another many aspects of that society's culture—its technology, its social and spiritual values, its economy and political structure. "Placemaking" then is the act of cultural incorporation, broadly conceived, into built form, relating culture to architecture and urban design, often within a planning framework and within an overall context termed "ecological." Thus, we introduce the concepts of architectural and cultural dimensions, which, we propose, always interact in an integrated manner. By "integrated" we mean that such an interaction is neither casual nor coincidental, that the architecture-culture complex is consistent and coherent at a point in time, that it evolves over time in response to certain forces, and that an understanding of this complex can tell us much about past cultures that have left no written record.

How, then, do we go about gaining such understanding? Our task in this book, as we see it, is to find how such integrated intersections "made sense" within the overall ecological framework of two prehistoric, preliterate societies; by posing the question in this way, we are adopting an *ecological perspective*. In this search for what makes sense, we must consider the *totality* of the context surrounding a presumed built environment-culture relationship—

Breaking Ground for Placemaking

hence the use of the term "ecological." This implies, first, an interdisciplinary and dialectical perspective; and the second, the necessity to re-pose questions in this total context, questions that may have been asked before from only a single discipline point of view.

The study of placemaking involves spaces from the micro-micro to the macro-macro, from a room detail through overall structure, construction, architecture, urban design, and regional planning, to extended context. To some extent, this is a "recursive" framework where the same questions are asked at each level. The evidence involved is of two types: internal to the specific place studied; and external, or contextual.

This chapter also introduces the central notion of *mode of production*, together with such related classical Marxist concepts of bases, forces, relations, means of production, use and exchange values, superstructure, etc. For those already familiar with Marxist theory, this is merely a review of basic ideas and terminology. As indicated in the introduction of this volume, far from attempting to "squeeze" reality into a specific theoretical perspective, we are experimenting: using a collection of Marxist concepts as an alternative "window," an "heuristic" in a certain sense, onto an elusive ecological reality. Thus, ours is not a hypothetico-deductive approach providing a "critical test" of a single theory. This book does not propose that the Marxist concepts we employ provide a "better" explanation than others used by students of the built environment-culture interface; rather, it tries to broaden the explanatory context by opening another aperture on a set of phenomena.

How and why people appropriate and alter certain spaces to provide shelter, sustenance, security, and satisfaction is a central concern of *placemaking*. Placemaking includes architecture — and a good deal of what is often called *vernacular* architecture — but is not concerned with architectural history, theory, and criticism in their conventional sense. It is concerned with issues of *settlement*, but is not about urban design, per se. We have taken two case studies and attempted to illuminate these with a perspective that is diachronic, ecological, and comparative:

(1) it is *diachronic* in the sense that prehistorical and historical *continuity*, particularly in the sense of societal development, plays an important role;

(2) it is *ecological* in the sense that no single line of explanation, such as the traditional "determinisms" (environmental, cultural, etc.), is assumed; placemaking is the result of a *combination* of forces acting together and, in that sense, is *ecological*. The most fruitful path to both description and explanation of what was actually occurring in both these locations is not a view that separates

culture from environment from economics. We shall be as much concerned with questions of movement — who migrated in and who migrated out, with whom, from and to where, and under what circumstances — as with stasis. Our concern with the past has led us from that past in both directions — toward the even more distant past, and toward the present;

(3) our perspective is *comparative* in the sense that it attempts to relate two widely separated societies whose *ages* differ greatly but whose *stages of development* show certain similarities.

What we are attempting to do herein is to determine how much about societies — preliterate societies, in particular — can be "read" from their placemaking activity. In doing this, we are unquestionably "pushing the bounds" of explanation, and hopefully expanding these bounds. Our aim is to be not only explanatory but critical. The "new" approaches of man-environment relations (MER) or person-environment relations (PER) or environment-behavior studies (EBS) (which actually *were* new a quarter of a century ago but have since become "institutionalized") have been limited to an extent by the positivist approach to the exploration of visible behavior; as such, they could be, and have been, only narrowly diachronic. Most studies have involved a single slice through time or brief longitudinal assessments, spanning at most a few years.

Data concerning placemaking activity during prehistoric times among preliterate peoples are necessarily partial. Our field studies have added a bit to the historical record, but we have been forced to rely, for the most part, upon secondary sources in several languages for both the nature of early placemaking and a possible explanatory framework. Our explanatory framework relies heavily upon certain concepts drawn from Marxist dialectical and historical materialism, developmental sequences of modes of production in particular, especially as related to the resource base, social relations, labor, value, and conditions of existence. Necessarily, therefore, some sections of this book are abstract presentations of theoretical concepts and relationships defined in Chapter One.

Where has this taken us? It would have been fruitless to attempt a book of this sort if it said nothing new. What *is* new is our approach as set forth earlier, and some considerable attempt to explain the *co-existence* of various modes of production and possible *retrograde* movements in modes of production. Also new is the framework set forth in Chapters Six and Seven for understanding the forces affecting the shaping of domestic dwellings in the process of placemaking. Furthermore, given the partial nature of available information, even more so in the case of Anasazi economy and culture than in Anatolian, some of our most tentative conclusions are unabashedly conjectural. In other words, we ask, given that such-and-such a condition prevailed, what might have happened if thus-and-so also occurred.

The *context* of placemaking — local, regional, and global external forces — is assumed to play an important role in "shaping" built form. Conversely, built form, when viewed as part of an ecological whole, can provide us with information concerning societal and other forces operating concurrently in the absence of written records. Our concerns, among others, are the *processes of* placemaking, the *products* of placemaking activity, and the *use* of ancient places as an evidential system enriching our knowledge of pre-literate societies.

Built forms as architectural products are sets of spatial organizations used for a given function: making architecture in general, and placemaking in particular—a purposeful activity and a means of production through and for other activities. Treating architecture as production allows us to penetrate beneath the physical attributes of built form to reveal its substantial characteristics included in the broader processes that are involved in its production. The development of built form as a productive force is no different from the development of other productive forces. Being material implements of historical acts gives built forms as productive forces an historical character. In growth, where production relations correspond to a definite stage in the development of productive forces (defined as *mode of production*), architecture becomes the physical expression of those relations.

Human factors shaping architectural objects — the manner and degree of response to needs (function); efficiency and application of knowledge in handling materials and construction (technology); and expression of artistic ability and innovation including shared, collective meanings in form-giving (aesthetics) — both form and are formed by the dialectic between production relations and productive forces. The manner of approach and treatment of built form and its environs and the degree of concern, articulation and expressive choice demonstrated are directly interrelated with production relations.

A basically materialist approach such as ours is not solely economic and socio-political, nor does it deny the existence of latent functions, such as expressive needs (meaning, symbolism, etc.). We do, however, suggest that these are at least closely related to, and probably a derivative of, the fulfillment of more basic needs. The reason for stressing certain things is to correct a balance; we feel that the role of expressive aspects of placemaking, particularly visual form, have been overemphasized in earlier work.

Finally, there is a two-part question, related to the nature of placemaking and to the human condition, involving architecture, planning, archaeology, anthropology and sociology: (1) to what extent can placemaking tell us about the nature of the human condition, both in past eras and at present? And (2) to what extent is the human condition (at a specific moment in the historical stream) capable of providing information about placemaking? First, both are concerned with material conditions and social relations at a point in time (part of the diachronic flow); second, neither is detached from everyday praxis; and third, neither the substance of the questions (on the human condition and placemaking), nor the questions themselves are abstract categories. We will attempt to use the above characterizations of the foregoing two questions to demonstrate that material conditions and social relations do in fact play a primary role in shaping human actions at all levels and in all realms, including that of placemaking.

On the nature of placemaking

Placemaking is used here in three senses. The first is the placemaking *product*, literally a *"made place."* Made places include but transcend what is usually considered architecture. The Plains Indian great "medicine wheel" in northern Wyoming, U.S., an open ceremonial site, is certainly an example of placemaking but not of architecture, as are earlier butchering sites in Anatolia. Classic Greek and Egyptian temples are illustrations of both placemaking and architecture, as are Catal Huyuk and Pueblo Bonito, both described in this book. The second sense is *process*, the "making of places," distinguishing between space-defining and space-delimiting activities under different modes of production.

The third sense of placemaking is *perspective*. A placemaking perspective, as elaborated in a later paragraph, refers to the scholar's or researcher's point of view, to the identification and evaluation of made places defined by actions of the human mind and hand, in accordance with societal norms. Placemaking, moreover, is the production and consumption of built forms — especially homes, houses, residential environments, and shaped and defined exterior spaces—and of such qualitatively different architectural products as temples and palaces (a dwelling is no more a small-scale palace than a palace is a large-scale dwelling, in ecological terms). Placemaking is also a way of living incorporated into everyday praxis. The difference between the dwelling environment and other built forms resulting from architectural activity is in production and consumption patterns as well as distributive relations which reflect socioeconomic class in a way which, in comparison with other architectural processes and products, is unique.

A placemaking perspective divides the generation of collective environments of use values — the creation of community — from qualitatively and quantitatively different organizations of space for other functions and purposes.

Breaking Ground for Placemaking

New contradictions thus emerge between placemaking activity at the community level (vernacular placemaking) and at other levels of architectural production, with changing conditions of existence. Thus, not only are property relations involved but also the territorial differentiation and cultural heterogeneity associated with intensified urbanization. In other words, by viewing placemaking activity as community creation, apart from placemaking as a generation of other built form, this perspective forces consideration of the relationship between diachronic qualitative changes in built environment and associated sociopolitical changes in society as a whole. Clearly, we are suggesting that the process of placemaking is inextricably intertwined with the productive forces of a society. We therefore propose that an *ecological perspective* whose elements are dialectically rather that dichotomously related gives a better account of the nature and function of placemaking than does a determinist position, whether that determinism be environmental, cultural, or other. Our global objective is to account for cross-cultural parallels and differences in vernacular *placemaking* activity, parallels and differences not adequately handled by unilinear or unidisciplinary determinisms. The search is for an understanding of interactions among diverse factors and underlying processes rather than for mere "cause and effect" connections.

In other words, so-called "mainstream" approaches to the architectural analysis of vernacular built form, which stress solely *artistic* or *expressive* aspects as explanatory, can be termed "formal;" these, as with ideological explanatory systems rooted only in *symbolic* meaning are mainly product-oriented. "Process" approaches, too, tend within architecture to stress modes and manners of construction, omitting underlying and facilitating social relations. Functional/behavioral approaches, many derived from the social sciences, stress such concepts as "perception," "stimulation," "territoriality," and "crowding." But placemaking is not a "controlled experiment." Thus, unidirectional explanatory systems do *not* control variables treated by other approaches, but simply *ignore* them.

Our approach must be diachronic as well as ecological, directed to the examination and explanation of development and change in the built environment and its social context. In this, we are attempting to build upon and extend the excellent work of a diverse body of searchers, researchers and theorists in placemaking including Adams (1966), Aksoy (1963), Brunskill (1971), Fitch (1961), Flannery (1972), Glassie (1975), King (1984), Knowles (1974), Lekson (1982a), Naumann (1975), Oliver (1969), Ozguner (1970), Rapoport (1969), Redman (1978), and Rudofsky (1964). Our amplification of their work draws upon concepts derived from the writings of Amin, Marx, Wolf, and others, and attempts to relate these concepts to specific placemaking activities in the two geo-cultural contexts under study. The result, presented in a later chapter, has been the incorporation of a modified form of dialectical materialism into our theoretical approach.

The dialectical character of the person-nature dialogue. Nature forces people to build suitable environment, and thus, to search for certain objects *in* the environment. To make use of these objects people must transform them to suit their purposes. The need for shelter is "natural," yet, with the exception of human knowledge and skills, what is necessary to meet this need — construction materials, solar energy and other environmental elements — is external. It is for this reason — the integration of external and internal resource — that people are coerced into *placemaking*.

This action coerced by nature is a unity of opposites: human needs and the environment. Environmental conditions produce the needs, but meeting these needs depends upon both human and environmental resources. The opposed needs are unified in production of the built environment, or placemaking. In this process, a transformation occurs: the perception and use of resources are altered in such a way that both the natural environment and the built environment go through *quantitative* changes. During this process *qualitative* changes also inescapably follow as new values, new knowledge, and new needs arise under new sets of conditions through direct experience with the environment. To understand all aspects of this developmental process, we need to consider three non-independent dimensions: culture, architecture, and the reflection of collective needs at the individual level.

The cultural dimension. Central to an understanding of placemaking processes is a definition of culture. The view that we support goes beyond the consideration of ritual, symbol, language, and transmission of cultural traits to an inclusion of traditional economy, resources, political systems, and ideology. In our view, then, culture is actually the totality of the society's treatment of these dimensions of existence. It is an ecological view in the sense that, rather than some of these aspects being central and others peripheral to the culture, all are viewed as contributing equally and interactively to the cultural matrix.

The foregoing view of culture is not shared by all researchers. Cameron (1973), for example, claims that the use of "culture" to signify the whole of the socio-cultural processes of society is incorrect; rather, he sees economic, social, and political aspects of society as "primary" and cultural processes as "secondary." Rapoport (1983b), among others, says somewhat the reverse:

> ... site, climate, materials, economics, political context and so on ... are important since they become constraints which will modify or distort the ideal (they are what one might call secondary or modifying factors)

Breaking Ground for Placemaking

> ... They can also be seen as the "how" — the enabling and constraining variables. (p.266).

Our own view attempts to formulate an ecological perspective by giving equal value to the various components of the socio-cultural processes of society, both dialectically and diachronically, through the overarching concept of *mode of production,* which will be defined later. The present view is conceptually fairly close to a statement provided by Wolf (1982):

> The concept of social labor ... makes it possible to conceptualize the major ways in which human beings organize their production. Each major way of doing so constitutes a mode of production—a specific, historically occurring set of social relations through which labor is deployed to wrest energy from nature by means of tools, skills, organization, and knowledge (p.75).

A similar position is represented by Steward (1955), who originally framed the concept of culture "core" and centered this concept on "the constellation of features which are most clearly related to subsistence and economic arrangements." (p.37).

The architectural dimension. What is vernacular architecture? ... Or, rather, what is vernacular architecture *about*? A suggestive answer to this reformulated question is given by Ozkan, Turan, and Ustunkok (1979): "the dialectical nature of ... vernacular architecture is characterized by four major points: experiential value; participation; environmental adequacy; intended meaning" (p.134).

Experiential value refers to a direct relationship with the environment that constitutes both the source and the context of vernacular building. *Participation* is an extension and deepening of this direct involvement. It signifies people interacting with other people in the process of building, and underlies the *relative* non-specialization of vernacular building activity (as elaborated later, this does not exclude the presence of specialists within the societies producing vernacular architecture, but refers rather to the building activity itself). The components of *environmental adequacy* are flexibility, identity, and economy. Thus, vernacular environments can be changed without having (as with more institutionalized building) to be *exchanged*; the designer is not separated from those for whom he/she is designing, and the building process can be adjusted to accommodate conditions of relative scarcity or abundance. Finally, *meaning* is *intended* rather than *attributed*: the product is integrated with, rather than alienated from, the environmental context of which the building is both a significant and a comfortably embedded part.

As just *one* aspect of built environment, dwelling is, in a limited sense, an architectural object. It is an environment in which part of everyday life is sustained through various activities and where social relations are accommodated. The dwelling provides for social activities, qualitatively different than those accommodated by other architectural products. Through structural characteristics, it is possible to explore the transformations in spatial organization in which internal and external contradictions help to identify the restructuring norms of placemaking in different periods. How the dwelling becomes an element of production relations can be examined through the constituents of placemaking. The dwelling environment simultaneously represents productive force (a means of production) and labor power, and provides experience contributing not only to the quality of everyday life of individuals but also to the development of the dwelling itself. The growth of constructional faculties, design concepts, and the ability to implement these, modifies the placemaking process. Coupled with developments in other productive forces, built environment contributes to the productive potential of a society. Therefore, it becomes essential to consider aspects of placemaking beyond its production and consumption. Through its social role in production relations, built environment is charged with political implications. Thus, the dwelling environment is a political implement, transcending its sheltering and domestic functions. To comprehend it, we must consider individual and social needs in domestic, community, and ceremonial environments—and even open sites—in an ecological perspective.

Individual and social needs. In common English, the most basic of human needs are just three: "A full belly, a safe and dry head, and hope for the future." These are associated in social terms with production, provision of shelter, and the formation of conditions favorable to social reproduction. The first relates to means of production, the disposition of surplus, and social relations; the second to building and settlement, including modes of technical and social appropriation; and the last to planning, insurance of continuity, and social organization. These are all, according to our position stated earlier, part of *culture*, and their interrelationship is central to the production and utilization of built form.

An ecological perspective. An ecological perspective, fundamentally, has as its task the search for concealed relations among apparently disparate elements; it is something like trying to solve a "diagramless crossword puzzle." The search for interrelationships implies the expectation that aspects of the same general system will combine in some sensible way. But it is not expected that the rules of combination will be contained in outward appearances: "… all science would be superfluous if the outward appearance and the essence of things directly coincided." (Marx, 1967; III, p.817).

Breaking Ground for Placemaking 15

The tasks of such an ecological perspective are (1) to pose (or re-pose) certain "big questions" and (2) to put these together with other questions asked by different disciplines from diverse theoretical perspectives, then to use information provided by the same or other disciplines to address these questions.

Several of the "big questions" are much like the "who, what, when, why, where, and how" of journalism. More specifically:
- *What* are the architectural/settlement manifestations in question?
- *How* are they achieved, both technically and socially?
- *When* do changes in built environment and associated society occur?
- *Who* is building and for *whom*?
- *Where* is the settlement sited?
- *Why?* What are the possible explanatory frameworks for the above?

On placemaking in dialectical perspective

A built environment varies *objectively* in terms of changes occurring and accumulating over time, and *subjectively* in terms of one's point of view. In this sense, all objects are therefore multimodal and all placemaking produces multimodal objects. No single description from one frame of reference is sufficient to reflect the different modalities of placemaking. The environment resulting from placemaking activity is realized in multiple frames of reference, multiple perspectives, and specific moments in history. Knowledge of the true nature of placemaking then must also be multimodal. This allows those inquiries concerning placemaking to handle appropriately the contradictions between the object and subject relations of the materialization process as well as the contradiction between form and content. "Subjective" and "objective," like "form" and "content," do not exist without each other. A discussion of the "objective" without reference to the "subjective" is misleading. Likewise, discussion of "form" without reference to its "content" is an idealist representation which not only limits the method of investigation, but also distorts architectural reality. Architectural form is *what* is produced, perceived and experienced, therefore "objective;" content is *how* it is produced, perceived and experienced, therefore reciprocally "subjective." In a similar way we can speak of the contradiction between collective property and individualized property or between ownership and non-ownership, or between commodified and noncommodified environments. This is part of the essence of dialectical thinking.

We have stated that ours is a dialectical approach. Gebhardt (1978) indicates that "dialectic" is neither ideology nor method "in the sense of a research technique" but that "its dual claim — to be both faithful to, and critical of, empirical reality — has given rise to a host of misunderstandings ..." (p.396). One of these misunderstandings concerns the nature of *contradiction* in dialectics:

> The concept of contradictions has undergone such attrition that it is often used synonymously with 'antagonism,' 'opposition,' or 'conflict.' According to Hegel and Marx, however, 'conflicts' are only the form of appearance, the empirical side of a fundamentally logical contradiction. (Habermas, 1975; p.26).

Nor are all contradictions necessarily dialectical: "The dialectical method of study consists in the recognition of contradictory elements *potentially in conflict with each other yet which constitute a totality.*" (Wilczynski, 1981; p.144, emphasis added).

Our dialectical approach, then, embraces truly dialectical contradictions but considers other forms of opposition as well. These are of three types (Parekh, 1982; pp.86-95; see, also, Marx, 1970a; pp.76-94): (1) those which share a common essence, such as male and female; (2) those which have mutually exclusive essences, such as human and non-human; and (3) those which are inseparable aspects of a common entity, such as idealism and materialism or individual and society. Of these oppositions only the third is truly dialectical, in that the task at hand is not to reconcile but to "*dissolve* or eliminate the entities involved." (Parekh, 1982; p.90). Thus, "when it is realized that the individual is a social being, and society nothing more than a network of relations between individuals, the opposition between the individual and the society or between the individualism and collectivism disappears." (Parekh, 1982; p.90).

Placemaking requires an examination relating each contradiction to the rest, setting up, at a moment of history, a specific structure in which the strength and limitations of each member of a constituent pair can be elucidated without truly dominating the other as in the "either-or" approach of positivism. A *critical* view of placemaking without dialectics would be difficult if not totally impossible. A materialist account of placemaking, emphasizing the material aspect of architectural reality, creates its opposite: idealism. This dialectical phenomenon provides materialism with its rationale. It is within this rationale that the contradictions between the constituents of placemaking at all three levels of articulation, introduced in Chapter Six and further discussed in Chapter Seven, help to trace those which share common essence (e.g., inclusive/exclusive and open/closed spaces), or which have mutually exclusive essences (e.g., stratified/nonstratified organization; commodified/noncommodified environments), or which are inseparable aspects of a common entity (e.g., natural/ideological environments; public/private realms).

Gebhardt (1978) lists several more misunderstandings concerning dialectics, but perhaps the most common (even if apparently trivial) is the confusion of dialectics with dichotomies. However, the postulation of "two sides" to an issue does not necessarily imply a dialectical relationship nor, on the other hand, does it necessarily imply a dichotomy. In fact, the study of placemaking has often involved the presentation of certain issues as dichotomies which force the student of built environment to make artificial choices. These include:

"Selfconscious" vs. "unselfconscious" architecture. This dichotomy, introduced by Alexander (1964), posits two fundamentally different approaches to architectural design, one of which is supposed to characterize "high-style," the other vernacular. This dichotomy is, unfortunately, much too reminiscent of the "noble savage" notion: the presumed nature of vernacular building is both "pure" and "backward." The facts contradict the dichotomy: indeed, vernacular builders are quite conscious of what they do and why they do it. They are societally rather than individually "self-conscious."

"Primitive" vs. "civilized" societies (and their products). Outside the industrialized West, most of today's societies are *transitional* and in the process of moving from one mode of production to another: Their economies are not pristinely primitive; neither is their architecture. We employ the term *primitive communism*, later in this book, to characterize certain modes of production, but this in no way implies the "primitiveness," in other respects, of the societies practicing this mode of production. Primitive communism also exists in extremely elaborated and sophisticated forms.

"Static" vs. "dynamic" societies. There is an understandable tendency to regard both vernacular architecture and the societies of which it is a product as somehow static, i.e. frozen in time. In some cases this is an artifact of method: taking a cross-section through time obviously does not facilitate a diachronic perspective. Indeed, the most successful producers of vernacular architecture are those which have also coped successfully with problems of incorporating change into a pre-existing framework: this is clearly related to ideas of *cultural core* and *periphery*, as suggested by Steward (1955), Stea (1981), and Rapoport (1983b).

On the meaning of production

Our purpose is to carry the understanding of the contextual relations underlying placemaking into the formulation of a new framework of person/environment relations. Fully realized, such a framework would transcend both what is sometimes termed "naive empiricism" and unilineal cause and effect. It would go beyond cultural relativity to the realization of some general relationship of built form to society. Our eventual intention is to uncover some generic dimensions underlying building activity in a variety of cultures by expanding the framework of discourse; (1) to provide a base for comparative analysis of similar phenomena occurring in markedly different culture areas; (2) to give central consideration to some factors (e.g., economic activities) often considered peripheral; and (3) to proceed, through diachronic analyses, to consider important temporal dimensions which relate changes in modes of production to changes in building production and use. Our initial search is for a structural basis of placemaking rather than for descriptions of particular buildings or settlements and concomitant behaviors. Viewed in this way placemaking is a type of economic activity, using the term "economic" in its broadest possible sense. Thus, the final product of placemaking is a manifestation of combined social, political, cultural, and material aspects of a society's mode of production.

We suggest that analyzing placemaking activity by means of *modes of production* will result in a more thorough understanding than would be provided by more compartmentalized approaches through technological, social, environmental, or cultural determinisms. The concept *mode of production* is composed of three important components: economic base; ideological superstructure; and politico-juridical superstructure, involving the emergence of the state and societal classes. By *economic base*, we mean that the placemaker not only uses certain *productive forces* but is involved in *production relations*: i.e., relations of producers among themselves, of producers to non-producers, or of *means of production* to producers (e.g., who owns the land that the producer occupies). Relations of production also set conditions for the distribution and redistribution of products.

Necessary labor is that required for the maintenance of what is conventionally termed "subsistence," that is, the minimal labor required by an individual to maintain himself/herself and for the *reproduction* of labor, the formation and support of a family. *Surplus labor* is labor which is over and above that required to maintain a subsistence level. However, surplus labor is not necessary to only ensure reproduction of the economy, but for two other reasons as well: (1) to secure subsistence for those who may be performing socially necessary functions but are not directly productive in the material sense, such as, in traditional societies, priests, "medicine men," and other ceremonial leaders; and (2) to secure subsistence for other nonlaborers such as children, the elderly, the chronically ill, and the handicapped. The concept "mode of production" is not meaningful in the absence of surplus labor, which in fact exists in all modes (Hindess and Hirst, 1975; pp.26-29).

Related to labor is the concept *unit of production*. The unit of production in modes of production, characterized by the presence or absence of politico-juridical component, may be the individual, the nuclear family, or an extended family unit. An important issue is *degree of specialization.* Construction of such specialized structures as temples and palaces requires specialized producers—carpenters, brickmakers, and masons—whereas the construction of such nonspecialized structures as peasant houses may be accomplished by the family.

Labor can also be ordered according to its "complexity." The labor involved in specialized building is more "complex" than that required for peasant dwelling construction, which, in turn, is more complex than the "simple" labor of ordinary hunting and gathering. Thus, a relation exists between complexity and specialization of labor, especially in the production of built form.

Production occurs in response to need; it yields artifacts which will be used, or consumed, and the need is satisfied by the consumption of the product. Consumption, in turn, creates the need, or motive, for additional production. The product must then be *distributed* or *exchanged* in some manner. The product of placemaking activity, whether a simple shelter or more elaborated dwelling, similarly satisfies a set of needs. The *use value* of a dwelling is a measure of its utility to the occupant as shelter and other purposes apart from commodification. Housing may be redistributed or exchanged without commodification; appropriation, and later utilization, assign a use value to an architectural product. Use value is acquired first through need, then through utilization.

However, if the dwelling is constructed not just for occupancy by the builder or the "built for" but for sale or rental, the dwelling acquires *exchange value*: it has been produced for the purpose of monetary exchange. But it must have use value before it acquires exchange value. Indeed, as in urban "squatter settlements" in developing countries, the dweller often constructs a dwelling with only its use in mind; the exchange value emerges later. Production for *use* takes place in all modes of production, production for *exchange* only in some. Exchange value is initially related (but not, in the long run, restricted) to the amount (time and monetary value) of labor required to produce a given product.

By *ideological superstructure,* we refer to those traditions which regulate production and exchange in many precapitalist societies, such as kin and clan relations. Our contention here is that ideological superstructures are derived from a society's economic base. Thus, ceremonies are not just ceremonies, totems are not just totems, and house decorations are more than just decorations. These are conventionally considered under "culture;" viewed as part of the ideological superstructure, they are related to the economic base in that they are part of an attempt to make sense of the world — including those parts of the world concerned with material and social relations — in the light of the knowledge that the society possesses. They are part of the society's *ethnoscience*.

The ideological superstructure includes the ideas, beliefs, sentiments, and types of thinking associated with particular ways of organizing production, the "mental" aspect of culture exhibiting the intellectual, organizational characteristic of a particular society — its "cognitive framework," so to speak. It provides the basis for normative behavior — the operations of values, ethics and morals — and for existential understanding of environmental elements in the external world. The ideological superstructure is descriptive, prescriptive, proscriptive, explanatory, and predictive; it bears an instrumental relationship to technical and social aspects of the production process. The ideological superstructure then is also a rule system: it regulates the production, use, and distribution of built environment, for example.

Thus, we contend that there is comparatively little "architecture without architects" (Rudofsky, 1964); that which appears so does only because those who have, use, and transmit architectural wisdom do not bear the title "architect" in many societies. The absence of a specialized title, and easily recognized architectural codes, however, cannot be taken to imply the absence of the function conventionally represented by the title nor of the codification itself.

We have not been able to consider some other interesting and actually, or potentially, fruitful approaches to studies of prehistoric settlement. Two outstanding representatives are investigations into the relationship between architecture and spatial (rather than decorative) symbolism (e.g., Doxtater, 1991) and "microscale archaeology" (e.g.,Tringham, 1991a,b). We have not made reference to the first because of our deliberate choice to emphasize other factors in attempting to explain settlement form and development, nor to the second because it transcends our knowledge and expertise. However, our route of exploration is not meant to divert attention from alternative tracks through the wilderness of comparative settlement study, and we commend the valuable work of these others to the reader's attention.

Politico-juridical superstructure is associated with the modes of production of those societies in which the state functions as an authoritative political power in the organization of production relations. Such societies are characterized by the presence of socioeconomic *classes*. The absence of a politico-juridical component of mode of production implies production relations based upon social relations, usually kinship, among individuals or sub-groups of a society, whose life and livelihood are based upon *collective* labor production and distribution. On the other hand, mechanisms for the employment or use of surplus labor in societies characterized by the presence of a state are jointly maintained by the political and ideological components of mode of production.

Breaking Ground for Placemaking

Patterns of placemaking and the features of its spatial morphology are dialectically related to changes in mode of production, structural transformations, social relations, and cultural conditions of existence. Placemaking as an architectural production process (Adam, 1975), and its product—dwelling environment—both belong to productive forces which are in a process of continual development. However, social relations bring about the development of productive forces and, therefore, the patterns of placemaking and its products. The sociospatial organization of placemaking, its morphological features and its production are as much ideological and political as they are economic.

While the specifics of the constitutive features of placemaking in different societies may vary, the common denominator that affects goals/values are productive forces, namely, the *means of production*, the *instruments of production* such as tools, equipment, instrumental materials, and environments providing implements and specific environmental factors to be incorporated into the creation of places. Also to be considered are the *raw materials* necessary for construction, the *land* providing the substance to work on, and *labor power*—the producing agents' faculties such as skills, strength, experience, knowledge, inventiveness, and innovative abilities. Stated slightly differently, according to Harvey, the basic constituents that remain constant from one society to another are the object of labor (raw materials and land), the means of labor (the tools, equipment, fixed capital, etc., accumulated by past labor), and labor power itself.

It is quite clear that there may be more than one mode of production in a society at a given time. These opposing modes of production in different spheres of the society, such as in the urban and the rural realms, are bound together with the aid of various institutions and traditions of an ideological, political, social or cultural nature. The existence of "carving" as a way of creating dwelling for millennia in Cappadocia, or the uninterrupted continuation of a particular form of dwelling for thousands of years in certain parts of rural Anatolia, or the rural means of dwelling construction used by "squatter" settlers on the fringes of urban areas in developing nations are all translucent manifestations of the coexistence of more than one mode of production whose corresponding socioeconomic forms intersect and oppose each other.

This multiplicity of modes of production implies the necessity to reevaluate "traditions" related to architectural activity in general and placemaking in particular. The traditional qualities of placemaking owe as much to modes of production as they do to experience gained over centuries. Traditional ways of building are continued until a more satisfactory and appropriate substitute is devised or discovered. The continuation of traditional means of construction is not as much a question of choice as of the requirements of specific production relations dominating a particular segment of the society in question. The availability of productive forces, i.e., the means of production and labor power, is one determining component; the other is the production relations that determine the manner of utilization of those forces. Access to material, techniques, labor power, and control over these are the primary dimensions of production relations that determine the manner of utilization of productive forces are used in placemaking. The exact way in which the different segments of the society utilize these forces is subject to variation, but the reliance on diverse "traditional" means of placemaking is a direct result of production relations. The transition from a "traditional" way of constructing to another is neither a simple evolution nor a mere whim of the builder/architect, but rather represents a necessary transformation in the realization of placemaking, as the contradictions between its internal structure and the structure of its external conditions of existence are overcome. It is a transformation that leads to a restructuring of placemaking concomitant with the restructuring that occurs in environmental and cultural conditions of existence.

Discussions in the sections that follow will stress changes occurring in the two societies and their contexts through elaboration of the concept of mode of production and change in mode of production. Specifically, we are talking about elaboration of what has been called, in Europe, Asia, and Africa, the *primitive communist* mode of production. Wolf has suggested an alternative but equivalent term which seems better to describe the identical mode of production in prehistoric North America: *kin-ordered* (Wolf, 1982). We will use these two terms somewhat interchangeably in our analysis, doing our best to avoid confusion and keeping in mind, as elaborated later, that not all preliterate societies called "kin-ordered" were in fact solely oriented to kin in their socioeconomic relations, their actual productive activities.

The next stage in mode of production is that called *feudal* or *tributary* (Amin, 1977; Wolf 1982). Since the term "feudalism" has rarely if ever been applied to any stage of development in North American prehistory, we will use the term *tributary* for the transition which may or may not have occurred in Anasazi society. The mode of production, in this tributary stage, divides "the population under (its) command into a class of surplus producers and a class of surplus takers" (Wolf, 1982, p.99).

It has not been at all uncommon among students of anthropology, archaeology, and general and architectural history to posit relationships between economic and placemaking activities, between such economic activities as agriculture, and such settlement types as towns, for example. Thus, the beginnings of sedentary life are supposedly associated with the "agricultural revolution" or "Neolithic revolution" (Childe, 1952; Cole, 1965), which is in turn associated with the existence of villages. This belief was based on the premise that agriculture, in freeing people from the need to hunt and gather food, enabled the redirection of energy to the construction of permanent settlements, perfection of handicrafts, production of household utensils, and creation of art forms, thus leading to "civilization" (Childe, 1951,1964).

An alternative view considers, once again, the relation between mode of production, surplus product, surplus labor, and social formation. Social formation is based upon mode of production, which is in turn based upon surplus product. Viewed in this way, what is necessary for placemaking to occur is neither agriculture nor sedentary life per se, but surplus product. Placemaking in its most primitive form results from surplus product produced by those whose "labour has been to some extent socialised..." (Marx, 1967; I, p.512). In other words, initial conditions of existence allow portions of necessary labor to be directed to placemaking.

Modes of production are not static entities; rather, they have evolved through prehistory and history in several different stages. By way of a brief introduction, three stages have been fully realized in human history. These with their alternative labels and associated abbreviations are as follows:

1. "primitive communist" (PCMP) or "kin-ordered" (KOMP) mode of production;
2. "protofeudal" and "feudal" (FMP) or "tributary" (TMP) mode of production; and
3. "capitalist" mode of production (CMP).

In this book we are concerned primarily with the first stage and indices of an incipient transition to the second; the capitalist mode of production, the third stage, is not treated at all. The *PCMP* or *KOMP* is represented by a range of economic activities including hunting and gathering, food collecting, food production through pristine agriculture, and limited pastoralism. The *FMP* or *TMP* is characterized by staple agriculture, pastoralism, developed commerce, and pristine commodity production. The *CMP* is associated with highly advanced commerce, industrialization, and the mechanization of production. Each mode of production is related to a particular structure of socio-economic relations and to specific conditions of existence, which are in turn dependent on the structure of that mode of production; placemaking activity is integrated with all of these.

As stated earlier, we will be stressing the relationship of placemaking to the elaboration of the "primitive communist" or "kin-ordered" mode of production and the beginnings of the "feudal" or "tributary" mode of production. In the development of the *PCMP* or *KOMP*, hunting and gathering gave way to food collection (involving less nomadism and more storage), and food collecting to food production and limited domestication of animals. The most distinctive characteristic of the *PCMP* or *KOMP* is the *collective nature of appropriation:* there are no classes of laborers and nonlaborers in this unstratified society which extends far back into prehistory.

Notes on the organization of the volume

The book is divided into three segments. Chapters One and Two are introductory: they present a *basic philosophical and theoretical framework*, with an *introduction* to the two geographic areas of the globe which are the central regions being compared: the Anatolian plateau of present-day Turkey and what was the Anasazi homeland of North America, now the "Four Corners" area of the Southwestern U.S.A.

Chapters Three through Five trace the development of nomadism, sedentary dwelling, and eventual "urbanization" in the Anasazi and Anatolian regions. Hypothesized parallels are indicated, as well as non-parallels (such as the development of fortified cities in Anatolia, described in Chapter Four; we both compare and contrast them). Some interpretation is made in these chapters of the interrelation between built form and social forces, but the major interpretive task, within a systematic framework, is left to the third segment of the book, particularly Chapters Six and Seven.

Thus, the first segment sets the stage for the comparative study and unfolds conceptually; the second describes the two areas being compared and unfolds historically; while the third, primarily interpretive, at first unfolds analytically and then attempts to provide a new synthesis, or "reconstruction." An alternative way of expressing this is that the order of events is: theory, data, a reformulation of theory in placemaking terms, interpretation, and conclusion.

It may help the reader to make a bridge between Chapters Two and Six if we "telegraph" here what is to follow. As indicated later, Chapter Six elaborates a dialectical/ecological framework introduced in Chapter One. This elaboration is accomplished through the identification of fourteen dialectically related or "contradictory" pairs germane to the conceptualization of dwelling as place. Each of these elements is identified as "form" or "content":

I. Global concepts
- ideological and natural environments (content)
- shelter and property (form)

II. Fundamental relations in domestic architecture
- subject/object relationships (content)
- living and working relations/environments (form)
- use and exchange value (content)

- commodified and noncommodified environments (form)

III. Realization - specific interactive social and physical dimensions
- cultural and environmental conditions of existence (content)
- participation and nonparticipation in placemaking (form)
- stratified and unstratified organization (content)
- hierarchically ordered space (form)
- ownership and non-ownership of place (content)
- inclusive and exclusive—open and closed spaces (form)
- individual/family identity and social identity (content)
- public/private values (form)

As indicated, the above pairs are further grouped hierarchically under three headings: (I) global concepts, (II) fundamental relations in domestic architecture, and (III) realization — specific, interactive social and physical dimensions. Taken together, they constitute the basis of an ecological analysis. The elements and approaches of each of the chapters are further described below.

Chapter Two begins by expanding, in broad strokes, the descriptions of Cappadocia and the preconquest Pajarito to most of prehistoric Anatolia and the Anasazi territory to what is now the American Southwest. With the aid of maps, environmental and landscape descriptions, and cultural highlights, certain key events in prehistory are summarized. Chapter Two is intended to "set the stage" for the more detailed cultural/environmental description in the chapters which follow.

Chapters Three through Five cover the settlement history of the two areas being compared, from the end of the last Ice Age through the emergence of urban societies in the two locations, to some of the more recent patterns of habitation. The emphasis here is on "stages, not ages"; in fact, it may be because parallel developments in these two geologically similar areas occurred at such different *times* that they have not been noted. Moreover, the many differences in culture and specific patterns of settlement mask basic similarities — at least to a point — in the evolution of human occupancy of the two places in question. Chapter Three covers the period from the earliest "found shelter" through the modification of caves and the development of early free-standing dwellings to the beginnings of organized "proto-urban" settlements displaying more advanced approaches to shelter and systems of construction. The period spanned is almost ten millennia in Anatolia and more than 8000 years in the American Southwest. Chapter Three, by briefly tracing the early phases of settlement in both regions, sets the stage for the more detailed description of the important but often ill-understood transitions which followed.

Chapter Four starts with the first "cities" tracing and surveying the development of urbanization in the two locations. Major "breakthroughs" in Anasazi and Anatolian urbanization processes are described and illustrated, as are their physical manifestations in spatial organization and likely cultural concomitants. The emphasis here is on the search for ways of utilizing knowledge of the built environment and techniques of environmental management, providing an index of the kinds of changes that may have been occurring in the two societies and their interaction with other contemporaneous groups. In doing this we are attempting to advance the decoding of world views and ways of life of preliterate societies. This chapter paves the way to further the groundwork for the development of an explanatory framework in Chapter Six.

In Chapter Five, we return to the distinct parallels with which we started the descriptive material in Chapters One and Two, those between Turkish Cappadocia and the American Pajarito Plateau. The physical environments are — and have been, throughout the period of human occupation — nearly identical, and both areas have been continuously occupied for a very long period of time. Thus, the "break" between the distant and recent pasts turns out, upon careful examination, to be more apparent than real; the linkage between the great pre-historic cities and their modest descendants is established through the Pajarito and its offspring contemporary pueblos, in the American case; and through continuity of conditions of existence and evolution in modes of production in the case of Anatolia.

While Chapters Two through Five are primarily descriptive and only secondarily interpretive, both analytic and synthetic interpretation is the subject addressed in Chapters Six through Eight. As indicated previously, Chapter Six elaborates a theoretical framework built upon the concept *mode of production* introduced in Chapter One, together with its constituent economic base, ideological superstructure, and politico-juridical superstructure. Other concepts introduced earlier are incorporated as well, including social formation and appropriation, necessary and surplus labor, and use and exchange values.

The above are components of the "global framework" or general model. The "special framework" or specific model attempts to relate this general prototheory specifically to built environment. Some ideas introduced implicitly in Chapters Three and Four are here related explicitly to a new dialectical/ecological framework, whose general elements are "content" and "form." Concepts related to nature, ideology, shelter, property, and territoriality are delineated by definition or by example, setting the stage for the further analytic effort attempted in Chapter Seven.

Chapter Seven applies the analytic framework developed in Chapter Six to the descriptive material presented earlier concerning Anatolian and Anasazi settlements, building upon the beginnings of analytic efforts in Chapters Three through Five. The purpose of Chapter Seven is to attempt an explanation that brings together a number of apparently contradictory or previously isolated (because they are the products of single disciplines and unilinear perspectives) bits of information. Such an explanation is intended to provide the beginnings of a dialectical/ecological alternative to traditionally dichotomous (or trichotomous) determinisms. The relations of technological change and innovation diffusion to changes in mode of production in the two geographical areas of interest are introduced here in Chapter Seven and further elaborated in Chapter Eight.

Chapter Eight, after briefly recapitulating and summarizing certain major points and key elements raised earlier in the book, continues with a critique of inquiry concerning placemaking. Here, the relationship between what is conventionally considered "architecture" and placemaking is examined, contrasting the "mainstream" approaches concerned primarily with architectural form, per se, with an ecological/relational approach that considers forces of socioeconomic, political, and cultural organization, informing and influencing both "objective" and "subjective" aspects of placemaking activity. The positivist claim to objectivity, and the purely formalist/vernacular aesthetic approach to an understanding of built environment, are examined together with contradictions between idealist and materialist perspectives and between static and diachronic views of built environment. Next, the "questioning" nature of research methodology is reintroduced, with reference to material initially presented in Chapters One and Six. Finally, certain major points and issues raised in earlier chapters are recapitulated and a "reconstruction"—a new synthesis—is attempted. Then, as must always be the case, suggestions for future directions of substantive research and methods of inquiry are presented and elucidated.

Chapter Two

SHELTERING LANDSCAPES AND VICARIOUS HOUSING

> Scientific cognition strives to become explicit theoretical awareness.... Without a certain quantum of information, especially about the origins and transformations of a system, a scientific undertaking cannot be accomplished. It is possible, if one has collected a few rules and a few facts about a society, to rough out a synchronic analysis, to sketch a "model" of what this society "might" be, and if one has a number of successive pictures of this society, to attempt a diachronic analysis by offering diagrams of "transition" from one state to another of the reconstituted system.
>
> M. Godelier, The object and method of economic anthropology.

Chapter Two sets the context for the presentation of two case studies involving prehistoric settlements in Turkish Anatolian Cappadocia and in the Anasazi-dominated region of the American Southwest and the later analysis of the form/culture relationships they exemplify.

We begin by examining the evolution of settlements — in size, form, and function — since the end of the last Ice Age; the dialectical relationship between city and country, urban and rural places, is examined in the context of economic and political "evolution," of changing modes of production, of new forms of social and spatial organization, of emerging new orders of societal and environmental management and administration. Built form is but one evolving product of these changes: its alteration over time is a function of changing needs and developing capacities to produce and exchange food, raw materials, and the tools and instruments of production, as well as the emergence of new forms of egalitarian or hierarchical systems of control, of new kinds of settlements, and the symbols — material, spiritual, and ceremonial — incorporated into vernacular architecture and urban design. Towns and cities are, thus, not just overgrown villages; they are qualitatively different in providing settings for newly-emerging productive forces and social relations.

With the above ideas as a starting point, this chapter presents, first and very briefly, the geomorphological context within which settlement evolution took place in Central Anatolia and certain principal areas of Anasazi habitation; second, and in somewhat more detail, the "nodal" role of these areas as places where trade routes crossed and both information and goods were exchanged. Strict environmental determinism is negated early on, but questions concerning relationships among agriculture, sedentarization, and settlement, and the extent of possible parallels between changes in built form and modes of production in the Anasazi region and Anatolia, are left open.

The long history of migration and emigration into both regions, by settlers who arrived, remained for a time, and were supplanted by others, is briefly summarized. In this, we draw parallels here and in the chapters that follow between prehistoric stages rather than ages: the development of proto-urban society in Anatolia preceded similar developments in the American Southwest by several thousand years. Thus, pre-Hittite urbanization in Anatolia prior to 2000 B.C. is probably paralleled to an extent by the emergence of the so-called "Chaco system" in North America some 3000 years later. The development of urban settlements and systems, of course, lagged far behind the establishment of the first ephemeral settlements; food-gathering existed as much as 10,000 years ago in what is now the American Southwest, and much earlier in Anatolia.

Setting the context

Placemaking is not only the creation of dwelling and establishment of settlements, but the consolidation of very small settlements into villages and the formation of towns and cities. Settlements at different scales appeared fairly early in both Anatolian and Anasazi areas, concomitant with the beginnings of sedentary agriculture. There is the common but erroneous belief in an invariant developmental sequence from isolated dwelling to village, village to town, town to city. In fact, in both of the geographical areas we are exploring, cities and villages have existed for millennia in dialectical rather than evolutionary relationship.

The rise of cities was neither the result of overgrown villages nor the direct consequence of agricultural development, nor was it an immediate outcome of technological advances. "The rise of cities," which is called "the second great 'revolution' in human culture" by Adams, "was pre-eminently a social process." (1972; p.137). On the other hand, cities were not really the cradles of "civilization" per se, as has also been claimed. No doubt, towns and cities together with their hinterlands played an important role in the development of "civilization" and culture by being the appropriate settings, by providing the necessary spatial organizational conditions, to patterns that were already in the process of development.

The "social process" of the rise of cities to which Adams refers is the process that is shaped with the development of class stratification and ownership (not necessarily legal ownership). As the concept of property and ownership develops, control of the main productive forces also grows and changes, enabling a minority (priestly class) to become the ruling group. The newly emerging political structure and slowly changing ideologies (religion, belief system, perception and cognition of nature, etc.) establish societal hierarchies which manifest themselves physically in spatial and territorial organizations. Thus, the political and ideological formations in the society, as a result of "maturing" material conditions, not only require further complex division of labor but also new settings, apart from older spatial organizations.

This highly complex division of labor, both physical and mental, is actually the germination of the dialectic between town and country. The emergence of "city" implies the necessity of a different order of administration, organization, and management. While the newly-rising city is forced to maintain its own existence, it is also in need of support for its economy and livelihood. The city proper cannot achieve this alone. Therefore, its food supply — animals, wild plants, or later, agriculture — must depend on a surrounding territory that is outside the city boundaries (Jacobs, 1970; pp.18-40). This territory is what is referred to as "country." Specialized communities dealing with hunting or collecting, and later with cultivation of the land (in the Neolithic), became the food-baskets in the hinterlands of the cities they were serving. While some of the old hunting villages may still have existed, the start of agriculture allowed new villages, using land for agricultural production, to emerge along with cities. However, these villages were only subordinate communities to the parent cities. As Jacobs conjectures, "city economies create new kinds of work for the rural world, and by doing so also invent and reinvent new rural economies" (p.39). Thus, according to the needs of the city, communities in the hinterland of that city became an essential economical part of the city as long as they serve the function that the parent city requires. With the changing needs of the city, the nature and capacity of villages determined whether they would continue to serve or become obsolete. With the advance of agriculture, for instance, hunting villages gradually lost their utility. On the other hand, as long as they served the purposes of the cities, villages became dynamic complementary extensions of those cities.

The primary reason for the formation of villages is production that can be consumed in the city. This production becomes the "rural production" to be used for "city consumption." Therefore, Jacobs' assertion that "rural production is literally the creation of city consumption" (p.40) describes the very nature of the city, a "settlement that consistently generates its economic growth from its local economy" (p.262). Here, the term "local" refers not to the formal boundaries of the settlement itself but to its broader hinterland, the landscape surrounding it, including rural areas.

City implies country, just as urban implies rural. Villages, for lack of a better term, or settlements that existed before the rise of the city, are of a different nature. Therefore, the village as an antithesis of the city, after the city's rise, is economically and politically different from the earlier village. With the rise of cities, villages became economically subordinate settlements where surplus labor was extracted for the needs and the demands of the city. Before the emergence of the city, material production was performed in the absence of political superstructure. The rise of the city was dependent upon different degrees of ownership or control of productive forces leading to a class stratification, eventually giving rise to complementary political and ideological hierarchies. Administration of territorially divided and economically differentiated settlements within the stratified society was based on specific economic forms determining social relations between the different strata. The way surplus labor was extracted from producers in the villages as well as in the cities was the foundation for "the entire formation of the economic community which grows up out of the production relations themselves, thereby simultaneously its specific political form." (Marx, 1967; III, p.791).

Since the "first historical act" was "the production of the means to satisfy" basic needs — eating, drinking, habitation and clothing — that is, "the production of material life itself," (Marx and Engels, 1947; p.16), any form of satisfaction of new needs emerging with the rise of the city was also an historical act. By generating the needs that led to the formation of villages, cities also reinvented "rural production" to supply some of their material needs. For the satisfaction of material needs, productive activity must be in process, which employs both means of production and labor power. The end result of this activity may be food (berries, meat, etc., and later agricultural products), raw materials (obsidian, wood, flintstone, etc.), instruments, tools, buildings, and the like. These material products needed by the city and produced in villages, regardless of their purpose (for immediate consumption, or for trade), are the results of some form of surplus labor and some mode of exploitation contributing to the economic well-being and growth of the city. In other words, as long as the contribution of villages to the city's economy was productively useful, the village became the setting for the productive forces that were supplying both the means of production and labor power.

The separation between town and country (city and land, urban and rural), according to Marx, is "the whole economic history of society" that " is summed up in the movement of this antithesis." (1967; I, p.352). If "history is nothing but the succession of the separate generations, each of which exploits the materials, the forms of capital, the productive forces handed down to it by all preceding ones, and thus on the one hand continues the traditional activity in completely changed circumstances with a completely changed activity," (Marx and Engels, 1947; p.38), then within this historical act the city reinvents the village primarily for exploitation. The antithesis between town and country exists as a result of the concepts of ownership, territorial division of labor, and mode of exploitation. While all cities change their form with changes in conditions of existence, the mode of exploitation can be realized by "other than economic pressure" (Marx, 1967; III, p.791), such as ideology, which was the case during the rise of cities. As the material conditions leading to an advanced level of productivity developed within the old economic structure to allow higher economic structure to emerge, which motivated one sector of society to dominate another was primarily ideological in the early stages; thus, "rural production" was manifested in its new physical setting, the village.

The dialectic between town and country "is the most crass expression of the subjection of the individual under the division of labor, under a definite activity forced upon him — a subjection which makes one man into a restricted town-animal, the other into a restricted country-animal, and daily creates anew the conflict between their interests" (Marx and Engels, 1947; p.44). While the spatial manifestation of this conflict is disclosed by the reinvention of the rural world to satisfy the changing and growing needs of the city, itself a new spatial organization, the antagonism between the two spatial entities increases further as the wealth and power of authority is centralized in the city.

At this point, it is necessary to draw attention to the distinction between the "social" and the "material" since "new superior relations of production never replace older ones before the material conditions for their existence have matured within the framework of the old society" (Marx, 1970b; p.21). This distinction brings out the differentiation between the content and form of a society, wherein the material content consists of the people and productive forces, mediated by production relations within the social form. Surplus product accumulation and production increase, beyond what was necessary to satisfy the essential physical needs of the immediate producers, led to the development of other productive forces, such as differentiation of functions in a dwelling and specialization of use in different buildings. Like the other constituents of means of production (tools, materials), buildings at a smaller scale and spatial organization at a larger scale developed. This was necessary to improve the productivity of means of production.

Together with labor power, i.e., the productive faculties of the producers (such as knowledge, skill, inventiveness), means of production constitute the productive forces. As the productive forces develop, needs also change. The development of productive forces is not only a social process in the human "interchange with Nature," (Marx, 1967; III, p.815), but also a natural and a material process. In this process, the material content of society develops within a form. This social form does not go through transformation "before all the productive forces for which it is sufficient have been developed." (Marx, 1970b; p.21). On the other hand, the development of productive forces, i.e., the material process alone, is an "abstract conception which does not define any of the actual historical stages of production." (Marx, 1973; p.88). With regard to building activity in general and placemaking in particular, built environment as material production is the result of broader productive activity which exists within social conditions. Hence, the rising city becomes the necessary setting for a newly-shaped social form to provide for developing productive activity different from the material production of earlier settlements, which in turn corresponded to the previous social form.

In subsequent chapters, we will be concentrating upon the area of Anatolian Cappadocia and ecologically similar environments of the prehistoric Anasazi in the American Southwest. But these cannot be considered in isolation from their surrounds, from their contexts. The context for Cappadocia is all of the Anatolian Plateau (Figure 2.1), while that of the Anasazi is much of what is now the American Southwest, northern Mexico, and parts of Mesoamerica as well.

We are concerned with two phenomena representing possible parallels between aspects of Central Anatolian and Anasazi settlements (Figure 2.2) at what we contend are equivalent stages of development. The first phenomena concerns the assumed relationship among agriculture, sedentarization, and settlement (the formation of villages and towns). The second inquires whether the indices of uncompleted change in mode of production in Anasazi society suggest parallels to changes in mode of production we know to have occurred in prehistoric Anatolia.

Whether human habitation in Mesoamerica and North America dates back quite as far as Anatolia is doubtful, but the existence of food gathering is well established at 5000 to 8000 B.C. (MacNeish, 1964), and probably dates to the end of the last Ice Age, or earlier. Since provision of food and shelter in Anatolia was a collective process at this stage, consumption, and use were communal. Relations of production were matrilineal and endogenously based in isolated social units (Berktay, 1983). Units of labor were based on environmental resources, and divisions of labor were based on sex. Environment was the object of labor, and the need to scour large areas for subsistence prevented the development of a strong sense of territoriality. Surplus product and surplus labor were insufficient to provide for either nonlaborers or the establishment of *permanent* settlements.

Placemaking even occurred at very early stages of societal development conditioned by the existing mode of production, collective appropriation, and non-sedentary existence; temporary "butchering stations" were occupied for brief periods of time and "base camps," the sites where most social appropriation took place, for longer periods (MacNeish, 1964). At the dawn of the PCMP or KOMP, shelter was provided by caves, and their "personalization" constitutes the earliest placemaking — perhaps as early as 300,000 B.C., according to Cameron's (1973) dating of "house" remains found near Nice, France. Later, of course, people used caves as environments to be further carved into dwellings (Cappadocia) or as building sites (Anasazi).

Vicissitudes of the landscapes

Shaping of the cones

By Oligocene times, the middle of the Tertiary period (approximately 35 million years ago), primarily granitic, crystalline rocks formed the ridges of the mountains in the central part of the Anatolian peninsula. Considerably taller than at present, angular, presumably Alpine looking, and articulated into several long ridges, the ancient crystalline rocks had been reduced in height and rounded in form as a result of long, continuing processes of erosion. The Miocene epoch (25 million years ago), with its moist and warm climate, led to even more intensive weathering and erosion, producing the gentle and rounded forms that are seen today. While some of the salt lakes in the region were being filled, a number of new lake basins were being formed in the deposits of sedimentary rocks, not very far from the present valley of Kizilirmak. (References, used in this section: Westerveld, 1957; Beekman, 1966; Pasquare, 1968; Andolfato and Zucchi, 1971).

The orogenic movements in the early Miocene times caused deep fractures in the crystalline foundations, as well as leading to the formation of new mountain ranges such as the Tauruses, the southern edge of the central Anatolian plateau. New depressions such as the Salt Lake immediately to the west of present-day Aksaray, and the plains surrounding it, along with the drainage valleys of present rivers such as Kizilirmak, Melendiz, and Mavrucan were also formed as a result of this fracturing. In this process of structural disturbance of the earth's crust and reformation of the landscape, large eruptive cones were also produced creating the conditions for underlying magma to push its way through the earth's crust. Formation of what was almost a chain of volcanoes in the heart of the central Anatolian Plateau was the beginning of a development which later led to the present landscape of the Cappadocian region. Erciyes Dagi and Develi Dag became the natural boundary of the Cappadocian region on the east, while the Salt Lake remained as a natural edge on the west; Hasan Dagi, Keciboydoran Dagi and Melendiz Daglari formed the southern border, and to the north, depression of the drainage valley (later the Kizilirmak Valley) completed the perimeter of this rather well-defined plateau. The area surrounded by these morphological features, as a result of orogenic movements in the early Miocene epoch, became a region of conic deposits, their principal peaks reaching more than 3000 meters, with numerous subsidiary cones. They constitute the landscape of the region now known as Cappadocia. (Figure 2.3).

Toward the end of the Tertiary period in the late Pliocene epoch (10 million years ago) the central part of the Anatolian peninsula went through another surface change as a result of the volcanic activity of the conic deposits. Masses of eruptive material, molten lava and basalt flows, formed thick layers of tuffaceous rock over an area of 10,000 square kilometers. Violent in nature and lasting several hundred thousands of years, alternating between quiescence and explosive phases, these eruptions continued almost until the beginning of the Quaternary period in Pleistocene times (about 600,000 years ago). Immediately following the volcanic activity, very humid climatic conditions set in during the Pleistocene causing the beginnings of the erosion cycle of recent (Holocene) times (12,000 years ago).

The top layer of volcanic deposits is fine-grained homogeneous tuff of highly compact structure; while this layer is hard and brittle, the layer below it is friable because of its medium-grained, pumice-like tuff of fairly loose structure; the third layer is again composed of medium-grained tuff, but of compact structure. After the first cracks, disintegration starts with the eolian and thermoclastic erosion affecting primarily the top layer and parts of the layer beneath it. The remainder of the second and most of the third layers are affected by precipitations, frost action, and erosion caused by the pre-existing cracks. Later, groups of cones form as a result of the disintegration of the tuffaceous rock, and cracks increase to become actual splits, separated from the main body of the rock. (Figures 2.4, 2.5). Since the second and third layers of the cones (isolated or in groups) are relatively easy to carve, they have provided shelter to the inhabitants of Cappadocia for millennia. (Figures 2.6, 2.7, 2.8). The hydrographic structure, one of the principal agents in reshaping the landscape by creating auspicious pockets of living environments and facilitating life-supporting activities, also provides the necessary means for human settlements in this otherwise barren, steppe land.

Tent rocks and canyons

Pajaritan geomorphology. Of all the Anasazi settlement sites, the area surrounding Frijoles Canyon of what is now Bandelier National Monument is perhaps the most volcanic. The Jemez volcanic field extends about 4,000 square kilometers. It is located on the east flank of the Jemez mountains of present-day New Mexico, mountains which reach an elevation of over 3500 meters and are primarily a product of late Cenozoic volcanism. During the Pleistocene, eruptions resulted in the enormous Toledo-Valles caldera complex, and also produced the formation known as "Bandelier Tuff" (Williams, 1986). This formation surmounts the Pajarito Plateau, to which reference will be made again later:

> The single most important event in the life of this volcanic field was also the one responsible for the most common rock type seen in the monument. During the two brief but catastrophic episodes that occurred 1.4 and 1.2 million years ago, many hundreds of cubic kilometers ... of silica-rich volcanic ash were erupted from the central portion of the volcanic field.... Within the lower, more "open" portions of the flow deposits, quite often immediately above a pumice fall deposit, *natural caves and depressions* were weathered into cliff faces. In these zones, the ash and the pumice deposits have considerable strength but *could be easily carved with blades and scrapers; early residents of the Pajarito Plateau expanded these caves into rooms used as habitations and for storage and ceremonial purposes.* (Heiken, 1980; pp.4-5, emphasis added).

Thus was produced one of the outstanding features of the Pajarito area, and its closest parallel with the geomorphology of Cappadocia's "cones." (Figures 2.9, 2.10, 2.11). Some of the tent rocks are located in Frijoles Canyon itself, with dense formations at its Rio Grande end; some are as far south as present-day Cochiti Lake; still others are located at the prehistoric Pajaritan site known as Otowi:

> Here is a cluster of conical formations of almost white [tuff], some of which attain a height of thirty feet. These are properly called "tent rocks." They are full of caves, both natural and artificial, some of which have been utilized as human habitations. These dwellings are structurally identical with those found in the cliffs. They present the appearance of enormous beehives (Hewett, 1938; p.47).

Natural caves perforate the northern face of the Pajarito Plateau; such caves, first excavated by water, continue to be enlarged by wind erosion. It was erosion, too, that "ate away" the volcanic "blanket" which once covered the plateau, leaving as remnants the long narrow mesas (*potreros*) which punctuate the valley of Rio Grande.

A mixture of water, ash, and cinders, resulting from the volcanic eruption, formed both brown strata and porous, white, unstratified masses. More relevant to processes of "carving to dwell," however, is a third form which in fact, dominates the plateau (Figure 2.12):

> ... the thick, non-stratified sheet, tending to columnar structure, ranging from a light, porous, gray pumice to fairly compact yellow tufa, in places approaching the hardness of sandstone, carrying a high propor-

tion of silicious material in the form of minute crystals. It is with this form that we have to do in archaeological studies. Rudely dressed from the irregular blocks into which it is already broken, it furnished a durable and easily worked building material. (Hewett, 1938; p.28).

Hewett goes on to emphasize the security and comfort offered by caves and carved dwellings in the "tent rocks," (Figure 2.13), and, important with regard to the question of Anasazi cave-dwelling, the fact that such homes require little labor for their creation.

Chaco geomorphology. Chaco Canyon is cut by the Chaco River, whose drainage covers about 11,500 square kilometers in the south central part of the San Juan Basin. The headwaters of the northward-flowing ephemeral Chaco River are located outside the Canyon. The Chaco River joins the San Juan River, and the Chaco drainage basin is thus a part of the larger San Juan Basin.

Chaco Canyon itself, 32 kilometers long, varies from 500 to 1000 meters in width and is bounded by moderately high cliffs penetrated by side canyons. Alluvial fans spread from these side canyons onto the relatively flat floor of the main canyon. Fajada Arroyo, which joins Chaco Arroyo at the southeast end of the canyon, does not flow at the same time as Chaco Arroyo, reducing the probability of severe flooding. The sediments of the lower canyon, where most prehistoric great houses were located (see next section), may be headwater-derived or locally derived.

San Juan Basin habitation dates back at least 13,000 years, with substantial populations beginning about 7000 years ago (Love, 1977). Thus, changes in the Canyon's physical conditions over time are of obvious relevance. Rainfall has fluctuated and the possible effects of this on settlement formation and settlement "abandonment" will be discussed later. Increased rainfall results in greater stream flow, depositing embedded gravel and locally-derived sandstone cobbles. Deposits formed under more arid conditions include talus blocks, colluvial deposits, soil, and cross-bedded channel sands.

The arroyo channels were alternatively cut and filled through the alluvium. The questions of arroyo cutting and filling, and of its effects upon agriculture and grazing in the prehistoric American Southwest, have been debated over some time (Bryan, 1941; Cordell, 1984; Hall, 1977; Love, 1980), as has the relationship between arroyo cutting and filling, and climatic change (Bryan, 1925; 1954; Cordell, 1984). Cooke and Reeves (1976) have provided a general discussion of "the arroyo problem;" we shall return to this and related subjects later on.

Anasazi climatic environment. Geomorphology is important in that it forms the foundation and, in many cases, the material for placemaking. But if, without invoking environmental determinism, we were to single out the single most important environmental feature in Anasazi society, it would be climatic variation.

Within the Colorado Plateau, two basic kinds of natural processes have been recognized that cause environmental change (Dean, 1988). These are:

(1) low-frequency processes (LFP), whose periodicities are longer than one human generation, approximately 25 years;

(2) high frequency processes (HFP), which are of shorter duration with shorter periodicities. These include wild food resource fluctuations, annual variability in climate, and seasonal cycles.

LFP and HFP are measured in various ways on the Colorado Plateau, including dendroclimatic analysis. It is in this way that the duration of droughts has been determined. Obviously, the duration of such droughts was important to the survival and expansion of the Anasazi; more important for our purposes, however, is that

> Human behavioral adaptation of LFP environmental variability is different from adaptation to HFP fluctuations. Most LFP variability is unlikely to be apparent to humans and probably is comprehended as stability. Basic economic and social adaptations are made to the environmental conditions established by low-frequency processes. HFP environmental variability on the other hand is much more likely to be explicitly recognized by human groups. (Dean, 1988; p.30)

According to Dean (1988), in the case of drought (which frequently plagues the Colorado Plateau), what is likely to be most important is not the drought itself but the interaction of drought with other stress factors. Thus, the "great drought" which occurred toward the end of the twelfth century, A.D. intensified adaptive problems because it occurred at the same time as (1) LFP hydrologic changes, which reduced the carrying capacity of the area, and (2) high population, which placed greater demands on that carrying capacity. We will consider further the related issues of long- and short-cycle, high- and low-amplitude climatic cyclicity in Chapter Five, as well as other possible causes of migrations away from, or actual abandonment of, the Anasazi homeland that occurred after the apex of Anasazi placemaking.

Crossroads of many peoples

Anatolia: Nexus and nodes

While the earliest recorded traces of placemaking activity in Anatolia go back fifteen millennia, habitation of the peninsula is not limited to this relatively recent time. The eastern part of the peninsula is thought to have been occupied continuously by people from the time of the lower and middle Paleolithic culture, as indexed by Acheulean stone tools (Cambel and Braidwood, 1972; p.137). There may have been other groups of free-wandering hunters and food gatherers in the remainder of Anatolia. Whether the conjecture of continuous occupancy of more than 100,000 years holds true or not, the recorded duration of fifteen millennia of uninterrupted habitation is long by any standards.

Anatolia, with so many resources and *generally*, a relatively moderate climate (ranging from semi-desert to subarctic), not only provided a reasonably suitable environment for the maintenance of human life but also acted as a link between east and west as well as north and south throughout this continuous occupation. Many different peoples with primitive to highly developed languages—varying from the indigenous Hattian to immigrant Indo-Aryan, Semitic, or Ural-Altaic among others—as well as peoples of different areas and races, lived on the Anatolian peninsula at one time or another in history. A number of civilizations flourished on the peninsula and added new dimensions to the earlier Anatolians; as each one left a mark of its own, they formed their own cultural as well as physical landscapes. As they modified the environment to accommodate their lifestyles and to secure their existence, they also established traditions and developed customs affecting all aspects of life.

Within this continuity of tradition, from the Paleolithic to the Neolithic, through the Chalcolithic to the present, placemaking activity went through different phases of development. Being highly dependent on conditions of existence, placemaking activity in certain places, especially in some rural areas, remained almost unchanged for several millennia (as indicated by illustrations in Chapter Four), although the material conditions of life in nearby cities varied with transformations in modes of production. If the architectonics, the main conceptual schemes, and the space-ordering principles of dwellings remain relatively unchanged or survive with very little modifications in an area for thousands of years—irrespective of cultural changes, invasions, extrinsic forces, constraints imposed by foreign agents, and technological developments—this *negates* the notion of a *strict* cultural determinism but cannot, however, be taken as supportive evidence for environmental determinism. To argue *for* strict environmental determinism would require (a) demonstrating that the environment *itself* has remained unchanged, (b) that other effects have been held constant, and (c) that there is supporting evidence for environmental determinism in other areas, particularly neighboring areas.

The uninterrupted accumulation of customs and the emergence of new traditions, soundly based on those existing for fifteen thousand years, certainly did not occur in Anatolia as an isolated and self-maintaining system. Nor did placemaking activity develop in isolation, independent of the level of social relations and cultural influences introduced from outside. However, while the history of Anatolia has been marked by a great variety of cultures in the course of fifteen millennia, the conditions of existence within each one of these have remained unchanged for long stretches of time. Consequently, so did placemaking activity. Since supportive evidences negate dependence on culture or environment per se, patterns of dependence relevant to placemaking must be sought elsewhere.

Even at the beginning of placemaking activity on the Anatolian peninsula, people were not in an isolated setting. Neither the mountainous terrain, nor the *occasional* harsh climatic conditions, nor the distances between settlements prevented the peoples of Anatolia and the peoples of the other surrounding parts of the Fertile Crescent from being in contact with each other. To obtain life-supporting materials, it was not uncommon for people to travel as far as one thousand kilometers. For instance, the use of obsidian by prehistoric people as early as 30,000 years ago continued until the coming of the metal ages after 4000 B.C. The sources of this life-supporting material are mainly limited to areas near those subject to volcanic activity. Two primary sources in Anatolia, one on the central plateau in the Cappadocia region, and the other on the eastern part of the peninsula, attracted people in the Neolithic from as far as Beidha, even further south than Jericho, as well as across the sea from the island of Cyprus. (Figure 2.14).

Archaeological studies indicate that the late Paleolithic sites — caves, cavates, rock shelters, or open settlements — had already established nuclear zones of consumption around natural deposits of obsidian, with radii as great as 400 kilometers. The need to obtain this hard brittle volcanic glass for use in the production of other tools, hunting, and related activities not only established a system of material exchange but, more importantly, became one of the earlier reasons for cultural diaspora. "No area of the world illustrates the power of the trader to bring peoples into contact as well as the Near East in ancient times, where even in pre-historic times, rare goods brought in from a distance, already appear in Mesopotamian villages." (Orlin, 1970; p.174). The network of human contact arising from the trade of obsidian as well as other goods, among which even perishable commodities are included, is seen by many to be a major factor in the economic and cultural development of people from hunting and gathering bands to spatially well-established, socially organized, productive communities. (Dixon, Cann and Renfrew, 1972; p.87; Mellaart, 1975; pp.276-282). Since the idea of community self-sufficiency, especially in earlier times, is almost untenable, and since long distance trade in nonperishable material such as obsidian has been confirmed, it would not be erroneous to surmise that the people of the Anatolian peninsula have been in continuous contact with each other, as well as with those from the surrounding lands outside the Anatolian plateau with outlying islands, since the latter part of the Pleistocene. Jacobs' conjecture about "creative city economy" also seems appropriate for settlements prior to the formation of cities: "... the incipient flickers of a creative city economy should actually be sustained ... only if several little cities were simultaneously serving as expanding markets for one another." (p.35).

Such a network of contact and continuous movement of new groups from all directions, with various customs and habits, either passing through or settling down, was sufficient for a rich cross-fertilization of numerous cultures in Anatolia. The peninsula had already become a crossroad as early as the beginning of the obsidian trade. With time, these heavily travelled trading routes developed into a spatial nexus for different cultures and peoples from various backgrounds and various economic and technological levels. The precocity of the development of Anatolia as a nexus and a node in the Near East can be explained by some physical factors, inducements, perhaps even preconditions. First, there were very valuable, in some instances life-sustaining, resources in Anatolia. In addition to obsidian, there were also metals — copper, gold, silver — which later became principal exports. The lack of some resources in Anatolia certainly drew traders from surrounding areas for purposes of exchange. For example, large quantities of tin constituted about half of the imports into Anatolia; other major items brought to the peninsula were textiles and clothing (Ozguc, 1972; p.244). Luxury items for personal use, such as dentalium jewelry shells and precious stones, were also among imports as early as 6500 B.C. Second, its geographical location was a determining factor. Allowing relatively easy access to, and being on the crossroads of three continents no doubt made its position favorable. Another aspect was its facile access to three major bodies of water, allowing contact with seafaring people. Quite early domestication of cattle in Anatolia, which had a powerful impetus on the growth of private ownership (Thomson, 1966; p.29), was certainly an addition to the wealth of the peninsula since livestock were more durable and much easier to transport than perishable goods. Finally, the rapid development of complex social organizations and the establishment of numerous cults in various Anatolian settlements, which became primary cultural centers rather than cultural backwaters, may have contributed directly to the attractiveness of Anatolia. (Figure 2.15).

As the religious and secular aspects of life began to separate, creation of a priestly class facilitated the centralization of authority in the society. A new building form, the temple, was on the rise. Then followed the palace. As society shifted its central focus from dwelling/shrine to temple, then from temple to palace, it was also stratified, allowing a minority to control ideology, politics, and economics. The shifting ideology and the emerging political power allowed the temples, and later the palaces, to crystallize new social organizations with a growing centralization of function, controlling the productive and cultural forces that were shaping the society (also argued in Berktay, 1983; pp.157-179). Spatial ramifications of such centralization were represented in the separation of town and countryside. The antithesis between town and countryside developed not only in the separation of barter and commerce, or agriculture and crafts, or custom and law, but in the division of labor through specialization; and in the centralization of power and authority, in social relations and in the shaping of environment.

Starting with the early Neolithic towns and developing through Hittite times, wealth and power were clearly expressed in the formation of Anatolian cities. Along with the exploitation of the hinterland and surplus labor, the city also controlled trade with other cities or smaller settlements. "Trade was not only the work of arranging exchanges of goods, it was also the activity that organized other economic activities" (Jacobs, 1970; p.235). The "mutually advantageous commercial system" that Ozguc mentions with reference to trade between the Hittites and the Assyrians, which developed by the second millennium B.C. (1972; p.243), also existed in pre-agricultural settlements. Settlements involved in the obsidian trade no doubt benefited mutually from the exchange. However, with the rise of cities and the reinvention of villages, cities benefited from the exchange more than villages. Not only was the surplus labor of the villages pumped out without equal return, but the gains of inter-city trade remained primarily in the cities. With agricultural advances, the antagonism of the two settlement types grew even more since the productivity in agriculture, which helped to shape material conditions in communities, led to new relations between producers and consumers. Advances in agriculture meant more productivity.

However, the higher returns from more productivity, rather than making the producers richer, were channeled to the parent city, causing more wealth and power to accumulate in the city. The shift from temple-city to palace-city was certainly the result of this accumulation which also made political formation stronger. By the time of the Hittites, this had developed into statehood with control over much larger territories, including numerous cities interlinked within a trade nexus.

Development in Anatolia from the Paleolithic to the Neolithic over the course of more than six millennia was remarkable. It was marked by a transition from food-gathering to food-production, from roaming bands of people to communities with complex social organizations, from natural habitats to the emergence of settlements with truly urban qualities. By the Neolithic period, "Anatolia rose to prominence as an important centre in the diffusion of Neolithic culture in the Near East" (Alkim, 1968; p.47). The peoples of Anatolia continued this trend in the developed food-producing phase of the Chalcolithic period well into the Bronze Age. By the latter part of the third millennium B.C., people of Hatti, natives of Anatolia, were enjoying an advanced level of development, fruits of a rapidly growing technology, elaboration of economic systems permitting the support of specialization in different crafts (exemplified in superb works of art in gold, silver, copper, and electrum), and highly ritualistic religious ceremonies which were attracting worshippers from surrounding areas. In short, Anatolia was experiencing a remarkable cultural growth and a prominent level of civilization. Impressive achievements of the people of Hatti from 2500 to 2000 B.C. were only the latest in the long chain of Anatolian contributions to civilization.

It was in such a cultural and social climate that successive waves of tribes belonging to different branches of Indo-European stock started arriving in Anatolia, presumably from northern Europe, to establish one of the most significant cultures in the area's history. The Hittite state which was clearly "the creation of an exclusive aristocracy" (Gurney, 1973a; p.252), within which there were certain distinctions of class and function, grew to be one of the most important states (along with the Babylonian, Assyrian and the Egyptian states) in the Near East in the middle of the second millennium B.C. The influx of the newcomers into Anatolia toward the end of the third millennium B.C. was first felt in the northwestern sections of the peninsula along the southern shores of the Dardanelles and the Marmara Sea, most notably in Troy. This was followed by further inland intrusions as far as Beycesultan; the Indo-European tribes successively reached central Anatolia (MacQueen, 1975; p.28), where their earliest presence at Kanes, formerly a Hattian city, was felt around the turn of the millennium.

While the history of the Hittites is classified into different periods, the development of economy, culture, and social relations was continuous. By the early Bronze Age, metallurgy had become as important as agriculture (Ozguc, 1963; pp.10-11): "the great prosperity of Anatolia ... was based mainly on the systematic exploitation of its metal wealth and on its ability to trade it to its neighbors, not only Syria and Mesopotamia, but Egypt, Greece, the Balkans and the Pontic Steppe as well." (Mellaart, 1971; p.370). As the economy of the region expanded and became more influential in people's prosperity, cultural life flourished within the realms of law, literature, religion, arts, and military architecture. Social relations were set by the rules of a feudal system where the forces of production, "the metal industry and especially the metal trade were probably under direct control of the local kings." (Ozguc, 1963; p.11).

The Hittites, as they forced their way into Anatolia and settled in the central plateau of the peninsula to build up their powerful and influential empire, exhibited "extraordinary abilities and exemplary powers of adaptation, based on a sense of reality and tolerance ... to unite numerous races of different languages and cultures under a common rule." (Akurgal, 1971; p.23). They also were able to develop their own autonomous culture. (Goetze, 1975; p.273). While the Anatolian autochthonous characteristics were a continuation of the marked Hattian tradition to some extent, Hittite cultural development "remained immune to the superficial elements of cultural assimilation" (Mellink, 1966; p. 129) of the Mesopotamian and Hurrian influences. In the process of being "Anatolianized," (Mellaart, 1971; pp.406-410), the Hittites "adopted the local culture and ... assimilated it making it function as their own culture and art." (Ozguc, 1963; p.4). While most of the "lesser citizens" (MacQueen, 1975; p.65) were engaged in the tilling of the countryside and while others in the cities were involved in service and industrial production (especially metalworking), "there is evidence for the presence of doctors, builders, carpenters, stonemasons, goldsmiths, coppersmiths, potters, bakers, shoemakers, weavers, tailors, fullers, tavern keepers (male and female), fishermen, cooks, porters and watchmen, although in many cases full-time professionals were employed only by the palace and temples." (MacQueen, 1975; p.78).

Early fortification of cities in the Neolithic period evolved into higher levels among the Hittites. The development of spatial defense systems, integrated and isolated, paralleled city growth, economic development, and changing social relations. The citadel, a defensive fortress, became a structure by itself separate from the rest of the city, providing necessary protection for the palace and the temple, which actually stored most of the wealth of the city. "Cities became focal points not merely for the safe storage of surpluses prior to the deployment, but for conspicuous expenditures for public building programs, for the maintenance of elites in luxurious surroundings, and for the enhancement of military power. With the concentration of wealth, early urban centers became both proponents of expansionism and powerful incentives for external attack." (Adams, 1968; p.48). Cities also provided protection for Assyrian trading posts, which were established with the permission of the local rulers. First, the local princes had control over their feudal domains; later the regional kings extended their control over larger territories of several feudal lords who allowed such trading posts. By the second half of the third millennium B.C. the political map of Anatolia was fairly stabilized and the "Land of Hatti" had already "become a land of small city-states, their rulers living in castles, their economies based primarily on agriculture, but their real wealth and importance residing in their metals and metal products." (MacQueen, 1975; p.17). Cuneiform tablets from Kanes — Level II — reveal a different order of territorial organization with regard to autonomy and dependencies. These facts indicate that "the system of *parity* and *vassalage* treaty arrangements which we know so well from the

Hittite state treaties of the New Empire" (Orlin, 1970; p.237), were already established much before Cappadocian trade began between Hittites and Assyrians.

While peaceful coexistence between the Hittites and their Mesopotamian neighbors flourished in commercial and cultural interchange (Orlin, 1970; pp.161-183), the Hittites, building up their empire, were not always on very peaceful terms with other neighboring states. Their expansionist policy not only enabled control over more resources and strategically important passes, but also the accumulation of more wealth, and the transformation of communal surplus into individual ownership. Their policy also institutionalized a social phenomenon already in the making, although on a smaller scale, in the previous millennia: slavery. Although not all scholars are in agreement, there is convincing evidence to indicate that early Mesopotamian society was feudal, based on private property (Gelb, 1955; pp.180-184). The situation in Anatolia before the Hittites arrived was similar; the social and spatial protofeudalism which started as early as 5000 B.C. in settlements such as Hacilar had already ripened, especially in northern and central Anatolia, by the third millennium B.C. The Hittites not only "adopted the local culture and ... assimilated it" (Ozguc, 1963; p.4) but expanded on it. The conditions were right and mature, the setting appropriate. The power and glory of the Hittite Empire, even at its peak, was not sufficient, politically or culturally, to put these "Anatolianized" Indo-European people in charge of the whole peninsula. There were at least five other languages spoken in Anatolia: native Hattian, Akkadian, Hurrian, Palaic, and Luwian (Gurney, 1973a; p.137). The latter two, in addition to Hittite itself, are closely related to the Indo-European family of languages. The linguistic and ethnic divisions of the Anatolian population in the second millennium B.C. are clear indications that the peninsula was not experiencing unified cultural development.

Following the Aegean immigration, about 1200 B.C., which caused the devastation of many Anatolian cities, a Neo-Hittite culture, strongly modified by the Assyrian, Aramaean and Phoenician civilizations, developed during the ninth and eighth centuries B.C. Descendants of the Hurrians, the Urartians established a powerful kingdom in the eastern part of the peninsula about the same time. Anatolia also became the setting for the Phrygian, Lydian, Carian, and Lycian civilizations during the same period. These cultures contributed significantly to the formation of the Greco-Anatolian civilization of the sixth century B.C. By this time, as eastern Greece or Ionia climbed to its zenith, the cultural leadership of the world once again passed to Anatolia. Between this and the Hellenistic revival in the fourth century B.C., Anatolia came under the domination of Persian governors, who usually confined themselves to recruiting mercenaries and levying taxes (Metzger, 1969; p.137). With the Hellenistic revival, native artistic traditions gave way in most cases to Greek forms. Native languages, especially in cities, were gradually superseded by Greek (Metzger, 1969; p.137). Under the Hellenistic monarchies, surrounding cities with walls continued. The Agora, the market place, gained special importance in urban organization. Throughout the Roman period (30 B.C. to A.D. 395), the Greco-Anatolian tradition continued as new Roman advances, specifically in construction, were incorporated into the building of cities. Anatolian cities such cities as Ephesus, Sardis, Aphrodisias, Hierapolis, Side, Perge, Aspendus, and Termessu were among the most influential cultural and artistic centers of the Roman Empire (Akurgal, 1971; p.25). These and many other cities in Anatolia, the important Roman centers, were also the cradles of early Christian and Byzantine art and culture.

Byzantine dominance of Anatolia was interrupted by newcomers to the peninsula. First the Seljuks (1071 to 1300), then the Ottoman Turks (1299 to 1923), brought Turkish elements from the steppes between the Ural and Altai mountains in Central Asia. They also introduced a new religion: Islam.

Anasazi: Nexus and nodes

The word "Anasazi" is Navajo, meaning "the ancient enemy" (Sando, personal communication, 1985); the term relates in no way to the people's name for themselves. The Navajo, Athabascan relatives of the Apache, arrived in the American Southwest over a period of time centering about the fifteenth century A.D. The "Anasazi" were presumably the ghosts of the people who once inhabited the stone ruins which the Navajo found scattered about their new territory. Because they feared the spirits of the dead, the newcomers shunned these ruins, the architectural remains of a society which had developed in the area over a very long period of time.

The earliest "arrivals" in the U.S. Southwest, referred to as "Paleo-Indians," are purported to have migrated to North America across a "land bridge" that once spanned the Bering Straits, connecting Asia with North America. The ancestors of various groups now called "Indians" presumably crossed at different times. The "Paleo-Indians" are likely to have made the crossing long before the Athabascans: estimates range from 14,000 to more than 20,000 years ago (Stalker, 1980; Horgan, 1992), with the strong possibility that migration continued over a considerable period of time, since the Bering land bridge was available at several periods from 23,000 to 8000 B.C.

Dating the first evidence of human habitation in the American Southwest has also been a problem. There is a debatable claim that Sandia Man-Cave, located approximately 25 kilometers northeast of present-day Albuquerque,

New Mexico, was occupied ca. 17,000 B.C. (Hibben, 1955) but general agreement that its habitation dates from at least 9500 B.C., contemporary with the Clovis complex (Cordell, 1984).

Paleolithic arrivals in the American Southwest hunted mammoths, primitive camels, bison, giant sloths, etc. By the so-called "Archaic period," beginning about 5500 B.C., all of these large mammals had become extinct west of the Rocky Mountains, including the variety of bison hunted by Paleo-Indians. The Archaic period was characterized by a continuation of hunting and gathering, but with hunting reduced to the pursuit of medium-sized and small game animals, and with climatic and vegetation shifts, consumption of wild plants increased. Communication (if not actual trade) with food sources in Mexico was established towards the end of the period, with maize first appearing in the American Southwest about 1500 B.C. (Figure 2.16).

The basis for Anasazi, Hohokam, and Mogollon settlements was effectively laid with the establishment of villages, between A.D. 200 and A.D. 700 in parts of what are now the states of Arizona, Colorado, and New Mexico in the U.S.A., (Figures 2.17, 2.18), and Chihuahua in Mexico:

> The appearance of the villages, of course, is ... a general characteristic of all New World societies at what has been termed the Formative stage or level of development ... This stage requires a secure resource base and social mechanisms that can integrate and sustain village economies ... in certain resource-rich settings it is possible to support sedentary communities without agriculture; however, in the relatively food-poor and marginal environment of the [American] Southwest, the production of crops is essential for the survival of even seasonally sedentary communities. (Cordell, 1984; p.137).

The culture stage called "Basketmaker" spans a period from A.D. 400 to 700 or so, according to the Anasazi Sequence in the Rio Grande valley proposed by Wendorf and Reed (1955). This was a period during which the use of ceramics spread; bows and arrows replaced spears, darts, and *atlatls* (spear-throwers); and the pithouse dwelling form became common. Importantly, too, it was a period of marked increase in the number of trade items.

The Anasazi also influenced the Mogollon of southwestern New Mexico and southeastern Arizona, perhaps before A.D. 800, a strong enough influence that by A.D. 1000 the Mogollon culture "had been so greatly altered and was submerged to such an extent that the resulting blend may be considered a new entity and given another name. This phase or culture is called the *Mimbres*." (Wormington, 1978; p.158).

West of Mogollon territory, the Anasazi appeared to have remained north of the Little Colorado area, separated from the Hohokam by the Sinagua (the latter with which the Hohokam had established contact during their movement northward up the Verde Valley) prior to the Sunset Crater eruption in 1066. It seems likely that it was the Salado Anasazi from the Little Colorado area who established direct contact with the Hohokam, then moved south into Hohokam territory about A.D. 1300 but their influence — in terms of architectural form — preceded their actual arrival by a century: "during the early part of the classic period (about 1200 A.D.), surface houses, sometimes with contiguous rooms, were built by the Hohokam. These changes were probably due to Salado influence, although the people themselves had not yet arrived in the area." (Wormington, 1978; p.140). Pueblo influence—and some pueblo people themselves—may have arrived even earlier. Kinishba, a great pueblo site on the Salt River just outside the junction of traditional Hohokam and Mogollon territories, appears to have been established about A.D. 1280 to 1320, approximately at the time of the Sunset Eruption: "Kinishba appears to have been something of a trade center, and pottery characteristic of many different areas is found here." (Wormington, 1978; p. 140). Starting as "Basketmakers" in the "Four Corners" area of Arizona, Utah, Colorado and New Mexico, and centering in the San Juan drainage, the people later called "Anasazi" by the Navajo spread west, south, and eventually east, covering an area from the Colorado River to the Pecos. In this process, they came into contact with many other peoples; the opportunities for transfer of information were undoubtedly considerable. In architecture, their rate of progress is truly astonishing: from the first masonry construction to the building of great communal houses, with several stories and hundreds of rooms, was less than 200 years (to the commencement of Chaco's Pueblo Bonito); Chaco Canyon National Historical Park contains 82 kilometers (32 square miles) and about 2000 archaeological sites (Hayes, 1981; Zeilik, 1985), with some 24 sites/square kilometer. The centers of Anasazi society apparently shifted eastward after the Great/Classic Pueblo period, from Chaco Canyon and Mesa Verde to the Pajarito and the Rio Grande/Pecos area, and westward to the present Hopi-Zuni region. But Chaco was the apex of prehistoric Pueblo; it is there and in adjacent areas that the answers to the "whys" of Anasazi society seem to lie. So far, however, as the next section indicates, more questions than answers have been raised.

The Chaco system. The great pueblos flowered in three locations in Anasazi territory: first in Chaco Canyon, next in Mesa Verde, and finally in the Kayenta area. Of the three, the Chaco system was the most geographically extensive, consisting of more than eighty communities. Earlier archaeological studies, in focusing only on the Canyon itself may have missed the true significance of the Chaco area, which includes, in addition to the visually dazzling megastructures on the canyon floor, a system of roads (noted by the resident Navajo and others but not firmly identified until the refinement of aerial photography) and of outlying sites (also called outliers, satellites, and colony sites) covering much of the San Juan Basin.

There are yet other possible names for the outliers. They may be similar to Hirth's (1978) "Gateway Communities." In the economic system of regional exchange, "affiliates" or "exchange partners" might be better terms (Snow, 1977). A regional perspective permits a better understanding of the Canyon's truly unique features, including "... 'engineered,' pre-planned buildings, high site density, complex water control features, high concentrations of prehistoric roads, astronomical alignments of structures, etc." (Marshall, Stein, Loose, and Novotny, 1979; p.355); and the relation among public, residential, and ceremonial buildings. The construction of the gigantic 800-room Pueblo Bonito, commenced in 920, but the "master planned" phase did not begin until 1020. If Pueblo Bonito was residential, it was, when completed, the size of the largest built "apartment house" in North America prior to 1880). But if, as has been suggested by many, it was part of a shift from domestic to public use of Chaco built environment, it was also no longer an "apartment house"—if it ever was (Lekson, Windes, Stein, and Judge, 1992). Thus:

> ... great kivas and Bonito phase buildings are considered to be public architecture ... A Chacoan settlement is a suite of several types of buildings including small domiciles, larger multistory public structures, and at least one great kiva ... We believe that a socially complex, but basically non-stratified, populace lived in the small structures ... and used the larger structures for storage, and for periodic sessions of special tasks related to public obligations and decision-making processes. These tasks were probably ceremonial, economic, and administrative in nature (Marshall et al., 1979; p.337).

Public function as well would explain the absence of burials and trash mounds near some great houses.

Major evidence for an extraordinary degree of community organization is the architecture itself. There is little evidence of growth by accretion in structures later than A.D. 1000. They were constructed over relatively short periods of time, and evidently pre-planned (e.g. Knowles,1974). Public function is evidenced in room size too; in multistoried Chacoan communities, rooms are more than twice as large, on the average, as elsewhere. There is a suggestion that "... the large room size is to accommodate large groups during Shalako, which is in part a redistribution ceremony ... when Chacoan sites are reoccupied by Mesa Verdean groups, and clearly used as domiciles, rooms are frequently divided into smaller units ..." (Marshall et al., 1979; p.337). Large rooms also probably served for storage since the Anasazi were threatened with frequent three-year droughts. The thick core-veneer walls of Chacoan buildings thus served more than structural purposes: the thickness provided insulation against temperature variations and the veneer substantial protection from vermin.

We are not certain about either the reason for the sudden spurt in monumental building or about why the great sites were "abandoned." The development of new strains of maize in Mexico may have sparked an "agricultural revolution" to the north, leading to the production of surpluses, extensive exchange, and the need for market centers. The ecology of Chaco Canyon could almost certainly not have supported anywhere near the populations of the great pueblos, had all the Chacoan megastructures been occupied primarily as domiciles. The major part of the agricultural production must have occurred in the outliers (affiliates, exchange partners), which, through the network of roads, probably supplied the centers: a "metropolis-satellite" relationship.

The usual reason given for abandonment of the area is drought. But the Anasazi were no strangers to dry periods: tree-ring data indicates alternating wet/dry periods, ranging from one year to 3 to 5 years (Jorde, 1977). Certainly, it required extensive organization to deal with such perturbations, but the fact that all possible productive niches were not "packed" with small sites and field houses indicates that even under the worst climatic conditions prior to abandonment, the area was not being exploited to its full productive potential. Why, then, were the sites abandoned? It may be that, as other evidence indicates, there was no mass migration, but rather a gradual drifting away. The social, political, and economic organization required for a massive exchange system may simply have been too fragile; the loss of even a minority of the population may have "forced the store to close down" — and with it the sophisticated transport system which Elbert and Hitchcock (1973), using indices of connectivity, ranked on the borderline of economic transport organization for modern, underdeveloped countries. There is the further suggestion that outliers were in fact specialized: some sites primarily for production, others for transport (Marshall et al., 1979) — but this still does not explain why the system finally failed; "The collapse of the complex Anasazi social system, in an area the size of modern England, is no small object lesson." (Marshall et al. 1979; p.339). We will return to all of the above issues concerning Chaco society in Chapter Four.

Comparative context

As Anatolia became the "crossroads of many people," so, much later, did the prehistoric American Southwest. However, the existence of interactive trade and information networks has been, until very recently, much more accepted for the ancient societies of the Middle East than for those of North America.

Visually and geologically, as earlier indicated, the Cappadocian region of Anatolia strongly resembles the Pajarito Plateau of northwestern New Mexico; there are some climatic similarities as well. In both regions, culture and architecture flourished (phenomena still not well-understood) prior to the invention or introduction of written language, and both apparently developed (directly or indirectly) extensive trade in "luxury" and utilitarian goods; but differences in the *resource bases* and general conditions of existence of the ancient Anatolians and the Anasazi are perhaps more marked than the similarities. The early Anatolians, for example, while dwelling inland, were not many caravan-days from the sea nor from the famed "Fertile Crescent;" the territory of the advanced Anasazi, on the other hand, far from both the sea and major river systems and plagued by chronic scarcity of water and the need for its control (e.g., LeBlanc, 1989; Pailes, 1989), could have been characterized as an "Infertile Crescent."

Large mammals, plentiful sources of both protein and transportation for ancient Anatolians, had become extinct in North America long before the flowering of the Anasazi. Among the latter, therefore, development of sedentary agriculture was perhaps more crucial than for Anatolians. This yielded a society that was, contrary to relatively recent belief, neither fully settled (e.g., Lekson, 1990; Powell, 1990) nor simple.

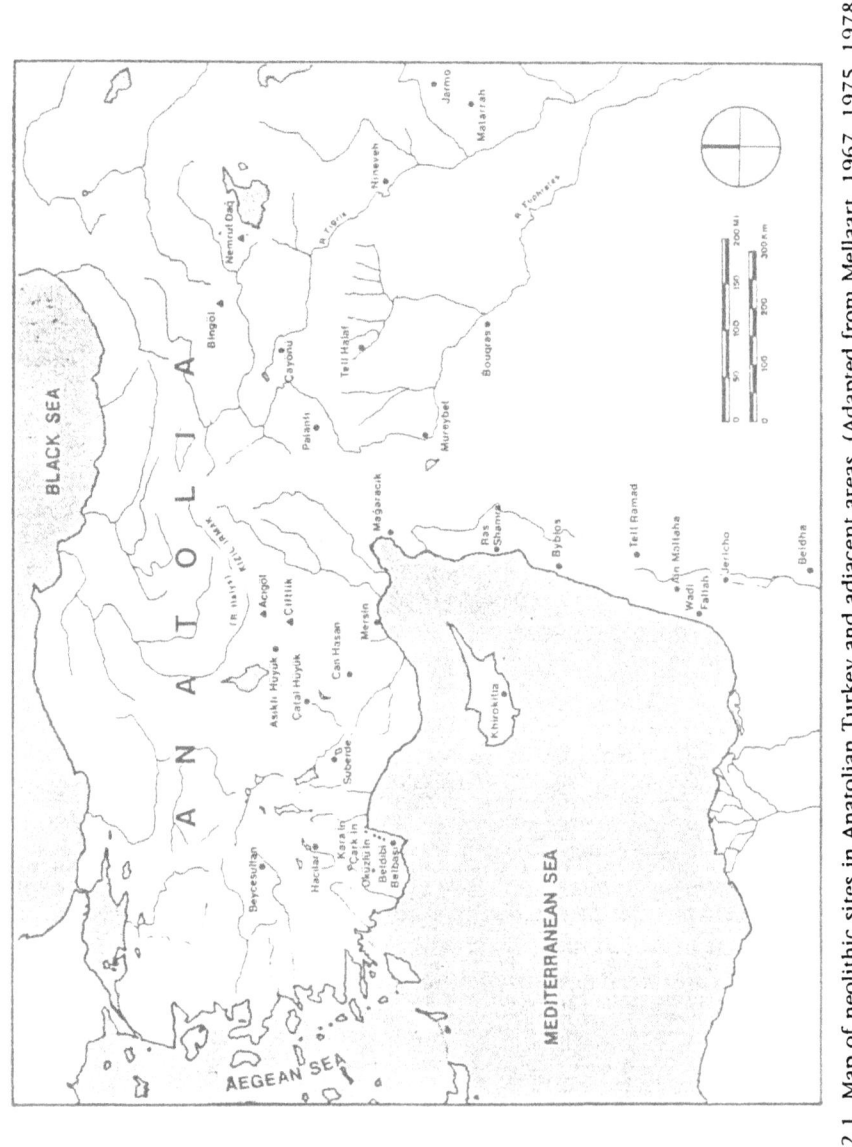

Figure 2.1 Map of neolithic sites in Anatolian Turkey and adjacent areas. (Adapted from Mellaart, 1967, 1975, 1978).

Sheltering Landscapes 53

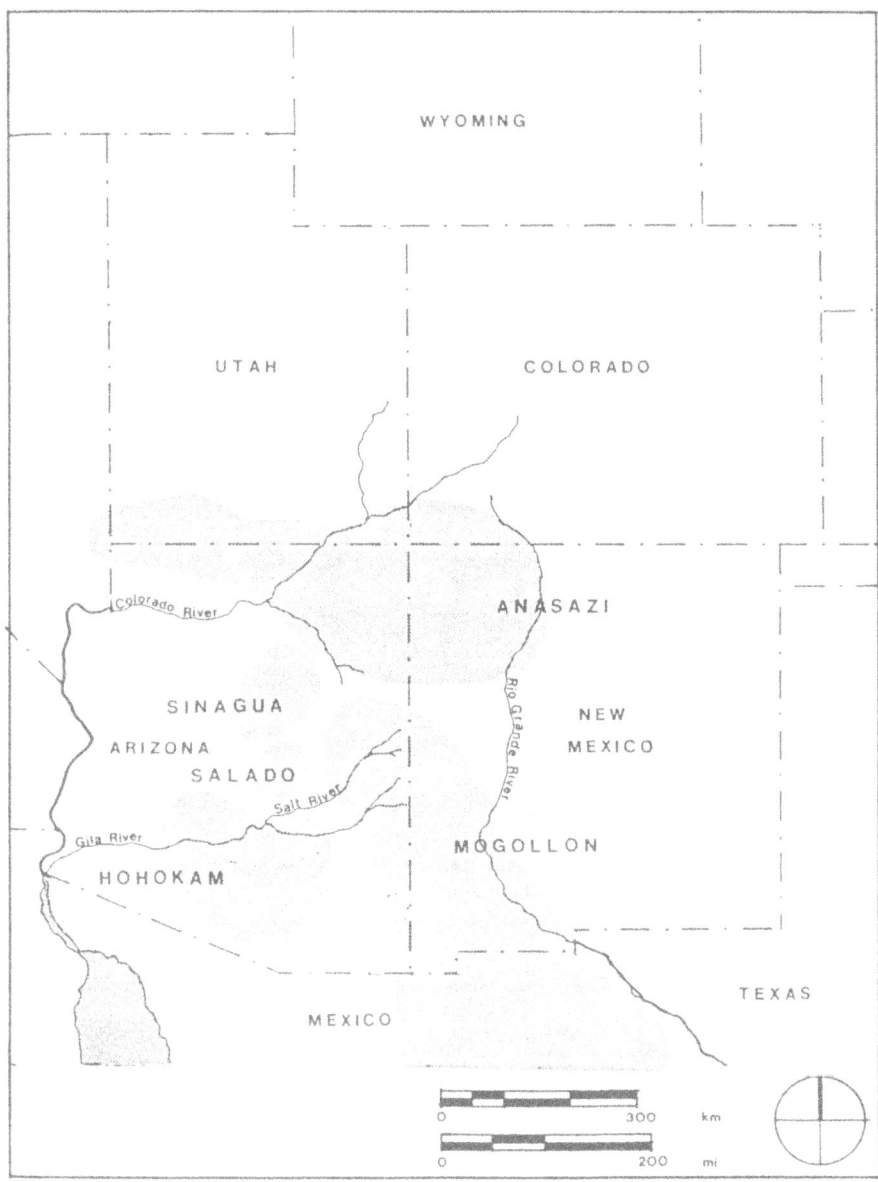

Figure 2.2 Distribution of major prehistoric cultures in the U.S. Southwest.

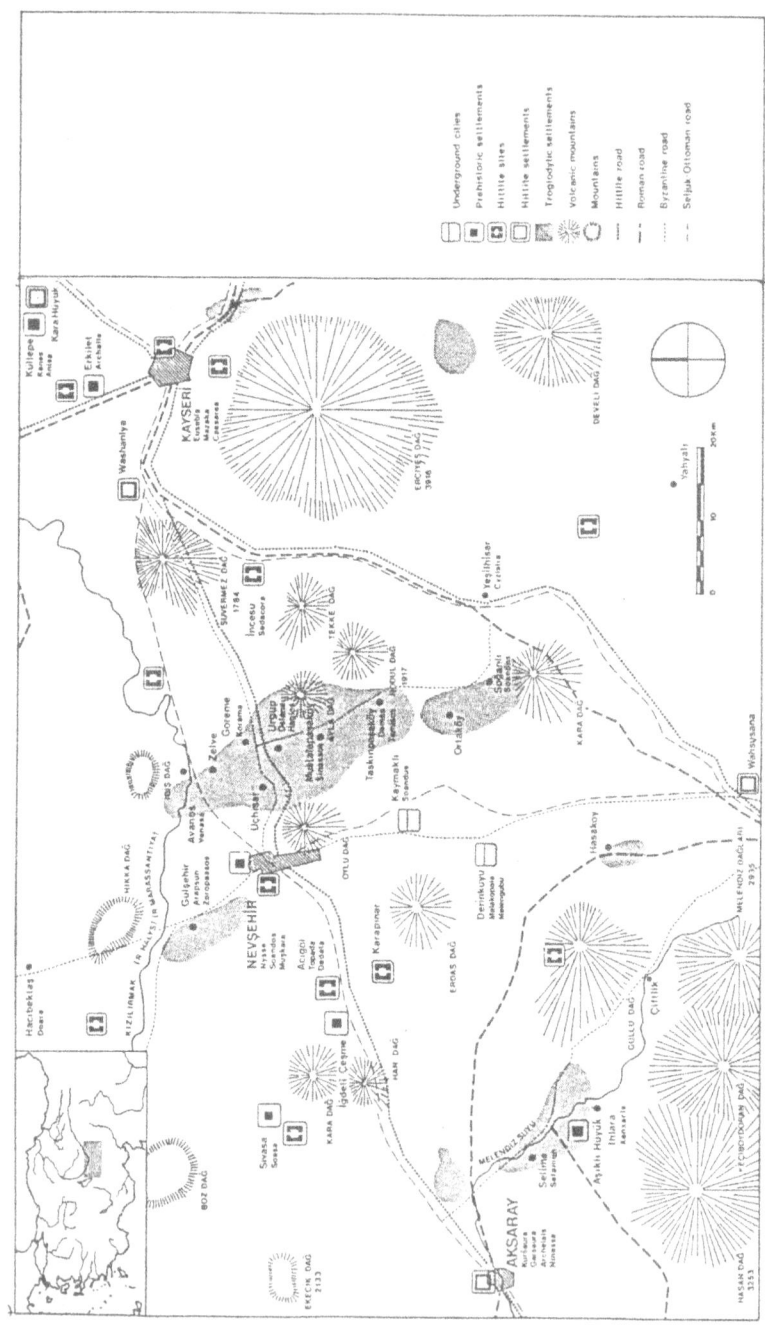

Figure 2.3 Cappadocia, with locations of major ancient sites and natural features. (Adapted from Giovannini, 1971).

Sheltering Landscapes 55

Figure 2.4 Cappadocia: landscape of "cones" not yet separated from the main body of the rock.

56   Sheltering Landscapes

Figure 2.5 Cappadocia: detail of gradual formation of free-standing "fairy chimneys" by erosion.

Sheltering Landscapes

Figure 2.6 Cappadocia: Zelve Valley.

Figure 2.7 Cappadocia: rock-carved dwellings in the Zelve Valley.

Sheltering Landscapes

Figure 2.8 Cappadocia: detail of rock-carved dwelling showing recent shearing of cliff face.

60   Sheltering Landscapes

Figure 2.9 Landscape of tent rock formations, Pajarito Plateau, New Mexico.

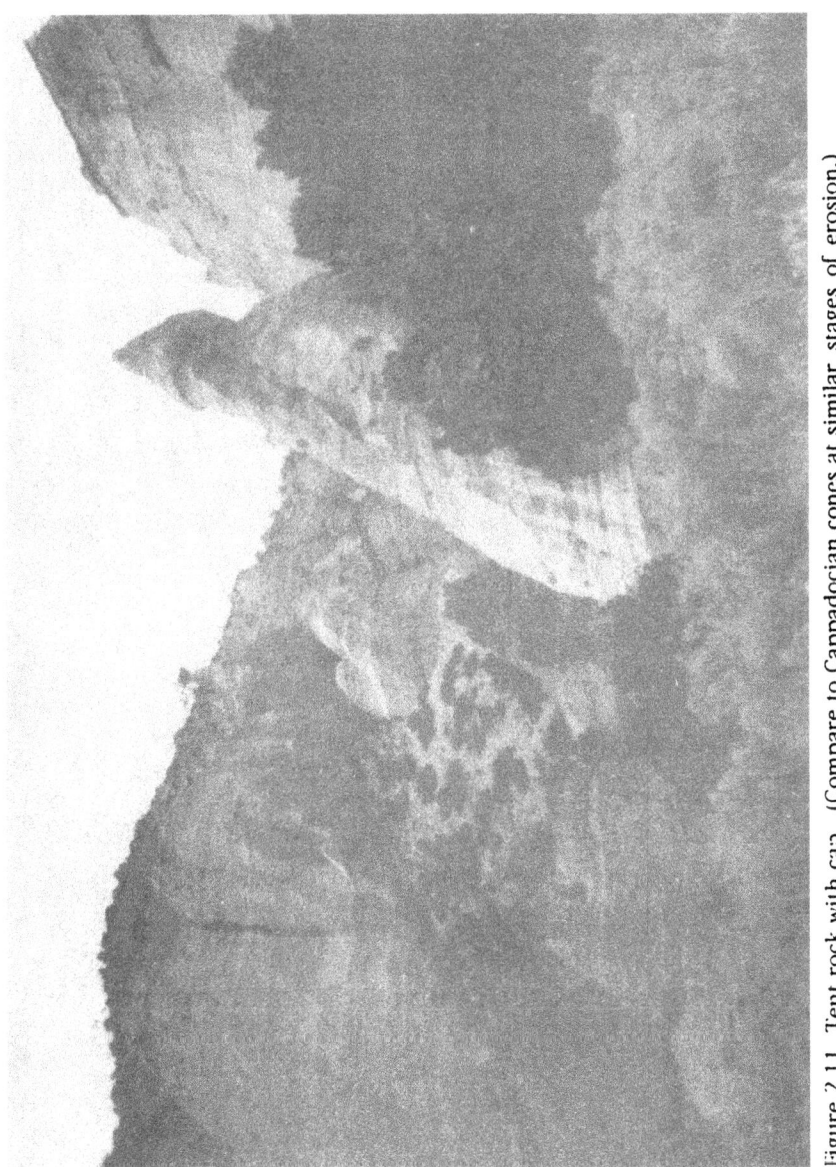

Figure 2.11 Tent rock with cap. (Compare to Cappadocian cones at similar stages of erosion.)

62   Sheltering Landscapes

Figure 2.12 Cave dwelling, southern face of Pajarito Plateau.

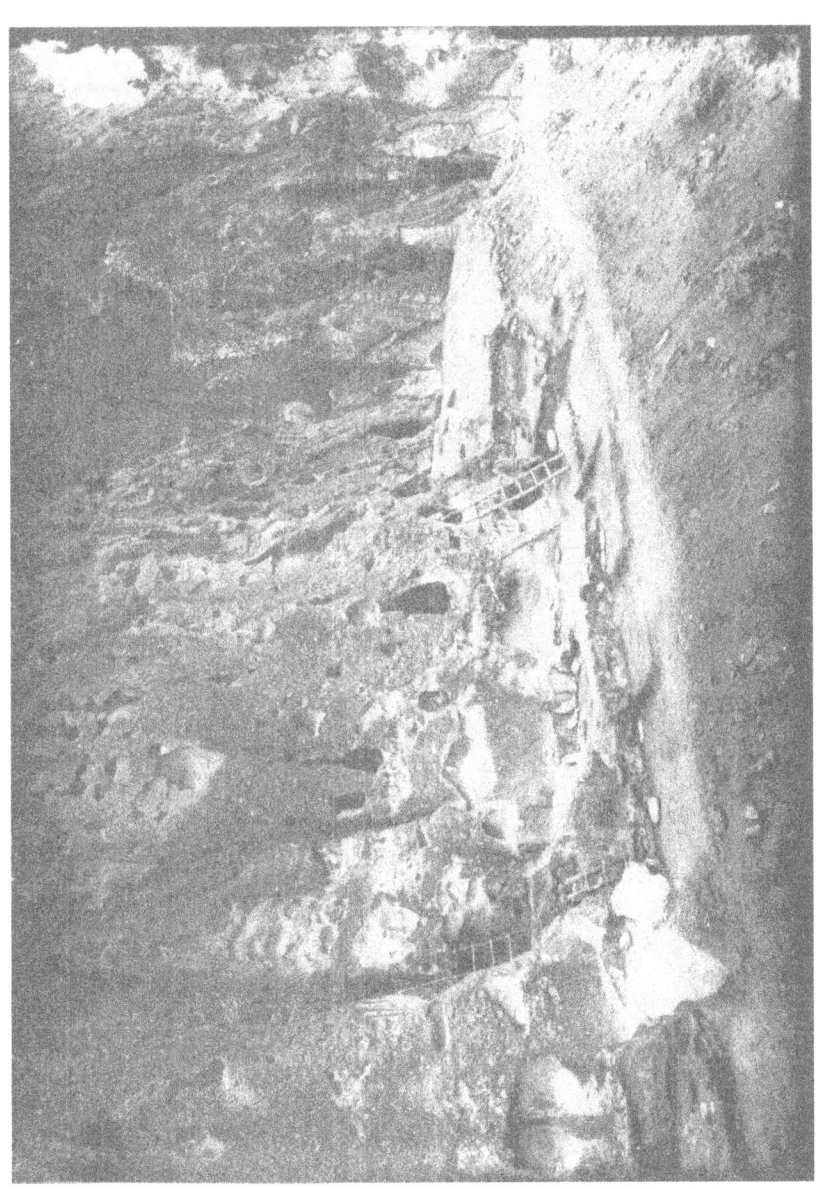

Figure 2.13 Rock-carved dwelling, Frijoles Canyon, New Mexico.

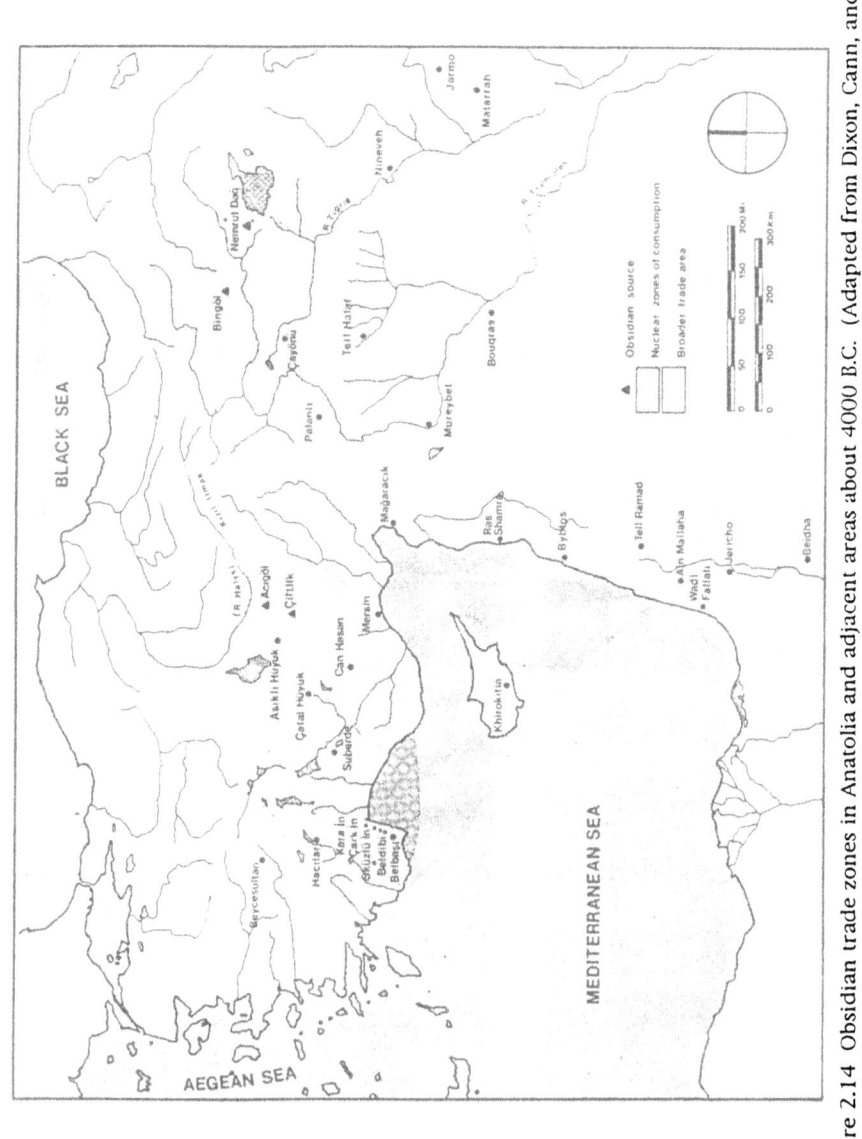

Figure 2.14 Obsidian trade zones in Anatolia and adjacent areas about 4000 B.C. (Adapted from Dixon, Cann, and Renfrew, 1972; Mellaart 1967, 1975, 1978).

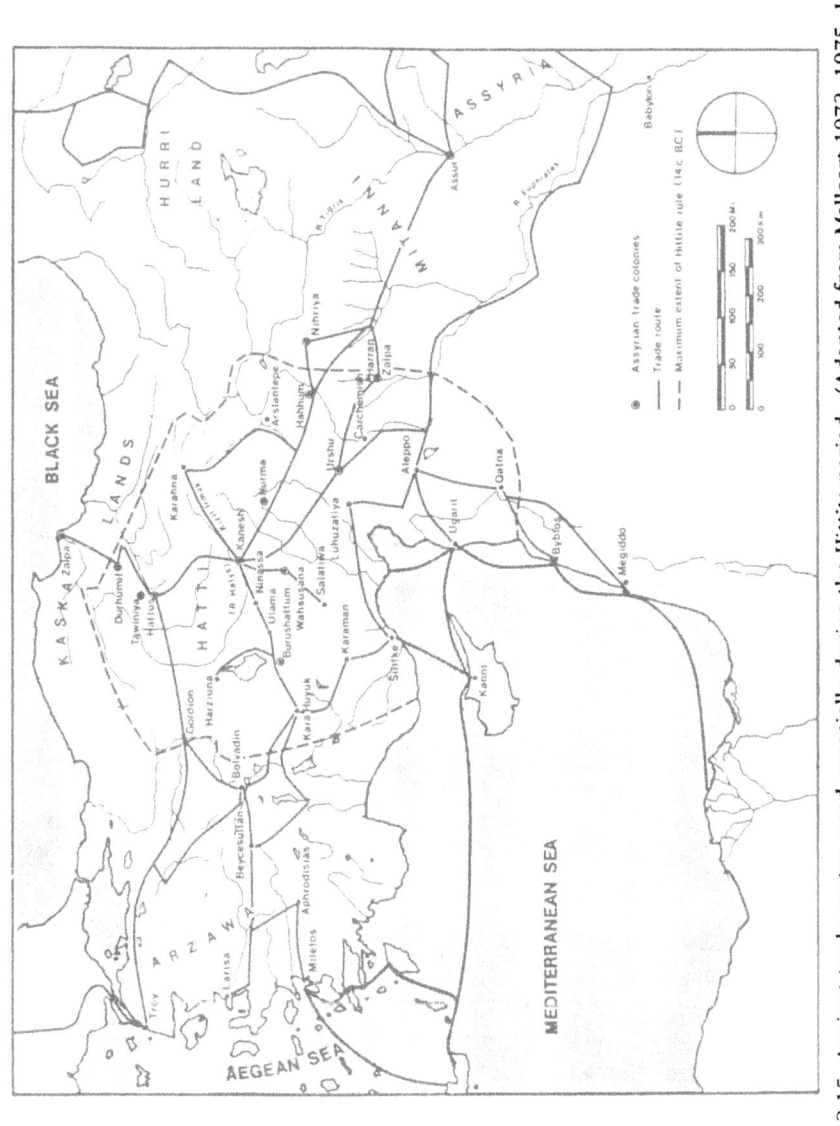

Figure 2.15 Ancient trade routes, used especially during the Hittite period. (Adapted from Mellaart 1972, 1975, 1978).

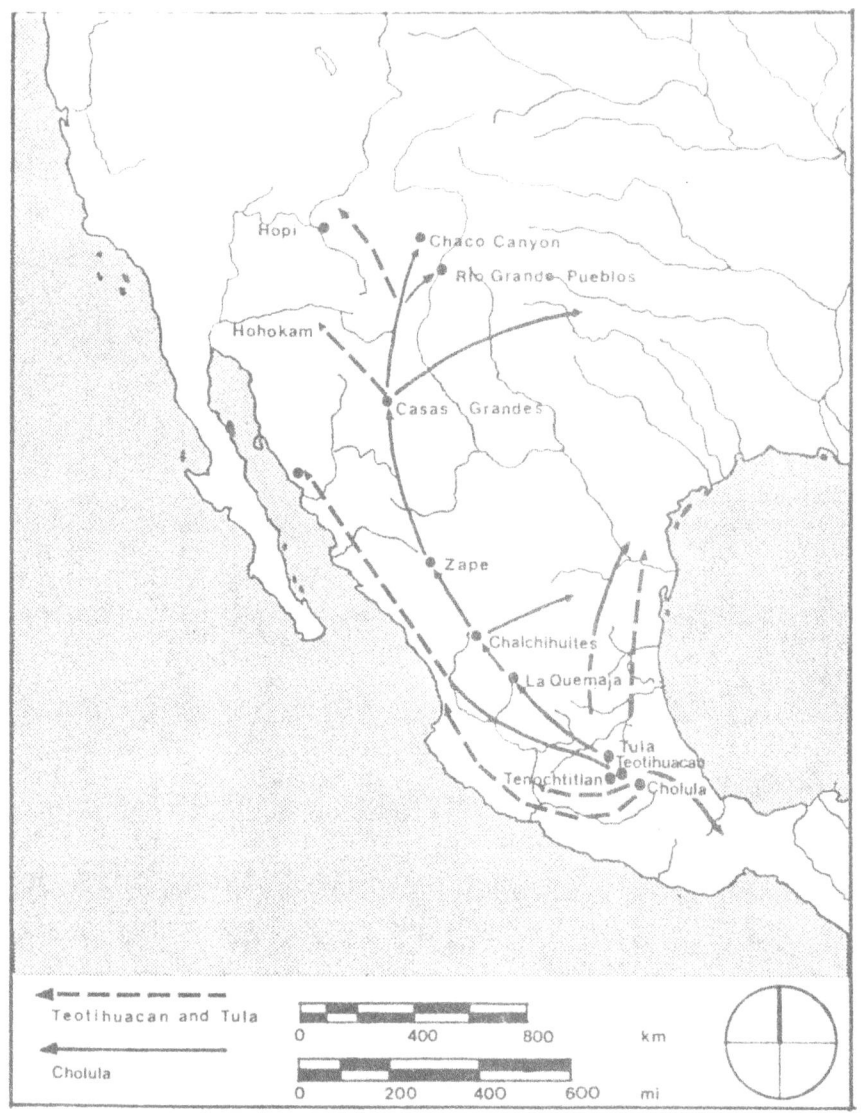

Figure 2.16 Probable major trade routes between Mesoamerica and "Oasis America" to A.D. 1400, prior to Spanish conquest. (Adapted, with additions, from Weigand, 1978).

Sheltering Landscapes

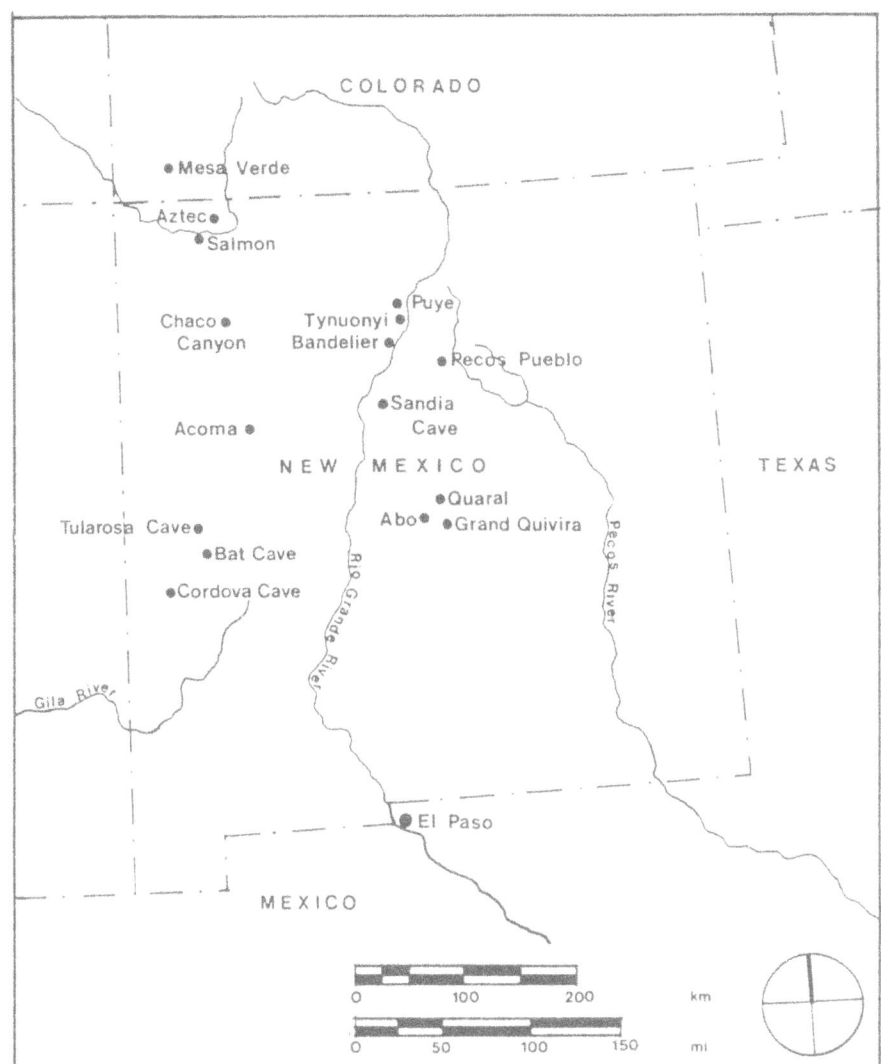

Figure 2.17 Major Anasazi sites in New Mexico.

Figure 2.18 Major sites of Anasazi and adjacent cultures in Arizona.

Chapter Three

FROM SHELTER TO SETTLEMENT

> The underlying bond between cities and their hinterland is that the existence of the former depends upon their capacity to mobilize and deploy the latter's agricultural surpluses ... we must deal with city and countryside not only as opposed abstractions on an economic plane but as intimately interacting parts of an embracing cultural and ecological system.
>
> R.M. Adams, The natural history of urbanism.

In this chapter, we proceed to a detailed examination of the transition from subsistence hunting-and-gathering economies in Anasazi and Anatolian territory to the development of horticulture, agriculture, and the production of surplus product. We start by exploring the caves that formed, for many peoples in both hemispheres, the earliest shelters, and the artifacts contained in these caves.

While larger caves, supplemented with defined open-air sites, may have formed base settlements, semi-permanent habitations, or smaller cavate shelters, were often used as transitory camps, as temporary bases for hunting parties, or for the subsequent extended butchering process. Some Paleolithic and Neolithic caves were "found shelter only," others were enlarged and even sculptured; there is even some evidence of early building inside caves followed in later periods by outside extensions of these rudimentary habitations.

Early post-cavate settlements consisted of huts and rude shelters, supplemented by storage facilities capable of handling a limited amount of surplus product. While these did not appear in the present American Southwest until about 2200 years ago (at the earliest), there is evidence of organized, pre-agriculture villages in Anatolia as early as 8000 B.C. in Cayonu, some 1000 years after the first evidence of sheep domestication. It is in Cayonu that we find the earliest indications of distinction between domestic and nondomestic building, and between individual and communal storage spaces and courtyards. There are also indications of decorated ceremonial architecture and of primitive metallurgy employed in working copper.

Asikli Huyuk, a city established a millennium later, evidenced the first advance over the use of "found materials" in architecture in the earliest recorded actual production of building material. Its contemporary, Aceramic Hacilar, may have been the first truly agricultural settlement in Anatolia.

Settlements indicative of sedentary living were not in evidence in the American Southwest until about two millennia ago, and were primarily composed of collections of semi-subterranean round or oval *pithouses* with contiguous storage rooms. Later villages combined pithouses, courtyards, refuse mounds, and above-ground shelters; and as stone began to complement mud as building material in certain areas, separate storage bins were constructed.

About A.D. 700, a marked shift occurred in Anasazi settlement form from pithouse clusters with exterior storage to multiple-room dwellings with interior, above-ground storage, later called *pueblos* (after the Spanish word for "town"). Compact villages made up of several pueblo buildings, containing anywhere from a dozen to 30 or more rooms, began to characterize the Anasazi region a century or so later; masonry construction began to supplant adobe-covered timber somewhat later, and separate, circular, subterranean buildings, or *kivas*, became common. But urban places, as we shall see, had yet to appear.

Even at the latest stages represented in this chapter, pre-agricultural horticulture did not provide all needed nutrients, nor was it sufficiently reliable as a source of food. Hence the Anasazi and Anatolian settlements here described represent placemaking in the service of mixed food-gathering and food-producing systems in which hunting and gathering, at more sophisticated levels, continued to supplement horticulture and small-scale animal husbandry for a considerable time, resulting in transitional, diversified economies. The still-popular notion that advanced systems of cultivation were a necessary precondition to urban development, that grain agriculture must precede the construction of immense architectural complexes, has been under fire for some time (see Quilter, et al., 1991, for some of the latest findings). The "settlements" to which we refer were not the product of fully-developed agriculture economies, nor yet the homes of fully settled people.

From subsistence to surplus

Existing evidence suggests that roaming bands of hunters and gatherers established themselves in Anatolia prior to 150,000 B.C. (Cambel and Braidwood, 1972). Eventually, small groups made up of several hunting and gathering units ("microbands," or family collecting units of 2 to 5 persons) formed "macrobands" and established semi-permanent settlements of 15 to 20 persons in Mesoamerica (MacNeish, 1964) and Anatolia, and 10 to 60 persons in some parts of the Fertile Crescent (Flannery, 1972). Since their material appropriation was not sufficient to produce surplus product requiring *secure* storage, larger settlements were not required; thus, transition from "compounds" made up of several production units to villages did not occur. These Anatolian compounds correspond roughly to Pueblo I and early Pueblo II Anasazi settlements, as shown in the figures at the end of the chapter.

The available evidence indicates that intensified food collection, some cultivation, and even pristine animal domestication characterized Anatolia by the ninth millennium B.C. "...[S]uch communities can be regarded as being incipiently *food producing*, in the sense that their inhabitants were doubtless already manipulating both plants and animals to some extent." (Cambel and Braidwood, 1972; p. 114; emphasis added). Settlement types to accommodate such conditions of existence were already under development in Anatolia during the late upper Paleolithic period.

At a later stage, the amount of surplus product (food) was sufficient to require not just provisional larders but secure storage, and more permanent settlements with at least *some* sedentary population. However, as Flannery (1972), Perkins and Daly (1972), and Mellaart (1965) convincingly argue, this transition was *not* dependent upon either agriculture as a specific type of economic activity nor upon wholesale sedentarization. Villages, as larger permanent settlements, require neither agriculture nor year-round, sedentary existence; sedentary life requires neither agriculture nor larger permanent settlements, such as villages; agriculture requires neither full-time sedentarization nor villages. In the PCMP, or KOMP with collective appropriation, such other activities as hunting and pastoralism can, with certain divisions of labor and under appropriate conditions of existence, be realized with or without villages and within sedentary, semi-nomadic, or nomadic frameworks. The major question, then, is not the relation of a *specific* economic activity to a *specific* settlement type, but whether changes in conditions of existence and *within* a given mode of production will affect transitions in built environment.

The required change *within* mode of production appears to be in the *forces* of production in terms of labor, labor units, and labor power. Increased hunting activity—particularly, the hunting of larger mammals—appears to be associated with greater division of labor between the sexes and a shift in the ideological base; in kinship lineage systems, increased hunting is accentuated by increased pastoralism and, with the accumulation of surplus product, the onset of wars (Berktay, 1983). Where these conditions exist (in Anatolian settlements, but not among the Anasazi), matriarchy is transformed into patriarchy, endogamy into exogamy, isolated groups into clans, and eventually, hordes into tribes (Berktay, 1983). More and more stable surplus product must be stored and secured. All of these changes in conditions of existence *within* the existing mode of production affect transition in settlement form from compounds to nucleated villages made up of related households.

As hunting started to complement gathering wild plants as a prime source of food, tribal living began to supplant mere wandering. The Anatolian hunt—and its product, large game — required more complex organization of labor, different forms of distribution, and alternative spatial patterns to those involved in mere gathering. Associated with this was a change in ideological structure, with totemic ideology replacing ideology of magic (Thomson, 1978). As the process of collective hunting became more refined, other tribes related by kinship were brought into the food production (and food sharing) process. This inter-tribal mode of appropriation was marked with ceremonies and celebrations of peaceful and cooperative co-existence, both within tribes—moieties and clans—and between tribes, resulting in the totemic character of tribal organization. Totemism, patriarchy, and exogamy in Anatolia constituted the main components of ideological structure. United by totem and influenced by more selective, intensive, and "regionalized" hunting and gathering practices, the tribes formed more permanent and more defined settlements.

Caves and cavates

A cave is undoubtedly one of the oldest of shelters. As "found shelter," it had obvious advantages over trees and tree branches, canyons, etc. As dwelling, a reasonably deep cave provided a degree of protection from enemies, predators, the worst of the elements, and even some temperature control. When the caves were not sufficiently deep but the material sufficiently soft, late Paleolithic man used stone tools to enlarge the cave in rough fashion, while even later Paleolithic and early Neolithic people began to carve more sculptured rooms. Neolithic folk in Anatolia, and in the American Southwest and northwest Mexico, subsequently *built* inside caves and, later, outside as well. Thus, patterns of cave dwelling differ and, overall, some may even display a certain sequence of development. There is evidence of the use of caves as dwellings among the early Anatolians and predecessors of the Anasazi, although in neither location were caves exclusive, or even frequent, living environments.

Along the Mediterranean littoral

Although few in number and limited in archaeological findings, the early cave dwellings of Anatolia provide some information on shelters and habitation of the hunting and food collecting peoples who lived 15,000 years ago. Most of these cave dwellings found in Anatolia are located on the southern slopes of the Taurus Mountains not very far from the Mediterranean coast; a few are situated inland on other slopes of the Taurus Mountains in environmentally protected valleys with mild microclimates. Before Homo Sapiens, their ancestors, Homo Neanderthalensis, must have found favorable environmental conditions on the slopes of the mountains rich with both flora and fauna. The discovery of the first

From Shelter to Settlement 73

fossilized remains of Homo Neanderthalensis in these Anatolian caves clearly indicates a deliberate attempt on the part of our early ancestors to meet needs for shelter as they roamed, in hordes, to find food for themselves. Obviously, these roaming bands, due to the scattered nature of their resources, could not establish permanent places to live. The large size of their "home ranges" (Lee and DeVore, 1968; Ch.I) forced them to have not only seasonal stations as shelters but also interim camps. The varying sizes of these shelters indicate that the hordes could break up into different work groups (labor units) to provide the necessary food by either hunting or collecting. It also indicates periodic trips away from semi-permanent shelters. However, a basic unit of settlement is estimated to have been able to accommodate 15 to 40 persons. Caves accommodating smaller groups in more temporary situations provided shelters for those on more special missions requiring intensive and skilled hunting. While the smaller caves were used as transitory camps and/or butchering stations, the larger caves served as base settlements. These were places of larger gatherings and longer-term living accommodations, places to distribute the food gathered and to carry out other collective activities, as well as places for shelter.

It is quite clear that habitation was not limited to caves or rock shelters. Open-air sites with scattered artifacts suggest very strongly the use of any appropriate place as shelter, with varying durations of occupancy, depending on environmental conditions. Both types of habitation were major forms of placemaking even prior to the first traces of Homo Neanderthalensis in Anatolia. Braidwood and Howe (1962) mention populations of food gatherers and free-wandering hunters to the south and southeast of Anatolia, who roamed in the middle elevations of the highlands on the upper Syrian steppe at least 75,000 years ago, and who made use of caves or rock shelters as their primary living quarters. This trend toward utilizing caves and rock shelters as major habitation places continued until the Mesolithic or the late Epipaleolithic period in Anatolia and the rest of the Near East.

Other forms of settlement, more specifically single buildings or compounds of buildings, did not appear before 10,000 B.C. in Anatolia and in the surrounding environments, at least according to the most recent archaeological findings. However, this does not mean that caves, rock shelters, and open-air accommodations were the only means of habitation elsewhere until this period. The encampment of the mammoth killers on the mountains at Dolni Vestonice in southern Moravia (Central Europe) not only displays a long period of continuous occupancy (27,000 to 22,000 B.C.), but shows the existence of huts constructed with roughly circular plans in the loess settlement (Klima, 1962). In spite of the impressive scale of these settlements and the astonishing early construction activity, these types of settlements do not seem to have been very widely spread nor as commonly used as caves and rock shelters. Although the advanced hunters of Central Europe achieved a high level of development in their placemaking activity quite early, it is very probable that in Anatolia, most of the Paleolithic people depended on hunting and food collecting for sustenance and "for the most part still lived in caves" (Alkim, 1968; p. 46). Nevertheless, in terms of organization and specialized labor, the semi-permanent hut settlements of the mammoth killers give a clear idea of a different settlement type inhabited by groups of advanced hunters, and of the collective living of a hoarding people in diverse environmental conditions.

The earliest cave occupancy recorded in Anatolia is around 13,000 B.C. (Mellaart, 1975). This is Belbasi cave, not far from the coastal town of present day Antalya. Its Epipaleolithic character is indexed by an array of microlithic points, triangles and obliquely truncated blades (Mellaart, 1975). Occupants are believed to have been hunters of deer, ibex, and wild cattle. Although the presence of harpoons in this area within close proximity to the coast may suggest fishing in addition to hunting and food gathering, no fish bones nor shell fish have yet been found in the vicinity of the cave (Bostanci, 1962; 1965). No art objects have been uncovered at Belbasi either.

Excavations carried out at Belbasi and the other caves helped to establish the stratigraphy of the Paleolithic in south and southeast Anatolia. Belbasi was occupied, on and off, for almost three millennia before Beldibi, whose first phase of occupancy dates back to 9500 B.C. (Bostanci, 1965; Mellaart, 1975). The second phase of occupation is thought to have been 8000 to 7000 B.C. with the production of wall paintings and pottery, and the use of obsidian. There seems to be a fairly extended gap between the first and second phases of occupation. Evidence of slightly earlier cave occupation is found in Kara In, Cark In, and Okuzlu In (all ca. 10,000 B.C.). All four caves are located immediately to the north of Belbasi. Considering the dates of habitation attributed to these caves, the early phases of Belbasi (ca. 13,000 B.C.) and the later period of Belbasi (ca. 7500 B.C.) span more than five millennia of occupancy (Kokten, 1949; 1952; 1963) which, no matter how discontinuous, suggests the high probability of favorable conditions for habitation, and for food collecting and hunting.

Certainly the living environment was not restricted to this region of the Taurus Mountains during the Paleolithic. Palanli (ca. 11,000 B.C.) (Alkim, 1968) near the modern town of Adiyaman, and Magaracik (Senyurek, 1956; 1958) on Samandag (not far from the modern Hatay), with their mammal remains (e.g., of wild cat, bear, rhinoceros, porcupine, red deer, fallow deer, ox and wild boar) and human skeletal remains, the petroglyphs of ibex, and microlithic tools, indicate fairly long periods of occupancy during the Paleolithic and Epipaleolithic periods. That the Epipaleolithic of southern Anatolia is contemporary with the same stage in Palestine shows the extent of human

From Shelter to Settlement

habitation in this area at that time (Alkim, 1968). The similarities in microlithic material found within the region suggest at least intermittent contacts, if not cultural continuity. Whether the interruptions in occupancy and the changes in the pattern of hunting and food collecting toward the end of the Epipaleolithic can be attributed to environmental conditions (namely, climatic events resulting in a neothermal age), as some archaeologists (Alkim, 1968; Mellaart, 1975) hesitantly argue, or not, one does not see much difference in the means employed to create habitation. A cultural sequence, at least in ways of placemaking, can be traced in all of these caves and rock shelters.

With the exception of Belbasi, all the caves mentioned above have yielded art objects either in the form of petroglyphs on the smooth rock faces, engraved pebbles and bones, or schematic wall paintings. There are even traces of very primitive pottery at Beldibi at the time of its last occupation (ca. 7500 B.C.). Human figures, geometric designs, and animal representations (ibex, bulls, deer, fish) constitute most of the art work uncovered in these caves. In addition to the decorative character and possibly idolatrous nature of these art works found on the cave walls and on different objects, other artifacts are covered with designs and decorations as well. The bone tools with representations of bearded male figures recovered in Kara In and Okuzlu In seem to be the earliest examples of decorated artifacts (Anati, 1968). They also seem to have Natufian parallels at Wadi Fallah on the eastern shore of the Mediterranean—the Levant coast— according to Mellaart (1975). The microlithic tool industry is of Epipaleolithic or Mesolithic type, and the tools resemble specimens found not only in the other parts of the Near East but also in Europe and Africa (Alkim, 1968). The sickle blades and grindstones dating from the first phase of Beldibi (9500 B.C.) strongly suggest the collection of wild grain on the slopes of the Taurus Mountains (Bostanci, 1965). Although the tools clearly indicate incipient agricultural activity, such activity certainly was not developed enough to enable the peoples of the Mediterranean littoral to depend on it as a primary source of nurture.

Although there is strong evidence of continuous human habitation to the south of the Taurus Mountains as early as the thirteenth millennium, B.C., traces of early human settlements on the central Anatolian plateau are scarce. There are no sufficiently convincing archaeological findings that clearly indicate long-occupied Epipaleolithic sites. However, open-air sites, believed to be used by Epipaleolithic groups, at least suggest that human habitation was not limited to only the region south of the Taurus Mountains. Both open-air sites found along the river of Macun Cay (Esin and Benedict, 1963) near Ankara and on Avla Dag (Todd, 1965) near the present town of Nigde seem to provide sufficient evidence of the existence of roaming bands on the central Anatolian plateau, and of the dependence of their periodic movement upon shifting sources of food. One conjecture, which supports the existence of food collectors and free-wandering hunters on the central Anatolian plateau, is related to obsidian and its presence in the Antalya caves (Kara In, Okuzlu In, and Cark In, all ca. 10,000 B.C.). It has been suggested that the sporadic presence of obsidian in these caves may be attributed to some contact with the people in the source area of obsidian (Renfrew, Dixon and Cann, 1966). Acigol and Ciftlik, neighboring settlements on the central Anatolian plateau, had been the main sources of the obsidian which was used extensively in Anatolian and Levant villages in the Neolithic period until the metal ages (after 4000 B.C.). The rare occurrence of obsidian on the southern slopes of the Taurus Mountains, it is conjectured, suggests that, rather than making special trips for obsidian over the mountains to the north, then over the plateau to the deposits, the inhabitants of the caves established contact with people living near the source who may have introduced them to this hard, brittle volcanic glass, most instrumental in tool making, cutting and scraping. (One such possible source is the settlement of Igdeli Cesme, although relatively sparse studies of this area have yielded no conclusive evidence to date).

The caves, varying in size between 25 to 250 square meters, were all natural, requiring little carving beyond clearing the earth to enlarge the usable area. Small openings providing access to the caves were perhaps blocked with boulders and dead tree trunks for protection from the possible threat of the incursion of larger animals which might have been a threat to the people. Conscious attempts to open ventilation holes are not evident. However, the caves are relatively shallow. Along the slope-facing surface, more than one access is sometimes available. While the natural contours of caves provide boundaries, open-air sites are without any territorial markings to indicate borders, and the area of scatter is much larger.

"Oasis America": Beyond the Mesoamerican frontier

"Oasis America" is the name given by certain Mexican archaeologists (Narez, 1991) to the prehistoric settlements of the present-day states of Arizona, New Mexico, Chihuahua, and Sonora that were situated across the "Chichimec Sea" (Mathien and McGuire, 1986b) from the northernmost Mesoamerican outpost in the Mexican states of Sinaloa and Durango.

Among the prehistoric inhabitants of Oasis America were the Anasazi. Anasazi chronology has always posed a problem, initially because of difficulties in dating (now practically resolved through dendochronology), and later

From Shelter to Settlement

because the original Pecos phases (Kidder, 1927) are no longer reflective of current knowledge concerning major environmental, architectural, and cultural changes. Vivian (1990) has summarized four classification systems proposed between 1927 and 1981, reproduced here as Table 3.1, and has suggested his own revised chronology specifically applicable to the Chaco area considered in the following chapter (Table 3.2).

Other chronologies have also been proposed, e.g., the Initiation, Expansion, Differentiation, Reorganization, and Aggregation periods suggested by Cordell and Gumerman (1989). In this book, use of Basketmaker and Pueblo phases will correspond more or less with the Pecos Classification since it is used in so much of the earlier literature. The initial word "pueblo" will frequently be abbreviated "P"; thus, "PIII" signifies the Pueblo III phase.

Archaeological findings concerning early cave dwellings in the American Southwest are even scarcer than in Anatolia, and there is little evidence that caves ever constituted a prevalent form of dwelling, even among Paleo-Indians. A few caves, however, have been studied in some detail. As indicated in Chapter Two, the remains of "Sandia Man," dated anywhere from 17,000 B.C. to 9500 B.C., were associated with cave occupation. Other indications of cave dwelling date from before 5500 B.C. to ca. A.D. 1300, both cases occurring long before, during, and after the climax of Anasazi society. There is thus evidence of the use of caves as dwellings in the American Southwest at least ten millennia ago, yet the *modification* of these cave dwellings through carving and building — a presumably more advanced form of *placemaking* — appears to be a relatively recent phenomenon, as will be discussed in a later chapter.

Bat Cave, located at the intersection of the Cochise and Mogollon culture areas north of the Gila River and east of the San Francisco River, exhibits signs of Cochise culture occupancy from 4000 B.C. and of Mogollon occupants from the beginning of first millennium A.D. to A.D. 1100 (Dick, 1965). Occupancy patterns and artifacts have been studied and well documented in caves to the south of Bat Cave (Cosgrove, 1947) and two other New Mexico sites, Tularosa and Cordova Caves (Hough, 1914; Martin et al., 1952; Heller, 1976), located respectively on Tularosa Creek and the west bank of the San Francisco River. Ventana Cave in neighboring southeast Arizona shows signs of occupancy by members of the Folsom culture, among others (Haury, 1950a).

As with Anatolian caves, the picture that emerges of the Paleo-Indian cave dwellers in the American Southwest suggests a hunting-gathering economy (Cordell, 1984). The best known inhabited caves appear to have been killing or processing sites, but this may be because killing and processing sites tend to contain the best "hard" artifacts, such as animal bones, stone by-products of tool manufacture, and especially projectile points, the latter providing the major

Table 3.1
Two Major Chacoan Classificatory Systems
(Hayes, 1981, modification of Kidder Pecos scheme (1927), and Chaco Center further revisions; adapted from Vivian, 1990)

AD	PECOS	CHACO CENTER	
-100	Basketmaker I (Archaic)	(Archaic) Basketmaker II	
100 200 300 400 500	Basketmaker II	----------?----------	
600 700	Basketmaker III	Basketmaker III	
800 900	Pueblo I	Pueblo I	
1000	Early Pueblo II	Early Pueblo II	Early Bonito Phase
1100	Late Pueblo II	Late Pueblo II	Classic Bonito Phase
1200	Early Pueblo III	Early Pueblo III	Late Bonito Phase
1300	Late Pueblo III	Late Pueblo III	Mesa Verde Phase

Table 3.2
Revised Anasazi Chronology from a Chacoan Perspective
(from Vivian, 1990)

Period	Types and Variants
100 B.C. - A.D. 400	Late Archaic (BMII)
A.D. 400 - 700	Basketmaker III
A.D. 700 - 850	Pueblo I
A.D. 850 - 1000	Early Bonito, Ackmen, Red Mesa
A.D. 1000 - 1080	Classic Bonito, Mancos, Wingate
A.D. 1080 - 1170	Late Bonito, McElmo, Wingate-Houck
A.D. 1170 - 1300	Mesa Verde, Houck

dating mechanism. Other artifacts, as data, suffer from the problem of selective decay or selective consumption: corn husks, being unattractive (and genuinely indigestible) to animals, tend to endure, while certain seeds are likely to have been consumed. It is thus difficult not only to determine whether the Paleo-Indian diet was "adequate," but even what that diet might have been.

For the above and other reasons, it is unclear whether any cave sites were permanent dwellings or whether all were primarily the loci of seasonal activities or special uses (Cordell, 1984). If the latter is true, the caves were certainly not the only temporary dwelling places complemented with rock shelters and open sites, especially during the so-called "archaic period" (5500 B.C. to A.D. 100) characterized architecturally by a transition from "found shelter" to the construction of "pithouses." Martin et al. (1949) report finding oval pithouses, excavated to about 0.5 meters below ground level, at Cochise sites in the Pine Lawn Valley of western New Mexico, and O'Laughlin (1980) has described the discovery of more than 23 shallowly excavated circular houses with mud brush and grass walls, located near present-day El Paso, Texas, which may have been occupied as early as 2500 B.C. Further refinement of pithouse architecture, however, appears to have occurred much later, and its development is detailed in a later section of this chapter.

Places for all seasons

Hut to hamlet

As food providing activity was achieving a level indicative of considerable cultural development, signified by extensive storage and later production (as opposed to mere gathering followed by selective collecting of plant and animal foodstuffs) — the distinction associated with the appearance of the blade-tool tradition, ca. 35,000 B.C. (Braidwood and Howe, 1962) — there was also a slight change in the pattern of placemaking. Both in the food-gathering, free-wandering hunting phase, and in seasonal food collecting, selective hunting phase, conditions of existence simultaneously required and permitted a continuously migratory life pattern. Some places offering sources of sufficient amounts of food for longer periods became more permanent settlements, provided that other environmental conditions allowed fairly comfortable habitation.

Collective living in the gathering and collecting phases resulted in the development of forms of social organization which facilitated the storage and distribution of foodstuffs. In addition to the caves and cavates and the temporary shelters built with branches and stones in open-air sites, construction activity was beginning to provide more suitable shelters both for storage and for living.

This newly emerging construction activity was necessary to meet the emerging need for storage resulting from increasing food supply. In terms of territoriality, proximity, and reliability, it was also a necessity to *secure* the food sources. In other words, more permanent settlements were the outcome of social organization developing concomitantly with the increase in food supply, a prerequisite for the further elaboration and implementation of such organization.

At its early stages, the built area of these compounds of huts/shelters and storage facilities was not much larger than that of the caves and cavates which accommodated 15 to 40 persons. Although the division of labor was still by sex rather than by families, the compounds were not necessarily one "large house" accommodating primarily hunting/collecting bands. One illustrative example of such a settlement is Ain Mallaha (ca. 9000 B.C.) near Lake Huleh in Israel (Flannery, 1972). The compound composed of circular, semi-subterranean, and rock-lined huts arranged around an open area formed an enclosure clearly defining the boundaries of the settlement. The settlement covered approximately 2,000 square meters and it is unlikely that at any one time there were more than fifty huts in use on the site (according to the excavator, Jean Perrot). The diverse sizes of huts, (diameters ranging from 2.5 to 9 meters), suggests numbers of occupants varying from one to three persons per hut. While some huts housed storage pits, the main storage seems to have been outside the huts, either in pits or in hut-like structures smaller than the huts used for dwelling.

One other example of this type of settlement is Mureybet on the Euphrates River, east of present-day Aleppo, Syria, established slightly later than Ain Mallaha, ca. 8250 B.C. Excavations carried out by van Loon (1968) uncovered huts, again circular in plan and with diameters varying from 2.7 to 4 meters. The semi-subterranean character of these huts with rock foundations, and the settlement plan surrounding an open area, clearly indicate parallels with those in Ain Mallaha. Like Ain Mallaha, there were storage pits in some of the huts, but primary storage must have been in larger pits outside the huts or in the smaller huts without hearths.

Neither these compounds of the Natufian period of the Mediterranean littoral nor the larger-scaled ones appearing sightly later in Anatolia can necessarily be considered capable of accommodating year-round sedentary life. These settlements presented opportunities for *comparatively* more permanent residence than cave dwellings, base camps, butchering stations, or open-air sites. It is obvious that collection of wild grains, wherever it was possible, and collection of other foodstuffs and selective hunting, still required extensive migration determined by the timing and spatial locus of food sources. However, more favorable locations — favorable in terms of food sources and environmental conditions — were becoming settled for longer periods than the places occupied more transitorily. It is quite probable that the same band could establish and build more than one compound provided that the locations were suitable for longer durations of stay. Available shelters such as caves and year-round open-air sites, along with food sources and environmental conditions, were decisive factors in the logistics of the moves.

Communities such as Ain Mallaha and Mureybet show no evidence of food production. Yet these settlements are qualitatively different from the caves and cavate dwellings of the earlier phase. First, they show a definite attempt to establish an enclosure as both a shelter/dwelling and a clear boundary for the settlement. Second, the site is more carefully selected than are natural caves. Third, there is strong indication of territorial organization of space. Although there is no significant qualitative difference in the provision of food, more selective collecting and more intensive hunting introduced a quantitative change in storage requirements; the increase in food supplies required more extensive storage, and thus, new and more innovative techniques beyond the simple provision of additional space. The development of social organization that is necessary for such manipulation, no matter how primitive it may have been, imposes its own spatial organization whose requirements transcend the caves, cavates and open-air sites that previously provided main shelters.

A couple of centuries later, or perhaps contemporaneous with Mureybet, settlements began to be established for longer occupancy; this constituted the next phase in placemaking. These settlements were more developed and larger than the compounds of huts that archaeological studies uncovered with Natufian affinities in the Mediterranean littoral, and in the middle reaches of the Euphrates in Syria. These are the settlements which will be termed "villages," only to indicate a difference in scale and size between them, their predecessors, and the larger settlements that followed, which accommodated more and newer functions into their structure.

Cayonu is one pre-agricultural village in Anatolia that clearly reveals signs of much more permanent residence and more highly organized community, indexed by the archaeological study of its architecture. Excavations, carried out over more than twenty years (with some interruptions), have led archaeologists to the remains of 10,000 year-old stone buildings. Most recent discoveries push the date of occupancy half a millennium earlier than the first estimated date of 7500 B.C. (Braidwood and Cambel, 1982; Wilford, 1985). However, more important than the specific date of initial construction are levels of spatial organization and architectural features which shed some more light on the living and settlement patterns of these Mesolithic or Protoneolithic people.

Cayonu, near the headwaters of the Tigris River on the Anatolian plateau, some five kilometers southwest of the town now known as Ergani, is referred to as an early "farming village" by its excavators (Cambel and Braidwood, 1972). Since the earliest evidence for domesticated sheep comes from Zawi Chemi (ca. 9000 B.C.), east of Cayonu on one of the tributaries of the Tigris River, and since the sickle blades appear as early as 9500 B.C. at Beldibi (as has been mentioned earlier), it is not surprising to find a community a millennium later (ca. 8000 B.C.) combining incipient cultivation — primarily garden tillage — pristine animal domestication, selective hunting (specializing primarily on ungulates), and intensive collecting (Braidwood and Braidwood, 1986). Because primitive cultivation and plant domestication were still at an early stage of development, villagers had to supplement these activities with more traditional ones, preventing a fully sedentary existence. Yet their architecture was marked by "the substantial proportions of the buildings and by the relative sophistication of their construction" (Cambel and Braidwood, 1972; p. 119), indicating that surplus labor was already being appropriated so as to enlarge placemaking activity from individual dwellings to public or sacred building units. The presence of communal buildings with decorative flourishes, apparently the oldest structures uncovered that were erected for other than domestic purposes (according to the excavators), suggests that the villagers at Cayonu could afford the time and resources for ceremonial architecture (Braidwood and Cambel, 1982). It also reveals that the people living in this "farming village" had advanced to a level of complexity in their social organization previously unencountered in explorations of both their nomadic forebears and contemporaneous pre-agricultural societies.

10,000 year-old stone buildings, constructed both for domestic and nondomestic purposes, exhibit sophisticated architectural techniques and features demonstrating the knowledge and skills of the Cayonu villagers. Conceptually, there seems to be both knowledge of measurement and appreciation for decoration. On the practical side, there is evidence in the construction technology that the builders of Cayonu must have experimented with different materials and made use of a binding substance quite similar to cement. As rudimentary as they may have been, measurements used seem almost standardized for certain spans in the rectangular plans of domestic and nondomestic buildings. Rows of masonry walls with stone foundations over one meter in width are spaced roughly two meters apart, defining the individual dwelling units. These rooms, about six meters in length, enclosed a net usable area of approximately 12 to 15 square meters. Open courtyards paved with broad smooth flagstones at one occupied level and fist-sized limestone cobbles at another (excavations so far have traced at least six successive layers of occupation), together with buildings considerably larger in size than the individual dwellings (approximately, 8 x 9 meters), and of a totally different geometric order, suggest that these spaces were used for more than mere domestic functions. The presence of public buildings and outdoor spaces with decorative flourishes, terrazzo floors, and well-polished stones, and the use of identical spans in the nondomestic buildings as well, suggests not only a high level of social complexity but also sophisticated construction technology beyond just conceptual advancement. On the practical side, burning limestone and then mixing it with sand to form the binding element for the terrazzo floor (composed of salmon-colored limestone and white marble chips) was certainly no small accomplishment for the builders of Cayonu. The great care given to polishing stones and carving human faces, along with other figures, on slabs of limestone certainly indicates that the people of Cayonu could afford the time and resources (both labor tools) for such architectural detailing and finishes.

The village, being near rich deposits of copper and such copper-related minerals as malachite, was further characterized by the earliest use of metal so far discovered. Copper artifacts such as pins, hooks, drills, and simple tools were shaped by abrading and hammering. There are even indications that some of the copper artifacts were heated before they were shaped. In addition to the advancement exhibited in construction technology, there is also evidence of the beginnings of pyrotechnology, a primitive level of metallurgy.

The advancement in architecture at Cayonu over the compounds mentioned earlier is certainly remarkable. However, the most striking feature of Cayonu as a settlement emerges in the spatial organization of various functions and their execution in a series of building types. Clear distinction between domestic and nondomestic architecture, the existence of communal and individual storage spaces, the construction quality, as well as common courtyards spatially defined and surrounded by both dwellings and public buildings reveal the highly developed architectonics of the builders in Cayonu. The existence of substantial surplus labor before 7000 B.C. is evidenced in copper artifacts shaped through hammering and abrading, as well as in architectural sophistication. Still, that this appropriation remained substantially collective is indicated by such products of placemaking as communal storage areas and work spaces, common courtyards, and undifferentiated dwellings.

Asikli Huyuk, (ca. 7000 B.C.) is another example of these Protoneolithic villages of the Aceramic period. It is located on the banks of Melendiz Cay east of Aksaray and some 50 kilometers northwest of the Ciftlik obsidian deposits on Gollu Dag. In addition to beads and belt hooks, and tools such as polished greenstone axes and bone awls, an abundance of tools and flakes made of Ciftlik obsidian has been found in the limited excavations (Todd, 1966; 1980). The significance of Asikli Huyuk, although excavation is still incomplete, lies in the use of sun-dried mud-brick. Asikli Huyuk was the first settlement in Anatolia to produce building material. Certainly this is not the first example of production in construction activity. The use of cement-like material directed to a binder or the shaping of branches and tree trunks in the flooring or roofing systems in Cayonu (and elsewhere in earlier times) are different levels of production. However, the process of shaping mud-bricks and drying them in the sun to give them the necessary hardness to be used as load bearing elements, is the earliest technological advance over the use of natural "found materials." This was the first attempt to produce one material to replace another, mud-brick replacing the naturally occurring stone.

The use of red lime plaster floors in the houses also conveys an idea about the development and/or diffusion of certain construction techniques originated earlier and elsewhere. Such a technique was applied and utilized about a millennium earlier in Cayonu, though in a different manner. The significance of its use one thousand years later lies in the fact that this is the first application of so sophisticated a technique in individual dwellings. It may, in certain circumstances, be a better way of dealing with the uncomfortable temperatures and humidity of the earthen floor than mere packing of earth. Furthermore, it indicates that the villagers of Asikli Huyuk had the time to implement such a labor intensive technique to produce more comfortable living conditions in the individual dwellings.

These applications of certain architectonic elements in rudimentary form in both Protoneolithic villages—Cayonu and Asikli Huyuk—are clear signs that placemaking activity in Anatolia became oriented toward longer residence in one area, if not to completely sedentary, more permanent types of buildings. Such spatial organization reflects the developing social complexity of their essentially communal way of living.

One indication of the emergence of social complexity in such village communities is the nature of the burials found below the floors of individual dwellings in Asikli Huyuk. How widespread this burial system was in Asikli Huyuk is very difficult to determine due to the lack of extensive excavation and insufficient evidence for generalization. Yet it is still significant since several centuries later this very system of below-floor burial manifested a pattern indicative of ownership in Catal Huyuk, for instance. Both the skulls found in Cayonu that had been deliberately cut above the ears and blackened in fire and the below-floor burials excavated in Asikli Huyuk suggest the beginnings of ancestor worship, developed in full-fledged form later on in Anatolia.

Aceramic Hacilar, although considered by its excavator the earliest evidence for an agricultural settlement in Anatolia, still belongs to the group of villages in transition from Protoneolithic to Neolithic (Mellaart, 1970). Contemporary with Asikli Huyuk, Aceramic Hacilar (ca. 7500 B.C.) is located at the southwest corner of the central Anatolian plateau, 25 kilometers west of Burdur. Archaeological evidence strongly suggests the practice of simple dry farming. Two-row hulled barley, some emmer wheat, and lentils found in abundance, in addition to meager remains of wild einkorn and naked barley, certainly imply some agricultural practice. However, it was still too early for Aceramic Hacilar to have been a food-producing settlement. Neither the technology of plant domestication nor social organization had been developed to the level of exclusive dependence upon agriculture. Perhaps a little more developed than the people of Cayonu, still displaying an incipient form of cultivation in garden tillage, villagers of Aceramic Hacilar supplemented this cultivation with hunting and collecting with only canine animal domestication. The bones of sheep, goats, cattle, and red deer are too restricted in quantity to be considered evidence of domestication.

Although the existence of completely sedentary life may be in question, permanent settlement was suggested by Mellaart (1970) after uncovering parts of the village. The contributing architectural features and elements are the ubiquity of courtyard ovens, mud plaster on walls and floors of small rooms, red burnished lime plaster on a bed of pebbles in the larger rooms, square bins both in the courtyards and in the one dwelling thus far excavated, and post holes in the courtyard, indicating that it was at least partially covered. Furthermore, evidence of burials outside the settlement not only supports the idea of permanent residence but also, in parallel with Cayonu and Asikli Huyuk, presents the first traces of possible ancestor worship.

The remains of one dwelling reveal an undivided rectangular room of 16 to 24 square meters, attached to what appears to be a smaller food preparation area opening to the courtyard. The walls were constructed of mud brick reinforced with straw. According to Mellaart (1975), dwellings consisted of large rooms surrounded by a few smaller ones. Mud-brick walls resting on stone foundations separated individual dwellings, the units resting against each other as in the "row houses" of Cayonu. Again, as in its predecessor, these row houses were clustered about a central pebble court. Its excavator also conjectures that houses (as the much later Anasazi pueblos and some of the dwellings in Cappadocia) were entered from the roof since doorways are not in evidence. The walls are not wide enough to have supported more than one story. There are no post holes in the dwelling indicating that the span from wall to wall could not have exceeded, at most, 4.5 meter, which is the size of the readily available timber logs used for the roof (Mellaart, 1970). The roof timbers resting on the walls were covered with branches and packed earth.

Another Aceramic site among the villages where food production, per se, was not yet practiced, was a "hunter's village" at the southern edge of the Anatolian plateau, north of the Taurus Mountains and near the modern village of Suberde. This "hunter's village" covering an area of approximately 2000 square meters was beside Lake Sugla, in heavily wooded, yet rocky terrain (Perkins and Daly, 1972). Faunal analysis indicates that the villagers of Suberde (ca. 6500 B.C.) were not solitary hunters, but engaged in compound labor — trapping, chasing, killing, butchering, and *schlepping* (a technical term derived from German, for "dragging") — to acquire meat in addition to tilling gardens and collecting.

The whole process of hunting, including social appropriation, and consumption and storage of the product, was a complex task requiring different divisions of labor than those of earlier periods; evidence of "slaughtering whole flocks at a time" (Perkins and Daly, 1972; p. 110) suggests the nature and amount of surplus that needed to be stored and secured. The point to be emphasized, however, is that the Suberde site was primarily a "hunters' village," with little evidence of either agriculture or pastoralism, indicating that it was not a specific type of economic activity (i.e., agriculture) that gave rise to larger and more permanent settlements, but rather an articulated combination of forces and relations of production. The presence of querns (primitive hand grinding mills), axes, and sickle blades certainly suggests the practice of some sort of agriculture, no matter how rudimentary it may have been. Hunting was nevertheless the primary form of food acquisition. Evidence of "slaughtering whole flocks at a time" definitely supports this conjecture. The residents of this hunting village, whose only domesticated animal was the dog, primarily pursued and killed wild sheep and goats, boar, deer, and oxen. While the larger game animals, after being killed, were butchered on the spot, their leg bones were thrown away after the forequarters and hindquarters of meat were stripped. The feet still attached to its hide, the animal was dragged back to the village. Smaller game, such as goats and sheep killed close enough to home, did not go through the same treatment as the larger prey.

The lower deposits of Suberde, i.e., the remains of earlier occupancy (ca. 6500 B.C.) do not exhibit evidence of permanent structures. However, the evidence of a couple of centuries later reveals plaster floors and mud-brick walls quite similar to the ones observed earlier in Aceramic Hacilar, perhaps contemporaneous with or slightly later than the earliest stages of Catal Huyuk. Attached single-story houses constructed around a common courtyard or on the edge of an open area partially defined the boundary of an outdoor space; most of daily life must have taken place there, in addition to the work connected with the game brought home. Open hearths and ovens seem to have been the common features both of individual dwellings and of communal courtyards. The number of these found outside the dwellings gives the impression that they were more frequently used than those indoors, perhaps partially because of possible fire hazard and partially because living was communal. Nevertheless, timber beams covered with branches and pecked with earth on the upper surface always posed a fire problem produced by open hearths. Furthermore, since the major opening to the outside was in the ceiling, with some small window openings in one or two walls, proper ventilation would have been extremely difficult, especially with a fire.

Aceramic Can Hasan, a Neolithic settlement still belonging to the group of villages mentioned above, is located on the southern edge of the central Anatolian plateau near Karaman in the Konya plain. Its earliest occupancy dates back to 6500 B.C. (French, 1962-1968). The agricultural activity which occupied the villagers of Aceramic Can Hasan must have been at a high level; however, the village was not a full-fledged agricultural community. While sufficient evidence has been uncovered to indicate considerable involvement in agriculture, there is also much evidence that Aceramic Can Hasan was not entirely self-sufficient in food production.

The compact village layout, with buildings rectangular in plan was constructed on a site covering an area slightly less than 10,000 square miles. Excavations have disclosed individual dwellings, courts, and passages. The complexity of the plan is nearly equivalent to that of the early levels of Catal Huyuk where the earliest occupancy dates from two centuries later. While the rooms range between 4 to 7 meters in length the width is almost "standardized" at 3.5 to 4.0 meters.

While construction techniques, overall spatial organization, and certain architectural features (such as roof access), including the relation of dwellings to courtyards and the sizes of rooms, are neither very different from nor much more developed than those of its predecessors, Aceramic Can Hasan exhibits two architectural novelties, still in rudimentary form: (1) settlement compactness (passages from one courtyard to another created blocks of building in a highly complex spatial organization); and (2) building ovens into the walls.

Compact spatial organization and concomitantly denser settlement produced complex plans, actually an early sign of what was to follow a century or two later when more "towns" inhabited by larger populations were established. This indication of the beginnings of town formation actually signified a higher level of social organization as well as an increase in the amount of food to be stored, and as its natural consequence, the need for defense (provision of a new spatial order). With respect to this point Aceramic Can Hasan is certainly a settlement that shows other features of the village and the town; it is an example of the transition from less to more complex social organization. Architectural ramifications of this shift include intricate networks of passageways connecting courtyards surrounded by dwellings. Plans of the excavated area clearly show the effort to provide each dwelling with at least one exposure to the courtyard or to the passageway. It is quite possible, as has been suggested, that most of the entrances were from the roofs of these one-story buildings. However, the network of open spaces between the buildings certainly must have provided the opportunity for ground entrance if desired or needed, since the network allows the dwellings to sit back-to-back with a clear exposure to a courtyard on either side. While the passageways and courtyards provided the area needed for circulation on the ground, the roofs of the one-story buildings must have enabled above-ground circulation as well, which was definitely advantageous for defense against attack or from other dangers.

The second novel feature, the ovens built into the walls, may have been a natural outcome in part of compact planning: there was an apparent desire to use space, both indoors and outdoors, more efficiently, as well as to provide a measure of protection against fire hazards by providing a place for smoke to escape somewhere along the wall. Construction of free-standing dwelling walls, with a gap between the dwellings, may have created a rudimentary chimney. That ovens were built into walls as a fire-protection measure finds supporting evidence in the lack of open hearths. Building ovens against the walls must also have heated the wall surface, whereas before, heat was lost to the outside. Whatever the reason, the innovation was certainly a significant improvement over the previous practice of constructing "free-floating" open hearths and ovens.

Common features shared by these villages can be summarized briefly. The yearly cycle of migratory movements continued but with longer periods of residence in permanent settlements. The economy did not depend entirely on one type of food-producing or food-gathering activity, such as hunting or plant cultivation alone. The settlements were occupied by communities of nonsedentary people, involved in a complex economy of selective collecting, intensive specialized hunting, and some incipient plant cultivation. They all can be considered pre-agricultural settlements, that is, communities without food-producing economies. These settlements provided ample storage space and exhibited the complex spatial organization characteristic of a newly emerging social order composed of larger populations. They reveal a clear distinction between public and private spaces as well as communal living. Although there are traces of religious practices among the people of these communities, and although there is differentiation between domestic and nondomestic functions, there seems to be no clear separation between the sacred and secular in the spatial order. Buildings not only show deliberate attempts, through architecture and construction, to create more comfortable and safe places in which to live, but also display efforts to make places more livable through decorative flourishes and artistic creativity.

Pithouse to pueblo

While the archaeological record suggests human habitation of the American Southwest since at least 12,000 B.C., permanent, primarily sedentary villages appeared only in the first millennium A.D. Berry (1982) indicates only seven structures actually dated between 185 B.C. and A.D. 1, and Cordell (1984) claims little evidence of sedentary villages before A.D. 200. This was long after the introduction of maize from Mesoamerica and its presumed domestication, another counterindication of a one-to-one relationship between plant cultivation and sedentarization.

"Pithouses," the earliest free-standing, fully constructed dwellings in the American Southwest, were semi-subterranean dwellings, partly round or oval in form, excavated to varying depths, and covered with a simple post and beam structure. (Figure 3.1). Architectural variations in early pithouses (A.D. 200-500) are difficult to ascertain because, unless the above-ground structure actually burned, wall and roof remains were rarely preserved (Cordell, 1984). McKenna (1982) suggests reasons for the wide architectural variation found in Basketmaker (A.D. 500-700) pithouses. The village occupying the Durango site (Soygenis, 1985) consisted of 35 houses, circular in plan and ranging in diameter from 3 to 10 meters. The subterranean portion, plastered with adobe, had a firepit in the center of the floor. The foundations of the above-ground structures were circles of logs supporting an inward-leaning wood and adobe shelter, presumably entered from above. McKenna (1982) indicates responsiveness to local soil conditions in early Chacoan pithouses, which were frequently slab-lined when sited in loose, sandy soil, but not in bottomlands. Later (post-A.D. 575) pithouses were excavated to greater depth with "benches" adding further support to the walls. To the main room an antechamber was attached, and accumulated surplus product was accommodated in corner bins and wall niches. "Modified Basketmaker" pithouses were larger in diameter and deeper. By the beginning of the Pueblo I period (ca. A.D. 700 in Chaco), fireplace design became more sophisticated: deflectors appeared and the antechamber was reduced to a ventilation shaft. The *sipapu* also became fairly ubiquitous.

Bridging the modified Basketmaker and Pueblo I periods was the village of Shabik' Eschee in New Mexico. Its most interesting characteristic is the *variation* in building types, including 18 pithouses, an excavated structure presumed to be a kiva, a courtyard, refuse mounds, and — perhaps most significantly — storage bins *not* contiguous with pithouses. The village of Kiatuthlanna in eastern Arizona, (Soygenis, 1985), appearing slightly later, exhibits the beginnings of *clustering*, containing four clusters of 3 to 6 houses each. Architectural variation is further increased by the inclusion of *jacales*, above-ground shelters of pole-wall construction plastered with adobe.

Later Pueblo I villages, such as Utah's Alkali Ridge Village, were habitations with fully contiguous rooms. At this time, stone began to complement adobe as a building material. The one-story habitations containing 6 to 14 rooms were "I," "L," or rectangular "U" shaped, with occasional long arcs in evidence (Soygenis, 1985).

Changes in the relations of pithouses to storage rooms are particularly interesting. In the Chaco area, contiguous storage rooms appear to have developed from scattered cists located west or northwest of pithouses and were fronted by roofed *ramadas* (McKenna, 1982), or "shade houses." Walls less than 1.5 meters in height, first made of adobe and later of masonry, marked certain domestic clusters.

An increase in what were becoming *room blocks,* as more contiguous structures were added, was accompanied by a decrease in a number of pithouse features, *particularly* mealing bins, storage pits, and wall niches (McKenna, 1982). These post-A.D. 700 changes are indicative of an important transition period, characterized by a gradual shift from pithouse-dominated villages, with scattered noncontiguous habitations to true contiguous pueblo dwellings. (Figure 3.2). The transition is marked, first, by the storage areas being moved *inside*, and later, by removal of storage to above-ground structures.

Flannery (1972) concludes that the circular huts prevalent in some parts of the Fertile Crescent were constructed to house one or two people, while villages of rectangular houses, such as those in Anatolia, accommodated extended households. This suggests that the family was the basic unit of production in Anatolian villages of the period. Whether the dwelling was occupied by a polygamously extended household or a monogamous, nucleated family, it seems to have been a precursor of the more developed family dwelling concept seen half a millennium later at Can Hasan and Catal Huyuk, and in subsequent stages of Hacilar; in these, where most property was still collective, family storage spaces began to appear, supplementing the communal storage spaces of the settlement.

We do not know whether the circular huts in the Fertile Crescent were fully analogous to Anasazi pithouses. It appears probable that the pithouses, which formed clusters that did not resemble villages, also housed nuclear families. But there are other questions to be asked about (1) pithouses, (2) early pueblos composed of contiguous rectangular rooms, and (3) the transition between the two.

Gilman (1983), using background material from the *Ethnographic Atlas*, suggests that pit houses are thermally advantageous: their semi-subterranean nature facilitates climatic control. Their size seems to vary with altitude, being larger at higher elevations, the availability of bigger trees facilitates fabrication of larger structures, and the longer winters, forcing people to spend more time inside, may *necessitate* greater size. A single large space serves unstratified labor well, but increasing specialization of household labor usually implies the accommodation of different activities in separate spaces.

The *Ethnographic Atlas* provides comparative data on a variety of societies around the world. The use of pithouses seems to be associated with hunting and gathering, often semi-nomadic societies characterized by low population density and small settlements in areas with cold winters. Most are unstratified without class distinctions. However, increased population density is correlated with increased reliance on agriculture. Pueblos — occurring primarily in North America — are associated with greater populations, higher population density, and intensified agriculture and occur in predominantly hot, dry areas with cold winters.

Why did pithouses become pueblos? The reasons should lie in the relationship of mode of production to conditions of existence, to *quantitative* changes *within* a mode of production preparing the way for a later *qualitative* shift from one mode of production to another. In fact, Gilman's (1983) research provides physical evidence for this. The key, according to Gilman, is the combination of increased population, increased production (intensification of agricultural technology) and variable environment (temperature variation and, in particular, unpredictable rainfall). Under these conditions, food must be stored for more than one year in locations resistant to moisture, wind, and pests, and must be protected from "social pressure."

An obvious form of "social pressure" is theft, but the emergence of theft is merely one aspect of a change in social organization correlated with the pithouse-to-pueblo transition, and also with increased population and production (surplus product); the shift from social organization based on the family to clan-based organization, are arguably better accommodated by contiguous above-ground structures, which, in turn, are formed more readily of rectangular units. Their thermal disadvantage — that it is more difficult to achieve minimum heat gain in summer and minimum heat loss in winter than in pithouses — is partly overcome by making storage structures contiguous to each other and/or to habitation. Contiguity to habitation also protects the stored product against theft, a major concern with the combination of increased, longer term storage bulk and higher population.

Some characteristics of regions with unpredictable rainfall are worth noting. Since the maximum productive potential of a particular technology is reached at lower populations in such regions than in areas of more predictable rainfall with population increase, either migration or improvements in subsistence technology may be expected. In the American Southwest, however, particularly in the important Chaco region, microclimatic variations occur over a relatively small area; there can thus be substantial variation in rainfall over just a few kilometers. Hence it is possible for a society to "even out" the effects of climatic variation by controlling an extended territory; "how large?" is the question.

Another issue is information transmission, particularly about how much food a household has and where it is stored. This is called the "food information network." With population growth in marginal, unpredictable climates, the food information network can be expected to contract, food processing time (storage, preparation for cooking, and cooking itself) to increase, and food storage time to lengthen (to greater than one winter period). With longer and more complex food processing, winter weather becomes more of a problem, and a reason to move storage, food preparation, and cooking (with the exception of large roasting pits) inside. These are then accommodated in above-ground structures, according to Gilman's (1983) hypothesis.

Determining room and room feature functions was a task begun by Mendeleff (1891): the original supposition that small rooms were for storage, and rooms with hearths for habitation, no longer seems tenable. Dean (1969) classified pueblo settlement spaces during late Pueblo I and Pueblo II into six categories: living rooms, granaries, non-food storage, grinding rooms, ceremonial spaces, and courtyards. Each of these can be further subdivided according to its various forms and manifestations. Ransom (1960) categorized prehistoric Southwestern building forms as caves, outside pits, cribs, basket granaries, bins, separate rooms, and rooms attached to other structures, the last associated with dense populations. Further, room function may have changed with season; since cooler spaces are better for food storage, outer rooms are better in winter and inner rooms better in summer. The most efficient storage rooms according to Gilman (1983) are cubic, oriented north or east (with respect to the associated room complex), protected from the sun, small, and hearthless, with openings of minimal size.

Gilman evaluated these ideas in the Black Mesa area near the conjunction of Colorado, Utah, Arizona, and New Mexico, finding evidence of increased spatial differentiation and specialization through time. Her functional typology suggests that pithouses were winter habitation and *jacales* summer habitation, while masonry rooms in this transitional pithouse-to-pueblo area were primarily for storage. If her conclusions are correct, they bring into question the population estimates for the period. If a society is assumed to be sedentary but is in fact semi-nomadic, population counts based on presumed year-round occupancy will markedly overestimate the actual population of the region. Gilman suggests that counting pithouses, jacales, and masonry rooms *all* as habitations leads to similarly erroneous population estimates. But things may be even more complicated. Anderson (1982) suggests that *both* of the above factors —semi-nomadism *and* room specialization—may have been operating at Black Mesa. Thus,

...a family may choose from four or five winter sites each winter depending on conditions at each site that might include proximity to the agricultural fields used that year, water or firewood supply, or the likelihood of good hunting.... The use of pithouses in the prehistoric Southwest may be associated with *a much lower population density* than that assumed if pithouses are used by (completely) sedentary, fully agricultural populations: each person or family may be associated with many more sites than has previously been suspected. (Gilman, 1983; pp. 262-263, emphasis added).

We shall encounter this problem of population estimates again later on. One lesson is that the number of habitations is likely to be very much less than the total number of structures and the number of households less even than the number of habitations. Another is that the "carrying capacity," particularly of the Black Mesa region, may have been much less than previously assumed making agricultural production, storage and processing more critical at even lower population densities.

The similarity of pithouse settlements to much earlier architectural phenomena in Anatolia has not gone without notice: "the appearance of pithouse architecture in the Southwest is but one example of a worldwide Neolithic phenomenon" Cordell and Gumerman, 1989; p. 9). However, architectural information on the period spanning the interval between the pithouse-to-pueblo transition period and the proto-urban Classic Pueblo is murky at best. Interest in vernacular pithouse architecture and the monumental great pueblos has largely eclipsed interest in, and information about, the smaller-scale and visually less impressive late Pueblo I and early Pueblo II architecture and settlement (Rohn, 1989): "the ninth century in the Chaco Cores is one of the most poorly known periods in the archaeological record" (Vivian, 1990, p. 165). Late Pueblo I and early Pueblo II in the Pecos chronology (Cordell, 1984) correspond to the first part of Cordell and Gumerman's (1989) "Expansion period" (770-1050 A.D.), for whose pueblo-style architecture the terms "unit house" and "unit pueblo" have been coined (LeBlanc, 1989; Rohn, 1989).

A unit pueblo originally consisted of a habitation room and a storage room, which evolved:

> ...into an orientation of storage-habitation-kiva-trash from north or northwest to south or southeast, which occurs over much of the Anasazi area... until about A.D. 1275, when it is largely abandoned. Even Chaco big houses preserve this pattern. That is, the orientation pattern is preserved through a considerable architectural sequence in both house forms and time. It is surely a diagnostic or fundamental aspect of Anasazi behavior. (LeBlanc, 1989; p. 340)

This orientational emphasis distinguishes Anasazi villages from their Mogollon neighbors. Anasazi small kivas in the Cibola region (now central-eastern Arizona and central-western New Mexico) during the early part of this period were of earth and very much like preceding pithouses (Rohn, 1989), while great kivas existed among the northern Anasazi but were rare in Cibolan settlements during this period. Particularly interesting is the absence among the Cibola Anasazi of "strong evidence for the use of above-ground habitation rooms until after the initial construction of multistoried pueblos in Chaco Canyon" (LeBlanc, 1989; p. 341). Thus, pithouse-to-pueblo transitions in some areas actually overlapped production of multistoried pueblos in others.

Houses with several rooms and compact villages were present in other parts of the Anasazi region by A.D. 800. Building complexes in forms described in the previous section appeared, with 4 to 8 habitations in front associated with 8 to 24 storage rooms to the rear. Later in the period, basic wall construction materials changed from adobe-covered timber to masonry. Between A.D. 850 and 920 (early Pueblo II), habitation was concentrated in a smaller number of larger villages. (Figure 3.3). Straight rows of as many as 30 rooms became common. Masonry-lined "kivas" (or separate circular rooms) contained benches, cribbed log roofs and smokehole entryways in the centers of the roofs. Some advances in size and construction continued during the following century. (Figure 3.4).

In summary, what is indicated by both the description of Anasazi settlement up to the end of the first millennium, A.D., and the accompanying illustrations (Figures 3.1 to 3.4) is undramatic, gradual change: (1) a shift from pithouse to pueblo (a major, but not revolutionary, architectural change); (2) a gradual increase in settlement size, that is, in the number of contiguous rooms in a pueblo; and (3) changes in the nature and location of kivas: kivas, elaborated in architectural detail, tended to be sited away from, instead of contiguous with, building complexes. It may be said that as buildings were going up, kivas were going down, becoming more like the subterranean spaces characteristic of later periods.

But these changes were by no means visually striking, which may be why the Pueblo I and Pueblo II periods seem to have excited so little interest among archaeologists and architects alike. However, from our perspective, we suggest that the increase of pueblo size, while it represents no major shift in mode of production, is probably reflective of increasing efficiency in production, increasing predominance of agriculture over hunting and gathering, and resulting accumulation of additional surplus product. While there is no apparent indication of fortification in these villages, need for additional security is usually associated with surplus product storage, is probably better provided for, as earlier indicated, in above-ground contiguous structures than in pithouses; the presence of such structures is one possible index of surplus product accumulation. We would further hypothesize that detailed analysis of the use of interior pueblo spaces would show the proportion of space devoted to storage increasing at a faster rate than that devoted to habitation, another indication of increasing surplus product.

By the beginning of the tenth century A.D., conditions of existence, with increasing population, appear to have become more strained, more difficult. The Chaco Wash may have become a less effective source of flood water for the fields. Whatever the reason, further increased yields through simple intensified agriculture, a quantitative change, were no longer feasible. A qualitative, technological change was called for: irrigation.

The water runoff which, during short, intensive rains, poured down the canyon walls into the *arroyos* below, was to be controlled through a system of check dams, ditches, and canals. This may have contributed to a *regional* organization of agricultural production—a further increase in yield with larger surpluses—and through these, to facilitation of the "Chaco Phenomenon," a prehistoric complex of urban settlements in the San Juan Basin of what is now northwestern New Mexico. Construction of a new settlement form was initiated at about the same time on six sites in the Chaco area: Pueblo Bonito, Chetro Ketl, Penasco Blanco, Una Vida, Hungo Pavi, and Kin Bineola. The so-called "Chaco Phenomenon" was underway.

Crossroads: A comparison

Anatolia was clearly a "crossroads of many peoples." In succeeding chapters we will try to indicate that this was directly or indirectly true of the Anasazi realm, as well. In the latter, hypothesized turquoise exchange (Pailes, 1990) along what Coe (1984) refers to as "the Turquoise Road" may have been analogous to the earlier, and better known, obsidian trade in the Middle East. Obsidian did play a role in Mesoamerican trade (Gaxiola, 1989), but not, apparently, among the Anasazi.

However, the interaction implied by the term "crossroads" has been much better accepted for Anatolia than for the American Southwest; in the case of the latter, how much interaction took place, when, and with whom, is still in dispute. Certainly, the dearth of large draft animals and the (associated) absence of wheeled vehicles during the late prehistoric era made Anasazi trade in bulky or semi-perishable goods much more difficult. That changes, initially within a mode of production, took place to facilitate trade in both locales is indisputable; some aspects of this will be examined later and in more detail.

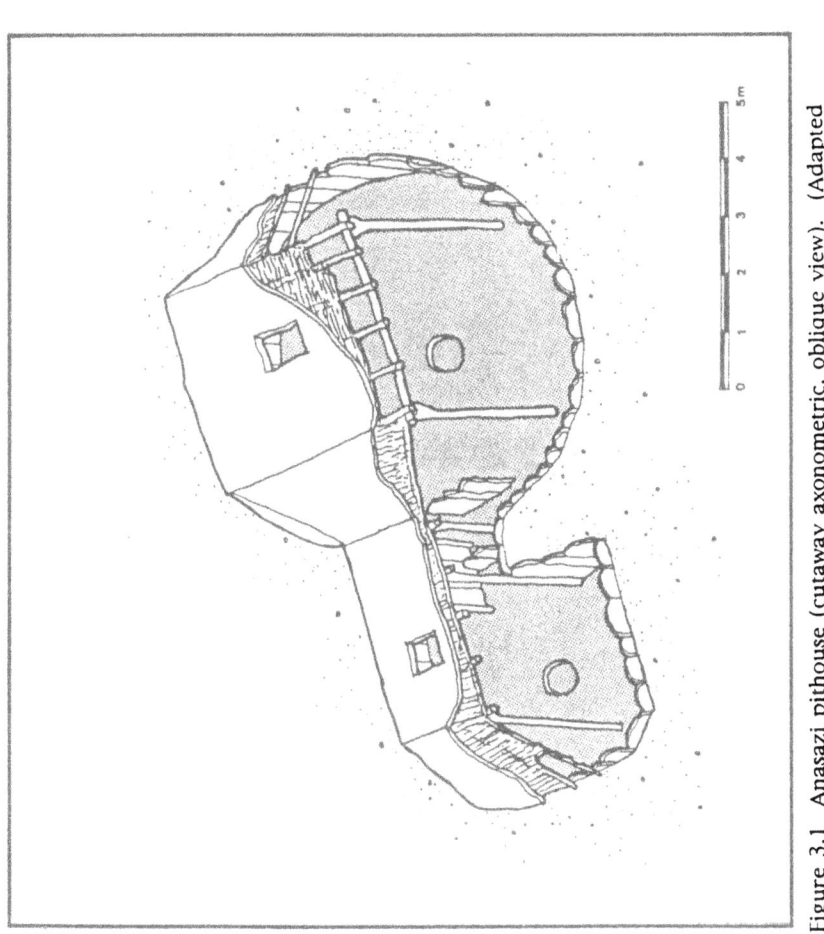

Figure 3.1 Anasazi pithouse (cutaway axonometric, oblique view). (Adapted from Ortiz, 1979 Lister and Lister, 1981).

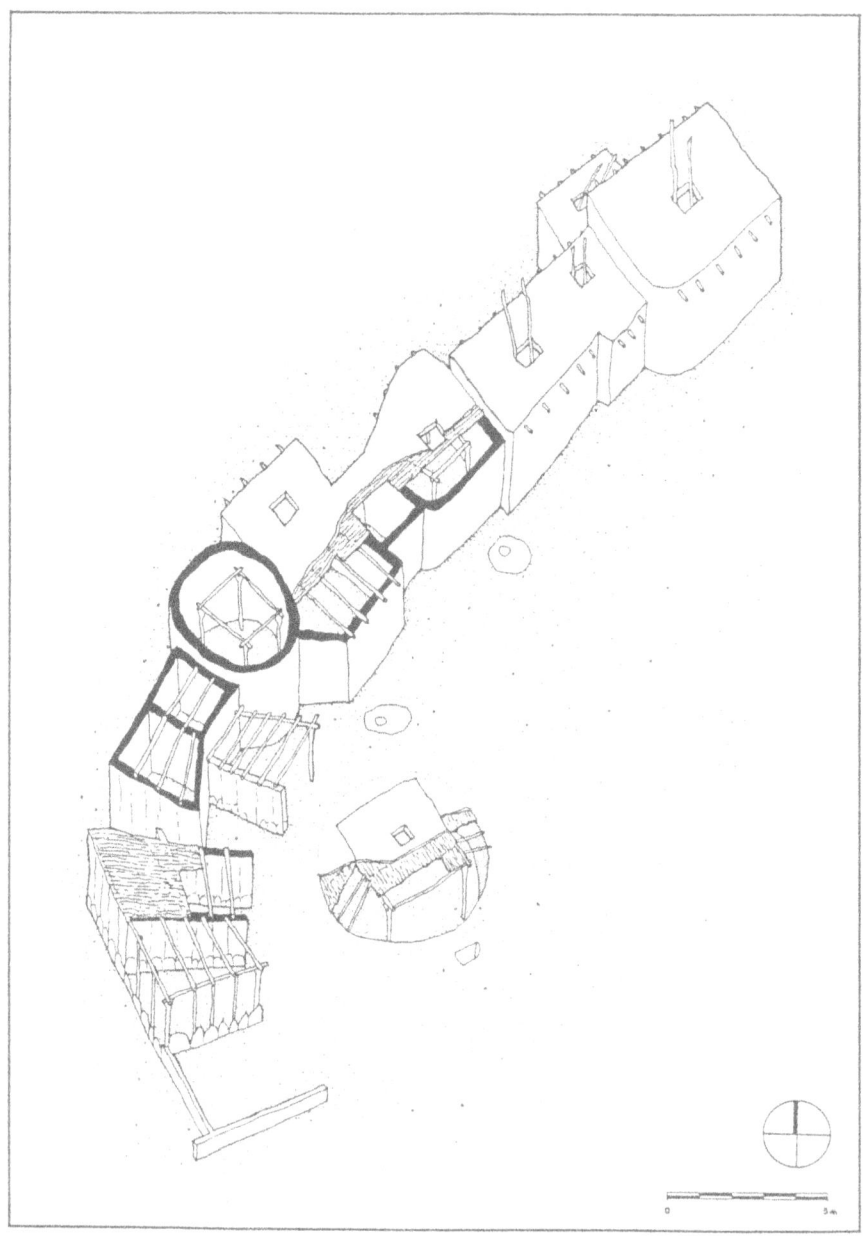

Figure 3.2 Anasazi early Pueblo I, reconstruction. (Adapted from Peckham, 1984).

From Shelter to Settlement 99

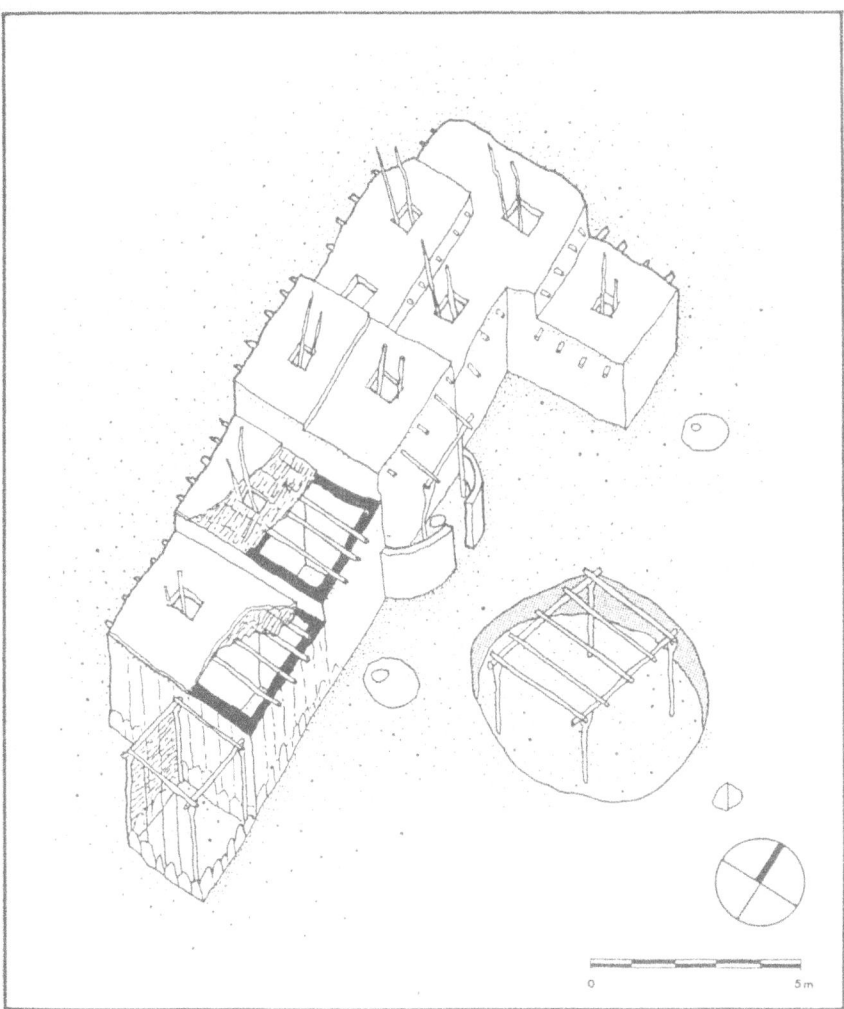

Figure 3.3 Anasazi early Pueblo II, reconstruction of part of a village. (Adapted from Peckham, 1984).

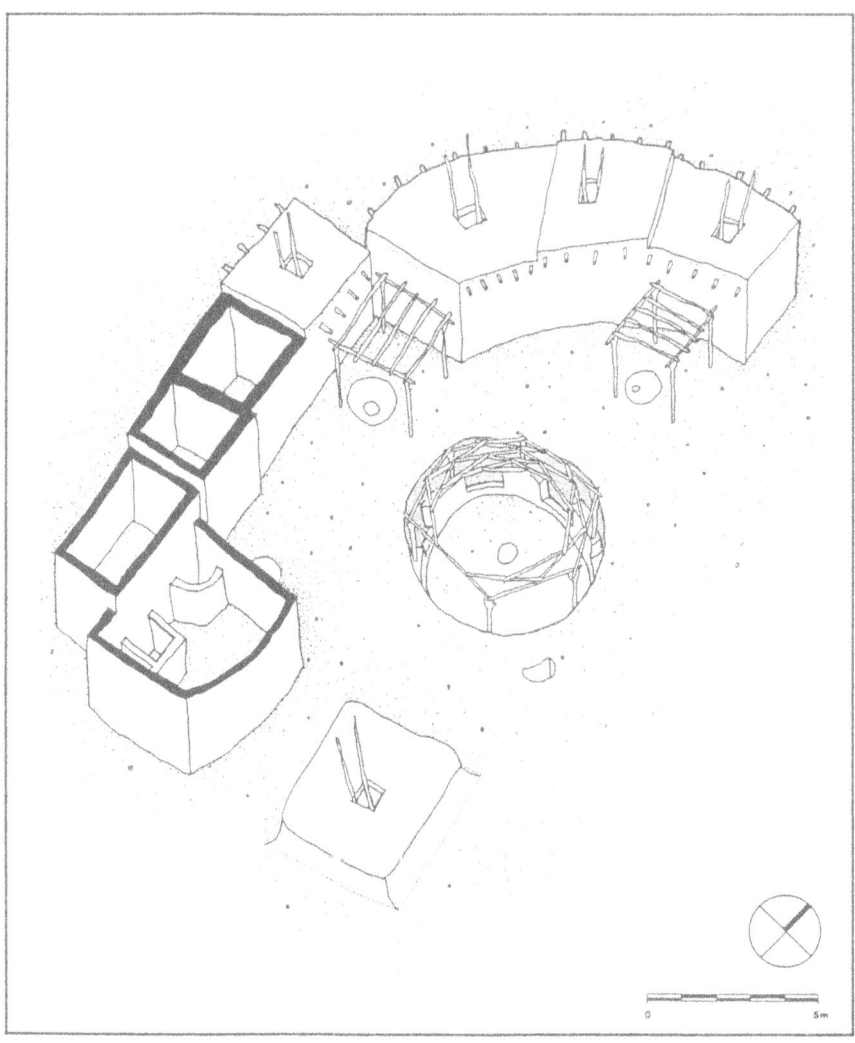

Figure 3.4 Portion of Anasazi village early Pueblo III, reconstruction. (Adapted from McKenna, 1982).

Chapter Four

URBANIZATION IN THE NEOLITHIC

> How can one understand the towns without understanding the countryside, money without barter, the varieties of poverty without the varieties of luxury, the white bread of the rich without the black bread of the poor? ... Everyday life consists of the little things one hardly notices in time and space. The more we reduce the focus of vision, the more likely we are to find ourselves in the environment of material life: the broad sweep usually corresponds to History with a capital letter, to distant trade routes, and the networks of national or urban economies.
>
> F. Braudel, *Civilization and capitalism,* v. I.

Over 8000 years ago, there came into being on the Konya plain of Anatolia what was probably the first Neolithic city: Catal Huyuk. At its peak, its population of some 6000 souls occupied one thousand houses. Its inhabitants, who practiced irrigated agriculture, were well-nourished on a balanced diet of beef, cereals, seeds, nuts, and other cultivated plants. This fortified city grew incrementally over a millennium from a Protoneolithic village of 100 people occupying some twenty houses to its later urban size and spread across 13 hectares in area.

Along with the cities of Can Hasan and Hacilar, Catal Huyuk represented several major leaps; its greater population was housed at markedly higher densities, and, while not entirely abandoning hunting and collecting as part of their economic base, its inhabitants employed advanced agricultural methods. Here, evidence is found of family property replacing collective clan ownership, and of the emergence of a separate priestly class concurrent with the construction of specialized shrines—the architectural manifestation of an incipient, stratified society.

On the other side of the world, and almost 7000 years later, a similar "revolution" occurred in the Anasazi region of the American Southwest with the appearance of the Chaco system, the apparent "quantum leap" in settlement development beginning at about A.D. 950. Where the Anasazi region had previously been characterized by apparently isolated villages consisting of storage rooms, the rather sudden development of architecturally sophisticated megastructures in Chaco Canyon and systems of relatively far-flung, outlying villages connected by well engineered roads to the main Canyon, among people who also practiced irrigated agriculture and complex trade, constituted a real phenomenon.

This "Chaco Phenomenon," as it has come to be called, has been studied and written about by many scholars and researchers over the past two decades, but their conclusions concerning "what was really going on at Chaco" still remain in the realm of conjecture. There is a fair amount of agreement that the Chacoan megastructures were not primarily dwellings but much less agreement concerning the balance of "ceremonial" use and economic exchange. In the realm of conjecture, as well, are answers to questions concerning the decay of the system, decline in occupation, and eventual abandonment of the megastructures, and what actually happened to at least some of the participants during the "Chacoan phenomenon."

As indicated in the concluding pages of this chapter, prehistoric building and associated artifacts from Central Anatolian urban places indicate a relatively unbroken line of progressively stratified societies with a clear but gradual shift from kin-ordered to tertiary modes of production. The Anasazi record, however, is much less clear. Most ethnographers viewing the unstratified nature of contemporary New Mexico pueblos, the presumed descendants of the Anasazi, earlier concluded that the Anasazi were also a uniformly unstratified society, which coincides well with assumed unilinear progression in the development of modes of production. But the placemaking and region-building record of Chacoan culture fits neither the simple and purely egalitarian model of the kin-ordered mode of production nor that of a traditionally stratified tertiary society, an apparent anomaly further explored in Chapter Five.

A town among volcanoes

Whether or not a settlement deserves to be called a town or city, as opposed to a village, according to the criteria of "a community with extensive economic development, specialized crafts, a rich religious life, a surprising attainment in art and an impressive social organization" (Mellaart, 1972b; p.120), the association between a specific system of social relations and a given ecological context remains ambiguous. The ecological form, in this particular case, refers to Catal Huyuk, the largest known Neolithic site, which Mellaart (1972a) refers to as a city. Certainly, the label "city" here, distinct from the settlements referred to as "villages" above, cannot be attributed to its sheer size alone — dimensions and density — nor, perhaps, to the heterogeneity of its population. The qualities and characteristics that give Catal Huyuk the title "city" existed at some level or form in the villages as well. Then what makes Catal Huyuk and other settlements referred to as "towns" or "cities" different from "villages"?

The answer to the above question must be sought in social relations and people's interaction with other human beings rather than in their interaction with their environment (Adams, 1972). For millennia, until the establishment of more permanent settlements, the major emphasis beyond the development of social relations had been upon experimenting with nature and increasingly intense exploitation of the environment through the development of new and better tools and techniques, and the discovery of more reliable modes of existence and reproduction. As social relations developed over a long period and the organizational level reached a point beyond mere search for foodstuffs, storage and redistribution became the major focus of attention. This gradual progress led to the rise of cities. Adams (1972) calls this preeminently social process the second "revolution" in human culture. The first, what Childe (1952) termed man's most profound revolution, refers to the shift from food collecting and hunting to a truly food-producing technology. Whether these were "revolutions" or not, they demonstrate the strong link between the evolution of ecological forms and social relations. In other words, the rise of cities such as Catal Huyuk was linked primarily to the development of social relations and to the organizational level that more complex social relations require. Settlements became cities as the product and expression of this social structure and of its laws of transformation (Castells, 1977). The heterogeneity and concentration of the populations of cities are the commonly accepted empirical expressions differentiating them from villages; in cities, the underlying social and technological complexities are further developed.

Catal Huyuk, considerably larger than the settlements of earlier periods, covering almost thirteen hectares, was inhabited without any major interruption over a millennium, from 6300 to 5200 B.C. It is not only the largest known Neolithic site but also one of the better documented (and the most publicized) of the cities of that period in the Near East. It is located on the central Anatolian plateau on the alluvial Konya plain about 50 kilometers southeast of the modern city of Konya and 11 kilometers north of Cumra. The founders and the earliest settlers of Catal Huyuk apparently started building their town on what were once the banks of a river; in later years the settlement grew out from this river bank. The excavations, started in the spring of 1961, uncovered 14 superimposed building levels.

The economy of the settlement depended on simple irrigated agriculture and animal husbandry. The hypothesis of a conscious attempt at irrigation is strongly supported by Helbaek's (1964) studies, indicating that the bread-wheat and six-row naked barley are hybrids that cannot be grown without some sort of sustained irrigation. It seems only reasonable to agree with the conjecture of Mellaart (1967), the site's excavator, that the domestication of plants at Catal Huyuk must have had a long prehistory somewhere else since the Konya plain could not have provided the right conditions of existence for the progenitors of these crops in their wild form. In addition to the more advanced, hybrid crops, cultivated plants also included emmer einkorn, two-row barley, peas, lentils, bitter vetch, and vetchling. Other food remains indicate the existence of pistachio nuts, acorns, almonds, hackberries, juniper berries, and crab apples. These were undoubtedly collected rather than carefully cultivated (Mellaart, 1978). However, there may have been a deliberate attempt to cultivate walnuts and grapes in orchards.

While cattle seem to have been the major domesticated animals, kept from the earliest times at Catal Huyuk primarily for meat, sheep and goats were later used for the same purposes (Perkins, 1969). Dogs were domesticated even before cattle. Ninety percent of the meat consumed came from domestic cattle (which also were used for transport) supplemented with meat from game, such as giant wild cattle (aurochs), wild sheep, onagers, asses, deer of all kinds, wild goats, boars, bears, hares, and birds. There is also indication of fishing in nearby lakes and rivers. However, since remains of fish bones are not in abundance, fish must not have been a significant element in the diet of the residents of Catal Huyuk. Also, residents did not depict fish or fishing on the elaborate wall paintings which featured hunting of such bigger game as aurochs and deer. Nevertheless, studies showing the excellent condition of teeth in excavated human remains indicate a varied and a well-balanced diet. This is not surprising since irrigated agriculture yielded cereals providing starch and legumes, meat supplied necessary protein, and seeds and nuts supplied vegetable fats.

A heterogeneous population may partially account, as Angel (1971) argues, for the creativity, inventiveness, and fast advance of the people in almost every realm of life in Catal Huyuk. Development and progress during the life span of the town was certainly aimed at changing conditions of existence in every facet of the social, cultural, economic, and technological orders.

Mellaart's (1975) conservative estimates suggest that the maximum population of Catal Huyuk was probably around 6000 and the number of inhabited houses about 1000. The initial settlement was undoubtedly much more modest, not unlike the villages of the Protoneolithic whose population of 50 to 100 typically occupied 10 to 20 houses. Although the very early settlements of Catal Huyuk were architecturally undefended, implying absence of aggressive enemies, occasional fire damage, subsequent rebuilding, and possible emigration of certain groups from time to time must have affected the monotonic growth of population as well as the expansion of the city. In this remarkably continuous sequence of growth, the resulting peaceful and comfortable existence must have contributed considerably to the prosperity and progress that generations of Catal Huyuk residents enjoyed and the level of organization thus achieved (Figures 4.1, 4.2).

Houses were built around courtyards ranging in area from 100 to 150 square meters to 500 to 750 square meters. As in the case of Aceramic Can Hasan, there seems to have been a deliberate attempt to expose at least one side of each house to a courtyard. While in some cases houses were built adjacent to each other in what appear to be independent rows, in other cases adjacent rows created a "back to back" layout. Even the smallest courtyard could provide outside exposure to a minimum of 6 to 8 buildings. Larger courtyards could accommodate as many as 20 to 25 units, including shrines as well as houses. Since there was no dimensional differentiation between houses and shrines at Catal Huyuk, there was no difference in the total number that could have been accommodated by the courtyards. Regardless of its size, the courtyard and the surrounding buildings together constituted the basic unit of construction. In other words, each phase of construction must have involved a *set* of buildings, the number of buildings depending on the size of the courtyard surrounded and defined by the buildings. Enclosing courtyards and bounding settlements seem to have been critical planning and construction decisions.

There are several reasons for this system of scheduling construction and physical expansion through incremental growth. The courtyard served a public function for the people living around it providing a place for daily communal activities and a relatively private place within the whole community, primarily accessed by the people living adjacent to it. The population of each sub-community (or perhaps "neighborhood") ranged from 30 to 100 persons. Subtracting the number of shrines around each courtyard from the total number of buildings leaves about 5 to 20 buildings primarily for dwelling. Dividing the estimated population by this figure yields an average household of six persons, which also matches the mean number of platforms per house. The estimated population surrounding a courtyard is also the estimated range of clan size. This all suggests the possibility that each courtyard was communal open space "belonging" to a particular clan. In the hierarchical order of space within the whole settlement, the courtyard was a public area primarily, yet not exclusively, for the people of the clan. In other words, it was shared by the people of the whole tribe: common property of the tribal system. It was "exclusive" in the sense of the clan's everyday functions yet "inclusive" within the tribal order; thus was the organizational aspect of social structure manifested in spatial order.

This system of sequential growth also provided for defense. The walls of the buildings which actually formed the boundary between the settlement and the outside were the first barriers which outsiders had to cross. The defender, in case of attacks from outside and given the weapons of the day, had the advantage, the strategic superiority, of being able to defend the settlement from the roof tops. Each row of buildings constructed on the outer periphery thus became the first stronghold against attack. Since there are no signs of massacre as a result of outside intrusion over the life span of Catal Huyuk, either there were very few attacks or this system of defense must have been fairly successful. Fires set from outside seem to have been the only serious danger unless accidental fires started within the settlement were actually the cause of damage that occasionally occurred in the course of eleven centuries of occupancy. Outside walls were also a check against occasional floods resulting from heavy spring and fall downpours common in the continental climate of the region. Furthermore, with each expansion, that is with each addition of a courtyard-buildings complex, the parts of the town built earlier were rendered more secure against both natural hazards and outside attack. While the river created a natural barrier on one side against possible outside intrusion for those near the river bank, the manner of physical expansion added subsequent defense barriers. Flooding must have been easier to control with the solid blank walls facing the river.

With increase in population new clans were forming. Each clan was given the opportunity to organize itself as a production group. From the spatial organization of dwellings, it is apparent that the division of labor was structured primarily by families rather than by sex. While the smallest production unit was the family, the clan constituted the next larger production group within the broader tribal system. Thus, while the clan maintained autonomy in production and organization of labor within the tribal system, it was evidently not an economically self-sufficient group. In spite of the independent domestic economy, which was primarily production for livelihood, there must have been a system of exchange within the tribal system to supplement the insufficient, locally produced foodstuffs. Autonomy in production, and perhaps even emerging specialization both in food production and collecting, also allowed freedom in the belief system, more specifically in the choice of totems. Both of these factors allowed the clan a social and cultural identity of its own. While the shrines of each clan were the formal places for expression of this identity, courtyards were the informal places. Clan courtyards consisting of individual dwelling units, shrines, and surrounding storage/work spaces completed the organized spatial array; the courtyards thus possessed a social identity.

The conjecture that incremental growth of the city was based on enclosing courtyards and outside bounds (with the buildings surrounding a courtyard constituting the unit of construction in accordance with the needs and size of the clan) seems even more plausible when the likely duration of construction (in labor terms) is considered. Conservative estimates, including a slow construction rate (Lekson, 1984a) and a technology applicable to the period, suggest that construction of a Chacoan great house, including storage and work spaces, would have taken roughly 6,000 person-hours (PH). While this does not include such finishing touches as painting and decorative elements on the walls (and elsewhere), the figure does include five general classes of construction labor representing, in approximate sequence: cutting and processing beams, transporting beams, excavating and building foundation walls, processing mudbrick (or quarrying stone), procuring other masonry materials, and actual construction. The preparation of the construction site and materials consumed about half of the time mentioned above. In other words, actual building time was about 3,000 PH. Assuming a 10-hour work day, a person working full-time could have constructed a house of approximately 50 square meters in less than a year, if all the preconstruction preparation sequence (appropriation and procurement of materials, preparation of foundations, etc.) were completed before actual construction started. All the evidence of standardized bricks at different building levels in Catal Huyuk (Mellaart, 1967), however, indicates that there was a production system. This, if true, reduces both the preconstruction preparation sequence and actual building to approximately 2,000 PH each. In other words, a person could have finished actual construction in approximately seven months, following completion of the preconstruction preparation sequence.

Since construction is rarely a solo activity, it seems safe to assume that people participated cooperatively in construction. It seems also valid to assume that the pre-construction preparation sequence was largely completed long before actual construction. Under these assumptions, 35 builders in a clan of 150 persons might have completed a 25-house clan unit in less than five months. With occasional secondary assistance, this task might have been shorter still. With standardized bricks, it is highly probable that the total duration of construction activity was even shorter than the conservative estimates made here.

The significance of the "unit of construction" and its duration is associated primarily with the defense of the town against its enemies; it was very important to establish barriers against potential intruders. These barriers, the outside building walls, formed the edge of the settlement, very much like the city wall of later periods. Individual families depended on division of labor within the clan not only in production, construction, and material appropriation — in short, in social relations — but also in different forms of cooperative defense against both natural hazards and enemies. In one sense, the more populated a settlement, the more desirable holding food production constant must have been. Therefore, the formation of a new clan or the introduction of one from outside must have been welcome. However, the security of both the new clan and the old depended heavily on the rate of construction of the new clan unit, that is, upon the new addition to the city (presumably, to its exterior). The faster the construction system, the more secure the unit and the entire town must have been for the residents.

Given the conditions of the times, it is very difficult to conceive of and argue for advance planning or actual "master planning" of the settlement. First, the life expectancy of people was too short, in relation to construction time, to realize such a plan or even a portion of such a plan. Even if it is assumed that the elderly played an important role in the establishment of continuity in conveying the hypothetical plan, in verbal form, to the younger generations, the predictions and presuppositions made at the initiation of planning are very likely to have been changed later on. Second, although the rate of construction may have been relatively fast, it is not very probable that in the life span of a couple of generations, more than three construction units, at most, could have been added to the existing settlement. In other words, the growth rate must have been one additional construction unit every 15 to 20 years. This is because survival and social reproduction require activities other than building, and also because large population increases, no matter what their source might have been, could not possibly have been accommodated within the existing economy and organization in so short a time. This inference is further supported by evidence of continuous emigration from Catal Huyuk to southern and western Anatolia. For the foregoing reasons, growth of the city probably occurred or was accomplished in increments of two or three construction units every 50 or 60 years. Third, occasional fire damage must have impeded implementation of preconceived plans, although rebuilding after a fire undoubtedly took less time than new construction. Different layers excavated reveal that only some parts of fire-damaged layers were completely rebuilt and that some construction elements were recycled. Nevertheless each rebuilding introduced a different layout. Finally, living patterns did not actually require clear distinctions between either domestic/nondomestic or secular/sacred areas to be manifested as separate functions in spatial organization. Therefore, there was no urgent need to produce or maintain a hierarchical order through functional separation of spaces. The absence of need for hierarchical order also reduced the need for — and the likelihood of — a preconceived master plan.

The above argument does not, however, imply absence of planning or order. On the contrary, there seems to have been serious concern for both, other than the "preconceived" planning level, as argued by Mellaart (1967; p.70). Furthermore, while Catal Huyuk seems to represent a considerable development over the Protoneolithic villages, this does not mean that the earlier villages were "disorderly and random agglomeration[s] of freestanding huts and hovels" (Mellaart, 1967; p.67). Any settlement has an order of its own at one level or another. By its very nature, the term "settlement," regardless of its size, represents some sort of order underlying the social organization. The shaping of a settlement depends upon both environmental demands and the technological capacity of the society. The development of urban order, observed at Catal Huyuk, must be interpreted as an outcome of the changing needs of the society and of developing social relations.

A typical dwelling at Catal Huyuk was composed mainly of two spaces: the living space, with fairly standardized dimensions of about 4.5 x 6 meters; and the storage/work space, about half the size of the major dwelling area. Although there certainly is a range in the floor areas in dwellings from about 10 to 48 square meters, the size of most dwellings probably depended on the size and the spatial requirements of the family: living quarters were about 25 to 27 square meters in mean area. Domestic spatial areas are replicated in what is interpreted to be the "shrine," or the space used for nondomestic purposes. The major difference between domestic and nondomestic spaces, or between "secular" and "sacred" spaces, is the absence of elaborate, decorative flourishes and cult symbols in the former. Goddesses represented in relief engaging in a variety of activities, such as giving birth (a sign of female fertility); bucrania and horn cores of aurochs embedded in built-in benches of mud-brick (representing the male); paintings on walls describing events such as stag- and boar-baiting and other hunting activities; and even an interpretation of human-nature dialogue represented by an erupting volcano behind an actual town layout (depicted in plan), are some of the richly varied and abundant works of art uncovered at Catal Huyuk (Mellaart, 1967; 1975). Also found in what are interpreted as shrines are statuettes and art objects of marble and baked clay representing human and animal figures (fertility and phallic symbols). Most of these artistic and cult-related objects and artifacts were uncovered in spatially similar but functionally different spaces. Apart from this difference, everything was architecturally and architectonically quite similar in domestic and nondomestic buildings.

Floors were divided into 2 to 5 platforms, as carefully packed and plastered as the rest of the surfaces. Usually those adjacent to three of the four walls were raised and joined, thus forming a U-shaped platform around the central portion of the floor, which hence appears sunken. Platforms with rounded curbs between them as dividers served not only as built-in furniture but also as architectural manifestations of the hierarchy that existed within the family. This hierarchy related to differentiation not only by sex but also by age. Platforms, which Mellaart calls "the prototypes of the Turkish sofa (and divan)" (1967, p.60) accommodated such household activities as sitting, working, and sleeping. While the woman occupied the main and largest platform in the house and never changed her place, the places of the man, children, and the elderly did change. This pattern of use is revealed by burial customs, indexed by the sex and age of the person buried below each platform. Although the corner platform, square in shape, seems commonly to have belonged to the man, the findings are not sufficiently definitive to establish this as a rule. However, as the woman's platform in the house did not change, neither did the food-preparation area. The woman's platform was along one of the two shorter sides of the rectangular room, the other being totally devoted to the food preparation area occupying roughly one third of the available space, with an open hearth near the sunken portion of the floor and an oven adjacent to the wall. Although the rooms were not actually divided by walls, a sense of space differentiated by activities and persons was established by rather subtle spatial "markers:" slight rises or rounded curbs between platforms and built-in benches. Thus, in the process of placemaking, space was defined not only by the boundaries of the room — the walls and the roof — but also by the subtle spatial markers which created different spaces within one volume.

Even the larger houses did not provide sleeping space for more than eight persons. The platforms averaged 3 to 4 in number. If this is an index of family size, then it can be inferred that an average family was composed of approximately six members, with children and the elderly possibly sharing a platform, or the mother sleeping with the young siblings and the man on a platform of his own. Sunken or unraised portions of the floor must have been used together with the food-preparation area for activities commonly performed by the household members, such as eating. It is also very likely that the roofs, weather permitting, were utilized for daily domestic chores. In addition to the individual ovens in the dwellings, larger ovens in the courtyards were undoubtedly utilized collectively for baking bread as well.

While the volume of the living quarters of the house, estimated at 60 cubic meters or more, seems to have been adequate for six persons, the smoke from the fire in the open hearth must have been a serious source of discomfort, since ventilation appears to have been very poor (with just one opening to the outside). This one opening, on the roof, served as the only access to the dwelling and as ventilation. However, as Mellaart (1967, pp.60-61) surmises, small window openings in the walls, especially facing the courtyard, may have alleviated the problem of smoke. These were necessary for admitting daylight as well. Yet this light must have been fairly soft and indirect. That the colors of the paintings in the shrines and the partially red-painted walls in some dwellings are still well-preserved suggests that interior daylight was certainly not strong and direct. Furthermore, any opening in the walls increased both the risk from potential enemies and heat loss to the outside. Efforts to retain as much heat as possible are quite understandable in a continental climate whose diurnal and seasonal temperature fluctuations are considerable. Further support comes from the observation of ovens partly set into the wall so that a larger surface, with a very high heat capacity and long time-lag acting as a heat sink during the day could reradiate the stored heat back into the room at night.

Having the only access into the dwellings through roof openings effectively protected against enemies. A removable exterior ladder, either on the side facing the courtyard or on the opposite side, provided the only access to the roof, as is the case among some contemporary pueblos in the American Southwest. Thus, the connected roofs must have furnished a widely used circulation area connecting one dwelling to another. A fixed ladder might have been used for access into the house from the roof in some cases, and a movable one in others (Mellaart, 1972b). The roof entrance was usually placed over the food preparation area of the house, which also contained the open hearth and the oven.

Mellaart states that the food preparation area was "always placed along the south wall" (1967; p.56). However, the irregularity in overall layout of the dwellings, as well as the odd shapes of the courtyards, could not have allowed such a rule to be followed uniformly, except around some courtyards and at certain levels (for example, building-Level V). Nevertheless, the excavator's deduction that the roof entrances must have provided a successful defense system, since there are no traces of massacre, seems both plausible and convincing (Mellaart, 1975).

Almost all the houses had a storage/work space, about 13 to 15 square meters on the average, attached to the living quarters. Some of the storerooms contained grain-bins of dried clay in pairs or in rows, and in others, coiled baskets or skins were used for storage. Excavations also showed that some of the storage/work spaces were not used entirely for storage of foodstuffs but also for stone tools, polishing stones, sling ammunition, knuckle-bones, and axes as well (Mellaart, 1967). Saddle querns and mortars were found on the floors of these storerooms and also in some of the living quarters of the houses. The existence of separate fire chambers and a larger, domed baking area in addition to the normal oven in some of the houses suggests that these fire chambers might have been used as pottery kilns, since plenty of pottery was found at Catal Huyuk. The presence of small ovens in all living units suggests that daily activities were then accomplished at the level of the family, while the discovery of large bread ovens, 1.5 to 1.8 meters in diameter, indicates the continuance of collective activity at about 5400 B.C. (Mellaart, 1967). The storage/work spaces were in most cases also entered from the roof. Some of those facing the courtyard had low doorways. No animals could be kept in the storerooms; even those with low doorways could not be used for animals since no access to the courtyards was available except through the roofs. It is quite likely that domesticated animals were kept in corrals surrounded by the outside walls of the houses on three sides and fenced on the fourth. The vulnerability of these to outside attacks must have been a problem. However, the strategy of rooftop defense was probably effective in reducing, if not totally eliminating, the risk of losing animals to invaders.

The construction of shrines was no different than the construction of dwellings: that is, they were built in exactly the same way using dimensions similar to those of habitations. Roof entrances, platforms, built-in benches, timber posts embedded partially in the walls, open hearths, ovens set in walls, storage spaces, the paneled appearance of wall interiors — in short, all of the architectural features observed in dwellings — were also present in shrines. One distinguishing feature of the shrines is the quality and degree of elaboration of decorative flourishes, as well as the cult symbols mentioned earlier.

Different building levels also reveal an important fact about a sociocultural trend of the people living in Catal Huyuk. Over the course of more than one thousand years of uninterrupted existence, a gradual separation of secular and sacred occurred in spatial organization, affecting other realms of life. In the town's earlier stages, there were two houses for each shrine. In other words, around a relatively small courtyard surrounded by six buildings, four buildings were used primarily for residential purposes and the other two as shrines. Around a larger courtyard, surrounded by, say, 25 buildings, eight of the buildings were used as shrines. In later stages of development the ratio of houses to each shrine increased to 5 to 6, implying that the number of shrines was decreasing, relative to residences, in each sub-community or clan of Catal Huyuk as time went by.

This certainly is not an indication that the belief system was weakening. On the contrary, the belief system, in organizational terms, was probably being strengthened. To state it differently, a more centralized authority emerged with increasing community affluence creating a special group of people: *priests*. Earlier, religion was an informal part of everyone's daily life; later, it underwent a formal separation from mundane daily functions, organized by a group of specialists in the society. Spatial manifestations of this development at the societal level include the gradual separation of secular and sacred functions of the dwelling. The house became the place for domestic and other secular activities to be performed, while the shrine became a place primarily for sacred functions.

The prosperity and the development of the art of life that are observed in Catal Huyuk—its levels of affluence, innovation, creativity, and achievement— are not only an outcome of agriculture or accessibility to material resources (which undeniably contribute to such progress). The latter may be necessary conditions but are not sufficient in themselves. Neither the high levels of trade nor those of production identified with Catal Huyuk are possible in the absence of a certain societal organizational level. Furthermore, Catal Huyuk's impact on outlying areas as far away as the Mediterranean coast to the south and the Cappadocia region of the central Anatolian plateau to the north is clear. Besides being a regional center for peripheral areas in the material sense, it is highly probable that Catal Huyuk was also a spiritual center, as Mellaart (1975) surmises. Johnson (1989), noted later, has compared social formation at Catal Huyuk with that of the climax among the Anasazi.

Early Anasazi and Anatolian "pueblo-like" settlements were inhabited not just by living families, but by the bodies of their ancestors and burials are, therefore, of considerable interest. Archaeological findings at Aceramic Hacilar suggest that burials were located outside the village. However, a number of skulls, purposely set upright, have been located, two of these supported by

Urbanization in the Neolithic 113

pebbles on the lowest courtyard floor facing the houses. One interpretation suggested by Mellaart (1970) is "ancestor worship," more fully developed later at Catal Huyuk. Perhaps the skulls served as a form of "deed," certifying that the territory was in fact occupied by one's ancestors, attesting to the collective ownership of property by clans (the smallest socially organized exogamous units) (Berktay, 1983). The dwellings of family units comprising the clan tended to be clustered together, while the cooperative nature of the clan itself was manifested in communal courtyards. The clan provided the labor power needed for the collective appropriation of food and for placemaking, but also contained the seed that would sprout into family ownership as surplus product increased. Thus, the tribal system incubated the later concept of private property.

Aceramic Can Hasan (French, 1962-1968) and Catal Huyuk (Mellaart, 1967) were well established agricultural towns (ca. 6300 B.C.) south of the Anatolian plateau, and east of Hacilar. Their layouts suggest that both settlements had to accommodate more people at higher densities than any of their predecessors. While primarily agricultural, these towns also engaged in hunting, pastoralism, and even some collecting, but the primary indicators of high, dense population are increased environmental control and the beginnings of full-fledged food-producing activity (Bernal, 1965; Berktay, 1983). More important for our own purposes, however, is the presence of defined family living quarters in both settlements which suggests that collective clan ownerships were beginning to give way to private family ownership.

Continued development of an ideology of descent is represented by burial of the dead beneath the sleeping platforms of houses at Catal Huyuk (Mellaart, 1967). Thus, while the dwelling still acted, for the most part, both as living area and shrine, totemic ideology was paving the way during this period for the later emergence of a class of priests. At this point in history, however, priests, both male and female, also engaged in productive activities. In later periods, religious functions were removed to separate shrines at about the same time that priests became nonlaborers, presaging the eventual emergence of political authority; but during the period of Catal Huyuk, exchange relations between lineages and between full-time and part-time (priestly) laborers were still reciprocal rather than redistributive (Polgar, 1975), and status relations still relatively egalitarian.

Anasazi status relations also appeared relatively egalitarian prior to the emergence of the great pueblos of the Chaco system, with no status differentiation evident either in under-floor or midden burials. There is some sparse indication, however, of status differentials among the relatively few burials unearthed in the Chacoan great pueblos (Frisbie, 1978, 1980; Reyman, 1978).

Architectural evidence of another transition to the clan's ownership of the built environment and its collective appropriation is found in Anatolia in the settlement patterns of Can Hasan and Catal Huyuk, where slight differences in conditions of existence, occasioned by changes in ideological superstructure, are manifested in the architectural features of dwellings. Large rooms with separate, almost enclosed, alcoves of 4 to 10 square meters may have been shared by more than one family or inhabited by an extended polygamous family. Some of the alcoves have raised platforms for sleeping and/or sitting; others do not, suggesting the use of the latter for storage. There is no indication, however, that surplus product was sufficient to enable the emergence of a class of priests, nor is there indication of separate, specialized religious buildings.

Anasazi urban systems

> The fact that a dwelling house is supposed to be at 'The Center of the World' does not make it any less a convenience, which answers to specific needs and is conditioned by the climate, the economic structure of society and the architectural tradition. (Eliade, 1957; p.177).

The "Chaco Phenomenon," mentioned toward the end of the previous chapter, was not an entirely unique event in the American Southwest of the last millennium; as Schroeder, in a personal communication in 1985, has indicated, the Hohokam experienced a "phenomenon" of their own only slightly later. This was followed by yet a third "phenomenon" in what is now northern Mexico: the Paquime phase of Casas Grandes. Thus, in the relatively brief period from A.D. 950 to 1260, three great urban spheres arose, flourished for a time, and then declined.

The achievements of two of these groups were notably architectural. The exception is the Hohokam, who occupied much of southern Arizona during their Sedentary (A.D. 900? to 1100?) and Classic periods (A.D. 1100? to 1300+), (Haury, 1976). Research by Haury at Snaketown (1976) and aerial photography (Ebert and Lyons, 1980) suggest that the Hohokam developed extremely impressive and technologically sophisticated irrigation works, consisting of canals, lateral ditches, diversion areas, head gate structures, and diversion dams. Nicholas (1981) and Dove (1982) differ on whether a precondition to the massive expression of irrigation systems that occurred during the Classic period was the development of complex sociopolitical institutions. Doyel's (1980) work suggests the existence of a hierarchy of settlements with each irrigation system associated with at least one town and a number of smaller villages.

The extent of social stratification among the Hohokam is unclear, as is the extent of Mesoamerican influence. Haury (1976) and Schroeder (1957, 1960, 1979) argue strongly for a Mesoamerican *origin* of the Hohokam, who are hypothesized to have displaced their Hakataya predecessors in the area. If

Schroeder is correct, the Mesoamerican connections of the Hohokam may have continued through the Colonial, Sedentary, and Classic periods as suggested by the architectural record; relatively simple domestic architecture was complemented by platform mounds and massive elongated structures oriented east to west, with expanded end courts. Those who support the hypothesis of continued Mesoamerican influence see the last as ball courts.

The "Chaco Phenomenon." A century and a half before the start of the Hohokam Classic period, an equally (or, according to some, even more) extraordinary development began in Chaco Canyon in what is now northwestern New Mexico. (Figure 4.3). So strikingly different was this development from the apparent previous evolution of Anasazi culture that it has been given the name "Chaco Phenomenon." The distinguishing characteristics of this Chaco development from A.D. 950 onwards include: (1) evidence of extensive long-term urban planning; (2) a probable distinction between "towns" and "villages," with marked architectural differences between the two; (3) an apparent relationship between the "great pueblos" (megastructures) of the Chaco Canyon area itself and the outlying settlements (outliers) employing Chacoan masonry and ceramics, connected with Chaco by road and a (still hypothetical) system of visual communication, and possessing towers/great kivas (Judge, 1979); (4) a sophisticated road system over 400 kilometers in extent, connecting the outliers with the central Chaco community (e.g., Vivian, 1990); (5) a system for control and direction of water flow; (6) the presence of such luxury items as turquoise and turquoise jewelry; worked inlays of mica, selenite, and turquoise on wood, shell, and basketry; copper bells; sculptured pottery; shell trumpets; various effigies and painted tablets; parrot feathers and other macaw remains, etc.; (7) the apparently utilization of solar energy and astronomical observation (Hayes, 1981; Knowles, 1974; Morgan, 1977; Reyman, 1976; Sofar, Zinser and Sinclair, 1979; Williamson, Fisher, and O'Flynn, 1977); and (8) a remarkable scarcity of burials (Hayes, 1981). While some investigators have referred to each of the Chacoan megastructures shown in Figure 4.3 as a "town," the appearance of the settlement group stretching at least from Kin Kletso to Chetro Ketl (less than 2 kilometers) is that of a single "conurbation," which will be discussed later.

A typical Chacoan "great house" is Pueblo Alto situated just above the canyon itself and at the terminus of one of the Chacoan roads. (Figure 4.4). Like its neighbors, it is distinguished from earlier pueblos by clear spatial definition and the presence of both great and small kivas. It is also distinguished from other great houses by its vast panoramic view and in being single-storied. Situated at the junction of major and minor Chacoan roads, it offered an opportunity for Lekson, Windes, Stein, and Judge (1988) to study the distinctive features of a number of road-related room suites, "completely inaccessible from inside the house" (p.105).

Other various aspects of Chaco architecture have been detailed elsewhere (Judd, 1959, 1964; Lekson, 1978, 1983, 1984a,b; Marshall and Doyel, 1981; Saile, 1977) but it is interesting to compare common aspects of Anasazi architectural construction and material use with that of the neighboring Hohokam and Mogollon, and to compare *within* the Anasazi realm the same aspects of "town" ("Bonito") and "village" ("Hosta Butte") architecture (Table 4.1). Chaco's settlement geography has also been intensively analyzed by Schelberg (1984), who suggests that:

> A hierarchy of settlement sizes and types is characteristic of the chiefdom or stratified level of society... The Chacoan settlement pattern in the San Juan Basin of northwestern New Mexico indicates that one such society evolved partially in response to a set of ecological conditions (p. 5).

Table 4.1
Comparative Architectural Features of Hosta Butte and Bonito Architecture*

Hosta Butte	Bonito
Average size: 16 rooms	Average size: 216 rooms
One floor	4+ floors
Small rooms, low ceilings	Large rooms, high ceilings
Oriented southeast	Generally southern exposure
Grew by accretion	Planned
Single compound masonry walls (Surfaced with adobe plaster)	Core-veneered masonry walls
Open plazas	Enclosed plazas
Small kivas	Small and great kivas
Kivas have vertical post or pilaster roof supports	Kivas have cribbed roofs supported by horizontal logs
Room-to-kiva ratio: about 6.5 to 1	Room-to-kiva ratio: about 29 to 1
On both north and south sides of Chaco Canyon	North side only
Burials in refuse or under floors	Burials very scarce
Absence of luxury goods	Presence of luxury goods

*Cordell, 1984.

Schelberg defends his contention that Chacoan society was ranked or stratified against the position (Altschul, 1978) that Chacoan society must have been organized along egalitarian lines because of the absence of ethnographic examples of hierarchical societies among contemporary pueblos:

> Such interpretations of archaeological facts in light of the ethnographic present may ... mask fundamentally important differences between the sociopolitical organization of the Chacoan Anasazi and the Pueblo Indians. There are clear-cut similarities between the two systems; however, if we assume that there is only a one-to-one correspondence in everything then we must also assume that nothing ever changes ... archaeological reconstruction of excavated sociocultural systems often takes the form of a direct analogy with a comparable living system. The result is that important variables may not be considered. (Schelberg, 1984; p.5)

We shall return later to this latter point of Schelberg. For purposes of the present discussion, we note that Schelberg rank-orders 67 Chacoan great houses and derives a three-level hierarchy among Chacoan settlements, with which Powers (1984a,b) concurs. Schelberg further suggests the possibility of even a four-level hierarchy using two indicators of hierarchical complexity other than size: (1) the number of distinct types of civic-ceremonial structures; and (2) the presence of organizational differences at the higher levels.

The identification of settlement hierarchy, of course, required the prior identification of Chacoan outliers with the "central place" of the Canyon itself, and of the road systems which linked these outliers to the center. The Chaco Phenomenon then, rests upon a number of quite recent findings: the missing link was probably the system of Chacoan roads, known in part to the Navajo at the turn of the century but not defined or mapped until the application of sophisticated aerial photography to archaeological survey (Vivian, 1972, 1974). Identification of the "Phenomenon," however, merely posed yet another issue; what was the nature of the Chacoan regional system and how did it develop? There are at least four basic interpretations: (1) Judge et al., (1981) suggest that a solution to the joint problem posed by highly variable rainfall and rising population within Chaco Canyon was to expand agricultural cultivation into high-risk areas, but to also "equalize" these risks through a resource pooling or redistributional system requiring centralized storage, management, and administration. Judge et al. suggest that Pueblo Bonito, Penasco Blanco, and Una Vida were tenth century redistribution sites, although Powers (1984b) rejects this proposition. Judge et al.'s contention is based upon the architecture of these three sites, primary considerations being their large size, multistoried construction, and well-crafted masonry. The Chacoan system, then, was an enormous "insurance policy" against localized famine, according to Judge et al. (2) Marshall and Doyel (1981) offer a quite different interpretation: rather than the central Chaco area having spawned outliers, they suggest that the outliers created the central Chaco community:

> Chaco Canyon may be envisioned as a central node *developed by the outlying communities* to create an intercommunity regional organization. From this perspective, it is possible that the great pueblos of Chaco Canyon *are regional affiliates* representative of certain community aggregates in the outlying provinces (p.72, emphasis added).

(3) Cordell (1984) suggests the existence of three types of adaptive systems, over time, in the Anasazi region: dispersed, nucleated, and aggregated. The Chaco Phenomenon, she contends, is uniquely representative of a *nucleated* pattern, which is not characteristic, for example, of the Mesa Verde Anasazi. The Mesa Verdean settlements are presumed to represent the more usual line of development from dispersed to aggregated communities, in contrast to the socially controlled, specialized, and (possibly) ranked or stratified Chacoan settlements. The Chaco Phenomenon, according to this interpretation, was simply a "flash in the pan"—an isolated form of urban development devised to cope with an ecologically unique set of conditions:

> What becomes abundantly clear when aggregated and nucleated community types are distinguished is that the nucleated structure of the Chaco Phenomenon was a very short-lived and apparently fragile mechanism of regional interaction. The aggregated pattern, on the other hand, appears to have been far more resilient and flexible, persisting in some areas into the late prehistoric and historic periods. (Cordell, 1984; p.270).

Why might the Chacoan nucleated regional system have been so fragile? According to Powers (1984); "... it is probably that once it was underway, interaction of social, political, agricultural, ceremonial, and exchange aspects resulted in increasing change and complexity..., [and] intercommunity strife and competition may have taken a cumulative toll." (p.34). (4) Finally, there is another group of scholars (e.g., Di Peso, 1974; Hayes, 1981; Kelley, 1986; Kelley and Kelley, 1975; Schroeder, 1981; Washburn, 1978, 1980; Whitecotton and Pailes, 1986) who view the Chaco Phenomenon (and, presumably, other Southwestern "phenomena" of the period) as part of a much larger system centered somewhere in Mesoamerica. This hypothesized "Mesoamerican connection" has been the subject of considerable recent debate (e.g., Mathien and McGuire, 1986); The question is no longer whether such a "connection" existed (there seems to be reasonable agreement that at least *some* prehistoric interaction, however indirect, must have taken place), but what the nature of that connection actually was. Such debate has removed the issue of the nature of Chacoan settlement, society, and interaction to another, larger level, but the "Mesoamerican connection" has also provided some additional hypotheses with which to address very thorny issues concerning Anasazi society. We shall return to this in a later chapter.

Chacoan urban design. The variety and combinations of Chacoan structures continue to baffle researchers:
> ... their exact purpose and range of use remains unclear. Some were almost certainly partially permanent residences ... but serious questions remain concerning whether they were community meeting or ceremonial centers... storage repositories ... elite residences or some combination thereof.... Given the hierarchical nature and complexity of the settlement system, it is proposed that at least a small elite population had evolved by the late eleventh century and was in residence at the large — and medium — size sites. Limited evidence for high status burials at Pueblo Bonito ... lends some credence to the argument. (Powers, 1984b; p.32).

The hypothesis of a stratified Chacoan society is one with which a number of researchers (e.g., Reyman, 1978; Schelberg, 1984) concur. This view is reinforced by the architectural record, which indicates both that the "Hosta Butte" and "Bonito" architecture were distinctly different and that they were contemporaneous. It may also be reinforced by the presence of different kinds of settlements with both small and large buildings, some so large that they have been called "megastructures:"
> The Cliff Palace, Mesa Verde, Colorado [is a] pre-Columbian *pueblo* ruin which is often claimed to be even closer to true megastructure than the conventional examples of 'group form,' the Italian hill town — chiefly because the carrying structure of the latter (the hill) is usually hidden under the town itself, whereas at Mesa Verde the massive slot in the cliff is clearly seen to carry the smaller accommodations within it ... (Banham, 1976; p.16).

With varied collections of buildings, themselves of various sizes, familiar terms like "town" and "village" have been bandied about, along with such less familiar terms as "Chaco system," "Chaco Halo," "outlier," "satellites," "ancestral communities," "scion communities," etc. and such attempts to shed light on Anasazi urban geography of the period have often clouded the issue.

Briefly, Chacoan buildings and settlements appear to display specialization of function, both within and between communities (Doyel et al., 1984; Lekson, 1984a; Powers, 1984b; Schelberg, 1984). This raises two important questions concerning Chacoan community structure: "One, what is the internal structure of these communities; how are they organized on a local level? And two, what was the role or roles of these individual communities within the regional system?" (Doyel, et al., 1984; p.38). The entire geographical area of the "Chaco Phenomenon," connected by 400+ kilometers of roads, including the periphery to the east, north, and west, is called the "Chaco system" (Powers, 1984a), as is shown in Figure 4.3 and Figure 4.5. The term "central canyon" is used to denote ruins along the north side of the Chaco Wash, stretching at least 5 kilometers from Casa Chiquita on the northwest to Hungo Pavi on the southeast (Lekson, 1984a), or perhaps even an additional 10 kilometers to include Penasco Blanco and Wijiji (Powers, 1984a).

> Outliers (Powers et al. 1983) or "satellites" ... are outside Chaco Canyon proper, yet they exhibit Chacoan core-veneer masonry, Chacoan ceramic assemblages, and either great kivas or tower kivas (or both) and they are connected to Chaco Canyon by means of a roadway or a visual communication system of signaling stations. About 70 outliers have been identified, varying in distance from Chaco Canyon from about 4.83 to 80.5 kilometers (Cordell, 1984, p.261).

In addition to the outliers, almost 5,400 small villages have been recorded in the San Juan Basin (Cordell, 1982). It should be reiterated here that the region surrounding Catal Huyuk was *also* characterized by the existence of outliers.

The "Chaco Halo" (Figures 4.3 and 4.5) is a term proposed by Doyel et al. (1984) —later evaluated critically by Vivian (1990)—to refer to settlements in areas adjacent to Chaco Canyon itself. Doyel's suggestion is that there existed a center-periphery relation between central canyon structures and "halo" settlements analogous to the relation between outliers and surrounding villages in more distant areas of the Chaco system.

Doyel et al. (1984) also distinguish among "ancestral communities," "scion communities" and "roadway related isolated structures" in the Chaco Halo. Ancestral communities are those with "significant time depth" dating back as far as the Basketmaker III period. Scion communities were apparently founded subsequently, usually in the late Bonito Phase:

> ... often smaller in size, [scion communities] lack features typical of ancestral communities, such as great kivas, and are often located in marginal environmental zones. Scion communities may have developed as a result of population growth, immigration, factionalism within ancestral communities, or as satellite communities to exploit locally available resources or markets (Doyel et al., 1984; p.39).

Urbanization. Lekson, in the following, rejects the town-village distinction for structures in the central canyon area:

> Several towns are literally a stone's throw apart, and the 'villages' are cheek-by-jowl.... For this later period [in Chaco Canyon] the "town-village" terminology is misleading.... Pueblo Bonito, Chetro Ketl and Pueblo Del Arroyo ... together with the numerous other structures in the central canyon — should be considered a coherent analytical settlement unit. It becomes necessary to shift our concern from 'towns' and 'villages' to the canyon itself ... as a larger settlement of significant complexity. It would not be unreasonable to see this complexity, when coupled with Chaco's regional centrality and relatively high population density, as nearly urban. By the middle 1100s Chaco was much closer to being a city than simply a canyon full of independent agricultural towns and villages (Lekson, 1984a; pp.69-71).

The alternative picture that emerges is of a dispersed multinucleated urban area with "suburbs" and a variety of specialized architecture, including "stratified housing, public ceremonial architecture, community storage facilities, extensive boundary walls, road, and road features" (Figure 4.5), (Lekson, 1984a; p.69).

We attempted a quantitative assessment of Lekson's "urbanization hypothesis" using the most central "towns" and "villages" of the central canyon area: Pueblo Bonito, Chetro Ketl, Pueblo Alto (Figure 4.4), Pueblo del Arroyo, Kin Kletso, and Casa Rinconada, as presented in Figure 4.3. The total area of these six sites is approximately seven hectares, although they are spread over much more of the canyon. But of special interest is the *maximum* pairwise separation between their sites — Pueblo Alto (one of the "Chaco Halo") to Casa Rinconada ("central canyon") — is 1.7 kilometers, which, even though Pueblo Alto is on the canyon rim and Casa Rinconada on the canyon floor, can be traversed in less than a half hour on foot (authors' pedestrian survey of Chaco Canyon). In fact, of the 15 interpair distances among these six major sites, the mean interpair distance is just over one kilometer (s.d. = 0.34 kilometers), with the minimum separation just 400 meters: quite literally, a "stone's throw." We agree then with Lekson; even among a people lacking horses or other aided transportation, accustomed to movement only by foot, such minuscule inter-settlement distances hardly justify classification of sites into separate "towns."

These six sites can be contained in a circular area of just 3 square kilometers. But area is much easier to estimate than population; indeed, estimates of Chaco Canyon populations varied as did the methods used to reach such estimates, which include (1) needed labor force for building and maintenance; (2) number of rooms; (3) number of kivas; and (4) number of hearths. Lekson (1984a) questions whether the labor involved in the construction of large Chaco sites was in fact as great as that suggested by, for example, Lister and Lister (1981). For example, Lekson sets up a hypothetical labor schedule, then estimates the number of man-hours per year required for construction (but not necessarily maintenance) during the period 1075 to 1115. Assuming a ten-hour work day, Lekson (1984a) concludes that the amount of work required for large Chaco sites, with no "breaks" during a 365-day year, could be generated by a work force as small as 16. He then uses ditch clearing in San Juan Pueblo (Ford, 1968) to estimate "a hypothetical labor investment in Chaco building," and the proportion of workers to total population at San Juan to estimate the total population in Chaco during the period in question. Lekson's estimate is 5,243, which, he states, "is alarmingly close to Hayes' (1981) peak population estimate for Chaco of 5,652" (Lekson, 1984a; p.64). But Lekson also cautions that both his and Hayes' estimates are likely to be on the high side.

Using the number of rooms as a population index, Hayes (1981) estimated the population of the *large* sites at 2,763. From the number of kivas, Lekson (1984a) estimated only 1,300. Finally, Windes (1984), using floor features — or, more specifically, hearths (Windes equates firepit rooms with single households) — arrived at yet lower figures, in comparison with others (e.g., Drager, 1976; Hayes, 1981; Judd, 1959, 1964; Pierson, 1949) — see Table 4.2. Samuels and Betancourt (1982), cited in Windes (1984), suggest that a population as

Table 4.2
Comparative Population Estimates for Chacoan "Towns"

LOCATION	ESTIMATOR					
	Pierson (1949)	Judd (1959, 1964)	Drager (1976)	Hayes (1981)	Lekson (1984a)	Windes (1984)
Chaco Canyon				5652	2660	<2000
Pueblo Alto	400		320	130		50-1000
Pueblo Bonito	1200	1100	500	800		100
Pueblo Arroyo		475	263	285		40-6

large as the highest estimates "must have imposed serious constraints upon available resources, for instance, denuding the area of wood needed for construction and fuel." (p.75). But the lowest estimates raise another question: from whence came the labor force for sustained construction *and* maintenance? — assuming that maintenance was a problem:

> ... it also seems likely that some of the massiveness in Chacoan construction reduced maintenance. Perhaps the labor force available for upkeep was disproportionately small — "caretakers," or perhaps the residents[,] were above replastering and reroofing after every rainstorm.... [I]n any event, after seven centuries of nonmaintenance, the larger buildings were surprisingly intact while their smaller neighbors were reduced to low bumps on the landscape (Lekson, 1984a; p.66).

If Chaco Canyon proper was in fact occupied primarily — or exclusively — by an elite population during the period roughly from A.D. 940 to 1115, as suggested by several (e.g., Lekson, 1984a; Windes, 1984), then the labor force *may* have been resident in certain "lower class" suburbs within the Chaco Halo (Doyel et al., 1984). Lekson (1984) hypothesizes that a major shift in both the architectural and economic spheres occurred between 1050 and 1075, a shift in "central place function" from the large Chacoan buildings as central places within the canyon itself to the canyon as a central place within the larger region. Lekson points out that accelerated construction seems to have reached a peak between 1075 and 1115, but that all effort was apparently concentrated on six major construction programs. Beyond 1075, there may have been a major shift in *room* function, as well:

> ... a great many of the rooms at larger sites were probably neither domestic units nor storage rooms associated with domestic units. This may indicate an added public function to the possible previous functions of elite residence. But even considering alternate functions for post-A.D. 1075 buildings, potential elite groups housed in the large sites were a disproportionate segment of the canyon population, if we are to continue to consider them local elites. (Lekson, 1984a; p.69)

Lekson (1984a) also suggests that application of the term "kiva" to all circular rooms may itself be erroneous:

> ... if by kiva we impute a function similar to ethnographic kivas (those present in contemporary pueblos), I suspect that the elevated circular room contained many of the basically domestic functions of earlier pit structures, and that great kivas found in the plazas of large sites are more likely prehistoric analogs for the modern kiva. (p.60).

We have suggested that one possible index of the transition from one mode of production to another in societies at the developmental stages represented here is the changing ratio of shrine or ceremonial rooms/spaces to the total number of rooms or total spatial extent of the community. There is, for example, some indication of a decline in the shrine/room ratio in Anatolian settlements of increasing size from the time of Catal Huyuk on, possibly due to greater centralization of religious/ritual functions and, perhaps as well, increasing power of the leaders of such functions ("priests"). There is some parallel suggestion of differences in relative "shrine density" (or "kiva density," in this case) among Anasazi sites of different sizes.

Kivas are a fascinating class of shrines and there are books devoted to them alone (e.g., Vivian and Reiter, 1965). Because such books exist, and because our focus is on placemaking as a whole, in its general context, we have not given special attention to kivas, but they merit at least a statement devoted to the relationship of these at least partially sacred spaces with the (presumably) more mundane.

Small Anasazi sites, probably consisting of one or two residence units, show no evidence of kivas or other ceremonial structures (Dean, 1989). Kivas begin to appear in larger complexes averaging a dozen or so rooms. The question alluded to above then arises: what is the change in room/kiva ratio as settlement size increases? Working with data on the Mesa Verdean Cliff-Fewkes Canyon pueblo, which contains between 530 and 545 rooms and 60 kivas, Rohn (1989) calculated a room/kiva ratio between 8.8 and 9.1. Our own calculation of the same ratio for four multi-room Chacoan structures covering 200 to 300 square meters, based on data from Powers (1985a), is 8.6.

A distinction must be drawn, of course, between great and small kivas: the latter are present only in the larger structures (generally in "great houses," or free-standing structures, as in the case of Casa Rinconada or Aztec Great Kiva). The room/kiva ratios for four Chacoan structures covering more than 15,000 square meters are 25.6 (including only small kivas) and 22.5 (including both great and small kivas).

These results are interesting but somewhat difficult to interpret because of (1) the small sizes of our samples, and (2) their dependence upon how the population per room differed from great to small pueblos—that is, whether the percentage of rooms actually devoted to habitation varied considerably with pueblo size. It must be reemphasized that the quantitative relation between rooms/kiva and kivas/family or habitation unit is at present unknown.

However, when combined with the views expressed by the researchers earlier cited, the above adds to the suggestion that additional analysis based on a combination of labor estimates, comparative populations, room sizes, household units, and public and ceremonial spaces ("kivas" and "plazas") may lend further support to the thesis that central canyon Chacoan settlements did indeed constitute a "city" (Lekson, 1984a) was capable of achieving the level of a tributary mode of production (Wolf, 1982) associated with a truly regional economic system (Powers, 1984b; Schelberg, 1984) and a nucleated settlement pattern (Irwin-Williams, 1980).

Chacoan science and technology. The achievements of the Chaco people in building technology were truly prodigious. Their dressed, core-veneer masonry walls exhibit fine craftsmanship, even by today's standards. They recognized the danger posed by "Threatening Rock" to the rear of Pueblo Bonito and engineered a protecting wall. They built masonry-lined roads between 4.5 and 9 meters in width that were, in some cases, straight to within 0.0001%. And all this was accomplished by what was, to all outward appearances, a late Stone Age society lacking draft animals, wheeled vehicles, metal tools, or surveying instruments.

Anasazi science was only slightly less impressive. While they seem not to have developed calendrical measurement into a high art, unlike Mesoamerican groups further to the south (the Maya in particular), they apparently did develop systems of, and aids to, astronomical observation. These aids included third story, exterior corner windows at Pueblo Bonito (Reyman, 1976), wall niches in the Casa Rinconada Great Kiva (Morgan, 1977; Williamson et al., 1977), and possibly the so-called Fajada Butte "sun dagger" (Sofar, et al., 1979). While the last may or may not have been Anasazi (Reyman, 1980), the first two were almost certainly used to observe solstice and equinoctial sunrises.

Certain elements of Anasazi architecture, too, appear to have been constructed in service of communications technology. For a long time the function of Chacoan towers was a complete mystery to researchers. An experiment conducted in the early 1980s, however, established the possibility that the towers functioned as communications nodes, since a fire lit at the top of one tower was visible from the tops of neighboring towers, often a number of kilometers distant.

Chacoan science and technology may have been indigenous or derived, or some of each. Given the rigid political boundaries between the U.S. and Mexico, and the only slightly less rigid boundaries between the U.S. and Mexican anthropologists/archaeologists, it is understandable that in past decades, Chaco was treated as an isolated phenomenon. It is less understandable now. To the authors of this book, the recently uncovered parallels in architecture, science, commerce, and other areas point very strongly to a high probability of contact — indirect or direct — between the Anasazi and Mesoamericans. Further support is provided by excavations at Casas Grandes in the Mexican state of Chihuahua (Di Peso, 1974), which indicate a peak of construction after the beginning of Chacoan decline, a combination of architectural influences from both Chaco and Mesoamerica (Table 4.3), and material execution in coursed, puddled adobe (perhaps related to the Hohokam). It seems likely that Casas Grandes was a trading node, intermediate between the (hypothesized) La

Table 4.3
Similarities Between Chaco and Casas Grandes Architecture*

Regional system based on capital (core area)
Satellite communities
Linked through system of roads and signaling devices
Elaborate water control features
Structural details: T-shaped doorways, shaped sandstone disks as timber seatings, square columns, stairways incorporated into buildings
Few burials
Planning
Luxury goods
Social control

*Cordell, 1984

Quemada and Chacoan nexes, and therefore an interchange point for information as well as trade goods. This possible "Mesoamerican connection" will be explored in more detail in the following chapter and in Appendix One.

Anatolian fortified cities

With the accumulation of wealth and surplus in the urban centers, Anatolian cities became targets for marauders quite early, as were other large settlements in the Fertile Crescent. Some of these also being cult centers, competing ideologies between different groups undoubtedly contributed to the hostile actions directed at cities. Exploitation of the hinterland by the city further widened the antagonism, which in turn made the city vulnerable to attacks from its own outlying villages. All of these factors caused cities in Anatolia to be concerned with defense. Built form, both at settlement and building scales, reflected this aspect of social relations in its organization, design, and execution. Not only were the cities fortified, on their periphery, against hostile actions from without, they also had *internal* fortifications against attacks upon parts of the city from *within*.

There is, by contrast, almost no evidence of fortification, per se, in Pueblo I and Pueblo II villages in Anasazi areas and little, in fact, (unless blank walls facing the exterior of Chacoan "great houses" are counted) until the decline of

Chaco and the establishment of "cities in caves" (with considerable doubt that the latter represented a form of "fortification"). Why is this? The absence of fortification usually indicates either (1) the absence of enemies, or (2) the absence of any attractive objective, either territorial, material, or ideological. The former has been suggested as characteristic of the Anasazi. The latter may also have been largely true: that is, the Anasazi at earlier stages of development may have accumulated insufficient surplus product to make marauding profitable; while the "Chaco Phenomenon" at a later stage *may* have represented— as has been conjectured—among other things, a cooperative, highly participatory system coordinated by "central planners" for redistributing scarce surplus product to the locations where, in a given year, it was most needed (another alternative is suggested at the end of Chapter Five).

Returning to Anatolia, Catal Huyuk was not the only center of its kind, at least not throughout its existence. Hacilar, reinhabited ca. 5750 B.C. after nearly a millennium's hiatus, grew to be a fortified settlement by 5250 B.C. The town of Hacilar started partly on top of the ancient site of Aceramic Hacilar and partly on new ground not previously settled. By this time the remains of the ancient village were reduced to a mound, hardly recognizable under the heap of earth accumulated over the thousand years of abandonment. The remains of the thirteen successive building levels at Hacilar, occasional destructions by fire, and other archaeological evidence show clearly that it was an important settlement of its period. Although it never grew to be as large as Catal Huyuk, even during its periods of great prosperity, the architectural development observed throughout its existence is as remarkable as that of its predecessor and of other contemporary towns, if not more so. Considering all the archaeological evidence revealing the life pattern, socio-cultural development, and spatial manifestations of growing organizational complexity as well as changing social structure, Hacilar represents a unique case in the history of placemaking, despite the claim that it never grew to be "larger than a village" (Mellaart, 1970; p.248). (See also, Mellaart, (1975; p.278) for a controversial view.)

Both the number of dwellings and of people inhabiting those dwellings fluctuated rather than displaying a steady trend. While the not-so-certain estimates (Mellaart, 1970; p.90) indicate gradual growth from a population of 100 to 250, between 5750 and 5600 B.C., with an increase in the number of dwellings from 20 to 50, both the population and the number of houses inhabited declined to 50 and 10 respectively in the next 350 years until 5250 B.C. There was a sharp increase in the following century and a half, climbing to a population of about 500 inhabiting nearly 65 houses (Mellaart, 1970; pp.85-90). Among factors contributing to the uncertainty with regard to population are two very important ones directly related to spatial organization at Hacilar. First, the average usable area of the living quarters is about 45 square meters, almost twice the floor space seen elsewhere, earlier (Mellaart, 1970; pp.10-20; pp.77-84). In the absence of platforms, as in Catal Huyuk, it is difficult to estimate the size of a family. Estimated household size used in the above figures varies between 5 and 7. However, if a ratio of floor area per person (4 square meters/person) similar to that used for population estimation in earlier settlements is adopted, a doubling of population is indicated. Even increasing the ratio to 5 square meters per person results in about 9 persons per dwelling, suggesting either two families or a large extended family per house. Second, there is a strong possibility that at least some of the dwellings had more than one story (Mellaart, 1970; p.85; 1975; pp.115-116). This again increases population estimates considerably, assuming that the second stories were not only used seasonally by the same household.

Evidence of frequent destruction by fire, especially fire started by hostile forces from outside, and of a few massacres, when added to the spatial features, first suggests that Hacilar was often under attack; second, that the population estimates for all the building levels are much too conservative; and third that the town definitely attracted outsiders. These lead us to conjecture that Hacilar was rich both spiritually and materially, and that Hacilar was an important regional center (Figures 4.6, 4.7), like its predecessor and contemporary, Catal Huyuk, in addition to being a local cult center (as inferred by its excavator, Mellaart, 1970; p.249). The attractiveness of Hacilar to outsiders may have resulted from economical or ideological factors, or both. Economic factors may have been based primarily upon surplus food and other wealth stored in the town. All indications are that it was materially a very prosperous settlement; its people were excellent farmers, expert weavers, and fine craftsmen. In the diversified economic and artistic stream, the people were very productive.

This material prosperity undoubtedly made Hacilar very attractive to outsiders. Ideologically, either the kinship system that was in historic transition, or the belief system (the old religion of Anatolia having its roots in the Great Goddess, her son, and her husband), or both systems combined, might have clashed with the ideologies of neighboring tribes or of newcomers to the area. Under these circumstances it is very likely that the people of Hacilar would have tried very hard to increase their population to a level higher than that indicated by the conservative estimates presented earlier for two reasons: first, to maintain the economic and production levels they had achieved, and second, to defend their wealth and themselves. For both of these, they needed as many people as their economy could support; maintaining abundance, diversification, and level of production in all realms of life would require a larger population than previously estimated. What is attributed to two or three generations at different phases of Hacilar seems very unlikely to have been produced by the numbers estimated earlier.

The economy of the city was not very different from that of Catal Huyuk, except that hunting and fishing were much less important. An abundance of statuettes and other cult objects have been found, such as ritual vessels in anthropomorphic shapes (e.g., drinking cups in the shape of a woman's head) and in the forms of animals, and jars painted and decorated in geometric and fantastic styles. Certainly their abundance suggests the possibility of a local cult center, perhaps even more important than Catal Huyuk ever was. Hacilar was destroyed by fire and rebuilt more frequently than either its predecessor or its contemporary. Trade, exchange, and outside contact seem to have been an important part of its economy and spiritual life. Its burial customs were quite different than those of Catal Huyuk; the dead were buried outside the settlement (Mellaart, 1970; pp.88-91).

Spatial organization and architectural development can be viewed on two scales: settlement and building. At the settlement level, courtyards were surrounded by a number of dwellings, none of which were free standing: houses were attached to each other; and in most cases in the earlier settlements, a shared "party wall" served the two dwellings. At some building levels, such as Level II-A and B (ca. 5400 B.C.), those courtyards that were on the periphery of the settlement were enclosed by a wall rather than a row of houses, also quite typical of Catal Huyuk (Mellaart, 1970; Figs. 19 to 22, pp.71-75; Figs. 25 to 27, pp.79-81; 1975; p.116).

It is very likely that in earlier phases of settlement such as at Level VI (ca. 5670 B.C.), the concept of planning was quite similar, at least in principle, to that of Catal Huyuk. That is, courtyards were defined by surrounding rows of houses, and the periphery was composed of the building walls themselves. Here, again, all the dwellings had access to a courtyard.

This level marks the last Neolithic settlement in Hacilar's life span. Evidence indicates that Level VI had a fairly short existence and was destroyed seventy years after completion (ca. 5600 B.C.). It was destroyed when it achieved the height of its prosperity, just a century and a half from the time the site was reoccupied. The end of the late Neolithic was the beginning of the early Chalcolithic, characterized by a developed food production phase and the first painted pottery (Alkim, 1968; pp.69 ff; Mellaart, 1970; pp.92-95; 1975; p.115). Also, new population groups of varying sizes flowed into Anatolia, creating a very heterogenous culture after mixing with the local people. However, the settlements of Hacilar V-II (ca. 5600-5250 B.C.) in the early Chalcolithic do not show recognizable influences from outside (Mellaart, 1975; p.115).

At the building scale, the spatial organization and architectural development of Hacilar exhibit one very important feature which evolved into a major architectural form, the megaron, a few millennia later. Although the collective life of the PCMP seems to have characterized almost all phases of Hacilar, the strongly established monogamous family and the developing concepts of property relating to family formation are clearly manifested in the domestic architecture of the later settlements. To one room houses, a semi-enclosed, occasionally divided space was added. This vestibule or entrance hall (actually the food preparation area, according to artifacts) was generally located in front of the doorway to the house. It was a form of transition zone from the courtyard to the dwelling. Adobe walls on stone foundations were not always shared by two units; in other words, the continuity of row houses was broken occasionally, but several houses still formed clusters around the courtyards.

Very early traces of a rough megaron, first observed at Level VI (ca. 5600 B.C.), developed considerably over the next two centuries. At Level II (constructed ca. 5400 B.C.), the design of houses took one more step toward the megaron; to the main room were added an anteroom and a porch (Mellaart, 1970; pp.25-28). In some of the houses the hearth/oven combination was still kept in the main room; in certain cases it appeared both in the main room and in the anteroom, in others, only in the anteroom. Obviously there was as yet no set rule—they must have been experimenting continuously since buildings were often destroyed by the rather frequent conflagrations experienced from the time of the early settlements. Another important characteristic of Hacilar II, in spite of being a "village," was, for the first time, marked differences in the sizes of some dwellings.

Hacilar I (ca. 5250), the developed fortress, exhibits a different trend in housing construction. The walls were built without any of the timber supports observed in earlier settlements, but with internal buttresses instead (Mellaart, 1970; pp.35-36). House plans and construction systems are very similar to those of Can Hasan, a contemporary settlement that rose on the ruins of Aceramic Can Hasan. One major characteristic of the fortress is its scarcity of doorways, i.e., the number of rooms that had to be entered from an upper floor. While the lightness of the construction system must have been advantageous, the highly inflammable materials must also have posed a constant fire danger. There is also the possibility that upper and lower stories were used seasonally; in summer, lighter construction and better exposure to air and sun might have made the upper story preferable, while the compact and heavier construction of lower stories could have provided a more suitable environment in winter (Mellaart, 1970; p.83). However, the absence of hearths in ground floor rooms casts serious doubt on such conjecture.

Urbanization in the Neolithic

There seems to be a "marked absence of cultural continuity between Hacilar II and I" (Mellaart, 1970; p.37). However, social relations, manifested in the architecture of the two settlements in the course of four centuries (Level II: 5400-5250 B.C., Level I: 5250-5000 B.C.), show continuous development towards more centralized power. "The extremely massive wall," "the extensive levelling operations," and "the intricate layout of buildings erected by the Hacilar I people" show that this was not another ordinary, defended settlement, "but probably a fortress of a ruler who had command of considerable human resources." (Mellaart, 1970; p.77). While other conservative estimates give an approximate population of 500, "there was certainly enough living room in the fortress for twice that number." (Mellaart, 1970; p.85).

The end of the early Chalcolithic corresponds with the next and last phase of the settlement. Hacilar I, which actually grew to be a fortified settlement in the course of a century and a half (ca. 5250 to 5100 B.C.) was deserted around 5000 B.C. after the destruction of the fortress, (Mellaart, 1970; p.87), and this was followed by desultory habitation of the ruins of the city, ending around 4800 B.C. (Mellaart, 1975; pp.119). A "highly conjectural" reconstruction of the fortified settlement by its excavator (1970; p.82) shows that the city was built around the earlier settlements, making little use of any but a small part of their remains (Figure 4.8). Obviously, the fortified settlement was intended for a much larger population. By any standards, it is again very apparent that the fortified settlement was also designed, from the beginning, for defense against anticipated attacks by intruders. Systems of courtyards serving each subcommunity, in this case the clan, prevailed in the overall planning. The circular plan was divided into segments suggesting separate quarters for different clans. Each quarter had its own courtyard either surrounded by rows of houses on each side (the other two sides being enclosed by walls), or attached to the buildings on one side and circumscribed by walls on the other three sides. Each clearly defined courtyard served about ten large dwellings. Two rows of buildings formed the perimeter of the circular plan, leaving a large area in the middle, 100 meters in diameter, whose center was the ruins of the earlier settlements. Both the courtyards and small passageways between the blocks of buildings provided entry into the settlement. Penetration into the settlement or the buildings from outside seems to have been impossible since the massive outer walls averaged 2 meters in depth, and in places, were as deep as 4 meters (Mellaart, 1970; p.77).

The concept of using the outer edge of a row of buildings as a defensive wall was not new. The builders of Catal Huyuk, as we have already seen, utilized the same system. However, the massiveness of the wall here is quite extraordinary. In Hacilar II-A, built in 5400 B.C., the fortress wall that was built deliberately as part of the defense system was comparable in thickness to the wall in Hacilar

I. Even that wall in places did not attain a depth of more than 3 meters (Naumann, 1975; p.247). Although the builders of Hacilar fortress saw no need to excavate foundation trenches for such massive walls, they leveled the wall bases with very little digging along the contours of the topography (Mellaart, 1970; p.75) as they were crowning the top of the hill.

The development of fortification at Catal Huyuk and Hacilar at different stages points to parallel development of social and political organization, and of concomitant spatial preparations for defense. In other words, the architectonics of fortification unfolded in parallel with social and political advances. When the expected enemy or prospective intruders were composed of less organized hoarding tribes, the defense system of Catal Huyuk was sufficient. The flat roofs of attached houses with no ground access from the outside certainly gave defenders a strategically advantageous position over attackers. Even when attackers could climb onto the roofs, each house could still be defended by controlling access to the roof entrances from inside. As developing social organization resulted in organized military units, and as advances in technology produced more versatile weapons — in short, as techniques of warfare developed — so did the defense systems of the settlements. The evolution of the architectonics of fortification gradually yielded elements such as walls with merlons, well-protected entrances with turrets, stairways with traps, and so on. Although even later levels of Hacilar did not include more refined and developed architectural elements for defense, the *conceptual* development of defensive principles is illustrated in the last two levels of the settlement.

The fortified city of Hacilar I left a very large open area in the center. Although this central "commons" was not meant to be part of the defense system nor did it contribute to it directly, its presence certainly suggests that during an attack upon the city and its vicinity, it could have been used by people in nearby villages and towns. As a temporary shelter for people and a storage space for animals, the central "commons" offered ample area. At the dawn of urbanization, Hacilar must had been a parent city to several rural settlements nearby. It is clear from the far too numerous objects, artifacts, and statuettes found at almost every level that a good portion of the population living in the city was not involved in agricultural and pastoral chores, at least not all the time. The abundance of pottery of varying shapes and sizes, monochrome and painted ware, anthropomorphic jars and vessels, stylized statuettes and small schematic figurines (Mellaart, 1975; pp.113-119) all suggest fairly intensive productive activity outside agriculture and husbandry. All of these present strong evidence that Hacilar, like its predecessor (before ca. 5700 B.C.) and contemporary (ca. 5700-5100 B.C.), Catal Huyuk, in addition to displaying material prosperity, was probably also an important spiritual center (Mellaart, 1975; pp.113-114).

In many ways, the quality of tools, and the quality and quantity of production, were at a considerably higher level than at Catal Huyuk. Further architectural evidence the beginnings of differentiation in the size of some dwellings, emerging private use of smaller courtyards by some households, more frequent two-story construction, the beginnings of the detached house, and less frequent use of party walls all suggest the gradual diminution of the communal form of life that once characterized Catal Huyuk. Also, the nature of fortification, especially that of Hacilar I, indicates that it was not only a protective measure against invasion by hostile communities, but also a safeguard against incursions from villagers in the hinterland related to developing antagonism between urban and rural areas. Domination of a relatively large group by a small minority is "not of one individual over another but of an individual personifying a function over community" (Godelier, 1978; p.222). The accumulation of surplus made more elaborate social differentiation possible, allowing the emergence of a small minority, the priestly class, who appropriated a share of the surplus and thus exploited the other people in the community.

While some members of the exploited community were in the fortified settlement, the majority were in the peripheral villages. The land in the rural areas and within the citadel belonged to the community. In other words, communal ownership remained, yet a higher status subcommunity, the small priestly minority, appropriated the surplus—both labor and product. Thus the gradual centralization of the tribal confederation and religious authority also led members of this higher status subcommunity to become landowners in the name of the larger community. It seems likely that antagonism between the rural and urban people developed concomitantly. Therefore, the concept of fortification acquired a second meaning with probable increased antipathy between village and city. It was no longer just an architectural obstacle against outside enemies but also an obstacle against aggressive action on the part of inside enemies. During the time of attack by outsiders, the central commons was a refuge for the villagers and mobile or portable belongings (e.g., domesticated animals) of the city; during an exclusively rural conflict, the fortified city protected the small minority against its own broader community.

A further conjecture is that the central commons must also have functioned as an economic exchange arena during peacetime. At the time of Hacilar I, perhaps, trade was "not the expression of commodity production within the communities but the transformation of the surplus into commodities" (Godelier, 1978; p.224). Nevertheless, the obsidian trade nexus that was established in Anatolia much earlier must have had a lasting impact on the cities, which were on the rise as well. Thus, fortification also provided protection for the commons, the forerunner of the marketplace that, several centuries later, appeared in the fortified cities of the Hattians.

Another city contemporary with Hacilar is Can Hasan, which was established on the ruins of Aceramic Can Hasan after a hiatus of almost a millennium. A settlement which lasted from early to late Chalcolithic, nearly two millennia (French, 1963, 1966), Can Hasan is notable for the special character of its dwellings. Each building had independent walls with adjacent walls separated only by an air gap, i.e., no usable lanes, courtyards, or other outdoor spaces existed between the individual dwellings. (Figure 4.9). The outer contours of the buildings formed a tight fitting, densely constructed, largely rectangular plan which allowed no access at the ground floor. From the fallen debris, French, the excavator of Can Hasan, conjectures that while the ground floor was used primarily for storage, the floor above must have been for living purposes (1962). Walls lacked stone foundations, but elaborate timber beams laid underneath served the purpose. Wider on the ground floor, walls were further braced by the slightly raised, densely packed, built-in benches (French, 1968), very similar to the ones found at Catal Huyuk. While hearths were common on the ground floors of Hacilar, the ground floors (or perhaps, artificially created basements) of Can Hasan did not have hearths. This, among other reasons, led the excavator to surmise that the ground floors must had been used primarily for storage (1962). While courtyards had a hard floor of packed white clay (1964), most of the ground floors were of beaten clay. Few of them had pebbles (1962).

From the compact site plan it is evident that the builders of Can Hasan had created a raised platform for most of the daily activities that took place on the roofs of the storage spaces. It also provided access to the individual dwellings. In this case, the fortification seems rather an unusual one since, instead of surrounding the settlement, it was apparently tucked underneath. While the planning principles employed indicate communal ownership, differentiation in the size of houses leads us to infer that the settlement was a habitat of a community in transition from communal to private ownership.

The system of attached dwelling units forming a wall, as seen in Catal Huyuk and Hacilar, developed into an elaborate defensive wall at Mersin by 4400 B.C. (Figures 4.10, 4.11). A town to the south of the Taurus Mountains and situated on the banks of a river, Mersin was one of the settlements inhabited the longest in Anatolia. The earliest traces go back to the early Neolithic, around 6000 B.C. However, the fortified city of Mersin was not developed until the end of the middle Chalcolithic. The fortress of Mersin (Level XVI), though not very large, had a central "plaza" like Hacilar (Mellaart, 1975; pp.124-129). The individual dwellings set against the thick circuit wall actually created a very powerful defensive system (Naumann, 1975; pp.247-250). The barrack-like rooms along the wall, "originally communicating but later turned into individual dwellings" (Mellaart, 1975; p.127), were provided with slit windows; and the battlement in front of the flat roof of these houses provided the second line of defense. Each room or dwelling had its own enclosed central court in the megaron style. The usual domestic furnishings — grindstones placed on raised mud-brick platforms, hearths, grain bins and cooking utensils — found in the dwellings are not much different than those located elsewhere. However, such heavy copper tools as axes and chisels appeared for the first time. The abundance of pottery with features of the late Chalcolithic cultures of the Anatolian plateau, plenty of weapons, and other military supplies unearthed during the excavations (Mellaart, 1975; p.127; Naumann, 1975; p.250) indicate Mersin's importance as an industrial and agricultural center where wealth and power were being concentrated, marking a transition from middle to late Chalcolithic as well as from PCMP to FMP.

As in Hittite cities such as Alaca Huyuk, Bogazkoy (Hattus), Acem Huyuk, and Alisar, the fortification system of earlier Mersin after 1500 B.C. developed into a typical fortress with compartmented ramparts (a double ring of walls frequently joined with cross walls, also known as "box walls" or "casemate-walls," whose compartments were filled with rubble) on a "sawtooth" alignment. With their rectangular towers, several major gates (subterranean passages built utilizing a corbeled technique), and posterns, the architecture of fortification became very impressive and monumental in character. Thus, from the local Anatolian style and tradition developed a distinctive military architecture, in which the line of ramparts, thick mud-brick walls on stone foundations, was adapted to the contours of the usually rolling topography.

The beginnings of social stratification and the slowly changing production relations early in the fifth millennium B.C. in Anatolia finally reached the feudal mode of production at the end of the late Chalcolithic, i.e., approximately two thousand years later. The protofeudal relations of the late Neolithic and the Chalcolithic were marked by the development of private property from the preceding numerous forms of communal property (Figures 4.12, 4.13, 4.14), the development of the monogamous family from various forms of polygamy, and the evolution of the state from the different forms of government characterizing primitive societies (Engels, 1942). Along with these transitions in social relations, Anatolian people in the course of two thousand years also went through a major shift from a reciprocal system of exchange to major reliance on redistribution. The gradual rise of cities created village communities composed of peasants who depended largely on the parent cities, since the cities owned the cultivated land. The farming people either worked as forced labor, or they rented land from the city.

In the following millennium from 3000 to 2000 B.C., small urban princedoms emerged in Anatolia. This meant the centralization of control over economic and political matters, initiating not only a rent collecting "aristocracy" who monopolized the land, but also a peasant class, the basic producers (Berktay, 1983; pp.329-376). The dependence of these peasants on the lord who owned their land developed in different forms, hinging on the circumstances. Central and north Anatolian princes of Hattian origin were living in rich and fortified cities when groups of Indo-European speaking Hittites started penetrating the Anatolian peninsula in the third millennium B.C. The "castles" (MacQueen, 1975; p.66), the royal tombs, and the artifacts of this period are evidence of their "provincial capitals" or "large cities." (Ozguc, 1963; Mellink, 1966; Bittel, 1970). Agriculture, metallurgy, and trade were primary productive and economic activities that brought "special wealth" (Ozguc, 1963; p.15) to the independent princes of an Anatolia "dotted with cities, towns and villages" (Ozguc, 1963; p.18).

The fortified cities of the Hattian princes developed into large production and trade centers, military complexes, and preeminent cultural compounds under Hittite rule (Bittel, 1970; pp.47-55). All the major settlements were surrounded by very impressive walls frequently punctuated with tall towers. Not only were they architecturally monumental but in sheer size, these walls and their great length must have awed an enemy (e.g., Bogazkoy (Hattus) 6 kilometers, Kultepe (Kanesh) 1.6 kilometers, Alisar: 1.4 kilometers), (Naumann, 1975; pp.223-237, 257-267, 286-296). Small fortresses within the citadels were not uncommon (Bittel, 1970). Since most of the Hittite cities grew from the formerly Hattian settlements, it is not surprising to learn that such monumental buildings as palaces and temples had been erected in the third millennium B.C. before the establishment of the Old Hittite Kingdom (Ozguc, 1964). While members of the ruling class lived in castles or palaces, the temples served more than mere religious functions. At the dawn of the protofeudal era, it was the temple that was on its way to housing the chief landlord, employer, and storekeeper. As the power of the central authority was assumed more and more by the temple, the temple gradually gained exclusive control over the means of production. Thus the temples became the spatial as well as spiritual centers of activities such as storing, distributing, lodging, working, documenting, and trading (Bittel, 1970; pp.54-62; Thomson, 1978; pp.23-24; Berktay, 1983; p.167). The architectural plans of these complexes together with their courts of different sizes clearly manifest these secular functions. "The rise of a strong executive system, under which the palace replaces the temple as the most prominent institution of the city or national organization, appears to have produced an alteration in the traditional balance of power between these two institutions." (Orlin, 1970; p.48). As the power and authority were shifting from temple to palace, so were some of the former temple functions. Royal palaces of the Hittite cities began to be planned with archives, audience halls, seal repositories, storage spaces, transaction offices—in short, with all the spaces formerly of the temples (with the possible exception of the adytum). Collaboration and consolidation of the clergy and the newly emerging secular aristocracy, headed by the prince or the king, enabled the centralization of the artisan, the laborer, and the bureaucrat in these complexes.

This social stratification had its parallel in the scale and differentiation of house architecture (Figures 4.15, 4.16, 4.17, 4.18); the differentiation among the dwellings that started in the fifth millennium B.C. at Hacilar had reached a new point where the detached individual family house for the wealthy and powerful — the *kabuti* (dignitaries), or *rabuti* (great ones, noblemen), or *hautezziyas* (men of the first rank) (Gurney, 1973a; p.253) — was clearly separated from the dwellings of the "lesser citizens" (MacQueen, 1975; p.65). Freestanding individual family houses, in some cases built around a "generally covered" (Ozguc, 1964; p.32) courtyard, were distinguished from other houses not only by sheer size, number of rooms, the existence of a central room, and abundance of storage space, but also by the protected property around the house. It was the "estate quality" that began to separate the residences of the wealthy from those of ordinary citizens. The latter lived in houses that were self-contained units, which retained the privacy and independence required by the family.

Blocks or *insulae* surrounded by alleys and divided into lots were composed of relatively dense residential structures. Commonly shared party walls of the past gradually turned into double walls between the units. The basic form of the most commonly used unit was only a refinement of the dwelling characteristic of Hacilar. On roughly rectangular lots, two adjacent rooms were built facing a court surrounded by walls. Entrance from the alley was to the court through a gate. Most of the examples of dwellings of the time give the impression that the court area was slightly larger than the enclosed rooms. However, in the case of a second story with connecting stairs in the court, the area of the enclosed space was larger. Ground floor rooms were usually paved with slabs of stones. (In the case of monumental buildings and residences of the wealthy, the stone pavements were composed of very regular and carefully placed slabs). Less frequently the courts were also paved, while the alleys were unpaved (Ozguc, 1964; Pl.XXII, p.47).

Most of these developments point to one phenomenon: the individualization of the dwelling. This is associated with the highly developed concept of property prevalent at the time. While we may concur with Naumann, who stresses the significance of social organization at a planning level (and acknowledges of individualization of the dwelling) (1975; p.376), we disagree with Bittel's attributions of high-level planning to a "communal basis" and of limitations on the individual concerning what he can do on his lot to the "regulations of a collective community" (1970; p.41). Only the *form* of collectivism, without the content, continued to exist. This was something that the ruling class needed to retain for the exploitation of the "lesser citizens" (Berktay, 1983; p.167). Under the relatively rigid stratification that the society was developing, the only remaining "communal" aspect may have been the long established tradition of collective work in placemaking.

Individualization of the dwelling was further accentuated by the emergence of servants as an institution during Hittite times. The introduction of slaves (Alp, 1949; pp.245-270) was another step taken in the direction of sanctioning this institution which eventually helped to separate the residences of the wealthy and powerful from those of the "lesser citizens" mentioned above. Each *nam.ra* (the civilian war captive) who was brought home from a victorious military mission had to at least be accommodated and fed in order to be able to perform his/her service. Regardless of how humanely the Hittites treated their *nam.ras*, the existence of such an institution, though in essence different from Graeco-Roman slavery, meant a master/slave relationship. While the productive use of *nam.ras* never became a dominant aspect of production in the Hittite cities since the absence of individual private ownership of land was the major obstacle to such utilization (Godelier, 1978; p.225), they nevertheless were employed largely in domestic activities. Thus they became part of the household and considerably affected both the size and the design of affluent people's houses. This change was not merely an adaptation but truly an evolution in housing design since the transformation it imposed was both quantitative and qualitative (Faris, 1975; p.241). It is highly probable that not all *nam.ras* were "fortunate" enough to be engaged in domestic chores. For such arduous activities as labor in the mines, the king, the princes, the priests, and the high officials must have used their slaves in addition to peasant forced labor (Godelier, 1978; p.225). However, this had at most a minor effect upon mainstream regional development towards the individual family house, whose scale (number of rooms) was increasing in comparison with earlier habitation. This started in the city and was spreading to the countryside as well. (Figures 4.19, 4.20).

One conservative estimate gives a figure of 30,000 to 40,000 inhabitants for Hattus (Bogazkoy), the capital which covered an area of 168 hectares (MacQueen, 1975; p.77). Other cities were not as large nor as populated as the capital. Almost all of the Hittite cities were larger than the largest city of earlier times, Catal Huyuk. Most of the estimates range between 5,000 and 10,000 inhabitants, skewed towards the lower end of the scale for Catal Huyuk, which covered an area of 12.5 hectares (Todd, 1976; pp.122-125). A six-fold increase in the population of any urban area over four millennia may not seem very striking. However, when the number of later settlements that were as large as or larger than Catal Huyuk is taken into consideration, the rise in urban population becomes much more impressive. When this gradual but fairly steady climb, with some fluctuations, is interpreted in terms of the growing obligation imposed on communities to create more surplus labor, it becomes even more meaningful.

For the feudal system to develop, the primitive communal system had to mature and give way to the beginnings of the protofeudal stages observed at Hacilar. Early cities provided the necessary environments, the conditions for maturations of the feudal system, leading to the later development of cities, exchanges, and commodity production. The most important condition was the existence of exploitable surplus labor. The city was the appropriate setting for the accumulation of surplus labor either in the city itself or in its hinterlands, with control always in the hands of an urban minority. In other words, the centralization of authority (economic, political and ideological) in early urban environments allowed the emergence of the economic structure of feudal society, which in turn led to the development of cities as well as commodity production and exchange. The city is considered an important development in the evolution of civilization. Yet the city, the product of the gradual but progressive breakup of communal relationships and solidarities, is also the outcome of the gradual development of inequality among people: the *city is the product of exploitation of one class by another*.

Whether it was a temple- or palace-city, the city emerged and developed as a "contradictory" reality in which the social form and the material content became the indissoluble unity of development (Godelier, 1978; p.231). On the side of material content, the important factor was the general development of means, i.e., productive forces. On the side of social form, the important factor was the development of forms of exploitation of people by other people. The contradictory reality is that the two are necessarily linked. According to Engels, "civilization is founded on the exploitation of one class by another" and "its whole development proceeds in a constant contradiction" (Engels, 1942; p.161). It is within this continuity that the city developed in Anatolia from the days of Catal Huyuk; within this continuity, each city prepared the conditions for the next phase in social relations; within this contradictory reality, each city made an enduring contribution to the development of its successors. And within this context, a study of the city in the Neolithic, its development in the past eight millennia, and its lasting contribution both to the development of other cities and to social form can provide a more meaningful explanation of the "urban phenomenon." Approaches with solely formalist concerns can only produce futile and misleading schemata along with concepts such as "abortive cities" that *supposedly* "made no enduring contribution to the development of the city in Anatolia, or indeed, elsewhere" (Hammond, 1972; p.98; for a contrary view, see Todd, 1976; pp.118-139).

Anasazi unfortified cities and their fortified southern neighbors

As far as we can determine from available evidence (e.g., Orcutt, 1990), warfare was rare or nonexistent among the Anasazi. Given the prevalence of war in so many parts of the world at so many points in history, this seems nothing short of extraordinary, implying the existence of a fairly unique form of social organization capable of avoiding this ubiquitous societal ill.

With no warfare, there would have been little need for defense, and that only against animal predators. Indeed, there are few indicators in either architecture or settlement plan of anything resembling fortification among the Anasazi. A few (mostly low) walls do exist in Pueblo III sites, including Chaco, apart from buildings; and towers proliferate, especially at Hovenweep. There is some suggestion, however, that the latter were primarily for communication. Cibolan pueblos in the mid to late thirteenth century were tightly clustered with at least one of their number at each site situated on a promontory with good views (LeBlanc, 1989b); this, together with other evidence, suggested to LeBlanc a shift to a defensive posture — but "defense from what?" is a question still unresolved. Further south, in the Mimbres Valley of the Mogollon region, there is also scarce evidence that warfare was the cause of the rapid abandonments of large settlements that took place there somewhat later than among the Anasazi (LeBlanc, 1989a).

Going much further south, however, beyond the Anasazi and Mogollon regions into the Gran Chichimeca, the scene changes. There is substantial evidence, for example, that Casas Grandes (Contreras Sanchez, 1982) in the neighboring state of Chihuahua, Mexico some 800 kilometers south of Chaco came to a violent end.

> Evidence for the destruction of Casas Grandes consists of collapsed and blackened walls, suggesting the burning of the city; the presence of breeding turkeys and macaws left to die in their pens; unburied bodies found throughout the city; the discovery of broken altar stones and figures ... and the fully articulated remains of two individuals within the Mound of the Offerings who were interpreted as representing guards (Ravesloot, 1988; p.6).

Davies (1982) criticizes Kelley for suggesting that "militaristic Toltec nobles" had penetrated the Casas Grandes region along with traders; perhaps an attack by neighboring nomadic Chichimeca is a more probable explanation.

Moving even further southward across the "Chichimec Sea" to the northern "Mesoamerican Frontier," one reaches the Chalchihuites site, called La Quemada ("the burned") by the Spaniards, in the Malpaso Valley of Zacatecas. While we are not sure why it was burned, it is architecturally evident that La Quemada, as attested both by its siting and by its defenses, is every bit a fortified city (Kelley, 1971).

Urbanization in the Neolithic   141

Parenthetically, we must note that a major problem in the interpretation of the Chalchihuites culture is that:
> Most of the large archaeological sites located north of the Rio Grande de Santiago in Jalisco, Zacatecas, and Durango are poorly known, and chronology for the region as such is little better than educated guess work (Kelley, 1990; p.487).

While La Quemada — whose culture, at the time of Kelley's writing twenty years ago was, like that of most northern sites, still "nearly unknown": — may have been an outpost to protect people even further south from Chichimec incursions, it may also during its long life have been threatened from the south; "Truly, La Quemada was on the northern frontier, ecologically, archaeologically, and culturally" (Kelley, 1971; p.777).

As in the Chaco area, undefended sites in the surrounding Malpaso Valley were connected to La Quemada with a system of well-designed roads (Hers, 1989; Lopez Lujan, 1989), resembling causeways or Mayan *sacbeob,* according to Kelley (1971). La Quemada itself was both elevated and walled, suggesting to Lopez Lujan (1989) that it served at least in part as a place of refuge for undefended valley settlements in the event of attack. Lopez Lujan is convinced that his findings indicate the former presence of a Malpaso Valley hierarchical society, and that the La Quemada site, beyond practical defense, also symbolized the subjugation of peasants by the elite.

The Mesoamerican frontier extended northward of La Quemada into the Chalchihuites culture area until 1350 (Kelley, 1971) when, because of changing climatic conditions or Chichimec incursions, or these combined with other factors (Davies, 1982), it withdrew some 750 kilometers to the southern part of what is now the Mexican state of Zacatecas.

The apex of La Quemada and Casas Grandes societies did not coincide with the culmination of Anasazi culture; La Quemada was dying as Chaco arose, and Casas Grandes was still thriving after the collapse of the Chaco system. There was no equivalent in Anasazi towns to the sophisticated fortifications at La Quemada, nor, at the time of their abandonment, to the evidences of burning that are found at La Quemada and Casas Grandes. Whatever sparked the need for defense, and whatever caused destruction by fire further south, was apparently absent among the Anasazi. Existing evidence indicates that defense against either hostile outside forces or internecine violence was thought unnecessary by the Anasazi and that whatever conflict occurred was settled peaceably. Why then did defended settlements come into being in Anatolia after Catal Huyuk and not among the Anasazi? One reason may lie in the possible development of a most interesting and unusual sociopolitical system in the latter, as suggested by Vivian (1990) and others, described in Chapter Five and further elaborated in Appendix One.

Retrospect and prospect

Thus far, we have confined ourselves to the presentation and partial analysis of built form in our two case studies, from the microscale of architectural details and elements through the mesoscale of individual buildings to the macroscale of villages, towns, and protocities. The architectural evidence considered or to be considered includes decoration and ornamentation; buildings, enclosures, and defensive walls; roofing and interior details; structural elements and construction systems (brickwork, core-veneer masonry, and puddled adobe); habitation and storage rooms; burial chambers and their contents; doorways, windows, and colonnaded passages; such probable public and ceremonial architecture as temples, pyramids, plazas, towers, and still-mysterious tri-walled structures; roadways and irrigation works; and, among the Anasazi, great and small buildings and kivas.

In the Anasazi case, the nature of the phenomena to be explained requires that we go beyond built form per se to the examination of regional networks and of possible interactions among these networks. These considerations, together with roles possibly played by Mesoamerican outliers in the evolution and devolution of the Chaco Anasazi, will be probed at the end of the following chapter.

In dealing with the ceremonial function of proto-urban centers, such as those in the two areas under consideration here, it is impossible to ignore the work of Wheatley (1971). While written over two decades ago, it remains seminal and relevant to our interpretive scheme.

Wheatley's book is an attempt to understand the beginnings of urban development in Shang China through exploring similar beginnings in seven other areas in Egypt, the Indus Valley, Mesopotamia, Nuclear America, and West Africa. His approach is "broadly hypothetico-deductive" and comparative, relating theory to reconstructed history.

A central thesis, and one with which we are in essential agreement, is "the role of ceremonial centers as the precursors of fully urban forms" (Wheatley, p. 316) outside the West. The characteristics defining a settlement as urban are, as Wheatley indicates, in some dispute; the classic Weberian criteria (Weber, 1925) were clearly based on the European city. However, while Catal Huyuk fails to meet Weber's stringent test, it is considered a city by Mellaart (1967). When Wheatley's book was being written, work at Catal Huyuk was at an early stage, the residential parts of Teotihuacan were under excavation, and the re-evaluation of Anasazi society had just begun; findings of the last few years, in our view, lend much validity to characterizing these as at least proto-urban and perhaps truly urban places.

Of special interest regarding our view of the importance of production relations in urban evolution is Wheatley's emphasis upon the "emergence of a redistributive superordinate economy focused on the ceremonial complex" (Wheatley, 1971, p. 267), upon "ceremonial centers, both compact and dispersed, [which] were pre-eminently instruments of orthogenetic transformation [representative of] a widespread functional and developmental phase in the process of urban genesis" (Wheatley, 1971, pp. 311, 316).

Unlike analyses of prehistoric settlement morphology which focus solely on abstract ritual and symbolic meanings of built forms and spaces, Wheatley's concern is with relations between the material and the ceremonial. His statement about the emergence of "a redistributive system whose reallocative demands were sanctioned by divine authority..., a new instrument for the organization of sacred, economic, social, and political space," is apparently as true of climax Anasazi settlements and Mersin as of the regions of primary and secondary urban generations which are his focus (Wheatley, 1971, p. 305). The need for such redistributive systems in regions such as Anatolia and the Anasazi area, as Adams (1966) has noted in the cases of Mesopotamia and Mesoamerica, may have been the need to compensate for ecological instability to ensure dependability of production.

In this connection, Wheatley's insightful remarks on the relation of social and ecological considerations to the emergence of ceremonial centers and, ultimately, of urban places, are germane:

> [While] a complex pattern of subsistence activity need not reflect a diversity of natural resources, but may itself be a product of social interaction... the integration of disparate ecological zones into a sociopolitically definable unit was a necessary concomitant of the rise of ceremonial centers.... [Diversity] would doubtless have been exploited as an assurance against natural calamity and, as such, in retrospect we can recognize it as an indispensable basis for long-term development... [D]iversities of environment and natural resources were exploited by, as far as the archaeological record has been unraveled, ceremonial centers in virtually all the nuclear urban realms (pp.273-274).

Figure 4.1 Plan of portion of Catal Huyuk. (After Mellaart, 1967). Here and in the drawings that follow, "C" indicates court or courtyard.

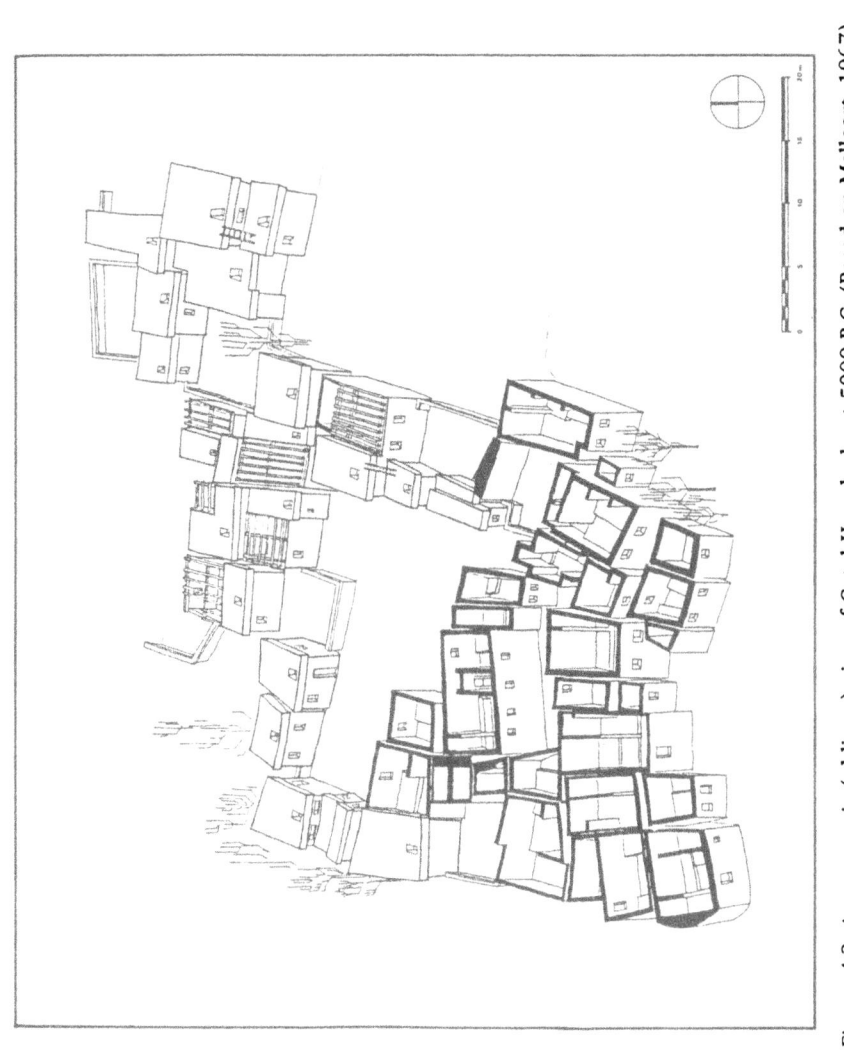

Figure 4.2 Axonometric (oblique) view of Catal Huyuk about 5900 B.C. (Based on Mellaart, 1967).

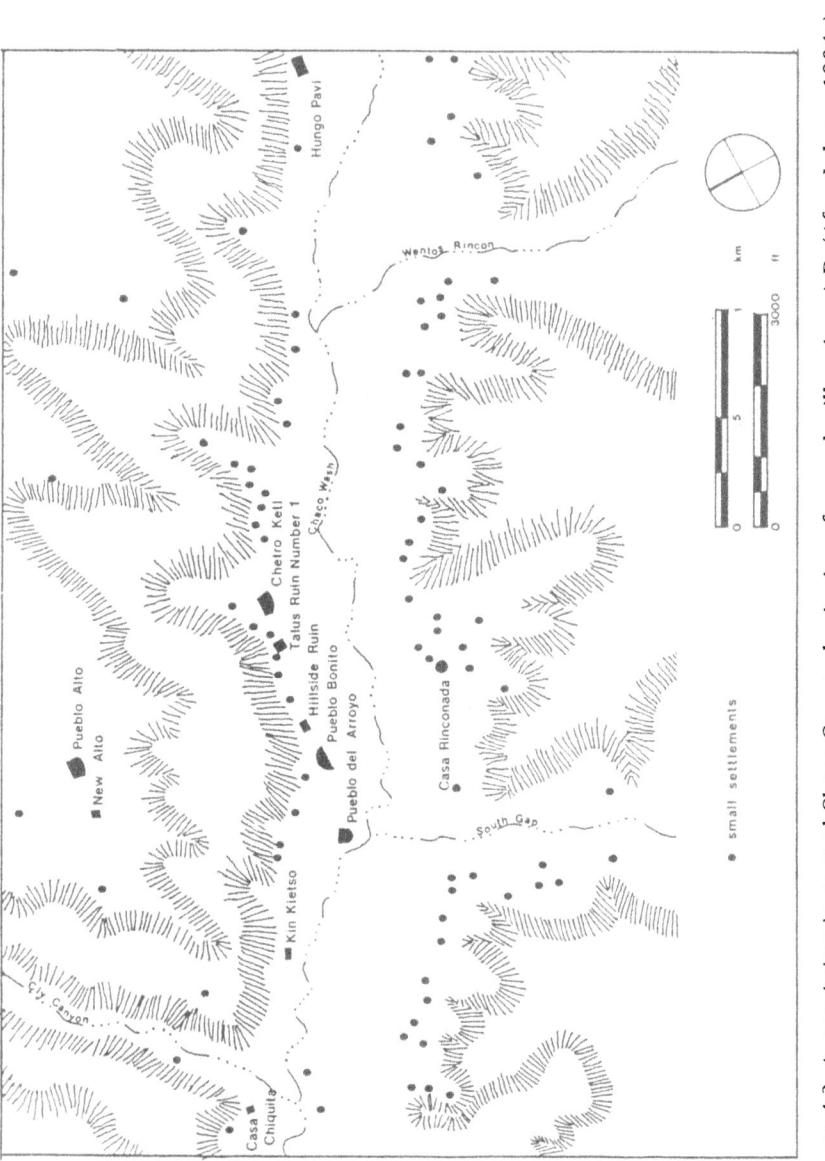

Figure 4.3 Anasazi sites in central Chaco Canyon beginning of second millennium A.D. (After Lekson, 1984a).

Urbanization in the Neolithic 147

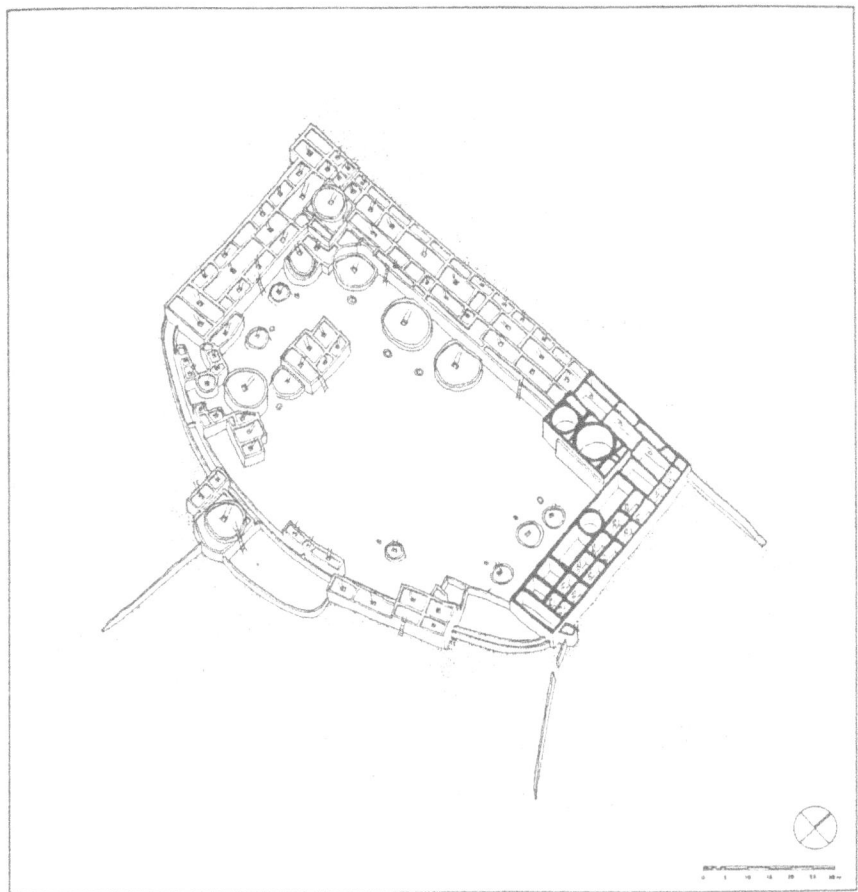

Figure 4.4 Axonometric view of Pueblo Alto. (Based on Lekson, 1984b).

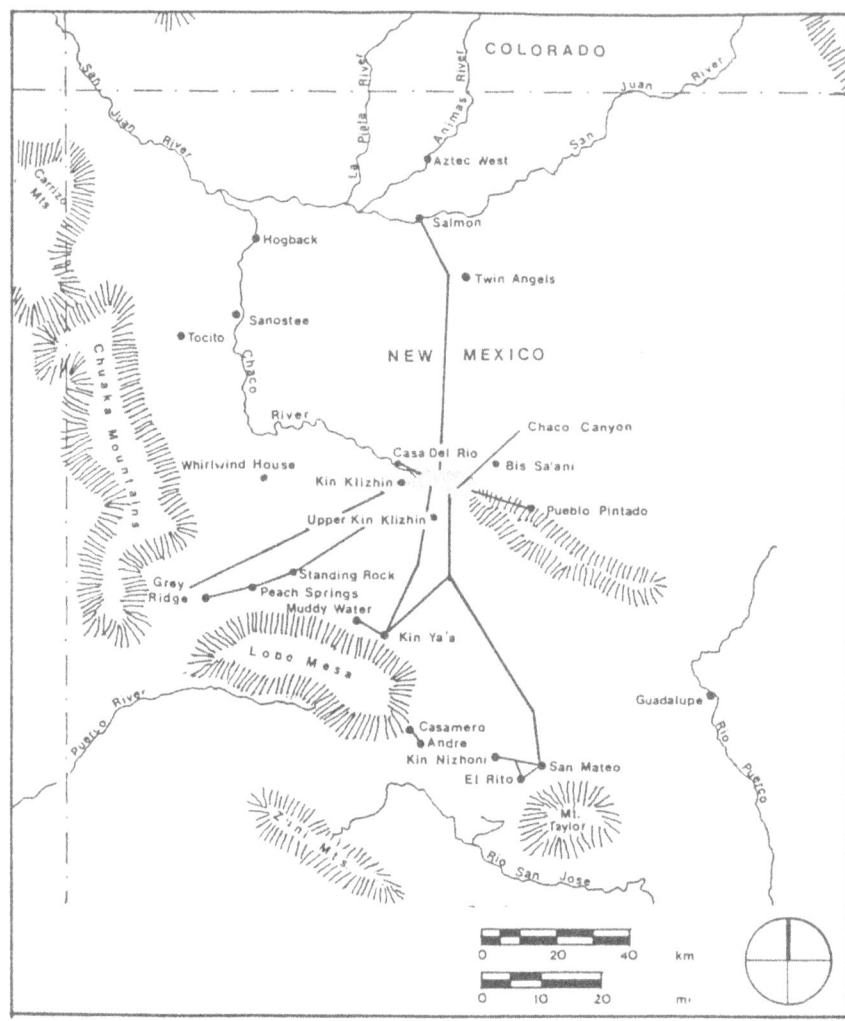

Figure 4.5 Major arteries of Chacoan road system. (From Powers, 1984b).

Urbanization in the Neolithic

Figure 4.6 Plan of Hacilar. (After Mellaart (1970).

150   Urbanization in the Neolithic

Figure 4.7 Axonometric view of Hacilar about 5600 B.C. (Based on Mellaart, 1970)

Urbanization in the Neolithic

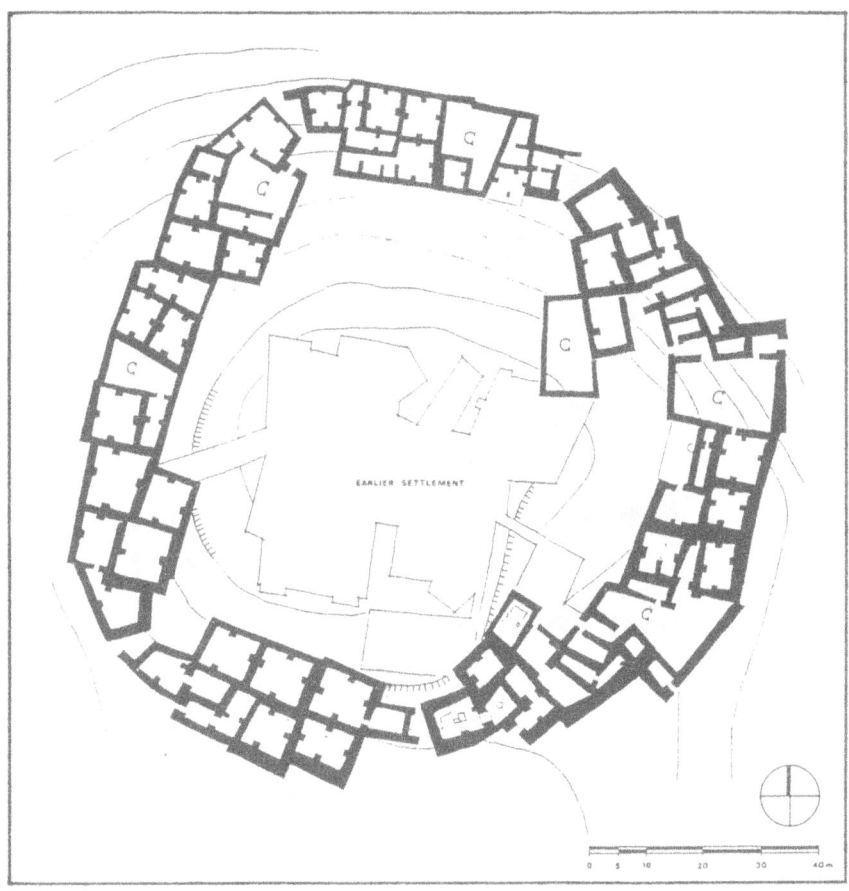

Figure 4.8 Fortress of Hacilar ca. 5250 B.C. (After Mellaart, 1970).

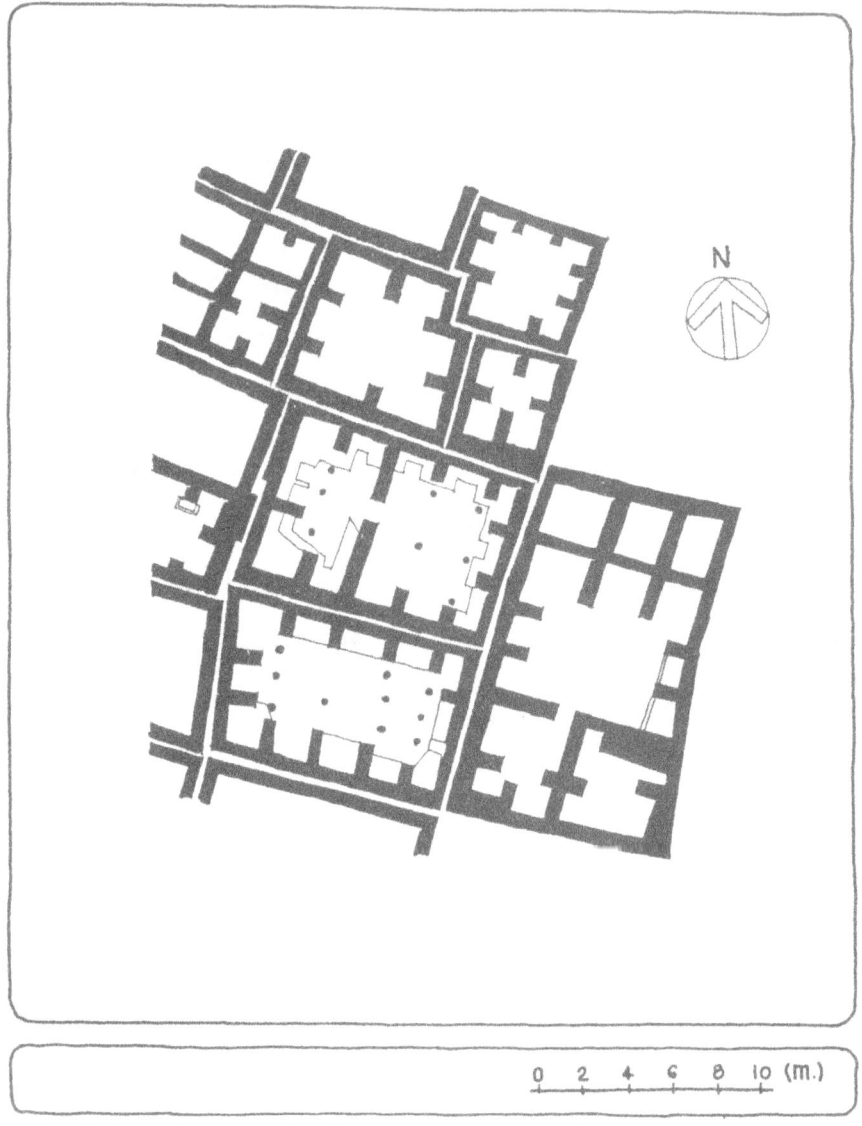

Figure 4.9 Plan of part of Can Hasan, Level II, ca. 5000 B.C. (Adapted from French, 1962, 1963, 1964).

Urbanization in the Neolithic 153

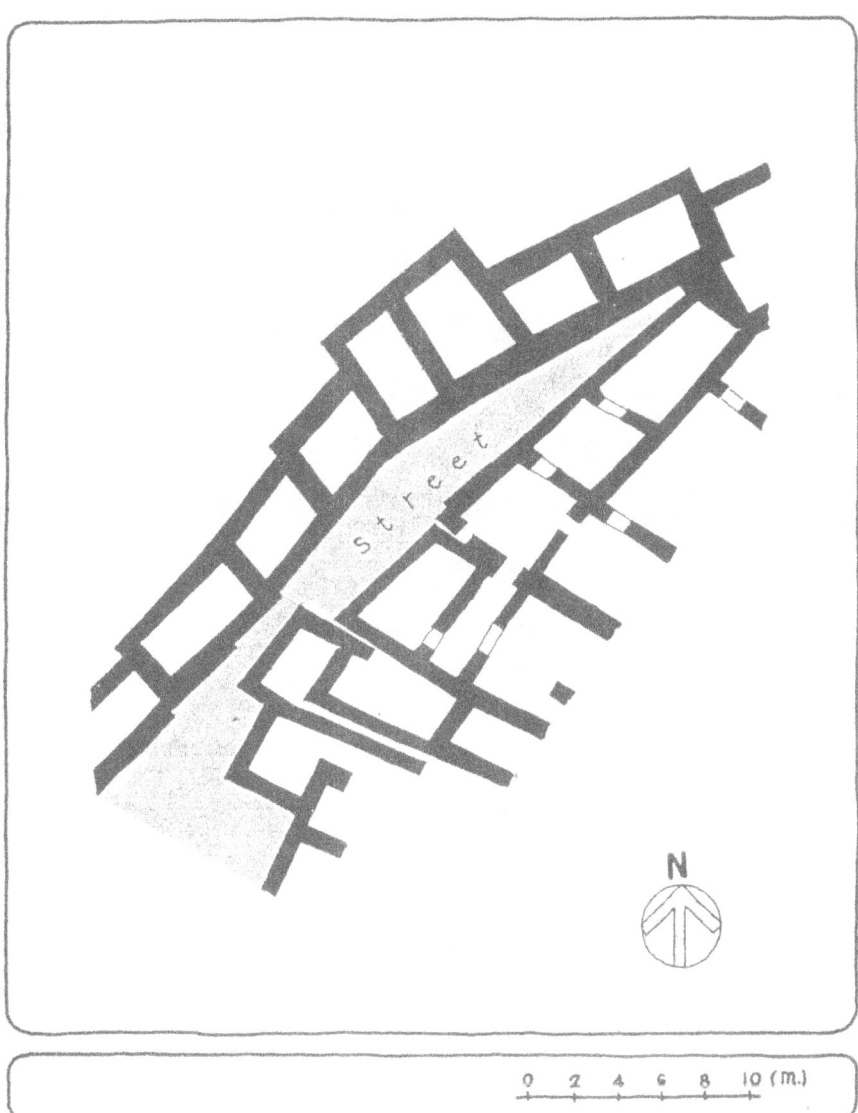

Figure 4.10 Plan of a portion of Mersin ca. 4400 B.C.
(Adapted from Naumann, 1975).

Figure 4.11 Axonometric view of Mersin. (Reconstruction after Naumann, 1975).

Urbanization in the Neolithic 155

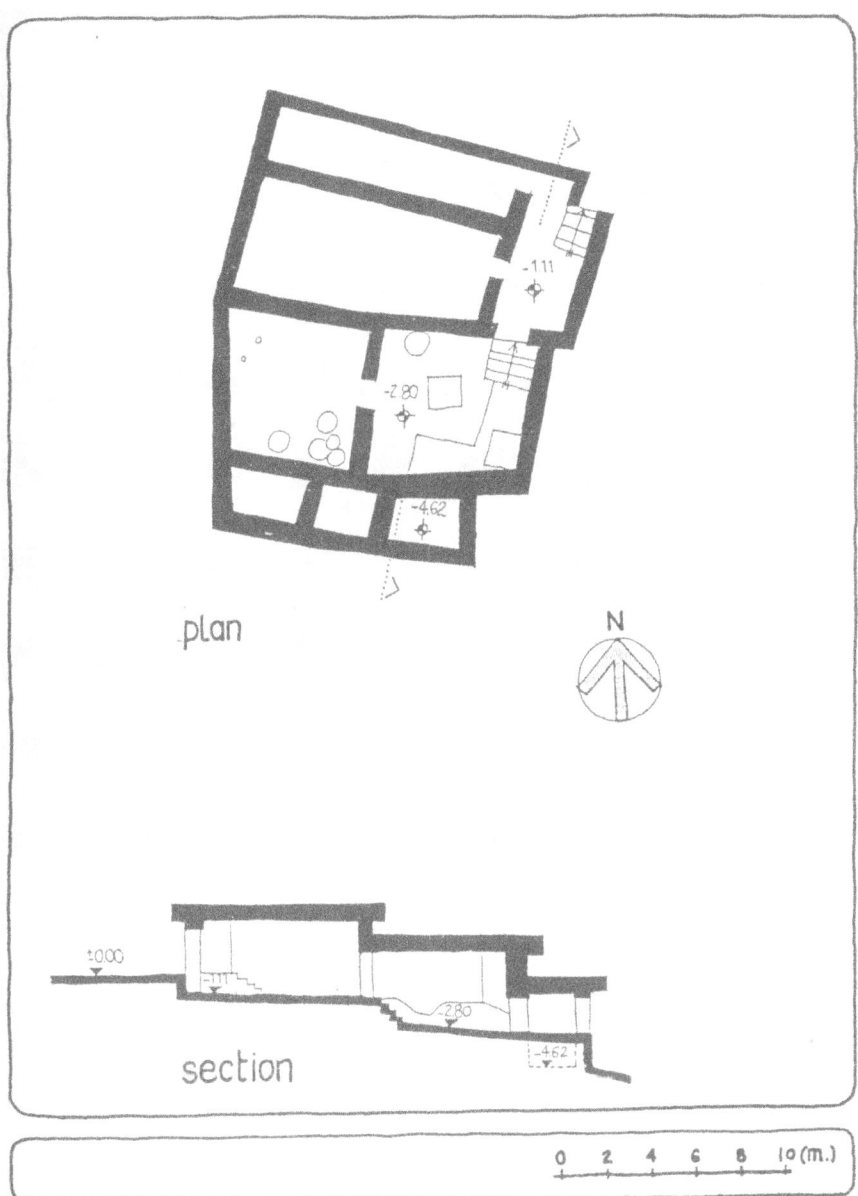

Figure 4.12 A private house in Bogazkoy (Hattus). (Adapted from Naumann, 1975).

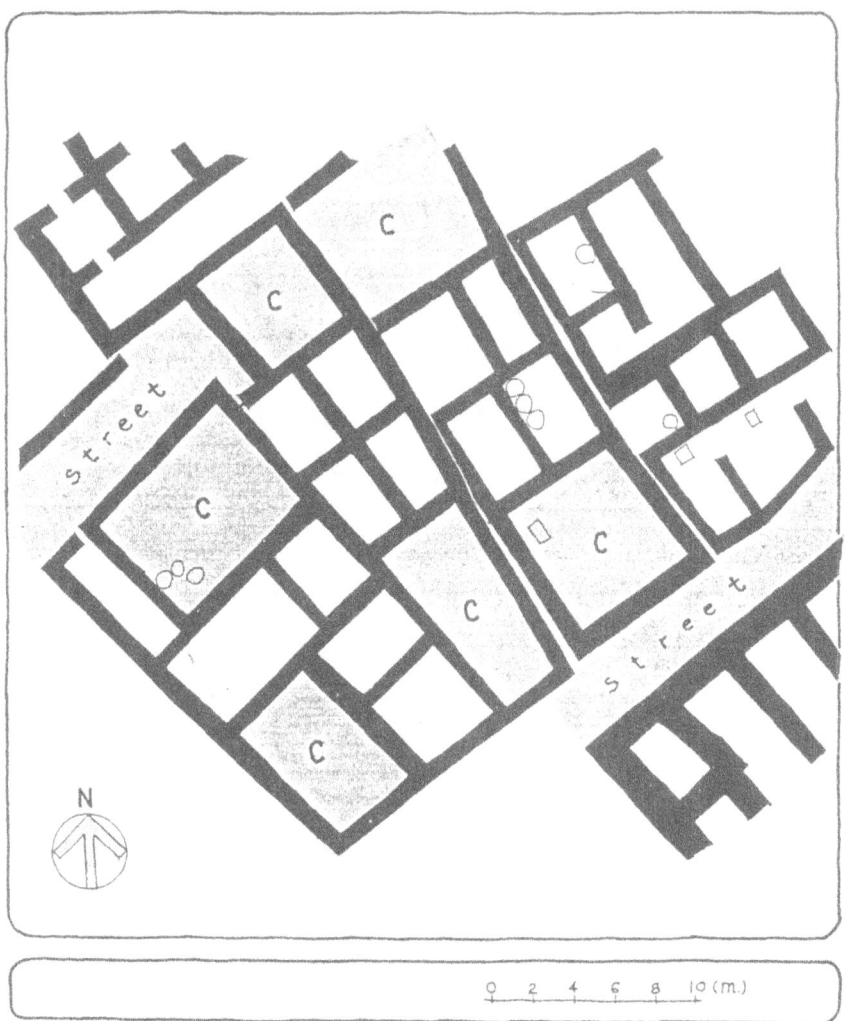

Figure 4.13 Courtyard houses from the Great Kingdom Period, Bogazkoy. (Adapted from Naumann, 1975).

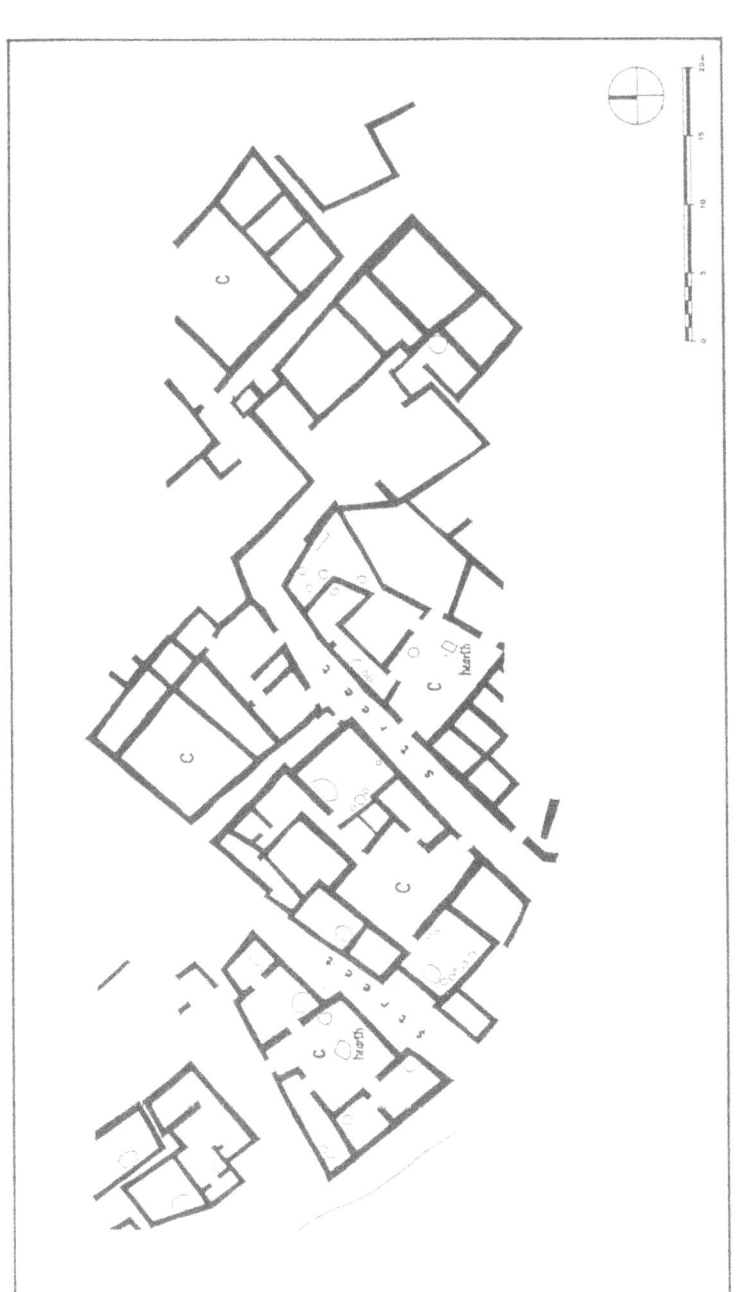

Figure 4.14 Courtyard houses in Bogazkoy (lower city). (Adapted from Bittel, 1970).

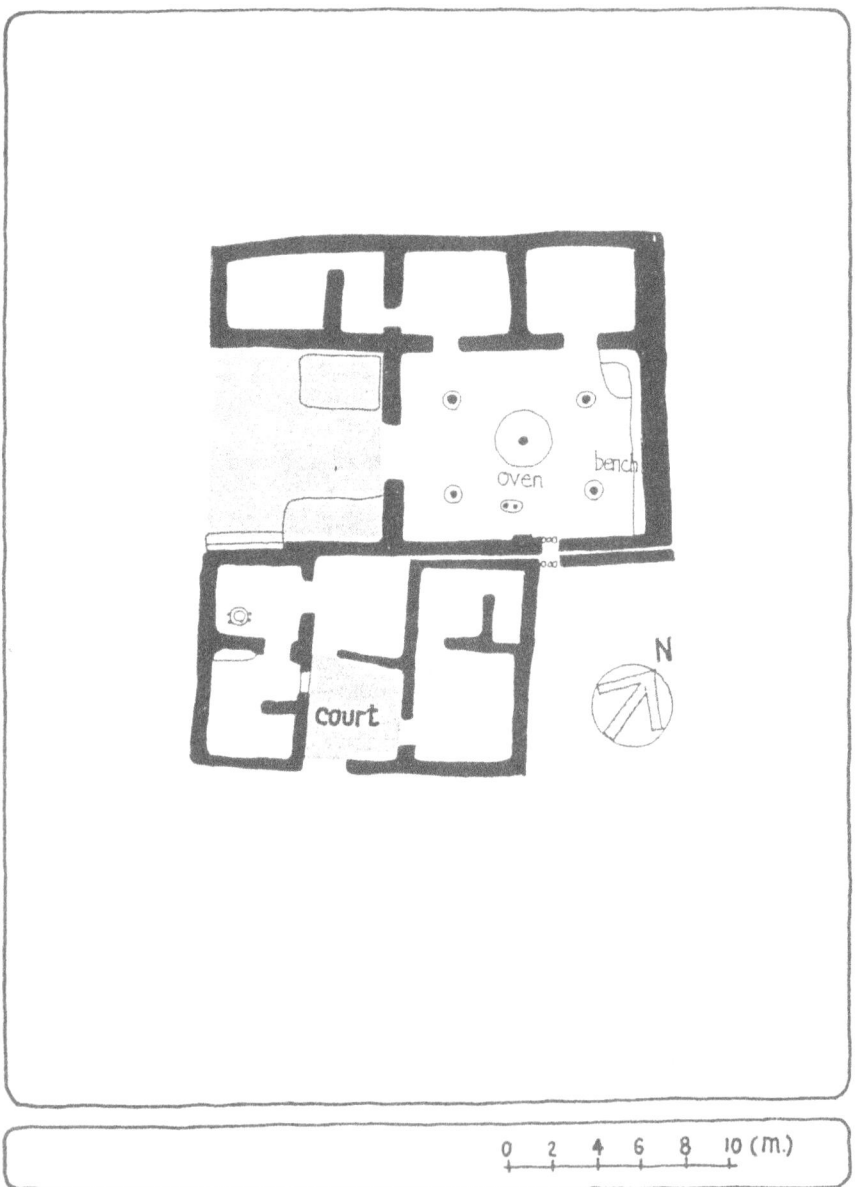

Figure 4.15 Megaron type house in Kultepe. (Adapted from Ozguc, 1963).

Urbanization in the Neolithic 159

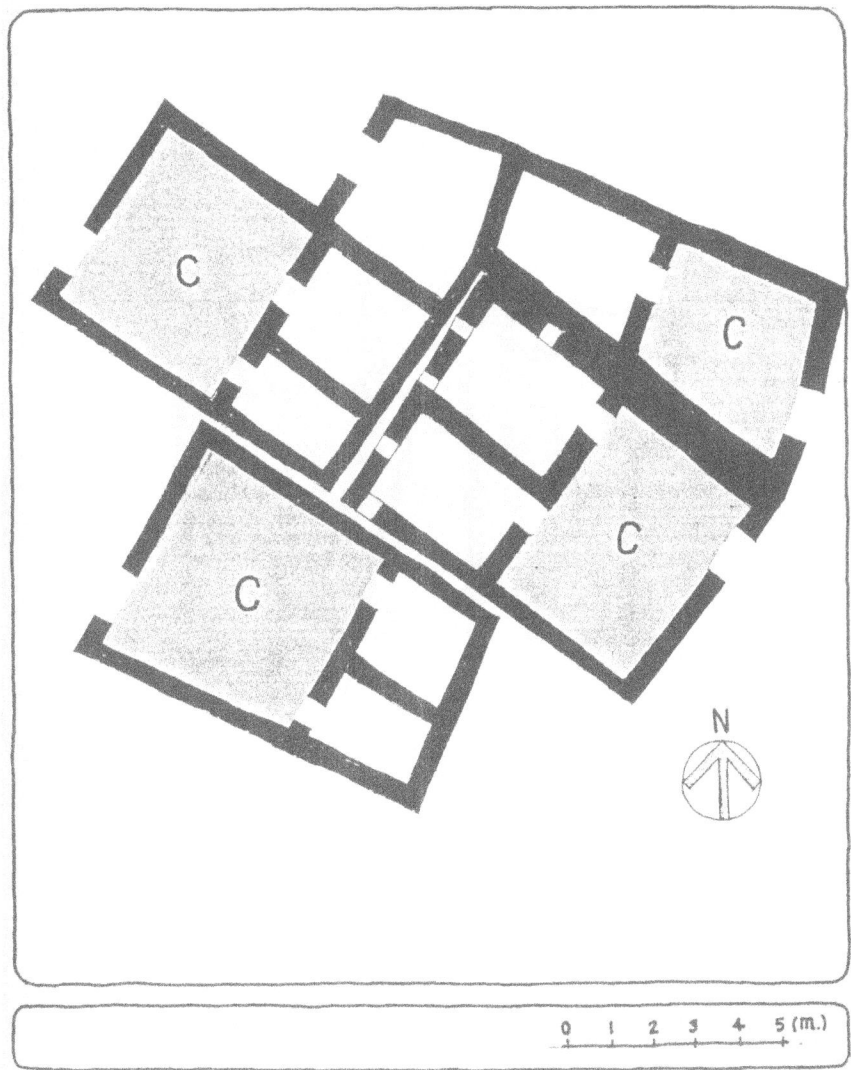

Figure 4.16 Courtyard houses in Kultepe, Level II. (Adapted from Naumann, 1975).

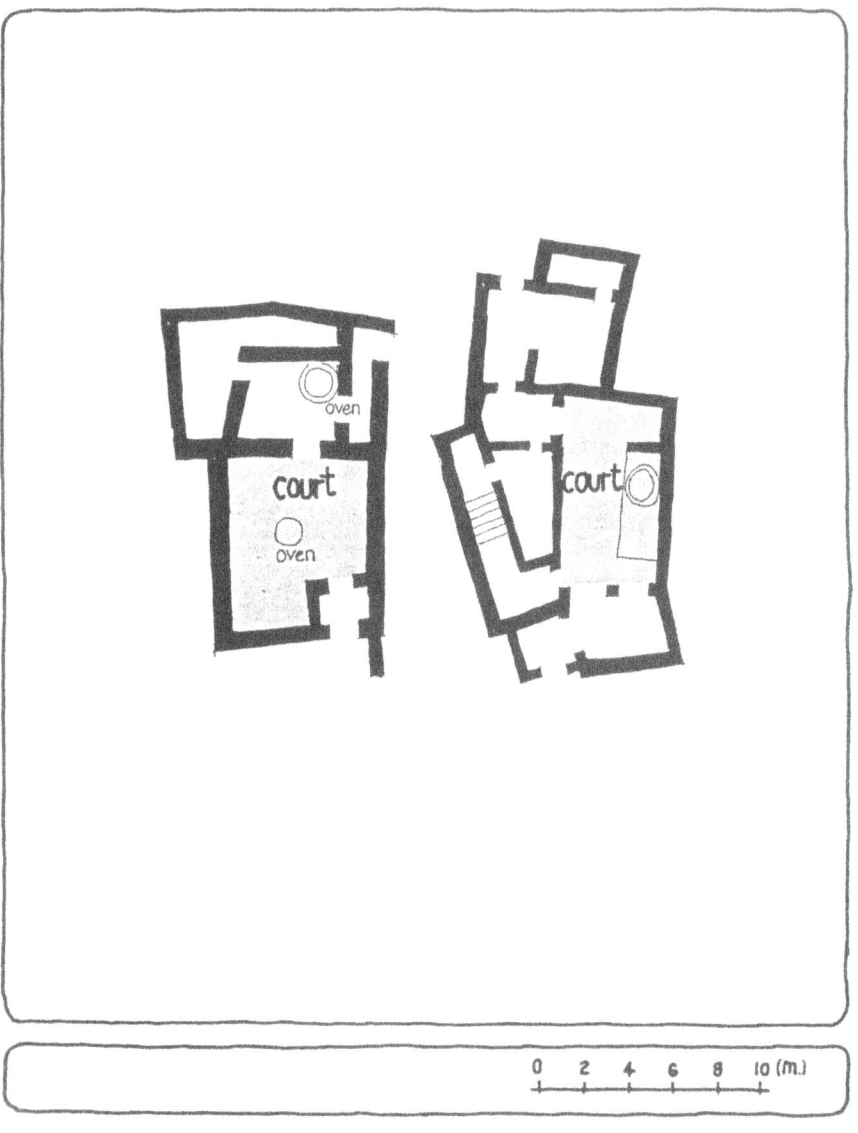

Figure 4.17 Courtyard houses in Kultepe, Level IB. (Adapted from Naumann, 1975).

Urbanization in the Neolithic

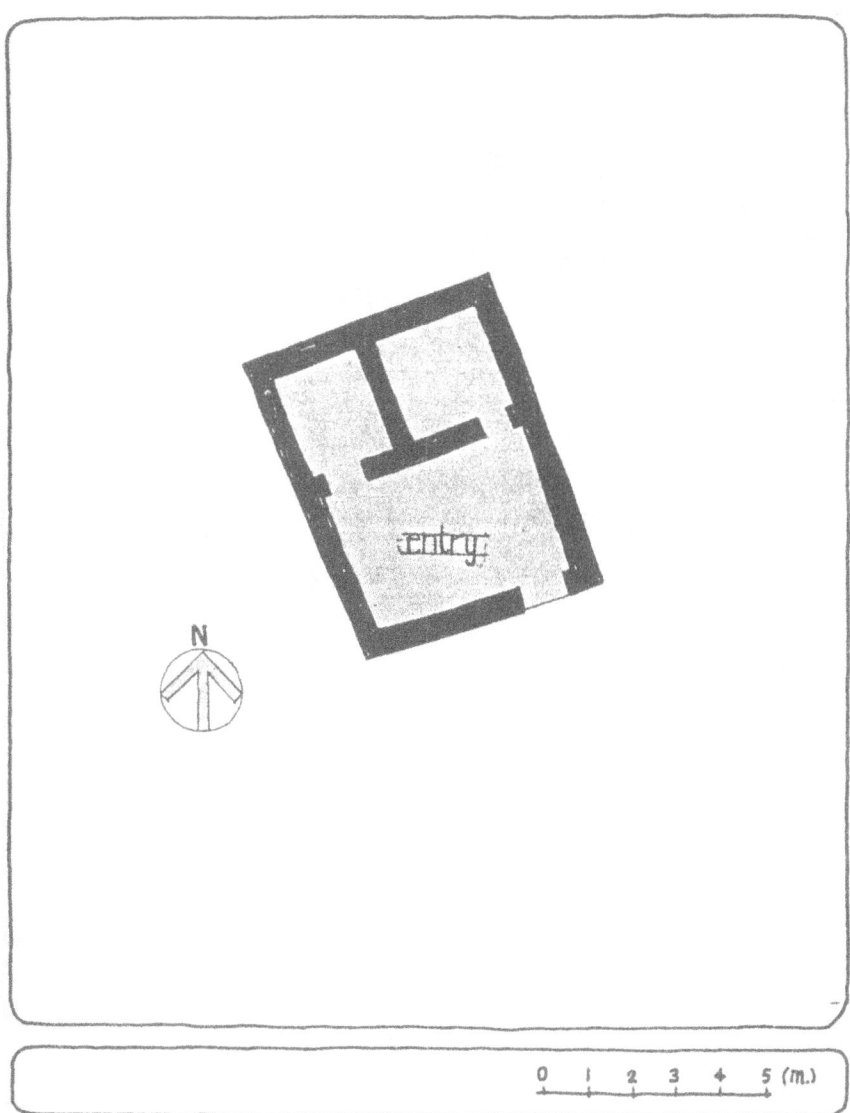

Figure 4.18 A courtyard house in Kultepe, Level IA.
(Adapted from Naumann, 1975).

162   Urbanization in the Neolithic

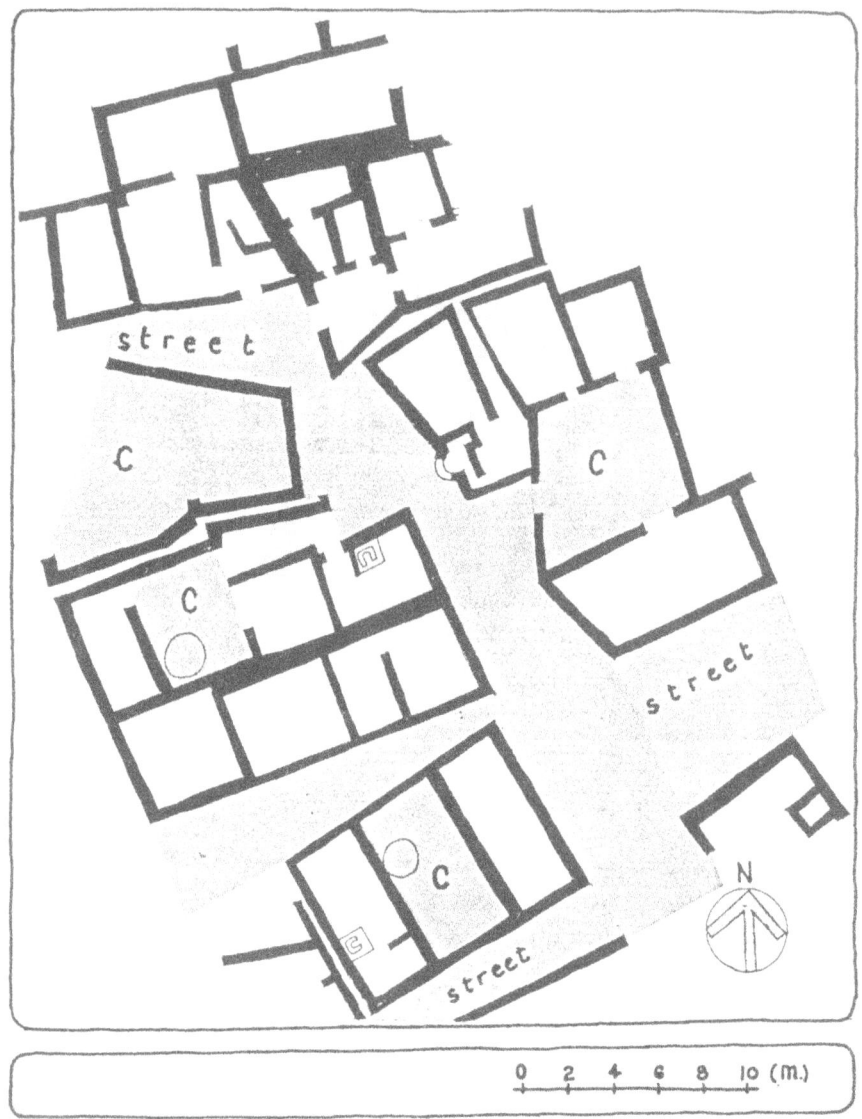

Figure 4.19 Individual family courtyard houses in Karum-Kanes, Level II. (Adapted from Naumann, 1975).

Urbanization in the Neolithic 163

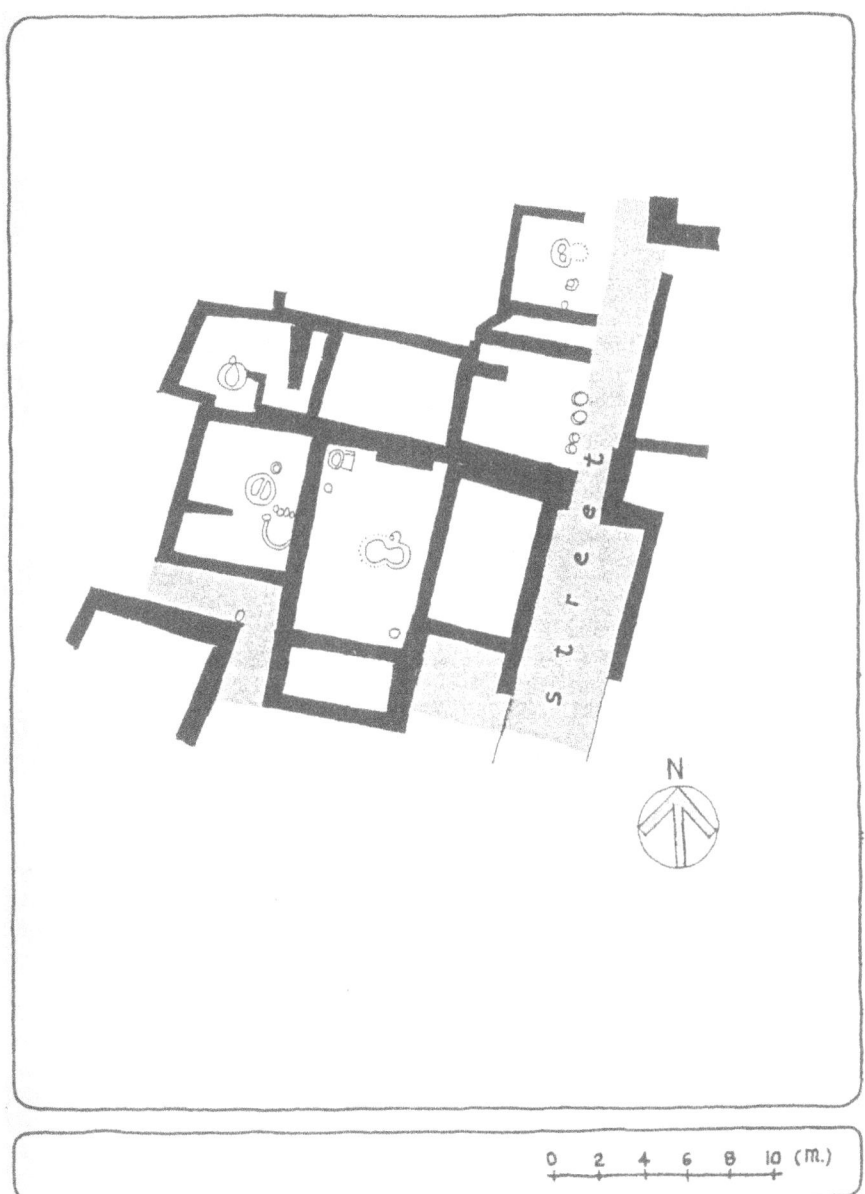

Figure 4.20 House in Alisar, ca. 2500 B.C. (Adapted from Naumann, 1975).

Chapter Five

CLIFF HANGERS AND TROGLODYTES

> At one stage or another in the history of almost any field of study, the condition may obtain that the more ample the facts that come to our cognizance the less do they appear to fit into a pattern.
>
> K. Polanyi, *Trade and market in the early empires.*

In the preceding three chapters, we have traced, in broad strokes, several millennia of prehistory in Anatolia and the American Southwest, from early post-glacial hunting and gathering societies to the beginnings of cities and urban life. The specific points in prehistory at which the transition from camp to village to town to city occurred vary from one location to the other, but the sequence is relatively clear.

Although there are many resemblances between Catal Huyuk and classic Anasazi megastructures, formation in the two areas differed rather markedly. The *collection* of *dispersed* megastructures that represented the Chacoan "urban revolution" among the eleventh century Anasazi had no parallels in the early cities of Anatolia (although the Hacilar fortress may be regarded as a single doughnut-shaped megastructure around the core of the earlier settlement). Similarly, the heavy fortifications of Hacilar and other towns mentioned earlier have no parallels among the Chacoan megastructures; with the exception of some low walls, these were entirely unfortified. In fact, there is no evidence of invasion or violent insurgency throughout the entire period of the "Chaco Phenomenon"; the closest possible Anasazi equivalent to "fortification" were "cavate towns," whose most famous examples are Mesa Verde, Kayenta, and Frijoles Canyon. Even so, there is no firm evidence that location of communities in massive caves actually represented an attempt at protection from enemies, as did fortification in Anatolia; in fact, as indicated in this Chapter, the establishment of large-scale cavate settlements by people in both the Anasazi region and Cappadocia during the first and second millennia A.D. has many possible explanations, among which defense is but one.

Cliff Hangers and Troglodytes 165

The formation of cavate towns during the second millennium A.D. in the American Southwest was not a ubiquitous occurrence and is *not* presented here as typical of the period, but rather as an interesting phenomenon worthy of examination in comparative perspective. It is a phenomenon, however, that seems to have been associated in some way with at least partial abandonment of Chacoan settlements. It would be as superficially glib to try to explain it solely as out-migration of an in-group from an incipient city as to explain rock-face dwellings in Cappadocia as immigration of an out-group (early Christians) from a "foreign" area. In the following sections, we will try to indicate some possible reasons for cave dwelling during and after the establishment of surface towns in the two areas under consideration, reasons why certain moves occurred, and finally, in the case of the American Southwest, why and in what way the Anasazi region was abandoned — if, in fact, it was abandoned at all. To accomplish this, both areas must be considered as part of much larger regions and broader economies, at significant intersections of routes both of trade and of information exchange.

Carving and building

Burrows and homes in cones

"Carving to dwell" has been a major form of placemaking in Cappadocia for some time. It has also been a way of life for the inhabitants of this quite unusual landscape. It is very difficult to determine, with precision, when living spaces were first hewn into the pliable rock covering over 10,000 square kilometers in the center of the Anatolian peninsula. This difficulty arises from the action of both nature and humans; the process of erosion has been going on for several millions of years. Continuous habitation of the region and of its friable environment so vulnerable to change, for several millennia, has prevented the preservation of much substantial evidence. Concrete evidences of placemaking certainly trace back to Christianity. "But," as Kostof puts it, "there is no reason to disbelieve that the practice was more ancient" (1972; p. 19). At the end of his journey in Anatolia during the summers of 1884 and 1885, Sterrett, referring to Cappadocia, also wrote: "Whether these rock-cut habitations date originally from an earlier epoch or not, it is at all events certain that they were used by the early Christians. But such habitation goes back to a period so remote that the Christian Greeks," currently living in the area, "have no traditions concerning it." (1888, p. 230-231). Strabo (1854; Bk XV), writing slightly before Cappadocia became a Roman province (A.D. 17), reports that the people of the Cappadocia region were under Persian influence and already had an established fire worshipping cult in the first millennium B.C. — also supported by archaeological evidence of "pyraitheia" found in the region (Bittel, 1956) — along with remnants of Hittite religious beliefs. Greek belief systems were brought into the region with the appearance of new powers and cultures. With this continuity of immigrants, it would not be unreasonable to assume a continuity of hostile encounters and persecution. This is another possible reason for people taking refuge in the isolated landscapes of the region.

The reasons to surmise that "the intimate relationship between man and nature" (Giovannini, 1971; p. 71) in Cappadocia was established at a period antedating Christianity are several. First, the location of obsidian sources in central Anatolia, Acigol and Ciftlik, are in the Cappadocia region. The very early and extensive use of obsidian from these specific sources in the surrounding environs and in other parts of Anatolia, as well as outside the boundaries of the peninsula along the Levant coast, leads to the conjecture that settlements in the vicinity must have been established for easy access to obsidian sources and to develop further the already widely-spread trade network. Access to and control of these sources required territorial domination. This could not have been achieved without some sort of settlement — perhaps transitory or seasonal in the earlier stages and more permanent by the Protoneolithic — in close proximity to the sources. Igdeli Cesme and Asikli Huyuk, (Todd, 1966), two of the numerous Protoneolithic settlements in the central Anatolian plateau and relatively better documented villages dating back to ca. 7000 B.C., happen to be very near these sources. In spite of the fact that these Protoneolithic villages were constructed rather than hewn out of rock, later examples (such as those in Figures 5.1 and 5.2) lead us to suspect that other settlements could have been carved earlier into Cappadocian rocks or were making use of some of the natural cavities. The microclimate of the small valleys themselves, the abundance of water sources, and the availability of food certainly must have been contributing factors to settlement in areas not far from the obsidian sources, since this volcanic mineral was essential, prior to the Chalcolithic, to survival and development.

In addition to the need to camouflage and conceal the living environment as a defensive measure against attacks by other groups of people as well as animals, there are also environmental reasons for cliff dwellings, caverns, and grottoes hewn out of soft rock. These provide an environment that is climatically very advantageous compared to other "built" structures because of the high thermal mass of the earth (Labs, 1976b; Hazer, 1976; Golany, 1983; Boyer and Grondzik, 1987). In the absence of other building materials, such as timber, carving, as opposed to "building," saves labor, allowing a response that is more along the lines of natural adaptation. Such a mode of dwelling also allows intensified land use and nature conservation in a region where opportunities for efficient agriculture exist only in limited areas, such as the valley bottoms. While environmental demands have been considered the primary reason for dwelling in subsurface structures by many investigators, the environmental determinism implicit in this interpretation raises many important theoretical questions. Although the great potential benefit of subterranean placemaking as a rational utilization of resources is obvious from a narrowly defined environmental perspective, a broader ecological view must include the social relations predominant in such a society.

The rise of cities, starting at the end of the sixth millennium B.C., not only made "settlements" into "villages" but concomitantly made social stratification, already in progress, more pronounced. Forced labor and centralized authority also gave way to discontent, unrest, and dissidence, among those at the lower end of the emerging social hierarchy. By the fourth millennium B.C., strong local authorities, political and religious, had already established a difference between the "served" and the "serving" people. With the ascendancy of the Hittites, serving people became slaves. (Goetze, 1975). In spite of the Hittites' relatively "humane" treatment of slaves (Gurney, 1961), it is possible that a level of dissatisfaction and general unhappiness led some of these captives to seek refuge in the isolated, well-hidden valleys of Cappadocia. "In all ages," as Giovannini attests, "Rocky Cappadocia was the region offering most scope for eluding the control or the direct influence of government authority and the ruling classes" (1971; p. 69). Some of the valleys are so geographically isolated and the hewn-out dwellings so adapted to the natural environment that the practice of carving into rocks and cones may have been well-established as early as the second millennium B.C. under the existing and emerging social conditions, although Rodley (1985) contends that troglodyte communities did not antedate Christianity in Cappadocia.

It is certainly true that local conditions contribute to the form of a place, both at the settlement and dwelling scale. However, it is also true that environmental response is not based solely upon physical conditions but in addition is affected and shaped by social relations in the community. For instance, in a stratified society, especially in one where slavery is a way of life, it is not very difficult to deduce, nor is it an idle speculation to surmise, that some of the "underprivileged" must have escaped from urban captivity into the countryside. Since antagonism between town and country existed from the beginning of the re-creation of villages, it is not unlikely that those fleeing the cities were received sympathetically by the rural people. It is also possible that these migrants established small communities in valleys in which it was easier and faster to carve into rocks than to build. Giovannini's remark about "the persistence in Cappadocia of the characteristics of human settlement which had been shown in earlier periods by the identification of varying racial and social strata in different physical and geographical environments" (1971; p.68) is not only social, dealing with form, but also materially substantiated, concerned with the content aspect of placemaking. Given the advantages of burrowed spaces in the tuffaceous rock and of labor-saving, the practice of carving may have begun as soon as economically and politically significant cities started to emerge in Cappadocia.

Xenophon's *Anabasis*, the epic which narrates the great march (401 to 399 B.C.) of roughly 10,000 Greeks from Sardis to the gates of Babylon and back to Greece by the coast of the Black Sea, gives a description of a troglodytic settlement in the far eastern part of Anatolia, north of Lake Van. The route taken by the Greeks in their march against the Persians to assist Cyrus, the satrap of most of Anatolia (who wanted the Persian throne, occupied by his brother), did not go through Cappadocia. Therefore, there is no possibility that he was describing Cappadocia. However, Xenophon's account of a village on the uplands of eastern Anatolia can be easily applied to numerous similar settlements of Cappadocia. If underground houses with entrances "like the mouth of a well, but spacious below," with "passages dug into them for the cattle," where "the people descended by ladders" (Xenophon, 1867; p. 128), could exist in areas where the problem of "hewing out" is more difficult, then it is possible that the practice of "carving to dwell" in such a place as Cappadocia might have started much earlier.

A few decades before Xenophon's *Anabasis*, Herodotus used the name Cappadocia for the first time, the Greek version of Katpatouka (or Katpatuka, or Katpatukya) whose Persian meaning may be the "land of fine horses," or "the place constantly exposed to sun and which has wide shouldered horses." In other words, the name of the region is at least four centuries older than Christianity. Also, the region must have been important enough for the Persians to make it a satrapy about a century before Herodotus' time. Such importance would have been unlikely unless the region were economically and politically significant, with well-developed urban and rural coexistence.

Apparently, the region was also of importance to Alexander the Great who marched through Cappadocia in 334 B.C., leaving a commander to govern. Until the region became a Roman province in 17 A.D., the local dynasties of rulers were not displaced and they retained a considerable degree of autonomy. Throughout history, the peoples of Cappadocia remained resistant to the different cultures imposed by the ruling groups, and retained their own identity. This was not very difficult since the rulers, primarily concerned with the control of the military roads in the territory, carried on their activities largely in the principal cities, leaving the rural population mostly on their own (except for rent collection). The native peoples in the rural areas continued to inhabit the

Cliff Hangers and Troglodytes 169

stretches of rocky valleys and to dwell in villages either hewn from the rock or built in stone. (Figures 5.3, 5.4, 5.5).

All of these reasons, while not conclusive in themselves, suggest that the practice of "carving to dwell" in Cappadocia began long before the arrival of Christianity in the region, which was relatively early in its ascension (but later in time). Furthermore, if the primary reason for the influx of Christian immigrants into the region was safety (refuge from persecution) in the cone colonies, bluff rock slopes, and underground cities, then it seems unlikely that the newcomers would have innovated, developed, and perfected the technique and tradition of carving in a short time, implying that the very reason for coming to the region itself may have been that they had heard of the tradition of carving homes into rock, and that it had attracted them. The survival of numerous secular communities as well as religious communities in the rock villages of the eroded valleys of Cappadocia was as much dependent on the greater security and fertility of these valleys as it was on the possibility of carved dwellings provided by local environmental conditions. The way of life and the excavation technique remained unchanged for millennia. If our conjecture is correct, that the beginnings of "carving to dwell" extend back to the proto-Hittite period (if not earlier), none of the numerous cultures since then have initiated a real change in the construction or excavation process in placemaking in the rocky valleys of Cappadocia.

Techniques for excavating, at present, are relatively simple and not very time consuming. Carving into a cone, or rock face, or even underground has not undergone substantial change. Excavation starts with digging a tunnel at the location of what will eventually be the access/exit of the dwelling/compound. Once the desired dimensions of this opening are achieved and the thickness of the outside surface is determined, then extraction of the relatively soft material begins and continues until the cavity roughly achieves the measurements intended. Digging is done with the aid of pickaxes and iron bars (very similar to crowbars). In present practice, it is common to excavate large boulders, approximately one cubic meter, by driving iron bars into the rock and cleaving to separate the semi-cut piece from the main body of the rock. Otherwise, excavation is done by digging with a pickax; this process is slower than removing large pieces but much safer. A pickax is used even when the excavators employ the first method since the desired relatively refined finish requires some precision, not easily achievable with the sole use of iron bars. A pickax, a chisel-like edge on its head, is often the only tool with which the final touches are put on surfaces; it is also used for the architectural and decorative details cut into the rough surface, and for the carving of shelves, benches, and steps. Once the rough size and shape of the room is realized by excavating and removing the debris of carving, refinement and work on architectural details proceeds, starting with the ceiling, followed with walls and floor at the rearmost part of the cavity, moving finally toward the immediate vicinity of the entrance. Scaffolding that might have been necessary for the higher ceilings of churches (Rodley, 1985; p. 224), for instance, is not used in the carving of dwellings since the ceiling height does not require it; standing on boxes, low tables, or stools is sufficient for work on the ceiling and the upper parts of the walls. Although there is no record of the carving technique used on spaces along the hillsides and rock faces of the valleys, it seems plausible to surmise that the present practice is a continuation of the older form of hewing. That "[t]he technique of excavation remained unchanged for centuries" (Giovannini, 1971; p. 70) seems to be correct. (Figures 5.6, 5.7, 5.8, 5.9).

In addition to the social reasons for establishing homes in the rocks of landscape of Cappadocia, there are also reasons of economy. The fact that people were still living "in these rock-cut dwellings, at least two hundred feet high on the cliff," took Sterrett by surprise more than a century ago; ("There is no earthly reason why they should live there, as the country is safe and land abundant...") (1888; p. 229). That this form of architecture in Cappadocia is only "a logical response to the local conditions" (Rodley, 1985; p. 7) has been observed by others. Scarcity of materials (especially of timber which needs to be brought from far away), relatively less time consumed in carving than in constructing, and the considerably more favorable climatic conditions of the carved spaces (very thick enveloping surfaces with large time lags appropriate for the continental climate, with relatively large diurnal and seasonal differences in temperature that prevails year-round), are the major factors contributing to rock face placemaking in Cappadocia. In this sense, "the nature of the environment is the determining factor, and the constructors of the dwellings were content to tunnel through the rock as natural conditions dictated rather than take the trouble to build up a structure from separate blocks of stone" (Giovannini, 1971; p. 75). In this way, as indicated earlier, they also preserved the fertile valley bottoms for agriculture and fruit orchards as well as protecting their dwellings from occasional floods due to sporadic but heavy downpours.

We can only conjecture about the life styles and the dwelling environments of the peoples in Cappadocia antedating Christianity in the absence of material evidence. However, both the present state of the art and that of the Christian settlements starting from the fourth century may help us to put some of the evidential elements into perspective, even if they do not provide a precise picture. It has been mentioned earlier that rural life style, as well as placemaking activity in the villages of Anatolia, has not changed radically in the past few millennia. The primary reason for this is the feudal mode of production that

Cliff Hangers and Troglodytes 171

determines social relations in the villages and their concomitant effect on placemaking activity, not much different in Cappadocia than in other parts of Anatolia. Therefore, there is not much doubt that "in the cone colonies and bluff rock slopes, villages and towns go on as they have since early Christian times" (Kostof, 1972; p. 35). This assertion is a direct reference to the physical environment that the people of Cappadocia are inhabiting. It is also a reference to the mode of production, the conditions of existence, and the social relations that shape placemaking activity. The arrival of Christianity in the region (Peter's reference to a Christian community there, in his First Letter, and the establishment of a center of Christian theology at Caesarea (Kostof, 1972; pp.5-6), one of the major provinces of the region by A.D. 200) and its early success especially among the rural poor people who could provide "no more propitious footing" (Kostof, 1972; p. 7) for its growth, are clear indications of both the split between town and country, and the heavily stratified society of the time. The conditions that swelled St. Basil's anger — where "[t]he rich who owned land and the livestock were very rich; the poor who worked for them very poor" (Kostof, 1972; p. 7) — are not much different at present. Nor is there any reason to believe that they were different in the three millennia before Christianity, after the full development of the feudal mode of production in Anatolia.

Whether dwellings of secular type, or places of religious nature such as monasteries, hermitages, and churches (Rodley, 1985; p. 150), or complexes used otherwise, (such as temporary or permanent residences of local princes, landlords — the palace-owning class — or *hans*, which were lodging accommodations for travellers, especially merchants, or military staging posts), the troglodytic settlements may be divided into two categories: those that are built into enlarged natural caves or hewn out of the hillside, carved into bluff rock surfaces, or into the isolated free standing cones; and those that are burrowed underground. The first type is composed largely of individual units with only a few spaces attached to each other, both horizontally and vertically. In the case of family dwellings, for instance, spatial organization is such that at the most, four or five rooms are interconnected on one level and two or three levels connected with lesser numbers of rooms on floors other than the main one. Vertical connection is achieved primarily through exterior circulation on the surface of the rock rather than through the interior. Functions other than dwelling are accommodated in more complex and intricate organizations of space, including oratories, churches, monasteries, and refectories; yet even these are relatively simple.

The only exception to this simple organization of rooms and to the prevalence of individual units in the habitable hewn-out spaces above the surface are the larger communal settlements, such as those in the Zelve valley.

Here, and in places similar to it, one can find interconnections among several units, such as interior horizontal and vertical passages. The second type, the underground burrow, is actually composed of settlements much larger in scale than individual units. They are practically cities, with spaces to accommodate all the activities of several thousand people. Simple spatial organization of the first type is replaced by very complex organization in the second. Accommodating a multiplicity of functions and large numbers of people certainly makes a big difference not only in scale but in spatial complexity as well.

Rooms in the individual family dwellings hollowed out in rock cliffs or cones do not vary in shape and size very much; the basic room shape is a rectangle three to four meters (in rare instances almost five meters) in width and six to eight meters in length. Adjacent rooms may be carved on either or both sides of the first one, or may be the continuation of the first, hewn deeper into the rock with a difference in floor level or in ceiling height or both. In other words, after the first room is completely carved, there is a possibility of expansion in both directions, producing individual rooms of about the same size. While natural ventilation and lighting pose a problem in rooms carved deeper into the rock, less heat loss makes these rooms more useful in the winter months. There may also be vertical ventilation shafts leading from the inner rooms to the surface of the rock or cliff. Adjacent rooms facing outside may be connected with inside doors. There is also the possibility of expansion. However, this is done, except for structural considerations, almost independently of the main floor. It is generally the rule that in individual dwellings the two floors are connected on the exterior surface by steps carved into the rock. The thickness of rock left between two floors is not less than 50 centimeters, and in most cases, nearly a meter.

In spite of the appearance of randomly hewn-out spaces, a geometrical order and certain systematic and methodical planning in fact prevail in this process of "subtraction" to form the rooms of the dwelling. The "subtractive" quality of the spaces is dictated primarily by structural and thermal considerations and is in no way disorderly or haphazard excavation. While additive methods of construction allow "rehabilitation" of ill-fitting or inappropriate construction details, subtractive space-forming is basically irreversible. Therefore, in hollowing, *ad hoc* decisions are "out"; the risk is too great, and the limitations that these may impose on succeeding expansions are too restrictive. The risk and the limitations are primarily of structural/material failures. The problems are fundamentally twofold: one of human errors, the other of natural causes. By employing systematic technique at every step in the process of hewing out, human error may be reduced if not totally eliminated; also, failures that may be due largely to natural causes — heavy downpours, erosion, rock falls, land-

Cliff Hangers and Troglodytes

slides, earthquakes — may be delayed if not entirely prevented. All of these processes and features are represented in the three houses shown in Figures 5.10 through 5.16.

Geometrical order, not only in a planar but in a three-dimensional sense, then, is an absolute necessity in the process of hewing out spaces. This order is derived from span length: dimensions of such structural elements as walls and floors, and of openings such as doors and windows; and from general, informal, broader-scaled planning considerations, such as what the person next door or above/below has done previously. As indicated earlier, there seems to be a rough standardization of dimensions.

Although slightly different in nature, the *yao dong*, the traditional underground dwellings of the Huang Tu Plateau — in the provinces of Henan, Shanxi, Shaanxi, Gansu, Qinghai, and in the Autonomous Regions of Ningxia Huizu and Xinjiang Uygur — of the People's Republic of China (Konishi and Aoki, 1986), and the subterranean villages on the Matmata Plateau of Tunisia (Golany, 1983; p. 5-10), eventually established a uniformity of dimensions quite similar to those of Cappadocia. Similar dimensions are observed in the troglodyte habitations found in France — in the grottoes of Cales (Bouches-du-Rhone), Perriers and Jonas (Puy de Dome), Lamouroux (Correze), La Madeleine and La Roque-Saint-Christophe (Dordogne), Rochemenier (Maine et Loire), and the village of Barry (Vaucluse); in the numerous settlements along the valleys of rivers such as the Seine (Haute Isle, La Roche Guyon), Loire (Blois, Vouvray, Langeais, Longue, Montreuil, Doue, Gennes, Cumeray, Brissac), Cher (Bourre, Villaines), Loir (Le Roches, Troo), Rhone (Tourettes, Cotignac, Villercroze, Cadenet, Le Baux, LesBeaumettes) — and in Sicily (Avola Vecchia) (Huet, 1982; Mulligan, 1983).

Quite clearly, the above parallels are neither coincidental nor something associated with the general needs of rural life; rather, the common denominator is a response to the limitations of nature imposed through the structural characteristics of the soil/rock, to which people are subjected. The three-dimensional geometrical order, the precision required in carving technique and the need for advance planning (conceptual design) are results of very demanding material and the irreversibility of the carving process. This is, in a way, a manner of economizing both labor and material — the earth — efficiently and effectively. An economy of scarcity stemming from a lack of choice of materials and shortages of workable land for agriculture, combined with the specific social relations of slavery and a feudal mode of production, gave rise to "carving to dwell." With time, this developed from less orderly and less regular spaces into very orderly and regular geometrical forms, and into very complex planning at the settlement level.

This development becomes very clear by comparing the more recently carved dwellings of the past three centuries with those in the hidden valleys which once provided troglodytic habitation for people living in the cenobitic, monastic, and hermetic communities of the early Christian period, and for people living communally, sharing a common faith, and hiding from authority, captivity, and the elite of the broader society of the region in the pre-Christian era. Hollowed-out churches and spaces serving other public functions, such as common eating and meeting rooms, are clearly more articulated in details and decoration, while most of the individual dwellings in numerous valleys of isolated landscapes—among them Zelve, Goreme, Mustafapasa, Taskinpasakoy, Soganli, Ihlara, Hasakoy, and Gulsehir—are very spartan. In addition to living quarters there are many storage spaces, also carved, either in or adjacent to the rooms. The number of interconnections between units through relatively short tunnels or passages and steep staircases, all carved in the rock, makes it very difficult to distinguish individual family units, (see also, Giovannini, 1971; p. 75). At the same time it suggests the high probability of a living style that was communally rather than individually oriented. Escape from oppression in the pre-Christian era and thereafter may have been the common incentive for the people of these hidden valleys to pursue what may have been a retrograde mode of production. While the basic unit of social organization was the family, the spatial characteristics of the living environment suggest communal production for livelihood. There is also the possibility of dual residence based on seasonal migrations for most of these people, if not all — a contemporary characteristic. Winter residence being more permanent, people at present still temporarily move to other carved dwellings scattered around the fields and orchards to be in close proximity to their daily summer work: cultivating, tilling, and harvesting. There are also environmental reasons for such moves: secluded and well protected valleys offer more favorable microclimatic conditions in the harsh winter days; less demanding summer conditions allow more choice of habitation.

The second type of troglodytic settlement, the underground burrows or "cellar villages," as Giovannini refers to them (1971; p. 76), are truly inverse megastructures. (Figure 5.17). Dug in from the surface downward, most of these underground settlements are in relatively close proximity and within the triangle formed by the religious centers of Goreme, Soganli, and Ihlara. Although the exact number of these three-dimensional, underground labyrinths in the region is not known, and despite the fact that there is a tendency to refer to some of the multi-story rock dwellings as "underground settlements" also (Gurcay, 1973), the two that have been cleared of debris and opened for public visits — Derinkuyu and Kaymakli — give sufficient clues as to their nature.

While one study estimated the number of "underground cities" at 41 (Urban, 1969), it is not very clear what criteria were used to distinguish underground settlements from the hillside rock dwellings in arriving at this estimate, (see also Urban, 1973). At the scale of the two underground settlements mentioned here, 41 cities would accommodate three times the population of the whole Cappadocia region, including the large urban settlements of the time. Therefore, the number must include some other settlements such as Zelve, Soganli, Selime, Uchisar, Ortahisar, and Goreme, which have been treated in this study as hillside settlements with many openings to the essentially vertical surfaces. On the other hand, underground settlements burrowed from the surface down, vertically deep rather than horizontally broad, have very few openings to the surface. The terminology used to differentiate between the far-subsurface ("lithospace") and shallow near-surface ("terraspace") cities in some literature (e.g., Labs, 1976a) is not of much help either, since almost all of the subterranean habitation in Cappadocia would be categorized as "lithospace." Other examples include the underground settlement at Goztezin between Nevsehir and Gulsehir (Gurcay and Akok, 1965), with its large meeting hall, burial chambers, chapels, dwelling units, and wine cellars. And it is highly probable, according to the talk of local people about long underground galleries that connect several of these cities, that there may be a "network of underground settlements" (Hazer, 1976; p. 27). But the number of these settlements cannot possibly exceed half a dozen or so. Neither was human labor so abundant at the time nor leisure so available as to enable relatively time-consuming and very strenuous placemaking activity; at the scale of a settlement such as Derinkuyu or Kaymakli to accommodate 3,000 people no less than 30,000 cubic meters needs to be excavated and removed; at present it takes one person about thirty days to carve only 100 cubic meters, i.e., approximately 3 cubic meters per day. (These figures are very close to Sterrett's estimates (1919; p. 318) made at the turn of the century.) Nor was there a need for that many underground settlements when 6 or 8 underground habitats, all roughly equivalent to Derinkuyu in size (conservatively estimated at 4,000 to 5,000 people), could house more than all of the rural population of the Cappadocia region.

There is practically no indication of these "inverse megastructures" on the surface except for very carefully and skillfully camouflaged entrances, openings of airshafts, and wells. Large enough to accommodate several thousand people at one time, they were not meant to be year-round permanent habitation. They were built for emergency when the security of the community was threatened. Most of the archaeological findings indicate the seventh century (A.D.) to be the earliest habitation date. This strange and drastic architectural effort, based on fear of being taken captive, was inhabited until the twelfth century when the authority of the Seljuk Turks was established in Anatolia.

Kayseri (Caesarea), the regional capital of Cappadocia, had by the third century A.D. become a center of Christian theology. During the following three centuries a majority of the inhabitants of the hidden valleys of Cappadocia were followers of this relatively new monotheistic religion. A great number of monasteries, hermitages, chapels, and churches were established and reached their peak by the eighth century, an indication of the religious importance of the region as a center of Eastern Monasticism.

In addition to its becoming a religious center, Cappadocia as a region, where lies "the most remarkable remains of early Anatolian history" according to Ramsey (1972; p. 28), has always been important strategically: it is at the crossing of the major north-south (Black Sea - Mediterranean Sea) and east-west ("Royal Road") axes. On the shores of the Black Sea, first Sinop, and later Samsun (Amisos) became the major harbor for central Anatolia, providing the closest sea connection for the region with fairly easy access. The "Royal Road," linking the western shores of Anatolia to the east for more than two millennia prior to the arrival of the Christians, went through the region without crossing Kizilirmak (Halys), providing a safer and easier route for trade and transport. This favorable geographical location and its strategic importance made it desirable to all powers who wished to control trade in Anatolia. It meant not only access to the shores and control of the heavy trade over Anatolia but also access to its own riches — agricultural, mining, and mineral — as well as the labor power of its population. Therefore, Anatolia in general, and Cappadocia in particular, were important to any political power in the area.

Persian attacks starting in the third century A.D., and occasional other invasions, were followed by Arab raids, the first of which occurred in A.D. 642. A majority of the Christian population, rendered insecure and distressed by the Persian attacks, had already taken refuge in the rural areas and were living in the hidden valleys. The population of rural Cappadocia was increasing rapidly, not only because of migration from the cities but also due to the hordes of Christian people coming from the south to escape Arab persecution. By the seventh century the rural population in the troglodytic settlements within the triangle formed by Goreme, Soganli, and Ihlara exceeded 30,000 (Gurcay, 1973; p. 163). When moving out to the secluded landscapes became inadequate, going underground was the solution adopted by the people who were caught in the conflicts, first between the Persians and the Byzantines and then between the Byzantines and the Arabs. Living on the strategic crossroads of east-west and north-south trade routes and in the fertile and rich lands of the Anatolian plateau had caused the peoples of central Anatolia, both natives and newcomers, to find new methods of shelter. The Iconoclast movement of the Eastern Orthodox Church in the eighth and the ninth centuries contributed significantly to this as well. It literally meant going underground.

An entrance to a typical underground city such as Kaymakli or Derinkuyu, well concealed on the surface, leads down steps to a modest chamber five meters below the surface. A gently descending tunnel starts at the other end of the chamber; approximately five meters down the tunnel is the first "security check point" with a room-like cavity on one side containing a round stone slab (about 1.5 meters in diameter and 50 centimeters in thickness), very similar to a millstone (Figure 5.18), that can be rolled across the tunnel to block the passage from inside. Its track is impressed into the bottom of the wall of the room-like cavity. The track ascends slightly toward the wall of the room; furthermore, when rolled to close the passage, a chord of the circular slab seats itself in a slot carved into the other wall of the tunnel. In other words, the round stone, supported by the walls of the narrow tunnel on both sides, cannot be moved in either direction, nor pushed or pulled open. This means of passage-blocking is repeated about every ten meters along the tunnel in the first fifty to sixty meters of a typical burrow. As the tunnel descends deeper and as the tributary tunnels branching from the main one form a network of passages, use of this blocking device decreases in frequency.

Branching tunnels go in all directions, with either descending ramps or steps, covering an area of several square kilometers. At some of the junctions of the underground "streets," or tunnels, are relatively larger spaces, or "squares," occurring at intervals of anywhere from twenty to fifty meters. Between the squares along the underground streets are the individual living spaces, divided with walls, columns, and irregular arches, providing privacy for families and rooms for storage. Most of these individual spaces are on split levels, very much in tune with the overall planning of the settlement, varying in size and shape. Almost all the rooms have special storage niches in the walls, in addition to separate storage areas, and into some are carved such furniture as sleeping platforms and tables, and cavities in the floors for large jars and other storage items. Winding down and descending further underground, the "streets" on either side connect not only living spaces but also such religious public spaces as chapels, churches, cemeteries, baptismal pools, wine cellars, and grape pressing chambers. Spaces serving religious functions, however, are encountered only after a certain depth is reached, at which the inhabitants must have felt secure: larger churches are generally hewed out at lower depths, reaching 85 meters in the case of Derinkuyu.

An underground settlement spread out over several square kilometers, reaching deeper than fifty meters and accommodating a few thousand people, poses problems in terms of air and water supply. Carefully excavated deep air shafts reach to the lowest levels from the surface. Some of the underground spaces are immediately adjacent to these shafts, almost spiraling around them; some are connected to the shafts with galleries. Because of a very low water table, the wells supply water at lower depths. A relatively constant and comfortable temperature, about 12 to 15 degrees Celsius, prevails throughout the year. Except for lighting and ventilation, the microclimate of the burrowed settlements, with their comparatively stable air temperature and humidity quite favorable to temperature regulation and metabolic processes of the human body makes them suitable as living environments (Huo, 1986). However, the inconveniences and discomforts they otherwise pose are obvious. In spite of the labor and hardship involved in removing tens of thousands of cubic meters of earth, this type of troglodytic settlement was not meant to be permanent. Such settlements were inhabited during periods of danger, for short duration at times and for longer periods at others, perhaps lasting several months. An abundance of storage rooms, elaborately hewn-out individual dwelling spaces, articulated carving details (especially in religious spaces), ventilation shafts and wells, and ingenious security devices—all carved underground—underline the determination of the Cappadocian people to survive. Digging deep into the pliant tuff certainly served far more than mere environmental concerns.

Cities in caves

While cave dwelling may have been both less prevalent and less central a phenomenon in Anasazi areas than in Cappadocia as indicated earlier, several outstanding (if perhaps atypical) large-scale cavate "urban" developments began to appear in present-day Arizona, Colorado, and New Mexico starting in the eleventh century A.D. But along with these cavates goes a *caveat*: contemporaneous with the developments in caves (e.g., Mesa Verde in southwestern Colorado) were a greater number of constructions "in the open" (e.g., the Montezuma Valley). On the other hand, eleventh century cliff dwellings were certainly not limited to the Anasazi (e.g., the Gila Cliff dwellings constructed by the Mogollon).

Cordell (1984), among others, suggests that late Anasazi settlements were representative of the more typical "aggregated" pattern of community development in contrast to the "short-lived and apparently fragile mechanism of regional interaction" represented by the Chaco system (p. 270). If so, then the later cliff dwellings were perhaps part of a scaled-down, post-Chaco organizational structure, representing, among other things, the disintegration of what may have been a far-flung trade and communication network. This may also have made the relative isolation (economic and otherwise) faced by cavate communities less important in proportion to the advantages afforded by this form of habitat.

Construction was completed at the major Chaco sites by A.D. 1120. During the late Bonito phase, between 1120 and 1220, some new construction was attempted at Casa Chiquita, Kin Kletso, and New Alto, but both population and the number of occupied sites in Chaco Canyon (even the few small pueblos built were of inferior construction) experienced a serious net decline: 282 pueblos were in use in early Pueblo III and 172 during late Pueblo III; during the same period, the number of occupied sites decreased from 400 to 221 (Hayes, 1981). Chacoan construction and, hence, the Chacoan influence on the forms of Anasazi material culture, appears to have ceased in 1132 (Jones and Cordell, 1985). The occupation of Mesa Verde caves had begun almost a century before (Wormington, 1978) and construction of the famous Cliff Palace began in the 1200s (Ortiz, 1979). Among the Kayenta Anasazi in what is now northeastern Arizona, Betatakin and Kiet Siel, both located in caves, appear to have been occupied for comparatively brief periods between about 1260 and 1284. The Aztec Ruin, built between 1100 and 1125 (Wormington, 1978), is located in the planar valley of the San Juan River — but an examination of the Anasazi "road map" indicates that it may have been, at least at that period, the largest outlier.

Early cave dwelling and above-ground settlement in Mesa Verde. Shallow pithouses whose antechambers were oriented to the south had begun to appear at Mesa Verde during the sixth century A.D.; they were of the "classic" form, typically constructed with wing walls with roofs supported by four posts, complemented with storage pits. Interior features included benches and circular hearths, usually lined with clay. While such pithouses, generally located on top of the mesas, predominated, some rock shelters continued in use.

Pueblos began to appear about 750 and the Mesa Verde Pueblo I period dates from then through the beginning of the tenth century. The large Pueblo I sites consisted of rows of adobe or jacal surface rooms: the rooms were roughly square in plan as were the associated pithouses. These large sites were also located on top of the mesas.

Early Pueblo II (900 to 1000) saw four changes occurring in the nature of Mesa Verde settlement; (1) the size of occupation sites diminished as (2) the space between sites increased and (3) slopes began to be occupied. Further, (4) circular kivas appeared, whose roofs were supported by four posts, and whose interiors contained *sipapus*, hearths, ventilator systems, and benches. Late Pueblo II sites (1000 to 1100) were characterized by improved masonry construction of both buildings and kivas: round towers were constructed and the size of kivas increased, the roofs of which were supported by six posts in place of four. Site locations became more varied, and it was during this period that sophisticated rock shelter architecture began to appear.

Isolated "cave-dwelling" phenomena have been noted in various parts of "Oasis America," the area comprising what is now the U.S. Southwest and northwest Mexico. Building in caves occurred in several locations surrounding the Casas Grandes site in Chihuahua: there are numerous examples in El Valle de las Cuevas (Guevara Sanchez, 1988) near Paquime and in Las Cuaranta Casas (Guevara Sanchez, 1984), slightly further south, the latter contemporaneous with Mesa Verde, and both possibly occupied until the fall of Casas Grandes. Johnson (1966) described cave dwellings in Sonora (in Arroyo Concho, a tributary of the Rio Bavispe) similar to those in El Valle de las Cuevas. Building materials used at these sites include rock, wood, and adobe; and many of the structures, like those of their northern neighbors, have T-shaped doorways. Domestically utilized caves have also been found in Zacatecas and in northern and southern Durango, particularly around the Alta Vista site mentioned later in this chapter (Hers, 1989).

Several of the cave dwellings in the Anasazi area, including the well-known Mesa Verde sites, are notable not just for their architecture but also for their size: they strike us as literal "towns in caves," but these examples, as earlier indicated, by no means represent a wholesale "return to cave dwelling." About 1150, coinciding with the cessation of Chacoan construction, village aggregation began to occur among the Kayenta Anasazi, and such "cavate towns" as Kiet Siel and Betatakin were built and occupied briefly during the latter half of the thirteenth century. Contemporaneous with these (but less visually striking) were the extensive cave dwellings in the canyons of the Pajarito Plateau, which continued to be occupied for a time after the abandonment of the Kayenta "cavate towns."

Mesa Verde, Kayenta, and the Pajarito are examined in more detail below.

"Classic" Mesa Verde. Early Pueblo III (1100 to 1200) saw the introduction of multi-storied buildings, more towers, interior kivas (especially keyhole kivas), and increasingly sophisticated agricultural and irrigation systems. The Mesa Verdean population peaked toward the end of this period, considerably after population began to decline in Chaco Canyon. The dominant influence over Anasazi culture had by then shifted to the Zuni area, although Mesa Verde sites north of the San Juan Basin, on Wetherill and Chapin Mesas, probably played an important role. Rohn (1977) suggests that rather than a single settlement dominating Chapin Mesa from 950 through 1300, the preeminent position passed from one site to another. After 1200, for example, the center of

population shifted from the Mummy Lake settlements (aided by the construction, probably between 950 and 1000, of an artificial water supply at Mummy Lake itself) to Fewkes and Cliff Canyons. During the thirteenth century (late Pueblo III), there were 33 sites, inhabited by 600 to 800 people, in Fewkes Canyon, including Cliff Palace which, with its 220 rooms and 23 kivas in a cave 125 meters long by 24 meters high by 24 meters deep, is the largest Chapin Mesa Ruin. There is little suggestion, however, either here or in the other Chapin Mesa groups characterized by large central sites, of the evidence of social hierarchy hypothesized at Chaco.

There are other substantial differences between the geographically close Chaco and Mesa Verde environments and cultures. Certainly, Mesa Verde was more lush, and its water supply, while not continuous, much more reliable than at any particular Chaco locale. Hayes (1981), in his comparative study of Chaco Canyon and Wetherill Mesa, found this apparent difference in carrying capacity reflected in site density, at least 2.6 times higher at Wetherill than at Chaco. Since many limited-activity sites may have been obscured, especially from aerial photography, by Wetherill vegetation and topography, the disparity was probably even greater.

There were disparities in architecture, and in the uses of architecture as well. Mesa Verde round rooms, presumably kivas, had above-floor vents in place of sub-floor vents, along with masonry deflectors and pilasters; single- or double-coursed masonry was employed instead of Chacoan core-veneer masonry; and underground burials were apparently more frequent (Vivian, 1959). Rohn's (1971) work on a 94-room cliff dwelling called "Mug House" suggested four levels of organization: (1) room suites (households); (2) courtyard units (a group of room suites clustered about a courtyard); (3) moieties; and (4) the larger community. Room suites at Mug House do not, according to Rohn, display the planned, simultaneous construction evident in Chaco settlements, but they do enclose (and use) space at the rear of the cave site. The roofs of the keyhole kivas doubled as courtyards for adjacent suites.

A wall divided the cave into two moieties and there are indications that construction of the southern segment of Mug House did not begin until the northern segment had reached considerable size. The larger community, here as elsewhere in Mesa Verde, is assumed to have been composed of such "central sites" as Cliff Palace (Figure 5.19) and Mug House, and adjacent smaller settlements. The larger communities display sophisticated architecture, masonry construction techniques, and water control systems, yet except for Knowles' (1974) analysis of Cliff Palace as an efficient utilizer of solar energy, there seems little indication at Mesa Verde of the physical planning or regional organization that apparently characterized both Chaco settlement and the "Chaco Phenomenon."

There are other distinctions as well. The northernmost site (outlier) reached by the Chacoan road system, some 50 kilometers straight-line distance from Mesa Verde, may have represented the northernmost reaches of the Chacoan trade system. However, some very recent data (reported in Lekson et al., 1988) suggests that the Chacoan road system may have been even more extensive, probing perhaps "as far east as the turquoise mines of Santa Fe and as far west as the Little Colorado Valley... as far north as the San Juan Range in the Rocky Mountains and as far south as the Mogollon Mountains" (p. 108). Thus, it is possible that yet-to-be-discovered "extensions" of the Chacoan road system did in fact reach as far as, or close to, Mesa Verde.

For a time it seemed that there was an astronomical significance to Mesa Verde architecture which paralleled that observed at Chaco, but this has since been disputed. Fewkes (1916) suggested that "Sun Temple," a mesa-top site at Mesa Verde, functioned as an indicator of the two equinoctial sunsets, and later (Fewkes, 1917), further claimed that the alignment of the front wall of Sun Temple was related to the summer solstice sunrise and winter solstice sunset. In a later study, Reyman (1977) confirmed the first but disputed the second. Reyman (1980) also disputed some of the hypothesized astronomical significance of Fajada Butte, Chaco Canyon, as suggested by Sofar et al. (1979).

Mesa Verde society is presumed to have shared some characteristics with the Chaco Anasazi. In fact, certain changes, including architectural changes, that occurred in Chaco Canyon between 1120 and 1220 are interpreted as the influence of Mesa Verdeans; these include aspects of the construction of Casa Chiquita, Kin Kletso, New Alto, and Tsin Kletsin, and modifications to Pueblo Alto and Pueblo Del Arroyo. Mesa Verdean double-coursed masonry and "keyhole kivas" began to appear, along with "pecked rock" wall facings, an increased number of burials, and — most importantly for our purposes here — the occupation of cave sites. This so-called "McElmo Phase" (Vivian and Mathews, 1965) has been alternatively interpreted as the result of actual *migration* of Mesa Verde people to Chaco during the twelfth century or increased economic affiliation between Chaco and Mesa Verde during and after the collapse of the Chacoan regional network, with the San Juan area (including Mesa Verde) perhaps succeeding Chaco as a regional center (Toll, Windes, and McKenna, 1980). Lekson (1984a) has put forth a completely different interpretation: "...the notion that McElmo sites represent site-unit intrusions from the San Juan is no longer tenable" (p. 69).

There is some continuity in Chacoan ceramic tradition suggesting that Chacoan residents were not wholly supplanted but that a mixing occurred between remaining Chaco residents and incoming Mesa Verdeans. There is, of course, the unexplored possibility that previous out-migrants from Chaco, perhaps departing during an earlier drought, returned to Chaco during a later, better time; it would be extremely difficult to confirm or to unconfirm such a conjecture. Whatever the case it is likely that there was considerably more interaction between Chaco and Mesa Verde than between either and the Kayenta Anasazi.

Other evidence comes from major "frontier" outliers of Chaco. One Chaco road runs north for a considerable distance, terminating at Salmon Ruin; another road begins at Aztec Ruin, heading northwest. Salmon is approximately midway between Chaco and Mesa Verde; Aztec is slightly closer to Mesa Verde. Both are referred to as "dual component" sites, since both display an earlier structure with clear Chacoan influences, and equally clear evidence of later Mesa Verde occupation. Kivas resembling those at both Chaco and Mesa Verde are found at Aztec (Lister and Lister, 1987). The Chacoan structure at Salmon with 290 rooms, appears to have been planned in three stages; construction, in Chaco style or core-veneer masonry, lasted from 1088 through 1106 (Irwin-Williams and Shelley, 1980). The secondary occupation of Salmon shows architectural changes in the direction of forms and styles more closely associated with Mesa Verde, beginning about 1130. Irwin-Williams and Shelley (1980) argue that in contrast to the architecture (or urban design) of Salmon's primary occupation, *the secondary occupation seems to lack coherent control and development*; indications are, in other words, that little remained of Chacoan planning, that Salmon had changed from a member of a *nucleated* system to an *aggregated* community.

Kayenta cliff dwellings. The Kayenta area of northern Arizona was another region of long-term Anasazi occupation. Pithouse villages developed between 200 and 750, with Pueblo I (750 to 975) and Pueblo II (975 to 1100) architectural developments roughly similar, in topographically varied settings, to those observed elsewhere in Anasazi country during the same periods. Aggregation of small communities into villages in the Kayenta area, however, lagged behind the same transition in Chaco and Mesa Verde. At about 1150, villages consisting of surface rooms arranged around an open courtyard began to appear, along with round (and even keyhole-shaped) kivas.

"Cities in caves" did not appear in the Kayenta area until toward the end of the thirteenth century. Kiet Siel (Figure 5.20) and Betatakin are outstanding but little understood examples (Dean, 1969). The area has been extensively surveyed (e.g., Jennings, 1966; Gumerman and Euler, 1976; Matson and Lipe,

1978; Powell, 1983) but the results of such survey have yet to be adequately synthesized (Cordell, 1984).

By applying dendochronology, Dean (1969, 1970) found that seventeen years intervened between the first occupation of Betatakin cave in 1250 and the construction of Betatakin "city" itself, in 1267. Three room clusters date from 1267 and a fourth from 1268; ten rooms and a kiva were added in 1275. Expansion then proceeded somewhat more slowly until a peak population of 125 persons was achieved some 20 years after the "city's" founding. An interesting aspect of Dean's work (1970) is the suggestion that the founders of Betatakin both anticipated and planned for in-migration to the cave in 1275. An obvious question is: from whence came these founders and in-migrants? At this writing, we do not know. Perhaps they came from somewhere intermediate between Chaco and Kayenta, such as the cave dwellings — Antelope House and White House — of Canyon de Chelly in eastern Arizona (Grant, 1978).

By the end of the thirteenth century, the cliff dwellings of Mesa Verde, Kayenta, and Las Ventanas, Chihuahua had been largely abandoned. At least some of the cliff dwellers joined the mesa-top dwellers of the Western Pueblos; while others moved east to the Rio Grande, which had been sparsely settled prior to the fourteenth century. Along the way they settled the cliffs of the Pajarito Plateau.

The Pajarito Plateau. We return now to one of the two locations that first excited our interest in this comparative study: the Pajarito Plateau of north-central New Mexico. Both it and the Cappadocian region of central Anatolia were formed by volcanic eruption and both were characterized by extensive areas of perforated cone-like volcanic tuff. Early Christians made their homes in the caves of central Anatolia, as described in the preceding chapter, and some Pueblo Indians in the cliffs of the Pajarito.

By A.D. 1175, small masonry pueblos had begun to appear on the Pajarito, with the now well-known "cliff-houses" established a quarter-century or so later. Behind the cliff-houses were often "cavate" rooms, carved into the soft tuff left by the volcanic eruptions that had occurred more than a million years earlier. Larger pueblos were established shortly thereafter and flourished until the great drought at the end of the thirteenth century.

Continued archaeological work has uncovered an enormous number of settlements, and many more undoubtedly remain to be discovered, but the 1,000 square kilometers of the Pajarito are now estimated to host 7,000 or so archaeological sites, or about 15 sites/square kilometer, some containing more than 200 rooms. The population probably numbered in the tens of thousands.

Cliff Hangers and Troglodytes 185

Hewett (1938) classified Pajaritan settlements into pueblos and cliff dwellings, and the latter into three sub-categories: open-front dwellings, excavated dwellings with closed fronts, and pueblo-like cliff dwellings. The large pueblos of the Pajarito Plateau are nearly all constructed of blocks of volcanic tuff. The blocks are large, ranging to over a meter in length, and laid in adobe mortar, which was also used to plaster interior walls. While Chaco pueblos were built with timbers sometimes twelve meters in length and a half meter in diameter, the diameters of Pajarito pueblo timbers rarely exceeded 15 centimeters. The blocks used in Chaco pueblos were smaller, and the overall effect more "finished," but this does not necessarily justify labelling Pajarito architecture a "degenerate" form since a finished appearance is much more difficult to achieve with tuff. In addition, masonry of volcanic tuff, by far, does not stand up to natural erosion as well as the Chaco sandstone: the result is that such Pajarito sites as Puye were found in a more deteriorated state than much older Chacoan pueblos. Against this must be set tuff's advantages of light weight, durability, and workability.

Puye, covering some 8,000 square meters, consists of four "houses" surrounding a court nearly a half hectare in area (Figure 5.21). The south "house" is detached from the court, providing entry from the east and west; it contains 173 rooms varying in length from 4 to 5 meters and in width from 1.5 to 3 meters. Other than fireplaces, the only interior features are sleeping ridges in the outer rooms, and doorways. The east house, less than half as large as the south house, has just one room containing storage bins.

Hewett's excavation in 1907 produced just one remarkable finding at Puye pueblo: three discs, or perforated stone rings, about 35 to 45 centimeters in diameter and 15 centimeters in thickness, were found, together with balls made of volcanic tuff, 4 to 8 centimeters in diameter. Hewett (1938) speculates that these are related to the ball game implements of pre-conquest Mesoamerica, the Casas Grandes region of Chihuahua, and possibly the Hohokam area of southern Arizona.

Puye is an example of a mesa-top pueblo on the northeastern side of the Pajarito Plateau. The Rio Grande Pueblos which claim descent from the Puye people (Santa Clara, San Ildefonso, and San Juan) all hold the surrounding mountains to be sacred, and few places provide so commanding a view as Puye. It was the largest by far (and a possible focus) of a number of villages, connected by Puye by a set of well-worn trails.

Opposite to Puye in topographic setting is Tyuonyi; while Puye is located on the mesa top, Tyuonyi is sited at the canyon bottom. Tyuonyi's form was roughly circular and its building material, volcanic tuff. (Figure 5.22). It was probably three stories in height at its outer perimeter. Hewett (1938) states:

Unlike the majority of large community houses in this region, this building was somewhat regular in construction. As a rule, these buildings seem to have grown by gradual accretions, single rooms or suites of rooms having been added to the building to meet the needs of increasing facilities. Here, *it would appear that the entire building was planned and built at once*. The curved walls were not produced by simply changing direction from room to room. The walls form curved lines. The thinnest part of the structure is at the southwest, where there is a flattening in the roughly circular plan due to the nearness of the creek. (p. 94; emphasis added).

The overall organization of Tyuonyi was apparently a courtyard containing three kivas and surrounded by tiers of rooms. There is only one break in the room block providing entry to the court from the east (the traditional direction of domestic entry among many Native American groups). The absence of doorways in the walls surrounding the court suggests that entry to the rooms was from the roof. The possibility that it was designed for defense was reinforced by Bandelier himself (1890, 1892), although reflection suggests that protection from animals and vermin is as likely an explanation as protection from human raiders. We will return to this issue later in the chapter.

Pajaritan cave and cliff dwellings are scattered around the plateau, but concentrations are found in three areas: Puye cliffs, Tsankawi, and Frijoles Canyon, in three forms: (1) carved dwellings without facades; (2) carved dwellings with rooms or porches added at the cavate entrance; and (3) houses of one or more stories built on the talus slope against a cliff face, and of which the cliff itself is the back wall, such as Talus House (Figure 5.23).

Ceiling beams of the last were seated in holes drilled into the soft cliff face. Stone retaining walls were built on the outside of ledges in some locations, and stairways connect cliff dwellings on the upper ledge of Puye cliff with the large pueblo above.

The north wall of Frijoles Canyon is a vertical escarpment, some 100 to 150 meters high. Against this wall are many excavated cliff dwellings just above the talus slopes. The largest of these groups of rooms is apparently a single continuous structure, originally 1 to 4 stories in height, extending along the north wall for a distance of more than 200 meters. Another much smaller group containing some 30 rooms and called Sun House is sited on a 50-meter terrace whose width varies from 3 to 5 meters.

In addition to rectangular rooms, there are a number of "cave kivas." The location of holes on the kiva floor indicates the presence of looms, and the origin of the still-extant practice of ceremonial weaving in kivas — all the holes, that is, save one:

Another hole, isolated from those in the rows, was found in the floor of nearly every kiva. In each of these a post was set. It always occupied a definite position with reference to the ceremonial opening in the kiva wall through which the sun's rays, entering and falling upon the post, produced a shadow which served to mark time. That it had such a function, I have been informed by trustworthy Tewa of the villages of Santa Clara and San Ildefonso. (Hewett, 1938; p. 92).

In Bandelier, kivas are located next to pueblos at the bottom of the canyon, adjacent to such mesa-top pueblos as Puye (and carved down into the rock itself), sunk into talus in front of cliff villages; or carved into caves along the cliff, isolated or in conjunction with other structures.

None of the Pajaritan kivas, however — nor, for that matter, any of the kivas at Rio Grande sites or sites in eastern New Mexico — resemble, in design details, the kivas of the Chacoan system, which ceased to exist between 50 and 100 years prior to extensive sedentary settlement of the Rio Grande area.

From whence came the Pajaritans and other settlers of the Rio Grande? "The sites of the Rio Grande and eastern New Mexico exhibit considerable variation in construction materials and techniques." (Cordell, 1984; p. 331). In the Pajarito case, the marked difference in available building materials may account in part for the absence of close architectural similarities to the pueblos and cliff dwellings of the San Juan Basin, such as Mesa Verde. But other sites, as well, display an absence

> ... of kivas and other architectural features that are closely similar to those of the Mesa Verde, which is also viewed as a population source for the Rio Grande pueblos... The major issue is that whereas the large, aggregated sites of the Rio Grande area do suggest a population influx, and the archaeological record of the San Juan Basin and Mesa Verde indicate that they are likely sources of population, there are no sites that are so closely similar to those of the population source areas that they can be considered evidence of a migrant community. (Cordell, 1984; p. 333).

Latter-day cliff dwelling: Analysis. In the fourteenth century, the Pajarito cliff dwellings were abandoned, never to be reoccupied. Most of the other sites in the American Southwest had been abandoned earlier, in stages (see next section). But a persistent question remains: why, in the first place, were these "new" cliff dwellings established?

At the onset, it should be noted that the "return to cliff dwelling" was limited in scope, and never represented more than part of the contemporaneous settlements in those areas in which it occurred. This means that "cliff dwellings" existed side by side with pueblos, to use Hewett's (1938) distinction, or rather, that cliff dwellings existed above and below pueblos.

A second major question is: why would people locate their dwellings so inconveniently, such that the inhabitants, in order to work the fields above or below and to secure water and firewood, would have to spend much of their time ascending and descending vertical cliff faces?

The first, most obvious, and still persisting explanation is "defense." Subsidiary questions include: defense of what, from what? The "of what" question is answered by the uneven distribution of subsistence or luxury goods, or of substantial surplus production in storage, if we assume that the defense required is from human marauders (defense from molestation by animals or vermin is another matter). If the "from what" question is answered by the threat of raids by "other people," there are three problems with the explanation:

(1) Not all settlements can be said to have been located defensively. Of the non-cliff-dwelling settlements (pueblos) extant in cliff-dwelling areas, a few, such as Mesa Verde's Sun Temple, Puye, and Tyuonyi show evidence of attempts at defensive architecture, but this is by no means universal. A response to this is possible *if* it is assumed that luxury goods or surplus product were present or stored only at certain sites: the defended ones. At present, there is little evidence to support this and much to refute it; Cordell (1984) indicates that crops and storage structures at Mesa Verde were located on mesa tops and could not have been defended by cliff dwellers.

(2) The most likely candidates for raiders, according to such writers as Gladwin (1957), are Athabascan in-migrants from the northwest. However, the Athabascans did not arrive in the U.S. Southwest until (at the earliest) sometime late in the fifteenth century, well after the cliff dwellings and their pueblo neighbors in Arizona, Colorado, and New Mexico had been abandoned. Furthermore, when the Athabascans arrived at the higher altitudes of the Southwest, they were small in number and, in proportion to the resident Anasazi, exceptionally poor candidates for the role of successful raiders until their acquisition of horses from Spanish colonists (Linton, 1944), which presumably did not occur until the seventeenth century. According to Schaafsma (1976) the seventeenth century is also the period of the earliest Athabascan archaeological material.

(3) If the hypothesized raiders were not in-migrants, they would have to have been other Anasazi. This possibility is suggested in Bandelier's classic novel *The Delight Makers* (1971/1890), and by Ellis (1951) and Davis (1965). The latter offer evidence that the "peaceful pueblos" may have been only a post-conquest phenomenon. But inter-tribal warfare appears to be an inadequate explanation for siting settlements in caves. As Cordell (1984) indicates, cave

Cliff Hangers and Troglodytes

dwellings offer no protection against ambush, a frequently employed form of limited attack.

The first explanation is climatic: in a widely varying climate, with hot summers and cold winters, caves offer a natural source of predictable shade, protection from wind and snow and — with clever prior planning — even an opportunity for maximizing solar energy in winter. (Knowles, 1974). This may relate to a reduction in available wood supply for fires, occasioned by earlier timber harvests and the need to clear additional land for food crops — both related to expanding population.

The second explanation involves energy. Two sources of energy must be considered: food energy (caloric intake) and human labor (caloric output). As population expanded, it may have been necessary to expand the amount of land devoted to agriculture; where arable land was scarce (as in most of the American Southwest and northern Mexico) it made little sense to use any of it for dwelling (Cordell, 1984). And if the need to cultivate more marginal land or to cultivate land more intensively meant additional labor input, then less labor would have been available for construction; using cave walls as building walls and for structural support would, under those circumstances, have been a more efficient use of labor.

The evidence available at the moment does not allow us to choose between the hypotheses advanced to explain the partial return to cave dwelling. They relate, however, to reasons advanced for the abandonment of *all* Anasazi sites, to be considered later in the chapter.

Building down, building up, moving out

Stories in stones

While dwelling in the hewn-out spaces in bluffs, cones, and burrows is the most striking feature of Cappadocia, extension of carved spaces with exterior masonry construction is also a conspicuous and a prominent characteristic of the region. In addition to carving into the rock, the inhabitants "built out," creating masonry structures actually adjacent to or detached from the rock. This constitutes the second major type of dwelling in this peculiar and outlandish landscape fashioned by volcanic violence and never-ceasing erosion. Blocks of pumice stone, quarried from the same rock that people have been carving into for millennia, were the primary material utilized to give form to rectangular exterior structure. Except for very rare cases wherein timber beams were used to span horizontal surfaces, even the floor system made use of the well-cut stones grouped in the form of arches to span the load-bearing masonry walls.

Thus the mass of tuffaceous rock is put to use once again; this time the process involved in transforming it to an architectural element is diametrically opposed to that of carving since a conventional construction process is involved. If carving as a subtraction process is considered "negative" space forming, then constructing as an additive process is "positive" space forming. While the two space forming processes, "definitive boundary elements," (Ozkan and Onur, 1975; p. 95), and the transformation involved in giving shape to their respective architectures are different in nature, what is common to the two is material appropriation to the purposive activity of making a place to dwell.

As with carved spaces, it is not certain when masonry construction started in the heartland of a landscape surmounted by pinnacles and perforated by isolated valleys with carvable rock faces. (Figures 5.24, 5.25). However, within the logic of the argument presented so far, we can surmise that the beginning of masonry construction was not as much for the purpose of forming "positive" spaces as it was to reinforce "negative" spaces. In other words, the most vulnerable parts of carved spaces—the surface openings, a product of landslides, erosion, or shearing—seem to have had support systems to prevent surface failures; therefore, before masonry as a construction method gave form to architecture other than carved spaces, it was employed as a support system in the form of a single arch, or a set of arches, to reinforce the architecture of hewn-out dwellings. In addition to overcoming possible surface failures, another reason that masonry construction may have come relatively late, especially to the rural areas of Cappadocia, was that people originally settled in the hidden valleys to escape and hide from authority, and/or from other enemies. The most concealed dwelling type is the underground settlement (e.g., Derinkuyu), and the next most concealed are dwellings carved in the rock faces and in cones; rectangular masonry structures are visually the most conspicuous architectural objects among the rock villages in the valleys, otherwise almost undisturbed by human-built artifacts. As long as there were reasons to hide and to escape, it was likely that inhabitants of rural Cappadocia would avoid building masonry structures, except, perhaps, for reinforcement purposes. (Figures 5.26, 5.27). However, masonry construction did exist in urban areas; and the people of rural Cappadocia were familiar with it.

After visiting the region at the end of the nineteenth century, Sterrett (1919) considered the masonry structures to be "facades," the facade being a "room which opens upon the street," "the only room with light" (p. 314), otherwise "nature-made apartment houses," (p. 281) "which extend horizontally into the bowels of the earth" (p. 312). Since they are not merely "facades giving entrance to the chambers" (p. 312), Sterrett's observation can only be interpreted as a figure of speech rather than an architectural fact. Regardless of their size and articulation, masonry structures were fully established, complete architectural entities, providing living accommodations with well-organized indoor and outdoor spaces. Well adapted to the rolling topography, in some instances to steep cliffs, most of the masonry buildings are two or more stories, allowing more than one entrance at different levels and on different sides, depending on natural contours and the position of streets (e.g., houses in Mustafapasa).

Common features of most of the prismatic forms, if not all, are carved rooms and built-out spaces. All the indoor and outdoor spaces are organized around a semi-enclosed space called *eyvan*, which serves as the main food preparation area (its oven dug into a hole in the earth — *tandir*) and also as the daytime living area. Enclosed on three sides, its ceiling supported by an arch (or a set of arches, depending whether it is totally or partially carved into the rock or freestanding with another type of connection to the carved spaces), the open end of the *eyvan* faces the courtyard. (Figure 5.28). The dimensions of the rectangular space range from about 4 meters to 5 meters in width and about 5 meters to 7 meters in length, with a ceiling height of 3 to 4 meters. Dimensions of other rooms are quite similar to those of the *eyvan*, with slight variations depending on the needs and exact organization of spaces. The number of *eyvans* may vary with the house size; in other words, there may be more than one *eyvan* serving different functions, while one, at least, housing the oven, is usually referred to as *tandir evi* (the oven-house), generally extended lengthwise into a carved space which serves as one food-storage area as well as a kitchen. (Figure 5.29). *Eyvans* may also function as the central circulation area which allows access to adjacent rooms and to the floor above. With its linear connection, the *tandir evi* /kitchen storage combination also provides an area for relatives and neighbors to socialize during the daytime.

Beyond the *tandir* (a hole in the floor roughly half a meter in diameter and depth, covered with a slab of stone when not in use), there are no other prominent objects in the semi-enclosed, arched space, except for cushions, pillows, and sometimes a platform, slightly raised from the floor, serving as the sofa. Most of the kitchen utensils are kept in the carved niches and on the carved shelves in the space next to the built-out *eyvan*. Further, in the hewn-out extension are more carved niches, shelves and special holes for earth containers storing food stuffs. Most of the houses still make use of the well in the courtyard for water supply; therefore, the designated kitchen area is quite different from the conventional. In terms of its use and function, the *tandir evi* /kitchen storage combination is also extended to include the courtyard as well. (Figures 5.30, 5.31).

While a distinction has been made only between carved and composite (carved masonry) dwellings as the two major types of placemaking in Cappadocia, Erencin's study shows many variations (216 among 410 houses) of the composite type of dwelling in one settlement — Avcilar — alone (1979; p. 53-103). In spite of these rich variations, derived from the combined use of carving and masonry construction, there is an incredible amount of standardization in dimensions, from the scale of the cut stone to the types and sizes of arches, and from the window/door openings to the floor spans and heights; there is also a strict geometrical order derived from the order of the carved spaces and from characteristics of the material related to structural and constructional considerations. Although there is not a distinctive plan type at the courtyard level, a typological attempt has been made in another study ("Ortahisar" ; p. 59-60) on the basis of the presence or absence of a room built with masonry construction: (a) *eyvan* plus a carved space, and a built-out room; (b) *eyvan* plus a carved space, with no built-out room. The upper story is closer to the conventional spatial organization because of its "constructed" nature; therefore, it is easier to establish a typology related to plan layout: (a) one or two rooms without an *eyvan*; (b) different combinations of rooms with an *eyvan* (most notably the "split-belly plan" — rooms on either side of a central hall, in this case the *eyvan* — otherwise known as the "Turkish house"). Both Erencin's study revealing the rich possibilities of architectural variations and the "Ortahisar" report, (p. 45-61), in which a typology is proposed, suggest the following as the major architectural elements to be considered in a study of placemaking in Cappadocia: carved-out spaces, built-out spaces (masonry construction), courtyard, *eyvan*, specialized and non-specialized spaces, decorative elements, window/door openings, arches, and massing of units. While these provide a helpful physical picture of the abodes, they supply an incomplete description; we interpret this as a conceptual reconstitution of the dwellings and the settlement, not only in terms of spatial and material characteristics but also in terms of the social relations of the actual "building process."

First, these examples of vernacular architecture indicate that there are specialists in construction and that people as users do not often build entirely by themselves. Second, the vernacular builder emerges as a skillful craftsman, a consummate designer, and a comprehensive planner endowed with a rare combination of visual delight and intellectual stimulation, while providing a design solution not only for the immediate present and the specific client he is serving but also for the future and the broader society. This is where the vernacular designer/builder draws upon the legacy of the collective significance of traditional architecture. Architecture of masonry construction in Cappadocia, with its rectangular geometrical order, its efficiency and rationality in the use of material, and its modest but elaborate decoration owes as much to the craftsman's skill as to the architect's imagination, vision, and knowledge. Therefore, the vernacular builder is a craftsman, an architect, and a planner. (Figures 5.32 to 5.36).

Third, within a particular mode of production and set of social relations, the nonvernacular builder works in a participatory manner in which the "client" is involved at every phase of the design/construction process. To arrive at 216 variations among 410 buildings, using the same material, working with highly standardized dimensions and components, making use of relatively few architectural elements, is neither a simple achievement nor an indication of the whims of the vernacular builder. It is a response to specific conditions and needs, to creative participatory processes, and to fine craftsmanship. These are matters of relationships: the relationship of life to the organization of spaces, of geometrical composition to the site, of ornament to the structure, of open spaces to enclosed spaces, of the construction technique to the material, of individual/ family identity to social identity.

"Building out" seems a logical and rational response to the problem of creating a more habitable environment to reduce or eliminate the disadvantages of carved dwellings. It certainly goes beyond dwellings hewn only out of rock. However, building out was achieved only when social relations permitted its realization, that is, only after the need for hiding from hostile authorities and other enemies was over. When the central authority was strong enough to protect its citizens, including those in rural areas, there was no need to seek dwelling underground. But this meant submitting to something new in return for protection—paying rent; slightly different types of authority allowed more religious freedom but required economic and political subordination; the newly emerging central power even allowed the peasants a sort of ownership. In contrast with the collective life and collective ownership manifested by the early troglodytes, new social relations, structured on private ownership together with the provision of security for lives and property, allowed some of the former troglodytes to build out in return for the payment of rent to the new lords.

As is characteristic of social relations and productive forces in a fully developed feudal mode of production, artisans and craftsmen such as stone masons, carvers, and builders, who specialized in construction, emerged. More than is the case with other trades and arts, these builder/designers had to work closely with users in order to respond to specific needs as much as to save on labor. Their services were paid in some form, enabling those who could afford to live in masonry structures to leave their carved dwellings. Building out also became a symbol of social respectability among the people of the newly stratified rural society. In other words, in the almost unstratified social system of collective existence, equality extended to the dwellings as well; with private ownership, regardless of the ultimate proprietorship of the means of production, social stratification was manifested in the places people lived, as at Hacilar several millennia earlier. Stratification that existed in urban areas and its concomitant manifestation in built environment began to affect placemaking in the hidden valleys of Cappadocia, which had once reflected equality in the dwellings carved into the rock.

Whether through size or decorative elements, the builder was required to express the owner's status in the society. Not surprisingly, the larger, more prosperous, more trade-oriented settlements had most of the masonry structures; these were also the embryo towns on the way to assuming eventual control of other smaller settlements. Both economically and politically, the new towns were still subordinate to the larger urban areas. Not only were there hierarchical relations between settlements but also within settlements.

For rural Cappadocia, the transition was from an entirely closed society, living in a collective economy characterized by little exchange with the outer world, to a relatively open society whose trade included agricultural produce, animals, and handicrafts, allowing more contact and exchange with people living elsewhere. The emergence of a secure minority who appropriated a share of the surplus allowed the transformation of this surplus into commodities.

In the built environment, this development was reflected in the differentiation of dwellings. While the house itself remained primarily without exchange value for a long time, collective life was, for ideological reasons, being replaced by individual estate feudalism. Bigger estate owners dwelt in the larger urban areas; the rising mercantile class formed the middle group between the wealthy landlords and the not-so-wealthy producers. Within the area, previously part of rural Cappadocia, small settlements, such as Urgup, Ortahisar, Uchisar, Avanos, Mustafapasa, and Avcilar, started gaining importance as trading centers and began differentiating themselves from the other remote settlements both in population and in wealth. The major connection of the larger urban areas — Kayseri, Nevsehir, Nigde — to the rural hinterland was established through the emerging small towns, which had direct access to the even smaller villages forming the urban hinterland. The earlier hinterlands of emerging cities, expanding both in size and population, needed to have control of larger areas.

This transformation, which occurred primarily during the twelfth and the thirteenth centuries A.D., was accompanied by a shift from primarily religious to more secular communities. The Turks arrived in Anatolia in 1071 from the east, and spread gradually over the peninsula. Along with the imposition of political control and new culture in large cities, towns, and villages, the new religion — Islam — was spreading among the urban and rural populations.

Cappadocia was no exception to this. While the smaller villages accommodated either Christian or Muslim populations, larger villages, towns, and cities accommodated not only members of both religions, but also Jewish people. Rather than ideological identity, economic structure constituted the basis of the developments of extraordinary settlements in the striking landscape of Cappadocia, which previously sheltered communities unified through ideology and collective existence. Settlements near the major trade routes grew faster, becoming important trade and cultural centers. With this growth and development, architecture also flourished within given material and environmental limitations.

In spite of certain decorative elements, the plainness of architecture in Cappadocia almost borders on austerity. The passion for simplicity and unassuming geometrical order among vernacular builders is not a whimsical choice but something determined by material conditions and the tradition shaped by those conditions. Flat roofs, whitewashed stone walls, controlled use of such forms as arches and facade decoration, are direct responses to the needs, environmental conditions, and social demands of the time. As components of "boxy" compositions, all of these seem as if they were precursors of the modern minimalist aesthetic. However, production of this architecture was unpretentious; architectural form was not detached from architectural content to give the former primacy over the latter. The house was not a commodity; since architecture as such had no independent existence, the builder was not alienated from his work in spite of designing and building for someone other than himself. Under the circumstances, environmental aesthetics were derived from building material, economy of scarcity, basic needs, canons of tradition, and pressing social demands: in short, from the relationship of design to everyday life.

The impressiveness of the unusual landscape and the striking geometrical simplicity of Cappadocia's architecture should not, however, be allowed to obscure the social relations involved in the making of places to live. Enhancing everyday life, which was the result not of choice but of social circumstances, took neither an architectural miracle nor a technological innovation. When social conditions allowed, surface architecture developed to supplement subsurface architecture. The latter continued in existence until the present, not just because the environmental conditions created were favorable — ecologically sound, energy efficient, and good for health — but because people could not afford to move out. The environmental advantages of carved spaces notwithstanding, social reasons were primary in some of the population remaining in the carved dwellings.

The emerging social relations of a feudal order clearly stratified Cappadocian society, allowing another minority to gain control over the means of production and to accumulate disproportionate wealth. While the newly developing social form led to the formation of new architectural content and concomitantly to considerably more advanced living places, hierarchically ordered spaces started to emerge within the new architectural form of the dwelling environment, and a hierarchical order appeared among dwellings.

The generation of new architectural form and spatial organization facilitated expansibility under specific conditions. Rationality and expansibility are those characteristics of architecture which are directly or indirectly associated with the material and spatial organization of architectural form, its external and internal modalities, and the construction process. (Figure 5.37). In the nascent form of Anatolian surface architecture, aesthetics involved both internal and external surfaces as well as overall form. For the "troglodytes" who had concerned themselves only with internal surfaces and relatively simple spatial layouts, surface architecture was a new experience and a new expressive form, not entirely without precedent, but achieved in the absence of accumulated firsthand knowledge regarding material, means of representation, sense perceptions, and modeling: the four components of the substratum of form according to Raphael (1968; p. 210-238). Although the material actually was the same pumice stone that had been used previously, its context and process were entirely different from those of carved dwelling. Also different was the content, i.e., associated, environmental, and social requirements, which set the agenda of the architectural program for the designer/builder. In this relational aspect of architecture the representation of content in a specific form determines universally valid, creative criteria. "If the content," writes Raphael, "is an experience rooted in objective reality, an experience revealed and completed in the process of artistic creation, it cannot be treated as a fixed, ready-made existent, such as might be 'recorded' or 'limited'" (1968; p. 226). Thus, the content that constitutes the architectural program reflects the society's conditions of existence manifested in architectural activity and form. This is the very point from which conceptual universality emerges, develops, and manifests itself in the particular (Raphael, 1968; p. 208).

It is in these architectural principles and values, the result of reflective judgments with objective responses as shaped by conditions of existence that one can meaningfully evaluate and compare the built forms of different places and even different societies. The nascent form of the composite placemaking process in Cappadocia, which incorporated carving and building, seems to have been strongly associated specifically with the use of the *eyvan* and with the overall layout principles of the later emerging "Turkish house" (Eldem, 1955). While this may be considered a natural consequence of physical and cultural proximity, different environmental conditions notwithstanding, there are striking similarities between composite placemaking in Cappadocia and in Tunisia, France, and China.

Between "abandonment" and conquest: pueblos of the fourteenth-sixteenth centuries

Abandonment of the San Juan Basin, Kayenta, and the Pajarito Plateau was the beginning of a locational transition: as old areas were depopulated, new settlements (Pueblo IV) were developed elsewhere: to the east, along the Pecos River, the Estancia Basin, and the Llano Estacado (beyond the southernmost extension of the Rocky Mountains), Pecos, Abo, Gran Quivira, and Quarai were among the now-abandoned villages that bridged the period from the end of the great drought through early Spanish occupation. The Western Pueblos include still-occupied Hopi villages, Zuni, and Acoma, all visited by de Coronado's expedition in 1540 (the beginning of the U.S. Southwest's "historic period," some 100 years after the probable arrival of the first Athabascan raiders).

Acoma is depicted schematically in Figure 5.39. Nabakov (1986) has presented detailed drawings of Acoma, showing the use of rooms on the ground floor for storage:

> ... in the average household more rooms (and total space) were devoted to storage than to living activities. For example, storage rooms in two three-story households accounted for approximately twice (about 80 square meters) the amount of room space used for maize grinding, living, and sleeping. Terrace areas in front of second- and third-story rooms at Acoma contributed an additional 10-20 square meters of space for communal activities such as cooking, but items were undoubtedly stored here, as well. (Vivian, 1990; p.444)

The Hopi use of pueblo terrace areas mainly for storage was noted by Mindeleff (1891). The general conclusion is that while space devoted to storage was in proportion to living space in historic Western Pueblos, at least at Acoma (1) all ground floor space was devoted to storage; and (2) storage space exceeded living space (constituting about 75% of covered space in Acoma). With reference to the preceding chapter, if this division of spatial function was typical of the earlier Chacoan pueblos, suggestions by Lekson (1984) and Windes (1984) that Chacoans were ground floor dwellers appear doubtful, and estimates of Chacoan living areas that equal or exceed areas devoted to storage are called into question.

West of Acoma, population shifts had begun to occur as western Cebolleta Mesa was abandoned in favor of presumably more defensible sites further to the north. Ruppe's (1953) finding of increased population in areas around Acoma suggests the possibility of immigration prior to 1400. Societal needs may well have been changing.

The most recent literature (1986-1990) sheds little additional light on the Pueblo IV period (Cordell and Gumerman, 1989; Gumerman and Dean, 1989; Vivian, 1990); like Pueblo II, it seems eclipsed by the fascinating and puzzling Pueblo III developments. Furthermore, while research appeared in previous years on the architecture of pueblos east of the Rio Grande whose occupancy overlapped the Conquest,

> ...little recent work has been done in Pueblo IV villages north of the Little Colorado River.... Excavations at Walpi... involve materials too recent to provide much information on the early protohistoric period. Earlier work in the 1800s and early 1900s produced large amounts of beautiful pottery but little in the way of information ... (Gumerman and Dean, 1989; p.127).

Pueblo IV overlaps what Cordell and Gumerman (1989) refer to as the "Aggregation period" (1275-1540), characterized environmentally by drought (Gumerman, 1988) and architecturally by very large sites which, in the western Anasazi area, were probable economic and social "focal" or "central" places. Relative homogeneity in artifactual styles and large quantities of trade goods have again suggested to some investigators a stratified society coordinated by an elite (e.g., Upham, 1982), but available data are once more insufficient to resolve the issues (see discussion later in this chapter). Gumerman and Dean (1989) propose an alternative explanation for western Anasazi developments in terms of cooperative societies; they also discuss possible relations between the probably new kachina cult (which, according to Adams (1983) may have been introduced in Pueblo IV, from the Mimbres — El Paso — Casas Grandes area) and environmental degradation, which made issues of rainmaking and fertility more critical to the Anasazi.

"Aggregation" refers to concentration of settlement, many sites containing hundreds of rooms. But if these settlements were uniformly large, they were heterogeneous in layout. There are sites (1) without central plazas, (2) with roomblocks enclosing plazas, and (3) with parallel blocks separated by plaza-like spaces (as at Acoma). Pueblo V (contemporary) sites are also characterized by heterogeneous construction materials and techniques; the nineteen Rio Grande Pueblos are predominantly adobe and the Western Pueblos stone, reflecting differences in the availability of durable construction materials.

An interesting sidelight, which we cannot consider here in detail, is placemaking in post-1540 frontier New Mexico mountain villages: Spanish adaptations of Pueblo IV architecture, construction, and material, and the transplantation of vernacular architecture, evolved in one cultural setting to vernacular production in another. Hanlon (in press), for example, suggests the origin of the Spanish mission church neither in European or evolving Mexican architecture, but in the pueblo kiva!

Certain Pueblo IV sites were surrounded by low walls, suggestive of weak fortification, but this practice was not ubiquitous. While we are quite sure that Athabascan raiders had not yet arrived in the American Southwest at the time of late Pueblo III abandonment, we are considerably less sure what nomadic groups were in the area just prior to the arrival of the Spanish. However, there seems little justification other than defense for the siting of Hopi villages (the only remaining contemporary Pueblo V settlements in Arizona) or Acoma Pueblo itself (Figure 5.39) on the tops of inaccessible mesas, far above the cultivated valley floors. Their defensible position may have served them well in more than one respect, as the Spanish influence over the Western Pueblos seems to have been markedly less than over those located in the more accessible Rio Grande valley.

Research biases and vexing questions

The architectural record examined in Chapter Five has expanded our list of unanswered questions presented in the last chapter, especially in the case of the Anasazi. Therefore, this section will emphasize those troublesome pueblo builders. Because so much research has been done on Anasazi society (as opposed to Anasazi artifacts) in the past five years in comparison with what went before, we will depart from our earlier emphasis upon built form and placemaking to examine the possible nature of Anasazi society as a whole, as revealed in this most recent work. As a preface, it must again be stressed that the new directions revealed (or old directions redefined) since 1985 have served mainly to sharpen the issues, rather than to provide definitive answers. It is not our knowledge of pueblo architecture, therefore, that has expanded so much as our capacity to seek alternative *interpretations* of that knowledge. Thus, we view this part of Chapter Five not as a digression, but as necessary illumination of what has gone before.

Biases in Anasazi research. A number of researchers into American Southwest archaeology and pre-Colombian architecture have recognized other conceptual, theoretical, and methodological biases in the interpretation of the Anasazi record, some of which are here elaborated:

(1) Positively-skewed distributions (Reid and Whittlesey, 1990). There is an understandable tendency to consider rare cases as "special"; thus, Chaco

Canyon and Mesa Verde have probably received more attention than the thousands of other Anasazi sites put together, and Casa Rinconada, more note than many hundreds of smaller, less visually impressive kivas. Similarly, the rare case is often viewed as more important, more significant; thus, the relatively few Anasazi burials associated with substantial quantities of luxury goods are seen, because of their rarity, as "elite," and as evidence of a hierarchical society. Note that this criticism does not hold in the case of the interesting work of Ravensloot (1988), which draws data from a large number of Casas Grandes burials rather than from a few unusual examples.

(2) Assuming that available data is representative of missing data. That, for example, extant Aztec codices do not show pochteca trading with northern peoples is cited as evidence against the "pochteca theory" of Anasazi-Mesoamerican interaction; apparently neglected is the destruction of a majority of these codices in the sixteenth century by the Spanish.

(3) Measuring, and then asserting (implicitly, of course) that what can be measured is what is important (Johnson, 1989): examples are numerous throughout social and behavioral science.

(4) Confusing complication with complexity, and complex social organization with the necessary existence of hierarchy (Upham, Lightfoot, and Jewett, 1989). This is a subtle bias, well-rooted not just in anthropology, but in cross-cultural and developmental psychology (e.g. the "organismic-developmental" theory of Werner, 1948) as well. In Anasazi research, cloudiness generated by earlier confrontations between "egalitarians" and "hierarchists" seems to be clearing and giving rise to an alternative to both lineage and elitist models of climax Anasazi society, as elaborated later in this chapter.

(5) Tribalism (Pailes, 1989). Although no one has spoken about Anasazi "tribes" in the literature, the implicit concept of "tribe," as in the contemporary American Indian context, seems to have percolated downward through time, influencing the once-pervasive notion that the Anasazi must necessarily have been egalitarian. Wolf (1982) warns against "the uncritical equation of the bands, tribes, or chiefdoms described since 1400 with the societies existing before European expansion and even before the rise of the state" (Wolf, 1982, p.76), while Fried refers to the tribe as "a secondary sociopolitical phenomenon, brought about by the intercession of more complex ordered societies, states in particular" (Fried, 1975, p.114). Pailes states simply that "so-called tribes are actually the creation of modern colonial states with no indigenous counterparts" (Pailes, 1989, p.215), a position with which Devalle (1991) concurs.

(6) Political boundaries as research boundaries. The frontier between the political territories of Mexico and the United States is the result of political treaties of 1848-1853, but it seems to have established intellectual territories as

well. Mexican archaeologists, for the most part, have concentrated their attention on Mesoamerica south of Tula, attracting the interest of many North American archaeologists and architectural scholars; the interest of other North Americans has tended to stop on the northern side of the border, leaving a large gap in between. There are exceptions, of course: a few intrepid U.S. scholars (e.g. Di Peso, Doolittle, Kelley, and Wiegand) have done valuable primary research in Sonora, Chihuahua, Durango, and Zacatecas, and their efforts have been joined in recent years by Mexicans such as Cabrero and Lopez Lujan (drawing heavily upon the work of their North American colleagues). Exactly how much this hypothesized "cognitive gap" has contributed to the paucity of data that can be brought to bear on possible Anasazi-Mesoamerican connections cannot, at this point, be determined.

(7) Misuse of ethnographic analogues (Cordell and Gumerman, 1989). In the absence of a written record, and when the present residents of an area claim unbroken and unaltered cultural preservation since before the conquest, it is attempting to interpret puzzling, prehistoric culture in terms of the present. The Spanish *conquistadores*, comparing the pueblos they encountered with the Tarascan and Aztec state-level societies they had conquered earlier, and with Spain itself, stressed the egalitarian nature of the former; but the archaeologists who followed in their footsteps centuries after went a step further, attributing egalitarianism to the Anasazi ancestors of the modern pueblos as well:

> Archaeologists tend to interpret the prehistoric Southwestern villages as though they were integrated by the same organization and ideological structures as are the modern pueblos.... [I]nterpretations... based on assumed continuity must... be reevaluated. (Cordell, 1984, pp.238-239).

There has been considerable criticism, recently, of what we, and others, have called the "ethnographic analogy" (e.g., Schelberg, 1984). Its roots may be traced in part to the reports of early contact; and in part to the reports of those who, in doing archaeological work before there was such a science as archaeology, and in trying to understand societies with no written language, used ethnographic information to aid in the interpretation of prehistoric ruins (e.g., Bandelier, 1890, 1892). These archaeologists were working within a nineteenth century theoretical framework which stressed unilineal evolution and homogeneous levels of development among all American Indian cultures; dendochronology had yet to be developed as an aid to calendrical dating, and the architecturally visible evidence was obvious and compelling: the most impressive remains of the Anasazi did indeed resemble the modern pueblos (Cordell, 1984). Finally, as Lekson indicated in a personal communication in 1985, some archaeologists and anthropologists came to act as informal advocates for Pueblo Indian land claims in the twentieth century. To an extent, these claims were based on both antiquity and continuity of habitation in the area. Such claims were strengthened by assertions not just of continuous occupation, but of continuity of culture, assertions which seemed well-founded in the evidence then available. Continuity of habitation remains unquestioned, but the "ethnographic analogy" *in toto* has been undermined by more recent findings.

A second and opposite manifestation is the creation of an ethnographic present in terms of supposed characteristics of a past culture, as when aspects of a cultural revival are justified by current interpretations of revered but only partly understood preliterate ancestors. A third form is the projection of historical fictions into the past, and one example is "spurious sedentarism" (e.g., Johnson, 1989; Lekson, 1990; Powell, 1990). In the early part of the century, archaeologists defended the land claims of modern pueblos through demonstration of continuity of residence. Later, they extended this laudable but politically motivated interpretation of the ethnographic present back in time to the Anasazi period; data on Pueblo III aggregation, the resemblance of great pueblos to modern pueblos, and associated dendochronology were used in support of "deep sedentarism":

> The very architectural clues that things were, to say, the least, unusual at Chaco inflate the impact of their dendochronology; the massive, multi-storied building (with consequent excellent preservation), overtimbering of roofs, profligate use of wood in every building context, all combine to ensure that the tree-ring sample from Chaco will be disproportionately large, and thus disproportionately compelling (Lekson, 1990; p.338).

Clearly, this variety of the ethnographic bias is closely tied to positively-skewed distributions; unusual architecture is again given much more attention, and more weight as evidence of, in this case, sedentarism. Lekson (1990) indicates that absence of burials and of large trash middens is frequently ignored or pushed into the background, and furthermore, that "to aggregate things must first be dispersed," citing evidence that if the Anasazi were ever actually dispersed, aggregation occurred long prior to Pueblo III (i.e., aggregation may be correlated with, but is by no means solely indicative of, sedentarism).

(8) The "Primitive Mind" (e.g., Levi-Bruhl, 1978; Werner, 1948). At one time it was assumed that non-Western people were nonrational, and therefore superstitious; and that they were practitioners, above all else, of ritual. This produced an understandable tendency to classify any architectural spaces, whose use we were not sure to be "ceremonial." Beyond this, it seemed unnecessary for earlier scholars of vernacular architecture to look at the social underpinnings of architectural achievement because they "knew" that they were

dealing with simple members of simple "unself-conscious" societies producing "architecture without architects" (see critique by Stea, 1990). Certainly, differences among peoples, among their conceptions of space (e.g., Pinxten, 1980), influence architectural conception and production, but difference by itself should not imply hierarchy of relative complexity, nor superiority or inferiority of the other.

A U.S. National Park Service employee once commented to one of the authors that if the Anasazi had spent as much time on ritual as the number of "ceremonial space" labels would indicate, they would have starved to death from lack of cultivation time. Our Western tendency to conceptualize religion separately from production may account for our failure, until recently, to perceive multi-purpose public spaces correctly.

Some vexing questions. Research into preliterate societies often yields puzzling questions to which, at best, only partial answers can be provided. In the Anasazi case, particularly significant general questions include the following:

(1) How and why did population movements occur, and how were they related to the nature of settlement (settlement initiation, in-migration, out-migration, abandonments)? If abandonments in fact occurred, where did the outmigrants go?

(2) What, if any, was the economic and informational relationship and associated exchange system — before, during, and after the Chacoan era — of the Anasazi (a) with other cultural groups in the American Southwest; (b) with present-day northern Mexico; (c) with the Mesoamerican frontier; and (d) with the Mesoamerican heartland?

(3) What was the actual nature of climax Anasazi societal organization? Was it egalitarian, hierarchical, or something else? How does the available evidence relate to a model based upon evolution in modes of production? This may be the most critical question of all.

Moving out: Anasazi abandonments

The following section deals with migrations among the Anasazi prehistoric pueblos, and out-migrations, which seem to have occurred beginning in the twelfth century A.D. As there are a number of possible interpretations concerning what the "Chaco Phenomenon" was about or even whether it was a "phenomenon" at all—so are there several alternative views of the "abandonment" of the great pueblos—including whether abandonment, as such, occurred at all. Possible interpretations are interwoven into the relatively scant data currently available. Those which follow from our theoretical model are indicated, and further elaborated in Chapter Seven. Contrary interpretations — those currently favored by a majority of anthropologists/archaeologists and anthropologically/archaeologically-oriented architects — are indicated as well at the end of this chapter. The questions "why abandonment?" and "whether abandonment?" are clearly still open, but we hope that our discussion will shed some more light on this important phenomenon.

"Abandonment" is a relative concept. In fact, the Anasazi region of the U.S. was not "abandoned" uniformly nor has all of Cappadocia been continuously occupied. There are still living pueblos, similar in form to some of the Anasazi megastructures, not far removed from Chaco (Zuni), the Pajarito Plateau (Santa Clara, San Juan, etc.), and Kayenta (Hopi). In Cappadocia, some carved dwellings have been occupied more or less continuously but not by the same people; others have been abandoned (e.g., Goreme, Zelve); still others are new.

Abandonment: the concept. Basically, "abandoned" means simply that "people don't live there anymore." But abandonment can occur in many ways:

(1) abandonment can be sudden or gradual—it is important to know whether people have moved out all at once, over a very short period of time, or in small groups over a considerable interval;

(2) abandonment can be evacuation of a single site, a local area, or an entire region (Cordell, 1984);

(3) long — or short — distance movements or migration may be involved. People may move to adjacent or nearby places (as happens in tropical areas using "slash-and-burn" agricultural systems, a well-understood phenomenon), or they may move far away;

(4) the "base state" (length and character of occupancy at the original site) is important. "Abandonment" implies being previously sedentary someplace for a period of time; we do not speak of "abandonments" by nomadic tribes, for example. Even "sedentary" is a relative concept: how long must people have occupied a place before they are considered sedentary?

(5) abandonment can be temporary or permanent. Occupation of certain sites was discontinuous, even periodic. How much time must elapse between sequential occupants before a site is considered "abandoned"?

(6) abandonment may or may not be correlated with population decline in a given area depending upon the *scale* at which abandonment is examined. Single site or local area abandonment may represent a population *shift* rather than a population *decline* for a larger region. Population declines, thus, may often be more apparent than real.

Anasazi abandonments. Single site abandonments were common among the prehistoric Anasazi, so much so that Parsons (1939) spoke of the "semi-nomadic" character of pueblos. This contrasts markedly with occupation patterns in, for example, Anatolia. For small Anasazi pueblo sites, the mean length of occupancy was less than 35 years; for all sites, about 80 years (Hantman, 1983). Moreover, numerous local areas were inhabited briefly or intermittently (e.g., Matson and Lipe, 1978).

We shall restrict our attention, for simplicity, brevity, and maintenance of focus, to large-scale regional abandonments. Cordell (1984) divides the explanations proposed for such abandonments into two categories: *cultural* and *environmental*. Among the explanations classified as cultural are those involving warfare with Athabascans (supported by Gladwin, 1957 and rejected by Linton, 1944; Schaafsma, 1976; and Brown, 1979). This is the reason often given as well, as indicated earlier, for the re-establishment of cave dwelling, following certain local area abandonments. It is still a popular explanation. Jonathan Haas (reported in Weisberg, 1985), for example, used a computer model to "predict" the location of previously undiscovered cliff and rock-face dwellings using, as predictor variables, those topographic characteristics most favorable for inter-site communication and defense. This was based on the assumption that such pueblos were established for defense, but not from immediately adjacent pueblos:

> ... accessible locations that had unimpeded views of other such locations seemed the most likely possibilities.... Because of the visual communication system, Haas was able to determine that the pueblos did not make war on their neighbors, but rather on more distant peoples (Weisberg, 1985; p. 9).

Other cultural explanations include factionalism, internal strife, and epidemic disease. The first of these fails to explain large-scale regional abandonments, while the second lacks any supporting evidence at all. The last relates, once again, to the hypothesized breakdown of an even larger-scale regional system centered in Mexico; we shall return to this later. Environmental explanations for abandonment center about the concept of one or more "great droughts"; such explanations date back to Hewett (1913), whose suggestions predate the more contemporary dendochronological research strongly indicating that severe droughts had in fact occurred. A particularly severe drought, between 1276 and 1299 in the northern San Juan area, coincided with certain large-scale abandonments. But this seemingly *prima facie* evidence, too, fails to account for other phenomena occurring simultaneously, including the establishment of *new* large communities (e.g., Kiet Siel) in the drought-stricken area (at the same time that others were abandoned) and *declines* in population among settlements in areas of highest rainfall.

But the "great drought," while at most a contributory factor, has had some heuristic value in leading to work on the *cyclical* nature of droughts in the area of the Colorado Plateau. The prehistoric peoples of the arid Southwestern U.S. were certainly no strangers to drought and had undoubtedly developed various techniques for coping with situations of markedly reduced rainfall. What *may* have failed, however, was a set of strategies based upon the assumption of a certain *amplitude* and *periodicity* to such droughts. Data collected by Slatter (1973) and Jorde (1977) suggest that low-amplitude, high-frequency variations characterized the pre-900 and post-1150 Colorado Plateau area. However, between 900 and 1150, the period of evolution of the most sophisticated agricultural and hydrological systems, as well as of the most advanced urban and regional architectural and economic development, cyclicity was characterized by high-amplitude, low-frequency variation. It is during this period that systems of adjustment to drought appropriate to larger populations and a more complex society were probably established. If so, such systems of adjustment may have proven inadequate or maladaptive in the face of changed patterns of rainfall/drought periodicity, which may also have affected "nucleated" and "aggregated" settlements differently.

Some recent discoveries of a most unique sort by Arizona-Sonora Desert Museum scientists Betancourt and Van Devender (Jaroff, 1992) provide additional evidence of depletion of Anasazi timber for construction and firewood, with corresponding farmland erosion, some 800 years ago. This conclusion is based upon a study of packrat middens in the area of Chaco Canyon. Specifically, the data consist of vegetation deposits associated with desiccated fecal matter.

Stress explanations: "pushes" (but no "pulls"). Attempts to explain large-scale "abandonments" of Anasazi pueblos may have been limited by certain biases: conceptual "blinders," so to speak. The "ethnographic present" analogy is a bias which has been mentioned before and will be referred to again later on. The "sedentary pueblos" bias may be a derivative of the "ethnographic present" bias, especially when contemporary pueblo societies are contrasted with their Athabascan neighbors; but, as mentioned earlier, the archaeological record seems to indicate that the prehistoric pueblos were actually rather mobile. If, however, operating from this bias, one takes sedentarism and a strong desire not to move as a baseline, it seems natural to stress "push" factors, such as the cultural and environmental explanations summarized earlier, as the causes of abandonment. It ought to be possible to differentiate explanations for abandonment along a dimension complementary to the cultural-environmental dichotomy, perhaps labeled the "push-pull" dimension. All of the explanations put forth in the previous section are of the "push" variety, actions and events that might have forced the Anasazi *out* of their dwellings and settlements. Emphasis solely upon these push factors, and upon *reactions* to cultural and environmental stress, has elicited considerable concern in certain scholarly quarters:

> I do think Southwesternists should beware of trying to explain too much by the "reaction to stress" model, and should be thinking hard about economic, social, and other factors which may generate their own developmental drives, which need not necessarily be augmented by environmental changes in order to lead to dramatic socio-cultural transformations (Cowgill, 1974; p. 38).

Therefore, it behooves us now to consider, however briefly, those "pulls" which may have existed in the economic, social, or natural environments of the time.

The "Mesoamerican Connection"

> Two streams of Mesoamerican influence were carried into North America after A.D. 1000. One of these may have been brought by Toltec colonists and traders into the arid Southwest. There the newcomers influenced the Hohokam, who lived on irrigated farmlands in the Gila River Basin, and the Anasazi of the Colorado Plateau, known for their large multihousehold complexes supported by intensive cultivation with irrigation and terracing. Most of the characteristic Southwestern ceremonial art derives from the end of the Toltec period (almost A.D. 1300) and appears to be a fusion of the Mesoamerican cult of the rain god with local religious traditions (Kelley, 1966). Soon afterward, however, the frontiers of sedentary life contracted sharply, as increasing aridity and warfare made it more difficult to occupy marginal agricultural areas. (Wolf, 1982; p. 68).

In earlier chapters, reference has been made to the likelihood of contact — perhaps prolonged contact—between the Anasazi and at least one of the cultural groups of Mesoamerica. The most likely candidate is the Toltecan society once centered in Tula, at the northern edge of the Valley of Mexico. Evidence for the contact hypothesis includes trade goods (particularly so-called "status" objects), architecture (as far north as Chaco's Chetro Ketl), and, for certain researchers, the kiva murals, which flourished in those pueblos founded between the "great abandonment" period and Spanish conquest: between the fourteenth and sixteenth centuries (Di Peso et al., 1974; Hibben, 1975; Brody, 1979).

To some scholars studying the issue of pre-Columbian contact, it seems reasonable to believe that this contact involved some degree of commercial exchange, and with that, the exchange of information. (Figure 5.38). Thus, it appears likely that those Anasazi involved in this exchange knew something about the conditions of existence of the Mesoamerican society or societies with which they interacted, of its products at least and, possibly, of its standard of living as well.

Mathien and McGuire (1986) present two earlier prevailing positions concerning the interaction or noninteraction of the Anasazi with other, more remote, societies, as follows: (1) that the American Southwest "was an island isolated in the sea that developed in its own right, taking on only those things of Mesoamerica that were tossed up on its shore like driftwood or brought by infrequent or sporadic voyagers across the sea" (Mathien and McGuire, 1986, p.1). The "sea" referred to here is the "Chichimec Sea," that vast, culturally little-known area of what is now northern Mexico, inhabited at the time by groups of semi-nomadic peoples who have been labeled "Chichimeca"); (2) that the American Southwest was the northernmost outpost of the great Mesoamerican civilizations. Such a categorization is, of course, specific to the Southwest and bypasses hypothesized (but empirically strongly-supported) relationships between the prehistoric civilizations of America's Mississippi valley and Mesoamerica (Wolf, 1982). Regarding the Southwest, the two positions indicated above have been called "isolationist" and "imperialist" respectively; during the twentieth century, archaeological thought has oscillated between one and the other, with some adopting a middle-ground, or "interactionist" perspective (Riley, 1986).

What is in question, currently, is not so much the *fact* of interaction, but the *mechanism*, the nature of the economic system, and the extent of the network over which it operated (Mathien and McGuire, 1986). More than a decade ago, Kelley and Kelley (1975), relating to ideas formulated earlier by themselves and Di Peso (1968a,b; 1974), among others, postulated that long-distance traders from Mesoamerica had taken control of Chaco between 1030 and 1040. Such long-distance traders have been given the label *pochteca*, by analogy with the Nahuatl name for such long-distance traders in the later-emerging Aztec society. The effect of this takeover was presumed to be the modification noted in the previous chapter: of socioeconomic organization, material culture, religion, and ritual from then until 1250 to 1300. Di Peso (1968a,b; 1974) had also seen the rise and fall of Chaco as tied to events further south among the Toltec and to a *pochteca* trade network operating through Casas Grandes, as well as to religious influence stemming from the hypothesized introduction of a Quetzalcoatl — or Quetzalcoatl-like — cult during early Pueblo III.

The hypothesized trade road between Mesoamerica and the Anasazi region may have been, at least in part, the same as the *Camino Real de Chihuahua*, the "Royal Road" that later conveyed the Spanish *conquistadores* and accompanying Catholic priests from the Valley of Mexico through the city of Chihuahua into what is now the United States, terminating somewhere north of present-day Santa Fe, New Mexico. Sauer (1932) termed this "the Road to Cibola" after the legend of the "Seven Cities of Cibola," whose fabled walls of gold inspired the greed of many *conquistadores*. In fact "the Road to Cibola" might have been several roads. (See maps, Figures 2.18 and 5.38). Another presumably paralleled the west coast of Mexico, entering the ancient Hohokam homeland through the present state of Sonora.

The archaeological evidence of the existence of these routes includes such trade goods as ceramics, copper, spindle whorls, cotton and cotton goods, tobacco, and smoking pipes. At some ancient settlements along these routes (such as Alta Vista, La Quemada, and Casas Grandes) there are notable similarities in architectural features: they appear to incorporate elements of Mesoamerican, Anasazi, and Hohokam architecture.

Though long-distance *pochteca* presumably required only oases and stopping places, the "*pochteca* theory" (first proposed by Ferndon in 1955, as reported in Kelley, 1966) has relatively few adherents. It seems more likely that any extensive trade between Mesoamericans and the Anasazi would have occurred through intermediary trading centers — perhaps with the aid of the "cultural mediators" described by Pailes (1990). The existence of sites that might have supported such centers has been known for some time, but, with the exception of Casas Grandes and La Quemada, mentioned in the previous chapter, these have received little serious attention until recently. This may be due to the "frontier bias" mentioned above or to the assumption that the Chichimeca were simply and entirely primitive desert nomads.

For the hypothesized trade connection to have flourished, however, intermediate centers would have had to gain something from the trading process: that is, they would have had to have been sufficiently advanced beyond the subsistence stage to produce and consume at least necessities and, presumably, luxury goods as well.

It now seems clear that there were sedentary as well as nomadic Chichimeca (Hers, 1989); and that advanced cultures did indeed flourish over a considerable period of time in the area between the Toltec Empire and the "Chichimec Sea" (e.g., Cabrero, 1989; Kelley, 1990). Outstanding among the cultures on the "Mesoamerican Frontier" south of Casas Grandes were the Chalchihuites and its Suchil and Guadiana branches east of the Sierra Madre Occidental, stretching from what is now northern Jalisco through Zacatecas and Durango to the Rio

Florida at the southern border of Chihuahua; and the Trincheras of northwestern Sonora (Braniff, 1990), west of the Sierra Madre Occidental, related to the Hohokam culture of southern Arizona. Northeastern Sonoran peoples also appeared to share cultural traits with Hohokam after 1100 A.D., as well as with Trincheras, and Mogollon, according to Johnson (1966), who also speaks of peripheral developments of Casas Grandes in this area, and of the resemblance of its architectural complexes to those of the American Southwest. Also mentioned is "the presence in southern Sonora and northern Sinaloa of a Huatabampo complex, which preceded the extension of Mesoamerican culture into this region" (Johnson, 1966; p.36).

Kelley (1966) wrote of two principal events linking the Southwest and Mesoamerica: (1) the southward and westward expansion of the Anasazi which, by A.D. 1100 to 1200, brought them to the frontiers of the Hohokam region, occurring at the same time as related peoples moved into the Mogollon-Mimbres area and the lower Rio Grande valley where New Mexico, Texas, and Chihuahua now come together; (2) establishment at Guasave, near the present Sonora-Sinaloa boundary, of a late Mesoamerican "Mixteca-Puebla" culture possibly introduced by migrants from central Mexico which, Kelley suggests, may have occurred prior to A.D. 1200.

Referring to the Alta Vista site north of Zacatecas (whole astronomical alignments are described in Brody, 1986), Kelley (1990) hypothesizes emigration out of this architecturally distinguished center at some time near the end of the first millennium A.D. "northwestward along the old turquoise trade route into the Southwest [U.S.].... The warriors leaving Alta Vista may [also] have fled southward ... or perhaps even further south to participate in the founding of Tula" (Kelley, 1990; p.488).

Harbottle and Weigand (1992) state that "Alta Vista... has the greatest turquoise workshop yet documented in North America" (p. 80). Nelson (1990) cites Weigand's (1977) suggestion, concerning La Quemada, of

> ... direct ties among Tula, La Quemada, and Chaco Canyon, implying that La Quemada and Chaco Canyon are part of a network constructed by the Toltecs specifically in order to acquire mineral resources. But, if our inferences are correct, La Quemada cannot have been an important nexus in such an economic network, and much less have been constructed to serve it. Chaco Canyon was occupied ... probably after the principal occupation of La Quemada (Nelson, 1990; p.526; translation by the authors).

The picture that emerges is not one of isolated subsistence but of continuous trade and information exchange among the cultures of "Oasis America." Whether such exchange extended to Mesoamerica rests on two criteria. One is a sufficient density of intermediate centers along the most probable trade routes: the central route, northward from Tula through Ranas y Toluquilla (Queretaro), La Quemada and Alta Vista (Zacatecas), Zape and Loma San Gabriel (Duranto), and Casas Grandes (Chihuahua); and the Pacific route through El Teul (Zacatecas), Ixtlan (Nayarit), and Guasave (Sinaloa). Kelley's (1990) reconstructed trade route map indicates better than ours a remarkable density of such potential centers, as does that drawn by Harbottle and Weigand (1992) of the U.S. Southwest-Mesoamerican turquoise trade. The second, and more difficult criterion is that these centers be occupied at the same time and contemporary with, or just prior to, the climax of Anasazi culture; the issue is one of dating, of radiocarbon dating in the Mexican sites vs. dendochronology in the Anasazi area. Nelson (1990) expresses doubts in the above quotation; Kelley (1990), as earlier quoted, feels that current dating in northern Mexico is "little more than educated guess work."

Pochtecas, progress, and "pulls." Having established the probability of Mesoamerican-Southwestern trade routes, and the further possibility that more than one existed, priority of use remains to be determined. The belief that the early Hohokam tradition comes from Mexico (Haury, 1976; Schroeder, 1981) implies a trade route west of Casas Grandes; Riley (1986) suggests that this trade route, from western Mexico through the Sonoran "statelets" of the time, returned to prominence between 1400 and 1600, after (and perhaps related to) the collapse of Casas Grandes.

Assuming — as seems likely — that trade or some system of economic exchange (periodic if not continual) was in operation between the American Southwest and Mesoamerica, disagreement exists concerning the *agents* of such trade. Were they actually *pochteca* analogues, long-distance traders coming directly from what is now central Mexico, or was there in fact a "middlemen" system? Kelley and Kelley (1975) clearly opt for the *pochteca* model, even suggesting that the great kivas of Chaco were *pochteca* headquarters in proposing that "...the great kivas were the actual base of operations for, and the creation of, *pochteca*... *the* archaeologically obscure (if not invisible) traveling salesmen of an expanding Mesoamerica..." (reported in Lekson, 1982a; p.p. 3,7).

Foster (1986) and others propose that actual travel took place over only moderate distances and was *intra*-regional rather than *inter*-regional, with exchanges not only of goods but of the carriers of such goods—the agents of trade—at places intermediate between the Valley of Mexico and their destination in what is now the American Southwest (Chaco Canyon in particular). Foster, indicating that Olmec and Teotihuacan long-distance trade considerably predated the period in question, suggests the possibility of trading groups from the Chalchihuites and Casas Grandes areas of Mexico reaching the American Southwest before 700. He cites evidence of social stratification in Mogollon settlements as early as 600, with status related to the presence of such nonlocal goods as rare items from Mesoamerica.

The question of the distances over which traders operated is of importance in determining the likely function and significance of large settlements located between Tula, or places south of Tula, and Chaco. If trade, in fact, took place through *pochteca* — *inter*-regional traders — then such sites as La Quemada (Zacatecas) and Casa Grandes (Chihuahua) were merely way stations: if trade was accomplished by *intra*-regional traders, then these sites were much more important points of actual exchange. In either case, however, it is quite likely, as earlier stated, that the exchange of goods was accompanied by exchange of information (Upham, 1986). Thus, as Foster (1986) states, "...local leadership at Chaco were dealing with or had knowledge of markets to the south." The issue comes down to the following two questions: did the *pochteca themselves* enter the Southwest (Whitecotton and Pailes, 1986)? Was the Southwest then, playing the role of periphery to the Mesoamerican core (or, was "the southwest... at best a periphery of a periphery") (McGuire, 1986)? The "strong" interactionist position on these questions implies that the American Southwest and Mesoamerica were intimately tied together; Schroeder (1981) related the collapse of Hohokam and Chacoan urban societies to the collapse of the Chalchihuites culture in the middle-to-late 1100s.

Schroeder further suggests that the *pochteca* system may have functioned through Hohokam intermediaries in what is now southern Arizona, and that the Hohokam could have been the "contact people" responsible for introducing Mesoamerican architectural elements to Chaco after 1050; he points to the coincident decline of Hohokam, the collapse of the Chaco system, and the diminished use of the west coast corridor in Mexico after the late 1100s when, according to Di Peso (1974), the Casas Grandes corridor became the dominant route of Mesoamerican contact:

> Whether by pochteca or other means, wherever changes occurred in the "Chichimec Sea" they were relatively rapid and pronounced and not locally inspired.... [A]fter the entry of the Hohokam, we do not have to look for pochtecas to leap out of Mesoamerican centers to affect the Chacoan area, but merely to the Hohokam where the last most northern Mesoamerican footprints seem to have their imprint prior to Chaco's ascendancy. As Erick Reed used to comment... "It is too bad that the United States acquired the Gadsden Purchase. If they hadn't the Hohokam would have been in Mexico where they belong" (Schroeder, 1981; p. 56-57).

Another difference of opinion is related to the "tightness" of the economic system in which the Anasazi, at the stage of most advanced development, participated. One issue concerns whether subsistence and prestige goods circulated together or separately. The term "spheres of exchange" (Firth, 1965; Nelson, 1986) has been introduced to denote a system in which subsistence and prestige goods may not be mutually exchangeable. Fried (1967) suggests that especially in ranked or stratified societies, status-linked objects may actually circulate in a restricted fashion, but the data are equivocal. McGuire (1986), Upham (1986), and Whitecotton and Pailes (1986) deal with a second issue: the possibility that the Anasazi participated in a *world system* (Wallerstein, 1979, 1982), probably centered in Mexico:

...There is increasing evidence that commercial systems involving considerably more than mere "prestige" exchange existed in Mesoamerica in the Classic and early Postclassic periods and that Mesoamerica constituted a world economy, not simply a world system with luxury exchange among elites, well before the elaborate market and exchange systems known from ethnohistorical accounts of the late Postclassic (Whitecotton and Pailes, 1986; p. 192).

Whitecotton and Pailes also argue against the notion that no "archaic" or non-European system could have achieved the complexity of a European world economy existing in the sixteenth century, an argument which, according to them, fallaciously implies "that some models must be used for some human societies while other models must be used for other human societies" (1986; p.199). Mathien (1986), however, finds the actual evidence unconvincing, asserting that the hypothesis that Chacoans participated in a world system, whose core area was in Tula, La Quemada, or some city south of the Tropic of Cancer, remains essentially unsupported.

Evidence indicating the possibility of ranked, stratified, or possibly proto-tributary Anasazi society includes a hierarchy of settlement types and sizes (Schelberg, 1984); the apparently organized construction evidenced at the sites of Chacoan great houses, requiring both advanced planning and a coordinated labor force (Lekson, 1984a); village turquoise workshops producing presumed "luxury" or "status" goods (Mathien, 1984; Harbottle and Weigand, 1992); the distribution of ceramics (Toll, 1984) and chipped stone (Cameron, 1984); evidence of high-status burials among the Anasazi and their neighbors (Kidder, 1958; Frisbie, 1978); and other indications of differential access to resources. Indeed, the Anasazi displayed many of the phenomena listed by Polgar (1975) as associated with transition from kin-ordered to tributary modes of production, including more specialized architecture, more sophisticated defense systems, and the availability of considerable surplus labor.

But the reports of early Spanish contact presented a different picture. Illustrative is the diary of Gaspar Perez De Villagra, who wrote in 1610: "We visited a good many of these pueblos.... They live in complete equality, neither exercising authority nor demanding obedience."

Certainly, the early colonial period had an effect upon the pueblos; had no societal change occurred previously, the ravages of widespread disease, particularly smallpox, the trauma of enslavement during the sixteenth and seventeenth centuries, and the attempted imposition of alien religious and sociopolitical ideas should have altered the nature of pueblo society and culture — and, by implication, its mode of production. But shifts within or between modes of production may have occurred considerably earlier, even before contact was first made in 1540.

Schaafsma and Schaafsma (1974) suggest that the still-extant "kachina cult" entered the American Southwest early in the fourteenth century. Brew (1943), and Kelley and Kelley (1975) put forth the possibility that kachina practices may actually be based upon Mesoamerican ceremonialism through the cult of Quetzalcoatl (hypothesized to have been introduced at the start of the Pueblo III period). McGuire (1986) provides a most intriguing argument along these lines, tying the kachina cult to the decline of trade with Mesoamerica, to abandonment of the San Juan Basin great pueblos, and to kiva ceremonial art: He disagrees with the argument advanced by some that late Anasazi society was hierarchical (proto-tributary mode of production); the social transformation and the crisis cult he describes are seen as occurring *within* the kin-ordered mode of production. But he also states:

> A decrease in production would have... threatened the prestige goods economy of the San Juan Basin Anasazi societies... [forcing] elites to modify their expenditures and lose power or to become more demanding in their extraction of surplus from the primary producers.... [T]he second could lead the populace to dispose of the elite (McGuire, 1986; pp. 257-260).

We will come back to the latter point later on.

McGuire's argument incorporates three important elements: (1) late introduction of the kachina cult (shortly before the beginning of the historic Pueblo V period); (2) introduction of the kachina cult from Mesoamerica; and (3) ejection of the Anasazi elite.

There is some evidence to support the first contention and none advanced, to our knowledge, to counter it. The second has been more debatable; the third, while in certain ways the most interesting, has received hardly any attention. Supporting evidence might shed light both on the possibility of "regressions" in mode of production and the hypothesis of a migratory stream starting southward at the end of the thirteenth century: such a *southward* path might have been trod by just these exiled elites.

While McGuire denies that the Anasazi had achieved a tributary mode of production, his argument is based upon the presence of a prestige goods economy, characterized by inequalities:
> Prestige goods economies are based on the association of political power with control of access to foreign goods.... Such economies are most commonly associated with kin modes of production and may link kin and tributary modes. (McGuire, 1986; p.251).

Complexity, hierarchy, and placemaking

There is a long history in Southwestern anthropology of correlating observed changes in architecture and settlement pattern with hypothesized developments in social and political organization (Vivian, 1990; p.435).

Here, we return to the fourth "research bias" and third "vexing question" mentioned earlier. The recent literature on Anasazi and neighboring contemporaries (e.g., Upham, Lightfoot, and Jewett, 1989; Minnis and Redman, 1990) is clearly replete with conjectures concerning ranked vs. stratified societies, and models based on Melanisian big men and Polynesian chiefdoms, etc. (Pailes, 1990). A detailed consideration of all the ramifications is clearly beyond our scope.

The conflicting views presented in the preceding section suggest possible confusions among "simplicity," "complexity," and "hierarchy" in the sense that the kind of complexity represented by Chaco seems necessarily to imply — to some, at least — a hierarchical society with a coordinating elite. The evidence of the past five years that seems further removed than ever from the concept of a simple kin-ordered mode of production in climax Chacoan society also provides inadequate support for conventional hierarchical structure; Gumerman and Dean state that "all scholars paint a much more variegated portrait of Anasazi society than had previously been observed" (Gumerman and Dean, 1989; p.137), while Johnson concludes that "if evidence for the presence of ranked or stratified social groups is not very convincing, attribution of these processes to the activities of egalitarian groups as we usually perceive them does not seem to be a particularly appealing alternative" (Johnson, 1989; p.378). Johnson proposes a "sequential hierarchy" model, described below.

If an egalitarian society is defined as "one whose members have essentially equal access to critical resources and to a relatively unrestricted flow of information about these resources" (Gumerman and Dean, 1989; p.132), then resolution of the above may involve an alternative to the "equality/simplicity" vs. "hierarchy/complexity" dichotomy—egalitarian complex hierarchies. What form these could take has been explored, among others, by Vivian (1990), who states that "our great dependence on architecture for charting Chacoan development has lulled us into accepting essentially a single element for measuring cultural complexity and growth" (Vivian, 1990; p.329); he has suggested an interesting model which, because it draws upon Chacoan Anasazi placemaking, merits consideration here.

In fact, both Johnson's and Vivian's models are derived in large part from characteristics of Anasazi placemaking. The evidence for Johnson's "sequential hierarchy" derives from his observation that "these people were almost maniacally modular.... [T]he Southwestern distributions seem to contain very distinct size classes in which larger sites had sizes that were common multiples of smaller ones" (Johnson, 1989; p. 378, 380). He proposes:

> ... a model in which small kivas or ceremonial rooms represent a level of *sequential hierarchy* above the household where such matters as interhousehold cooperation and dispute resolution were consensually resolved in a sanctified context. If this were the case, then the larger "special function" structures common on large sites (great kivas, big houses, concentric wall structures, etc.) represented one of more levels above a small kiva or "household cluster" level. Large sites would then have been organized in terms of smaller "social modules." The settlement size hierarchies that seem to be so clear in some periods may provide a direct reflection of the size of different suprahousehold cluster social groupings. (Johnson, 1989; p.380, emphasis added).

Judge (1989) proposes a three-level hierarchy for classic Chacoan settlement, as does Rohn (1989) for the northern San Juan; Reid's (1989) data suggest a four-level hierarchy at Grasshopper.

Johnson also brings together — at least implicitly — two other important but previously unrelated suggestions under the umbrella of his incisive analysis: the cooperative society model of Gumerman & Dean (1989) and Lekson's (1990) critique of sedentarism vs. mobility. In the case of the former, Johnson, without contradicting the notion of cooperation, neatly handles the issue, raised by Gumerman and Dean, of conflict resolution. Concerning the latter, he indicates (implicitly, once again) that Lekson's contention that the Anasazi may not have been as sedentary as previously supposed is not incompatible with the existence of a complex society: "A combination of low resource availability, egalitarian organization, and mobility with periodic sedentary aggregation and organizational complexity is not unknown in the ethnographic record" (Johnson, 1989; p.382).

Vivian's model is dependent, in general, upon Chacoan architectural variability and two aspects of its spatial organization (symmetry and planning), and specifically, the existence of "great" and "small" houses:

> ... spatial organization of suites in tenth century great and small houses was similar, but there were significant differences in suite and site scale. This pattern changed during the eleventh century to one marked by continued differences in scale but also significant variability in planning and symmetry (Vivian, 1990; p.430).

The obvious conclusion is that great houses were occupied by elite members of a "conventional" hierarchical society, in the usual sense of the term. But Vivian continues:

> If these patterns are real, planning and symmetry may be more reliable indicators of a great house architectural tradition than scale.... [If so], arguments for a great house-small house architectural continuum and rank-scale relationships have less empirical support (Vivian, 1990; p.430).

What is most often thought of as a hierarchical society is called a "simultaneous hierarchy" by Johnson (1982, 1989), in which a relatively small segment of a population makes most of the important decisions. "Sequential hierarchy," on the other hand, "is a structure for the organization of consensus among basic egalitarian aggregates of increasing inclusiveness" (Johnson, 1989; p.378). Vivian (1990) speaks of a "consensual sequential hierarchy" involving scalar changes in the decision-making unit, in which nuclear families and extended families *rotate* decision-making functions during the year; smaller units are thus integrated into larger ones when it is necessary to make consensual decisions at a higher level.

In other words, a rotating sequence hierarchy is a structure for "taking turns" at regular and predetermined intervals; those who are "leaders" at one point in time are "followers" at another. Such a structure allows things to be achieved in a society which are best accomplished by a hierarchical structure while building in a system of (sequential rather than simultaneous) "checks and balances," which prevents the continuous accumulation of power by any individual or societal segment. When "averaged" over longer time intervals, however, this structure may appear, to the external observer, to be a simple form of egalitarianism, perhaps contributing to the misleading conclusion that the society is much less complex than is in fact the case.

"Dualism" and placemaking. Based on the work of Ortiz (1965, 1969) involving eastern Tewa Pueblo "dual organization," Vivian then proposes a *rotating sequential hierarchy* for Chaco, wherein decision-making powers were trans-

ferred regularly between approximately equivalent units (a duality, emphasizing horizontal instead of vertical decision making), rather than from smaller to larger units within which they are embedded. Dozier (1960) suggested that sociopolitical systems observed in the organization of ethnographic Tewa (among whom kinship, according to Dozier, plays a functional role at the level of the household but not at that of the community) — and possibly Keres — might be of great antiquity.

Returning to Chacoan architectural variability, great and small houses seem to exemplify parallel development in suite form, joined suites, and the ways in which residential units are related to such architectural features as kivas. Some earlier writings (e.g., Lekson, 1984b) have proposed the existence of two scales of houses as evidence of stratification, and that the two were related within a single stratified system. Vivian (1990), however, differs, proposing that "small house sites were domiciles of a localized lineage whose nuclear families inhabited individual suites within the structure," while great houses were occupied by groups consisting of several extended families separated by walls without connecting doorways, "multiple households organized as a single corporate body on the basis of several aspects of dualism embodied within a rotating sequence hierarchy" (Vivian, 1990; p.p. 445,447). Vivian suggests that toward the end of the eleventh century, some great house groups may have aggregated in Chaco and Aztec, citing as evidence the wall partially enclosing the complex formed by Pueblo Alto, Pueblo Del Arroyo, Pueblo Bonito, and Chetro Ketl. He summarizes his argument by hypothesizing:

> ... that two essentially egalitarian sociopolitical bodies with diverging cultural traditions evolved simultaneously in the central (Chaco) Basin from at least A.D. 400. These traditions are identified as San Juan and Cibola.... Though the two bodies evolved along diverging cultural trajectories (expressed most visibly in great and small house settlement patterns) and functioned semi-independently throughout the Basin, they maintained economic, social, and ritual links that were expressed most clearly late in the Chacoan sequence when San Juan great house populations were established in Cibola small house settlements.... San Juan social relationships were founded on a principle and process of dual organization.... Cibola social relationships were embedded in the lineage and functioned through the lineage for the duration of the Chacoan presence in the Basin (Vivian, 1990; p. 449).

The plausibility of this hypothesis is supported by the suggestion that "coresidence of social modules of very different backgrounds should have been typical in a 'sequential' Southwest" (Johnson, 1989; p.383). This hypothesized complex pattern of sociopolitical relationships functioned, according to Vivian, to facilitate changes in "organizational trajectories" necessitated by climatic change.

Bridging the gap

In Chapter Five we began by examining the prehistory of cavate dwellings and troglodytic settlements in Anatolia—some of which are still occupied—and of late cavate dwellings in the American Southwest, and the eventual abandonment of the latter. In the process, a number of interesting questions came to the fore, particularly regarding the Anasazi, including why various large settlements were abandoned, and what trade, informational, and other connections existed with Mesoamerica.

Finally, while it seems clear that late Cappadocian society was hierarchically stratified, the record is much less clear in the case of the Anasazi; old adherences of researchers to simple kinship-ordering has given way and, while some evidence points to a prototributary mode of production in the Classic phase, it is by no means convincing. An alternative to both simple egalitarianism and simultaneous hierarchy has been presented here: dualism embedded in a rotating sequence hierarchy.

In an odd and interesting way, this third alternative may tie the divergent Anatolian and Anasazi case studies together. Here we quote Johnson (1989) once again:

> We have garden variety "chiefdoms" and "early states" stacked ten deep under the lab table, but elaborate sequential hierarchies may have been a rare phenomenon. Catal Huyuk in Anatolia ... with its pueblo-like architecture and numerous "shrine" rooms may have been an early Old World example (Johnson, 1989; pp.386-387).

The implications of this exciting possibility — that Catal Huyuk and its later Chacoan counterparts may both be representative of this rare phenomenon of rotating sequential hierarchy — are further explored in Appendix Two.

Figure 5.1 Cappadocian dwellings in cones.

Cliff Hangers and Troglodytes 221

Figure 5.2 Cappadocian cave and constructed cave dwellings.

Figure 5.3 Presently occupied cavate dwellings in the town of Urgup.

Cliff Hangers and Troglodytes

Figure 5.4 Ruins of cavate dwelling and church.

Figure 5.5 Contemporary cavate dwellings in town of Mustafapasa.

Cliff Hangers and Troglodytes

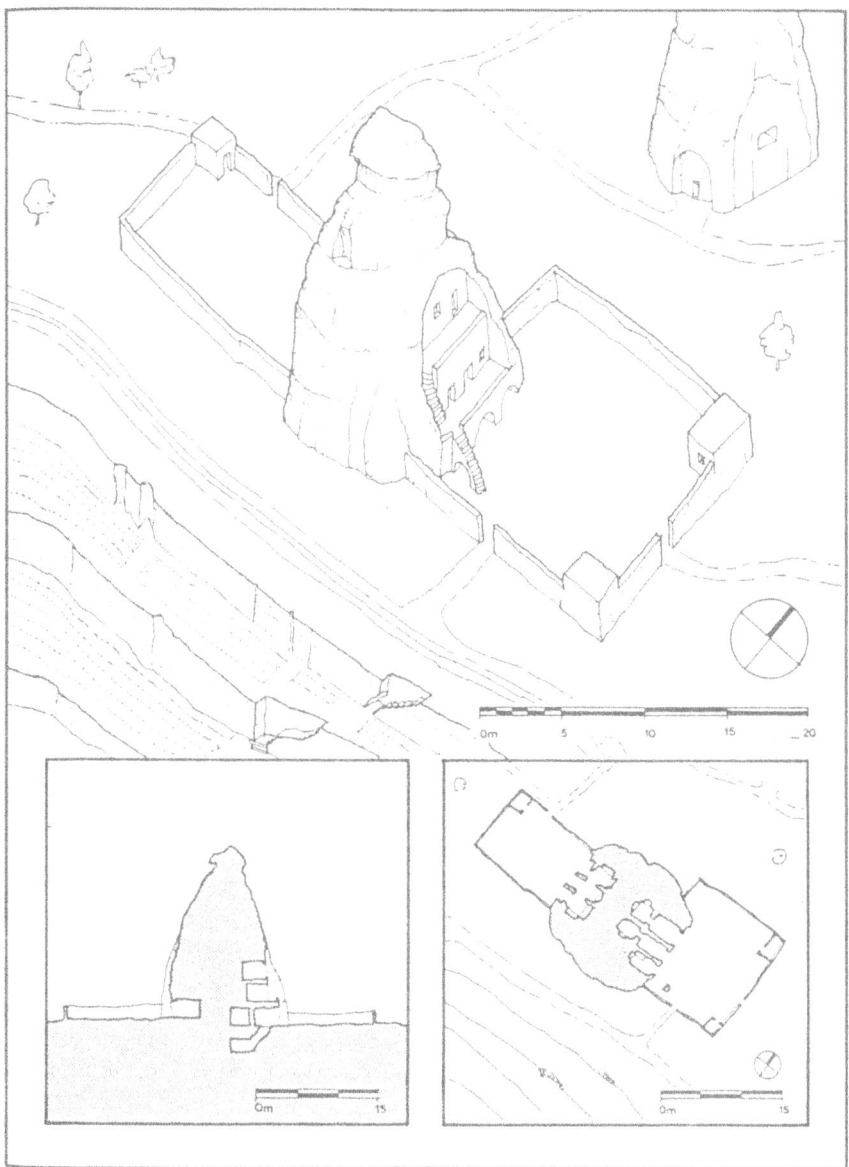

Figure 5.6 Contemporary carved structure in free-standing cone.

226 Cliff Hangers and Troglodytes

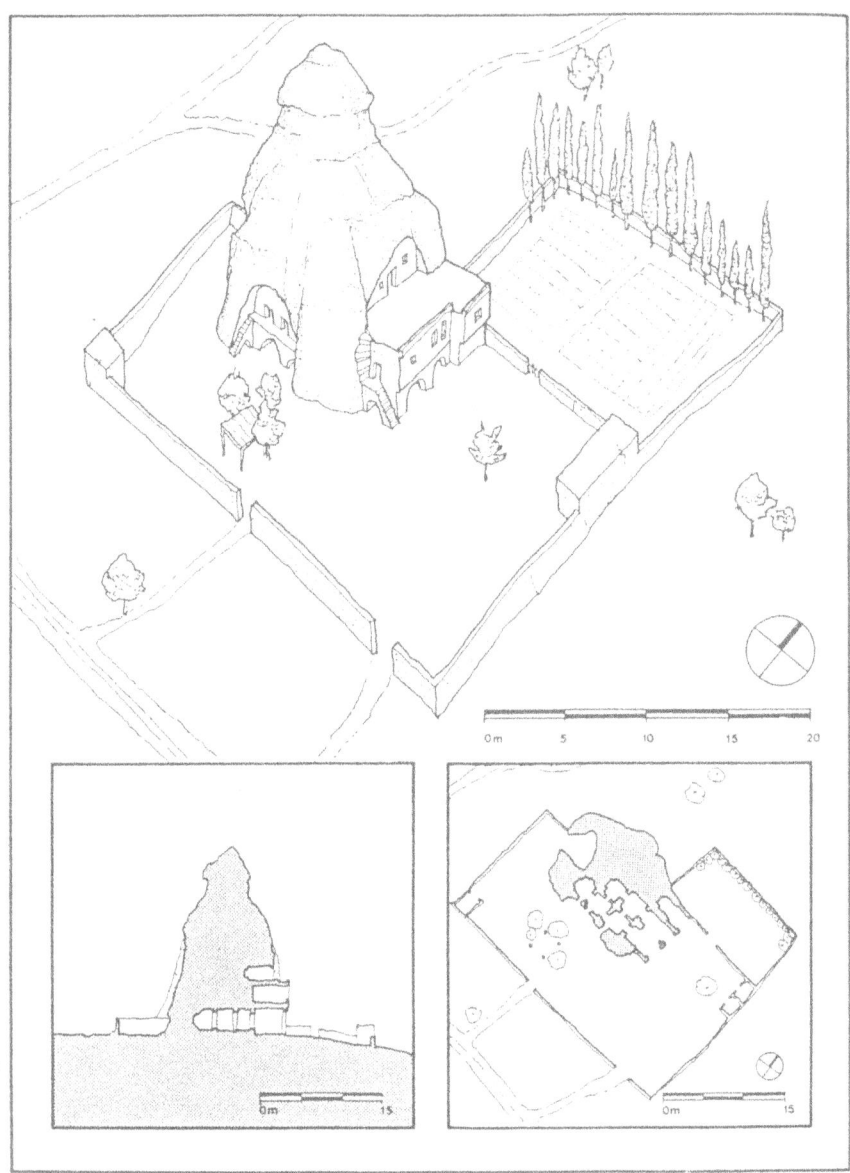

Figure 5.7 Contemporary structure: a combination of carving and dwelling.

Cliff Hangers and Troglodytes 227

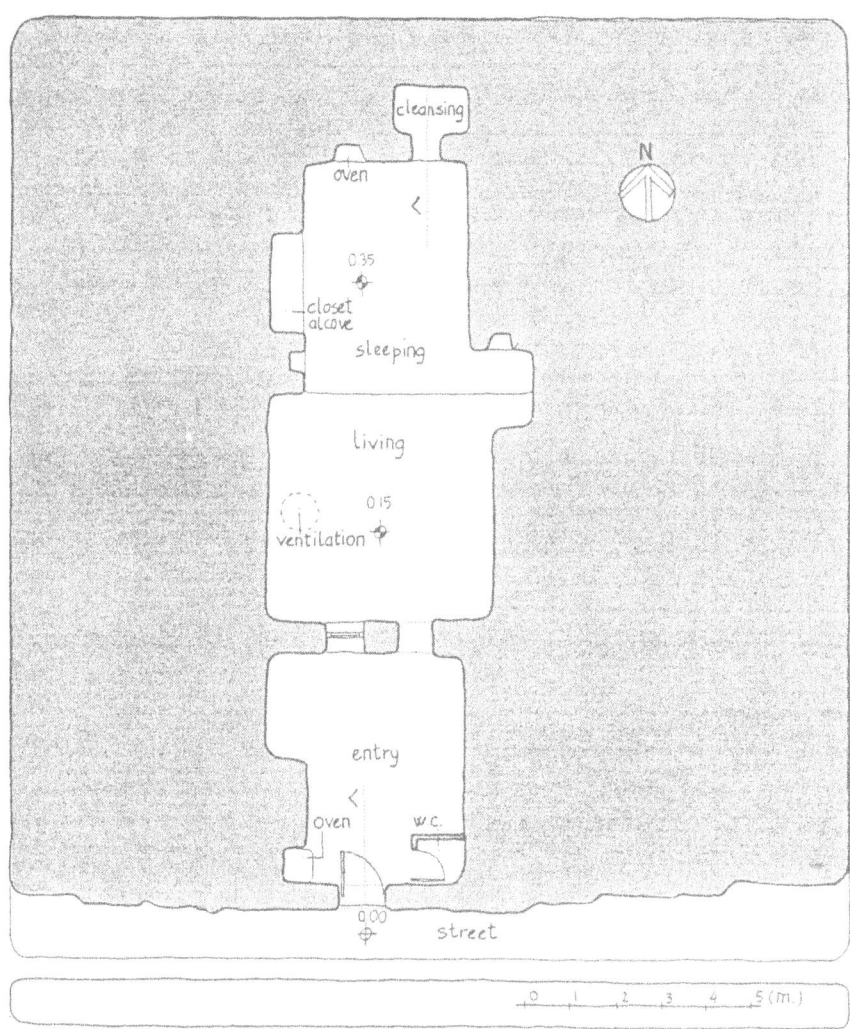

Figure 5.8 Plan of carved dwelling, Urgup.

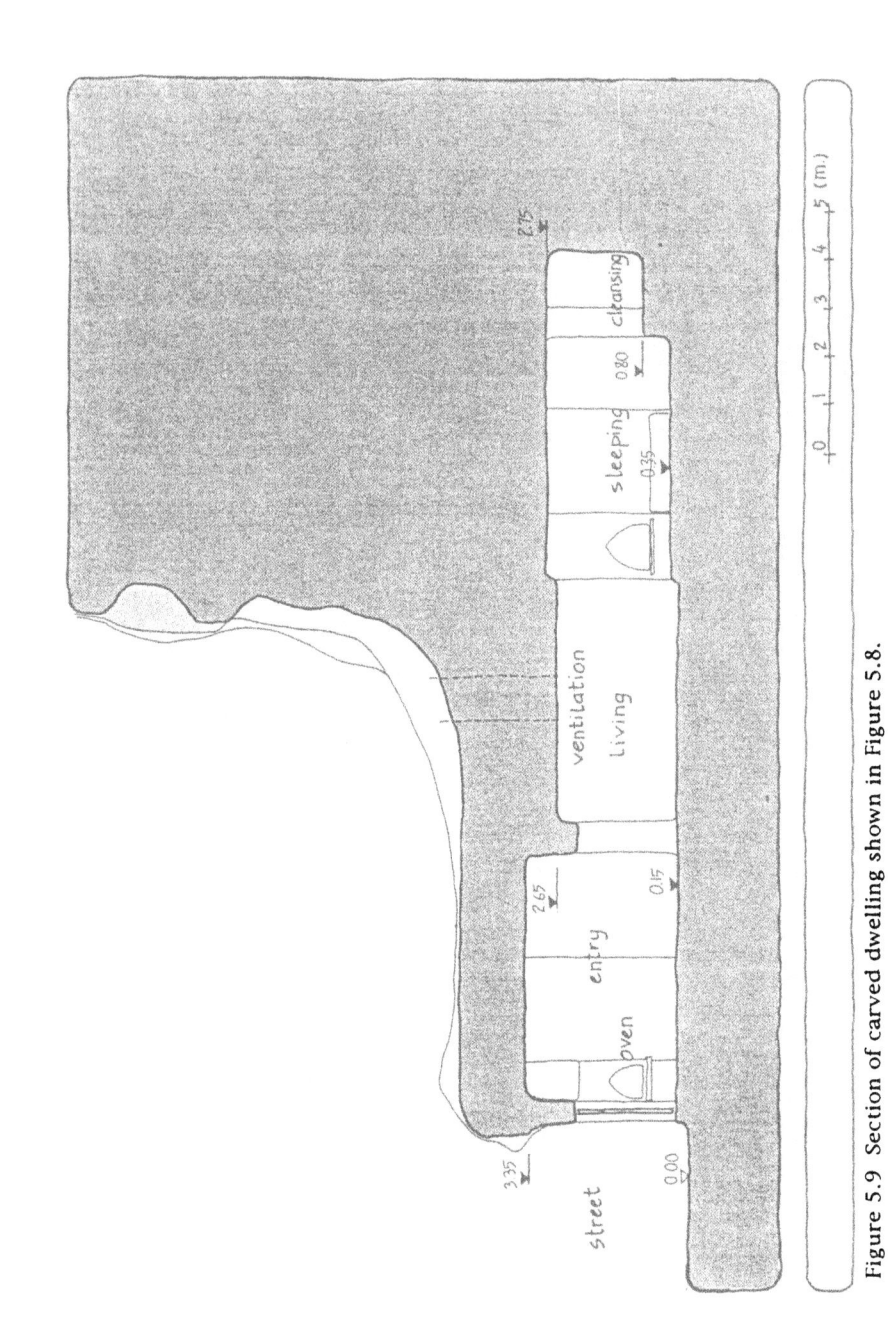

Figure 5.9 Section of carved dwelling shown in Figure 5.8.

Cliff Hangers and Troglodytes

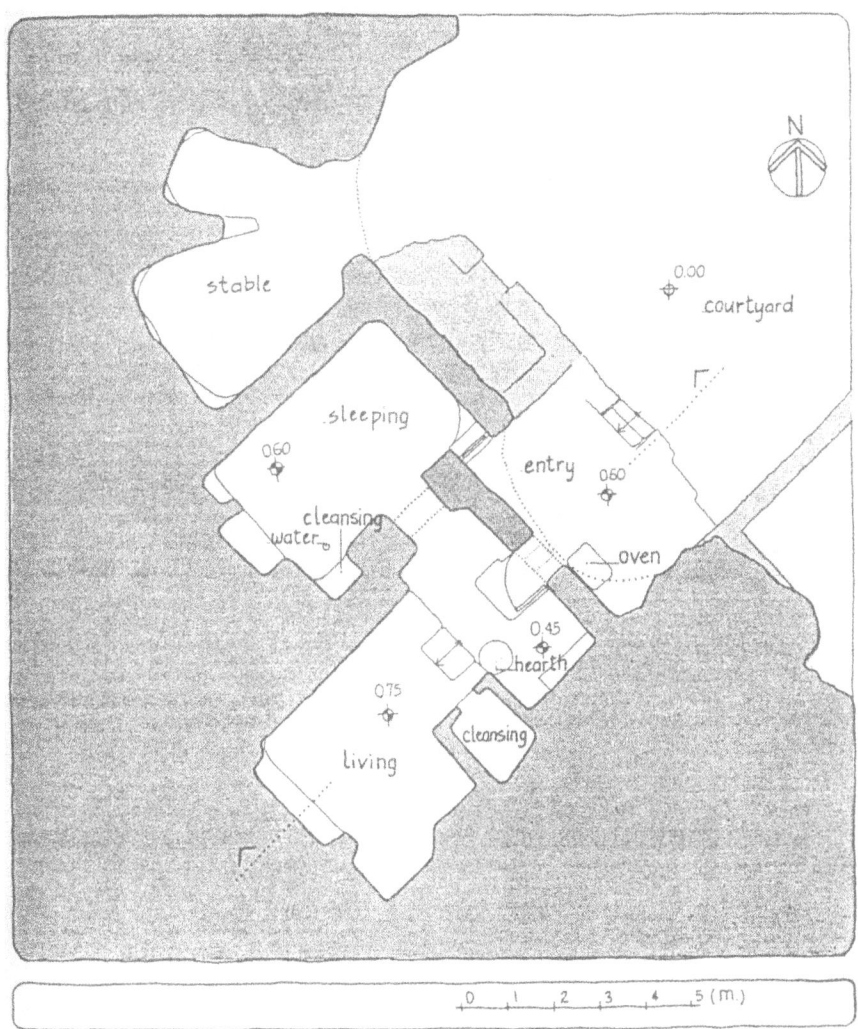

Figure 5.10 Plan of carved dwelling, Urgup

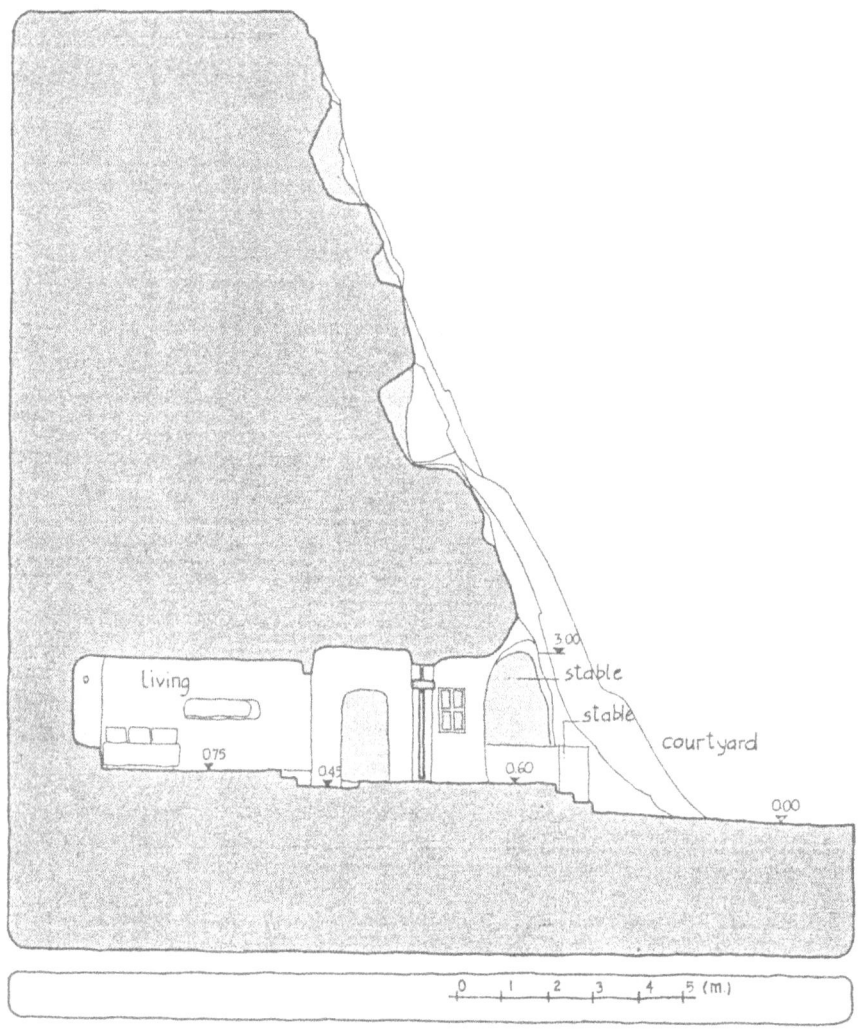

Figure 5.11 Section of carved dwelling shown in Figure 5.10.

Cliff Hangers and Troglodytes

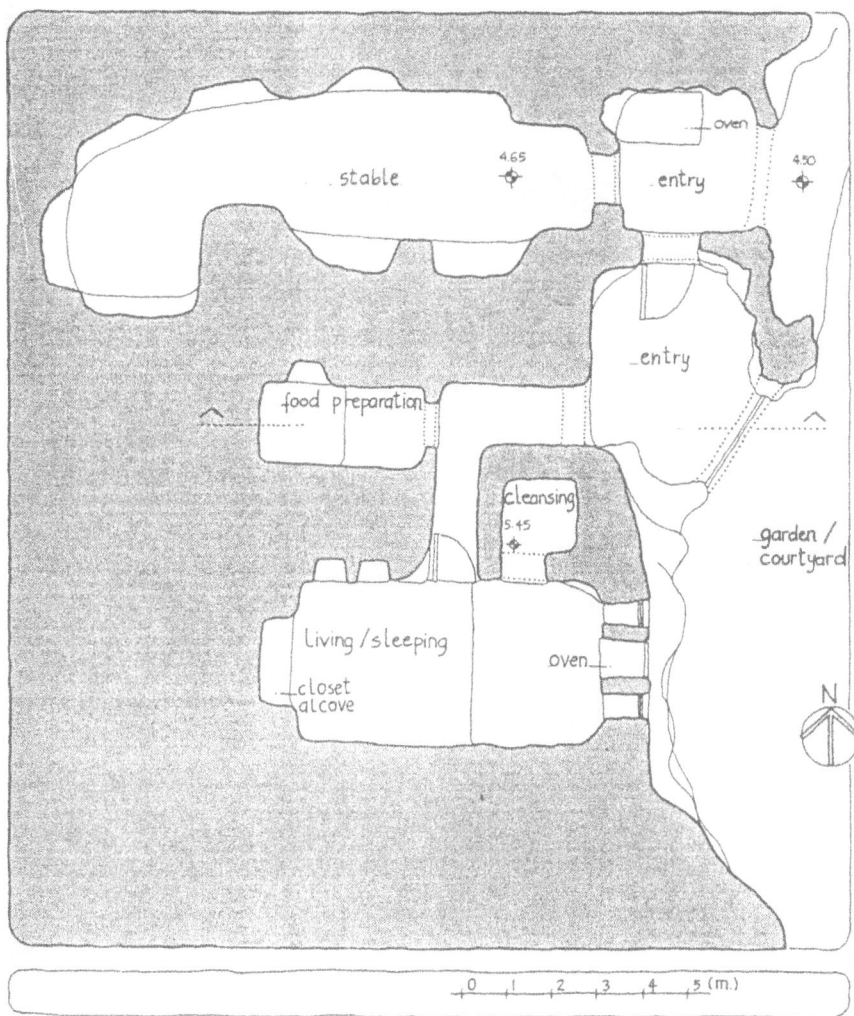

Figure 5.12 Plan of carved dwelling, Urgup.

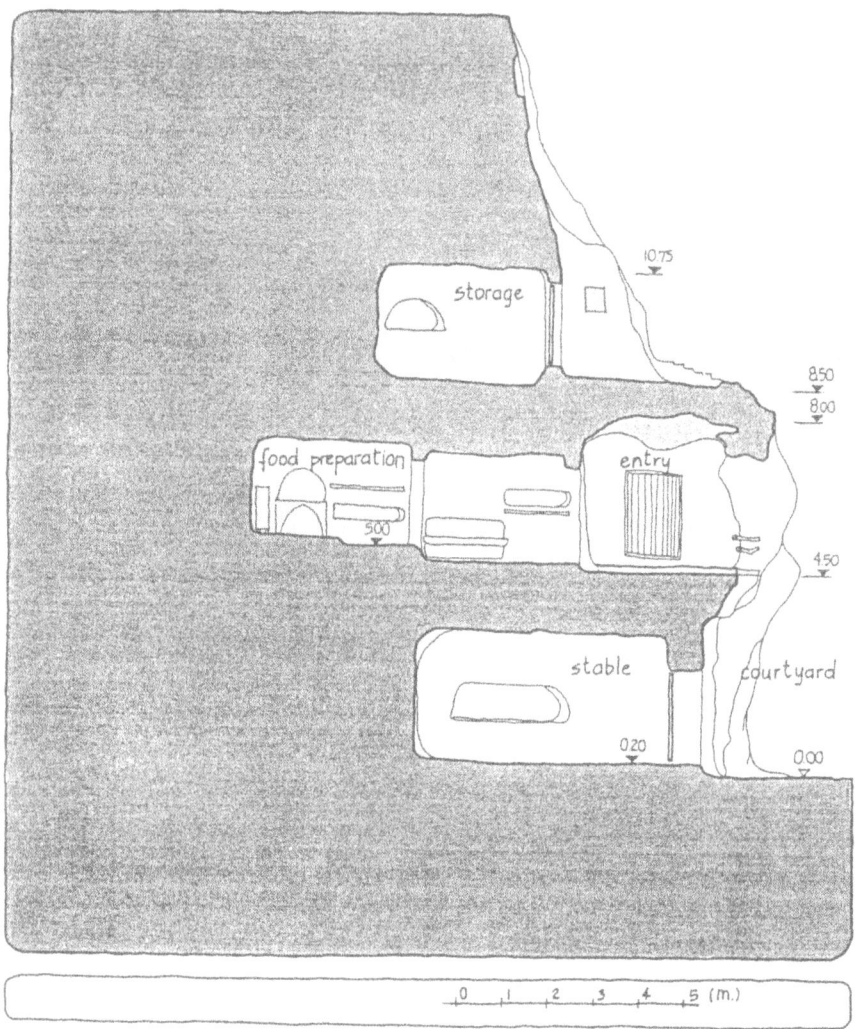

Figure 5.13 Section of carved dwelling shown in Figure 5.12.

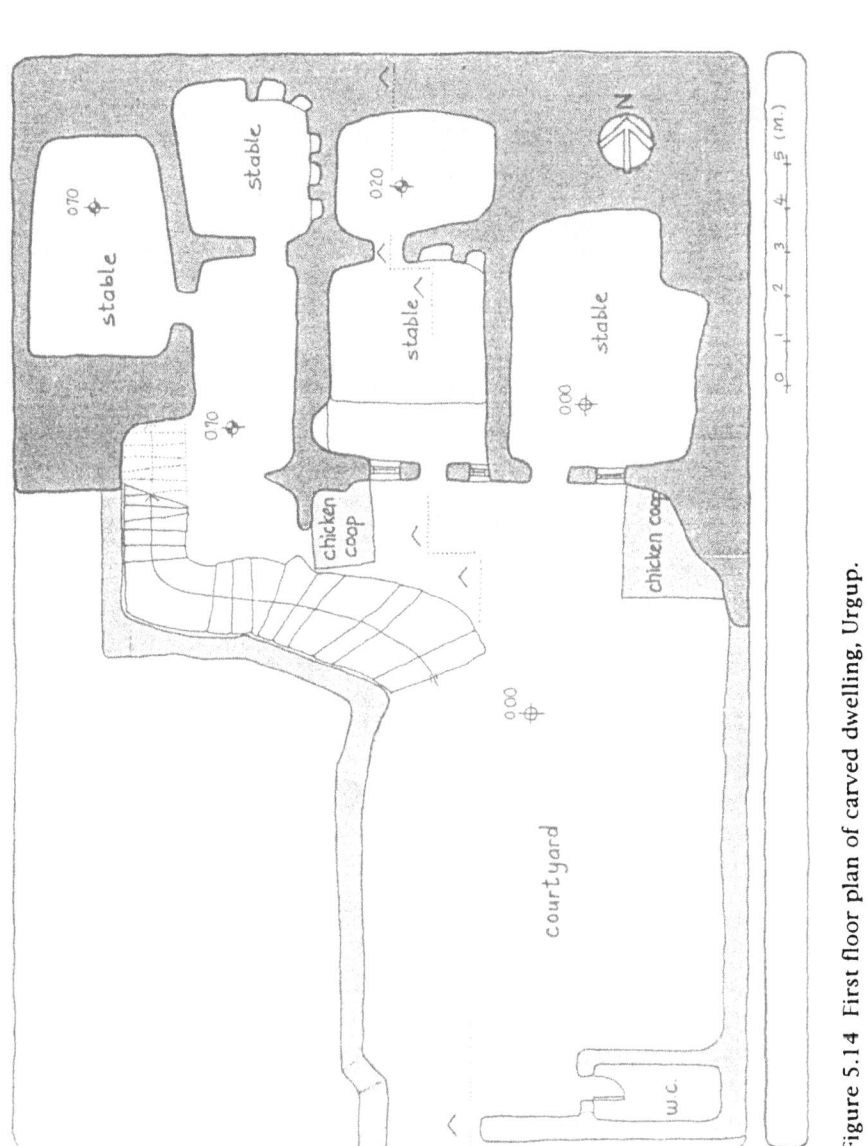

Figure 5.14 First floor plan of carved dwelling, Urgup.

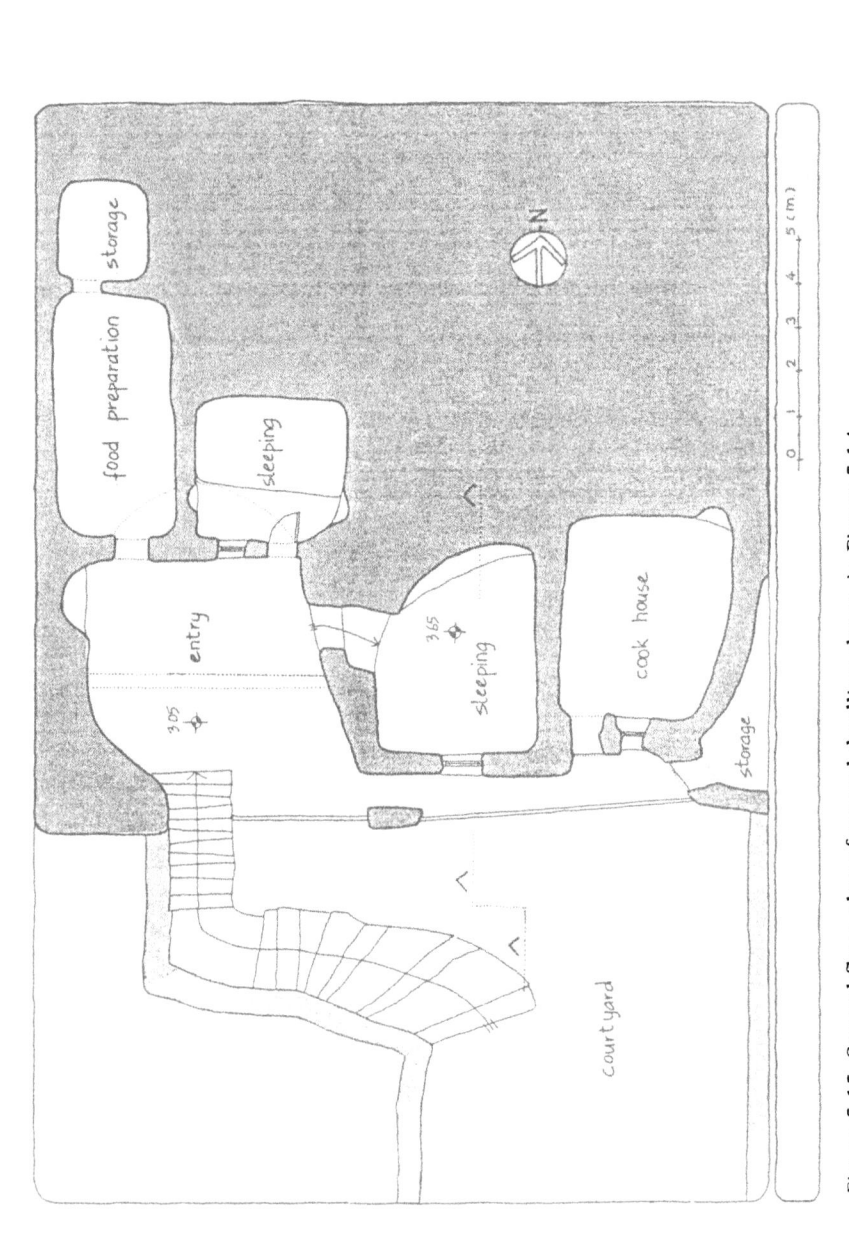

Figure 5.15 Second floor plan of carved dwelling shown in Figure 5.14.

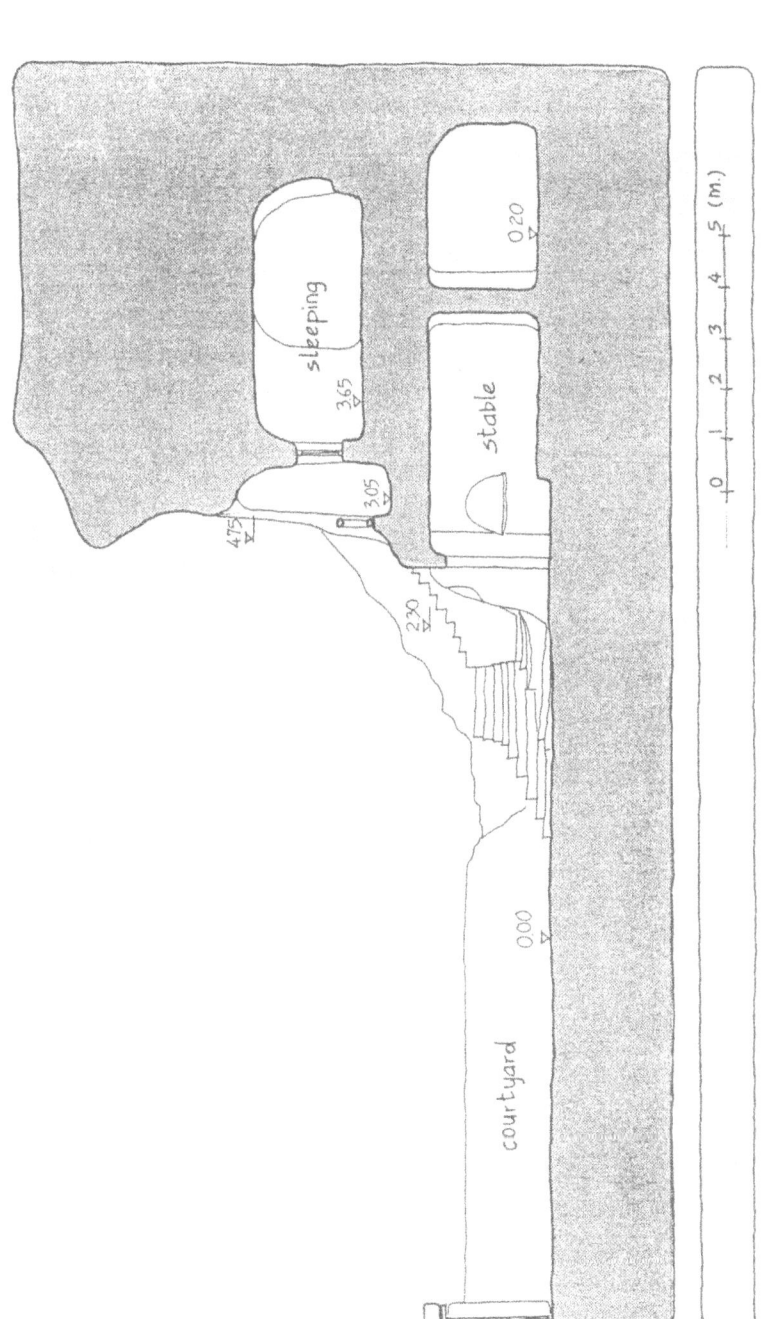

Figure 5.16 Section of carved dwelling shown in Figures 5.14 and 5.15.

236   Cliff Hangers and Troglodytes

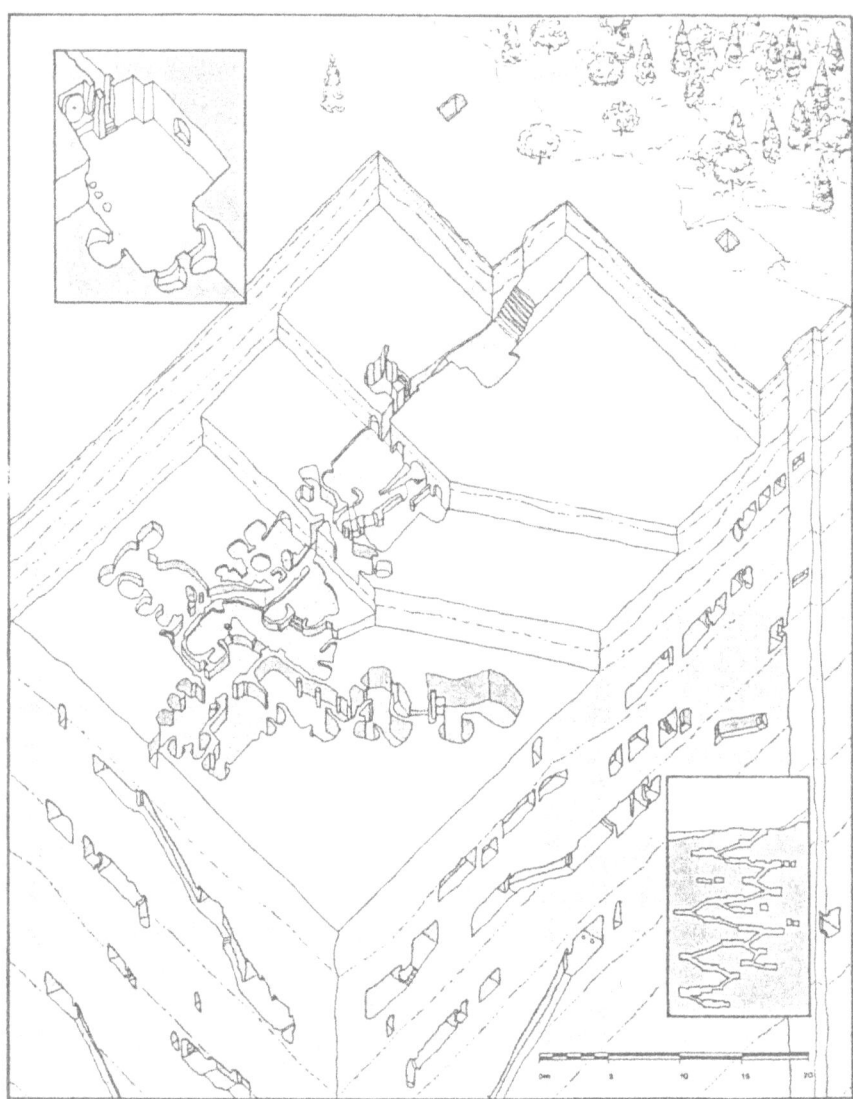

Figure 5.17 Cappadocian underground settlement.
(Based on Gurcay and Akok, 1965).

Cliff Hangers and Troglodytes 237

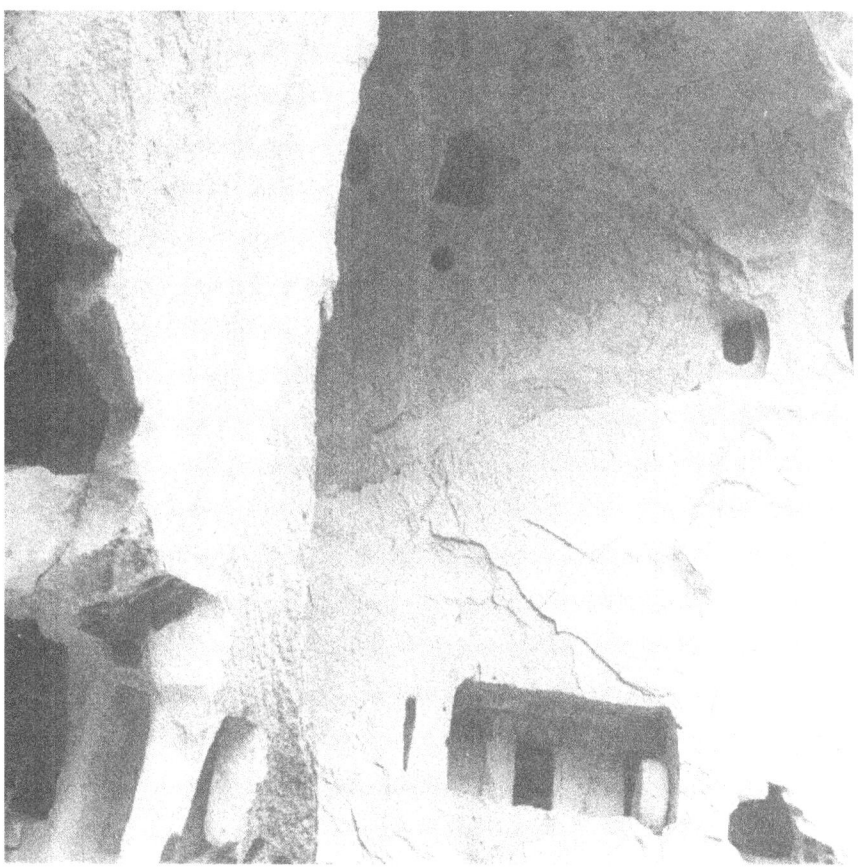

Figure 5.18 Interior carving detail, showing the rolling "millstone" to block the passage from inside.

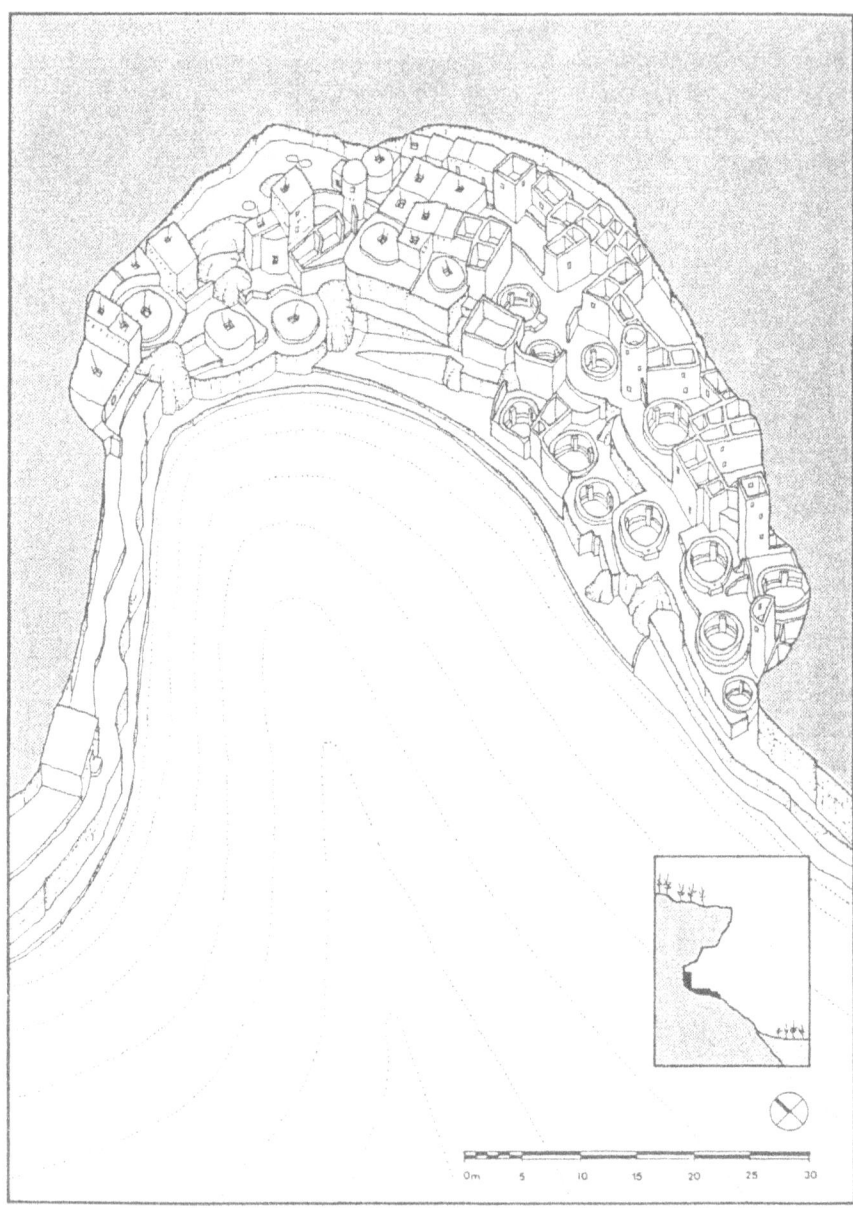

Figure 5.19 Axonometric view of Cliff Palace, Mesa Verde.
(Reconstruction after Fewkes, 1911b).

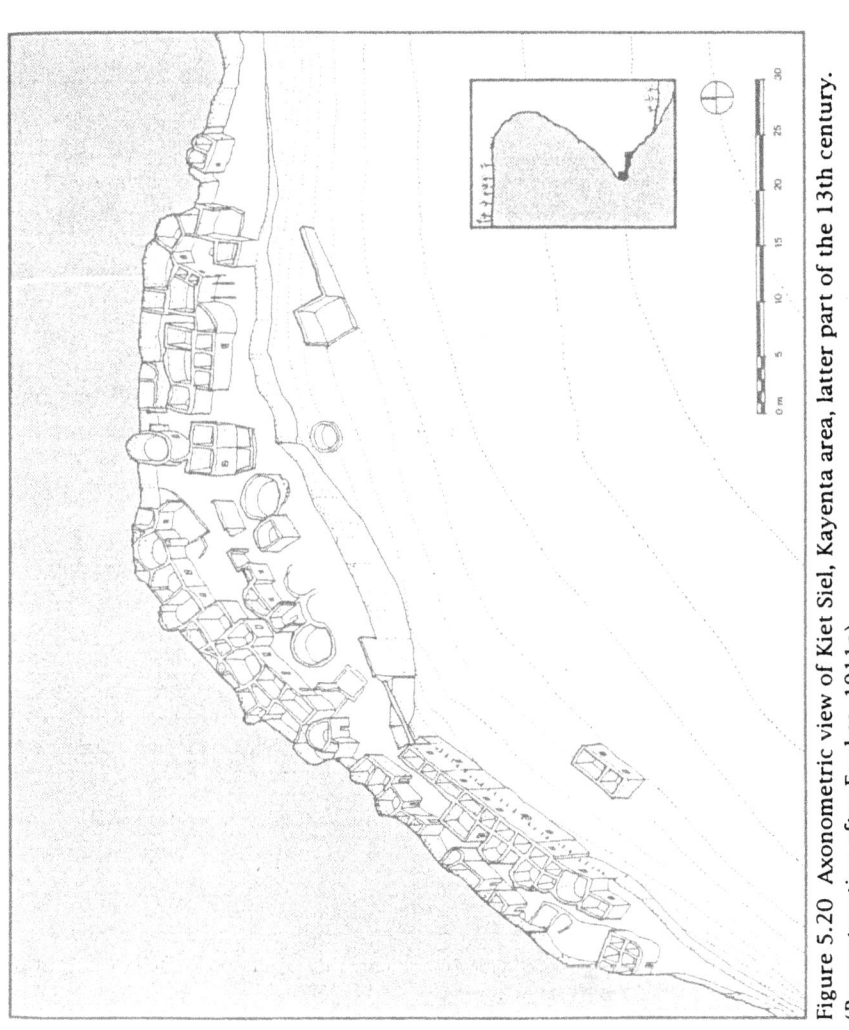

Figure 5.20 Axonometric view of Kiet Siel, Kayenta area, latter part of the 13th century. (Reconstruction after Fewkes, 1911a).

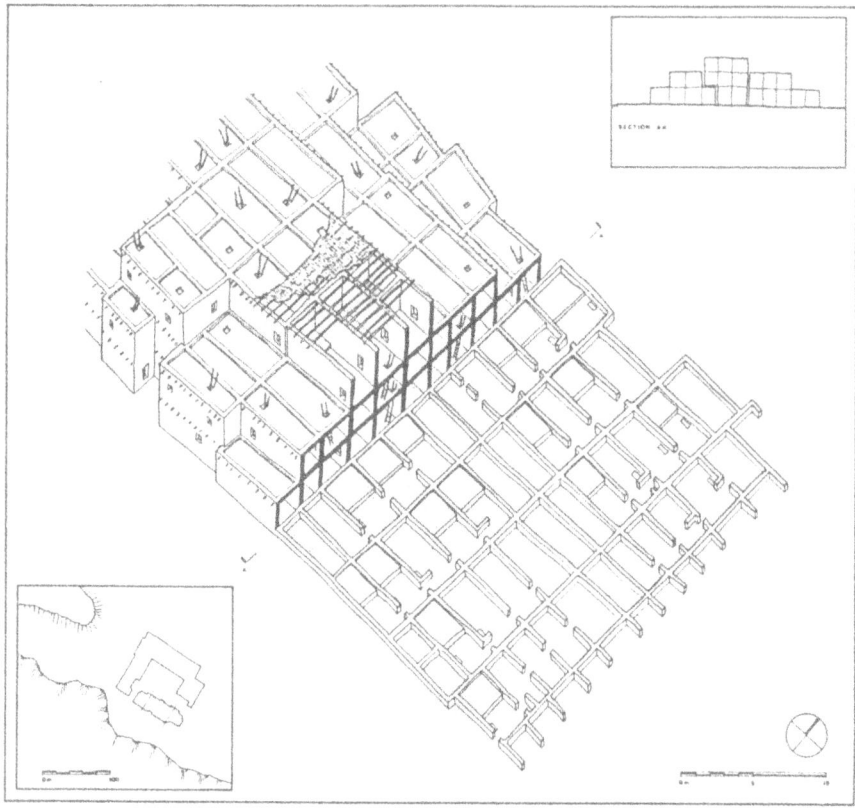

Figure 5.21 Plan and axonometric reconstruction of part of surface ruin above Puye Cliff, Pajarito Plateau, New Mexico. (Based on measured drawing of Peckham, 1984).

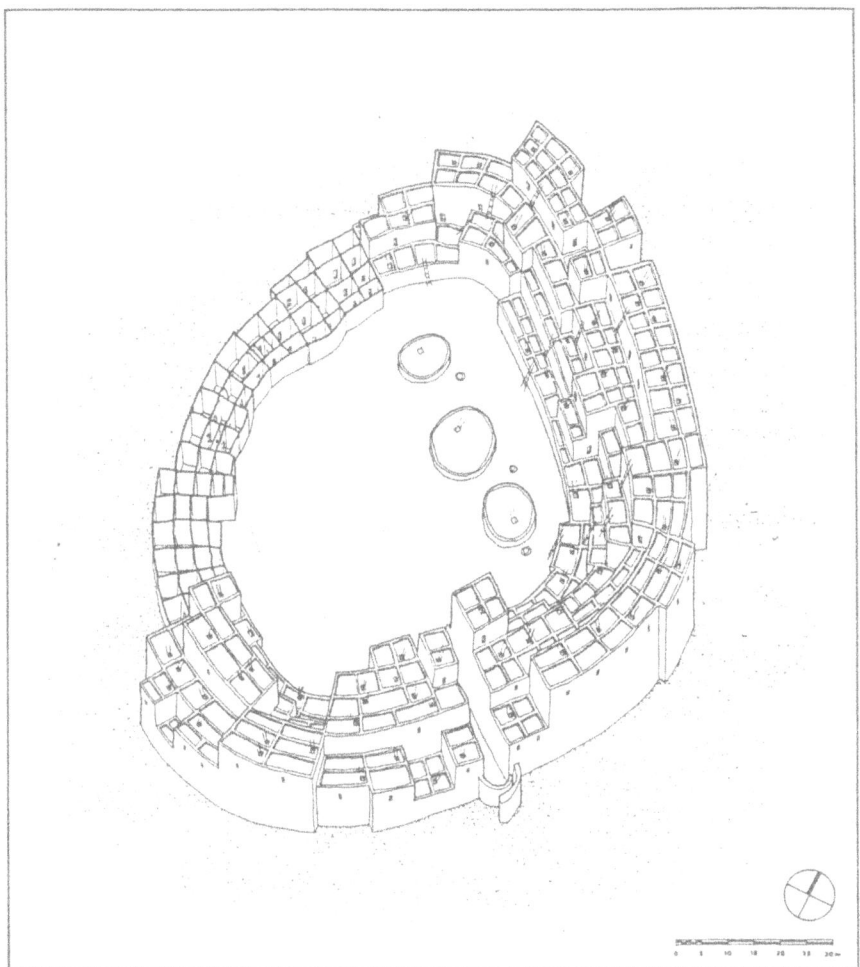

Figure 5.22 Axonometric reconstruction of Tyounyi, Frijoles Canyon, Pajarito Plateau, New Mexico. (Reconstruction based on measured drawing of Peckham, 1984).

Figure 5.23 Talus House: a Frijoles Canyon cliff dwelling.

Cliff Hangers and Troglodytes

Figure 5.24 Contemporary carved and built dwellings, Cappadocia.

Figure 5.25 Contemporary carved and built dwellings, Cappadocia.

Figure 5.26 Masonry reinforcement of carved structure, Cappadocia.

Figure 5.27 Masonry reinforcement of carved structure, Cappadocia.

Cliff Hangers and Troglodytes

Figure 5.28 Contemporary *eyvan* facade, Cappadocia.

248 Cliff Hangers and Troglodytes

Figure 5.29 *Eyvan* and courtyard combination, Cappadocia.

Cliff Hangers and Troglodytes

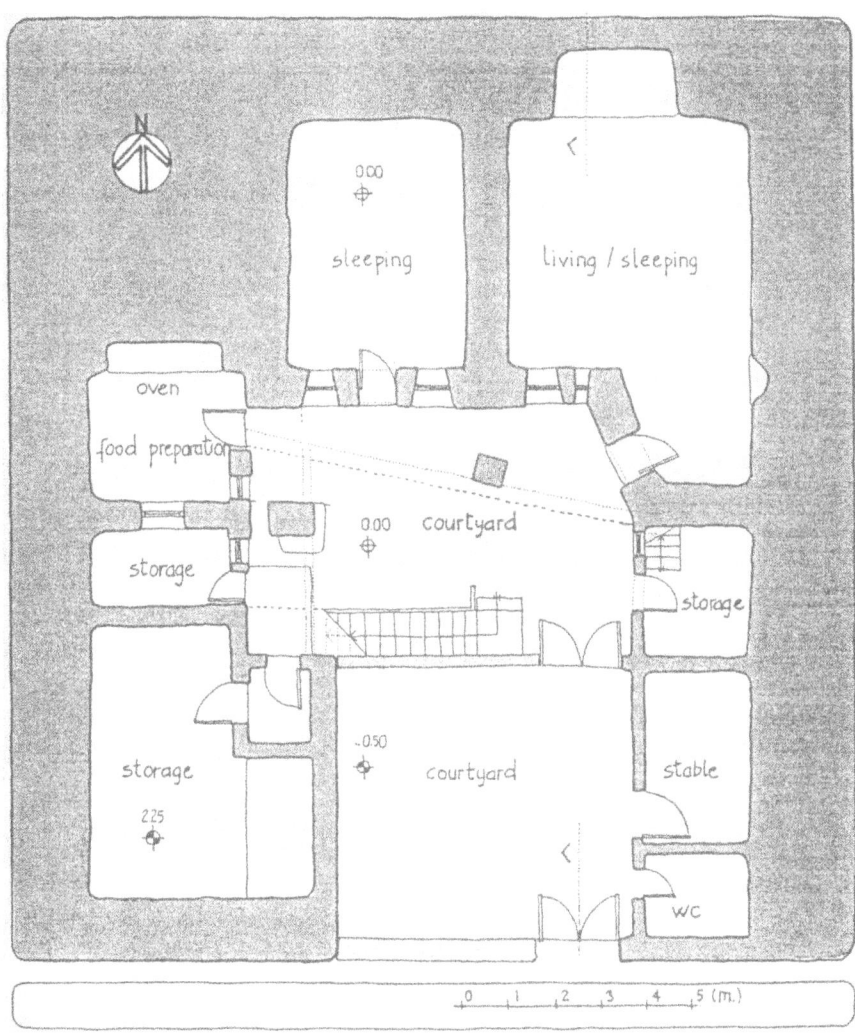

Figure 5.30 Plan of courtyard house, Urgup.

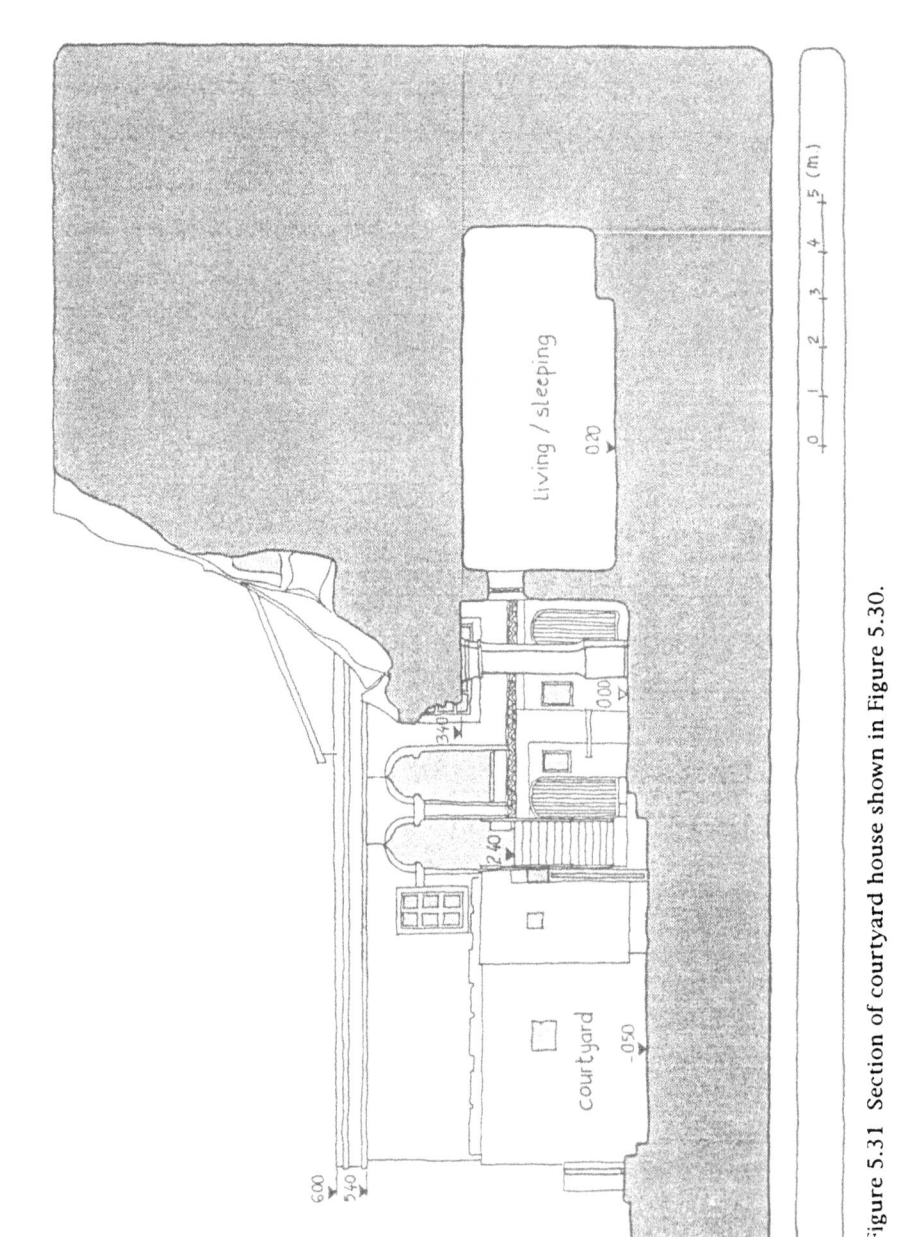

Figure 5.31 Section of courtyard house shown in Figure 5.30.

Cliff Hangers and Troglodytes

Figure 5.32 Facade masonry detail.

Figure 5.33 Facade masonry detail.

Cliff Hangers and Troglodytes

Figure 5.34 Facade masonry detail.

254   Cliff Hangers and Troglodytes

Figure 5.35 Carved interior detail.

Cliff Hangers and Troglodytes 255

Figure 5.36 Carved ceiling detail.

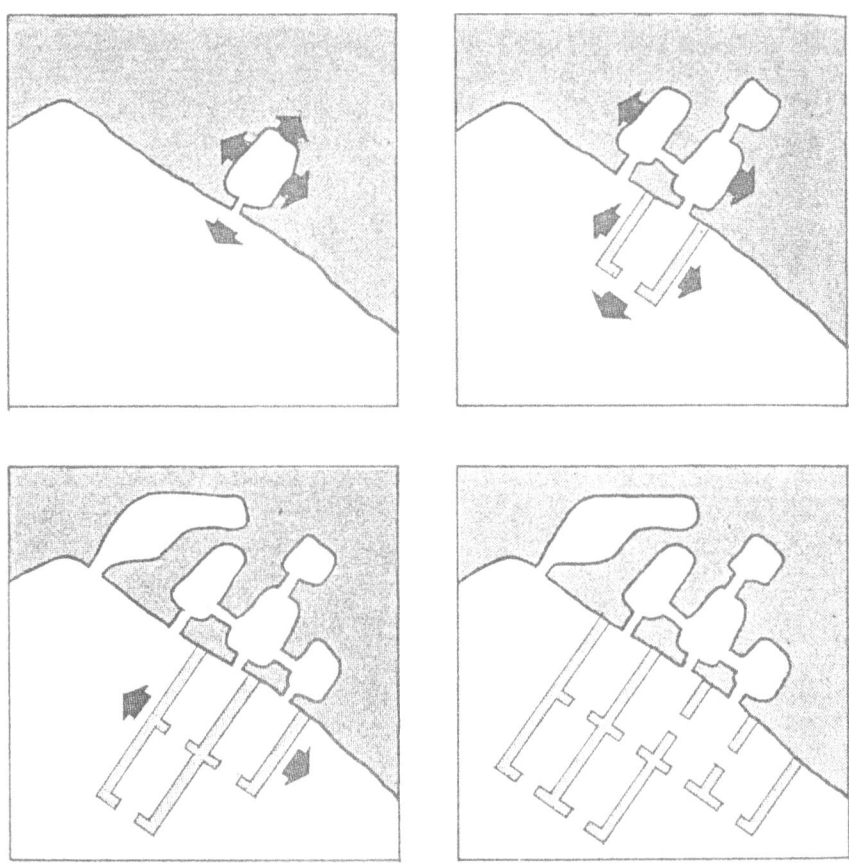

Figure 5.37 Schematic progression of carving and building.

Cliff Hangers and Troglodytes

Figure 5.38 Pre-Columbian sites and trade routes between Mesoamerica and the American Southwest. These trade routes are roughly parallel to the *caminos reales* of the Spanish Colonial Period. (Adapted from Cordell, 1984).

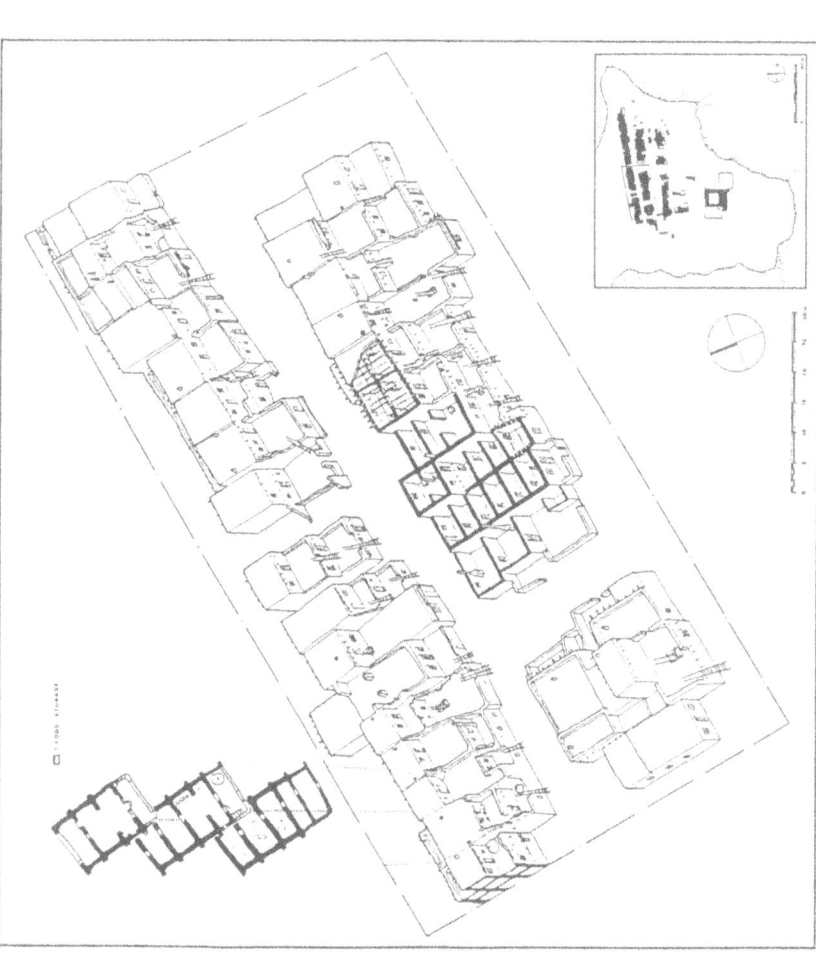

Figure 5.39 Axonometric and partial plan of a portion of contemporary Acoma Pueblo, New Mexico. (After Historic American Building Survey, 1934; Camilli and Cordell 1983).

Chapter Six
BEYOND IMPRESSIONS: STRUCTURING AN EXPLANATION

> Human history is like palaeontology. Owing to a certain judicial blindness even the best intelligences absolutely fail to see the things which lie in front of their noses. Later when the moment has arrived, we are surprised to find traces everywhere of what we failed to see.... And only by starting from there shall we be able to decipher our past again.
>
> K. Marx to F. Engels, 1868.

What we propose to develop in this chapter is a conceptual framework that will facilitate the understanding of placemaking. We anticipate that this framework will be applicable, not just to the two locations described in the preceding four chapters, but to other diachronically analyzed examples of placemaking as well.

One of our original purposes was to carry the understanding of the contextual relations underlying placemaking into the foundation of a new framework of person/environment relations/environment relations, utilizing comparative study. Our search is, hence, for an ecological theory that goes beyond simple environmental determinism and cultural relativism to the discovery of some general relations of built form to society; our purpose in presenting examples and descriptions of particular buildings and settlements was, therefore, to contribute to this goal. Placemaking is viewed as a form of *economic activity*, in the very broadest sense of the term, combining social, cultural, political, and material aspects of a society's *mode of production*. In this chapter, our statement on placemaking incorporates a *typology* of hypothesized relations which characterize the *context* of placemaking, placemaking *activity*, and architecture. In the next chapter we will attempt to apply this typology to the two locations presently under consideration: Anatolian Turkey and the American Southwest.

The task of moving from a general ecological theory concerning modes of production to specific person/environment relations is fairly formidable. Indeed, the argument could be made that the task has deterred architects in the past from building a theory-data bridge that others could cross comfortably. Our efforts will undoubtedly fall short of complete fulfillment, but we can start on the abutments and perhaps even string the suspension cables.

Some architectural treatises on prehistoric building have suffered from an emphasis solely upon *form*. We are introducing a form/content dialectic (related to function) which will run throughout the proposed typology. Because the relationship between the two is dialectical, there are formal aspects of content and content aspects of form. "Form" is the combination of the physical essence of placemaking and the most closely related social aspects; "content" includes the overarching sociocultural milieu which specifies function, gives meaning, and determines the ethnoscience of placemaking. The distinctions and relations between these two will become clearer as we delve into the typology.

A similar typology of relationships was introduced by Arel in her historical analysis of Ottoman house types (Arel, 1982). The content of the relationships in the typology outlined here is somewhat different than that in her inquiry, which focused specifically on the Ottoman house and its traditional qualities, and associated historical issues. While the present typology was clearly inspired by Arel's brilliant analysis and her quest for the roots of tradition in Ottoman domestic architecture, the changes we have introduced (for which, along with the generalizations proposed, we assume all responsibility) actually convey a meaning considerably different from that in her typology. These differences are the natural outcome of the differing foci of the two inquiries.

Establishing the framework

The dialectical relations between form and content exist on three levels, which, from the most inclusive to the most specific, are as follows:
 (1) global concepts;
 (2) fundamental relations in architecture, particularly domestic architecture;
 (3) the realization of domestic architecture: mutually interactive elements of what initially appear to be social "antecedents" and physical consequences.

Certain terms, which are well-known to researchers in the environment/behavior realm, are included in the third level above, under such labels as spatial ordering, public/private realms, ownership, and participation. Our description of these, however, may differ somewhat from that currently in common use.

The purpose of the framework that follows is to improve understanding of both traditional and transitional societies through introducing and ordering a set of dialectical relationships. In an earlier chapter, we presented dialectics as an alternative to the dichotomies, the contradictions reinforced by a thought system derived from the concepts of industrialized Western society. Dialectical ideas are not mutually exclusive: they coexist in a relationship of "and" rather than "versus." Thus, while dichotomies are mutually exclusive, dialectical

Beyond Impressions: Structuring an Explanation

elements coexist; indeed, it is the interplay between elements that defines the dialectic.

We have defined fourteen contradictory relationships related to dwelling as place, and have searched for a way to represent these diagrammatically. No uniquely clear manner of diagramming these has emerged, however; therefore, we present two alternative ways of viewing the typology we propose. The first is a loose "tree diagram," relating form to content, attempting to show that

Table 6.1

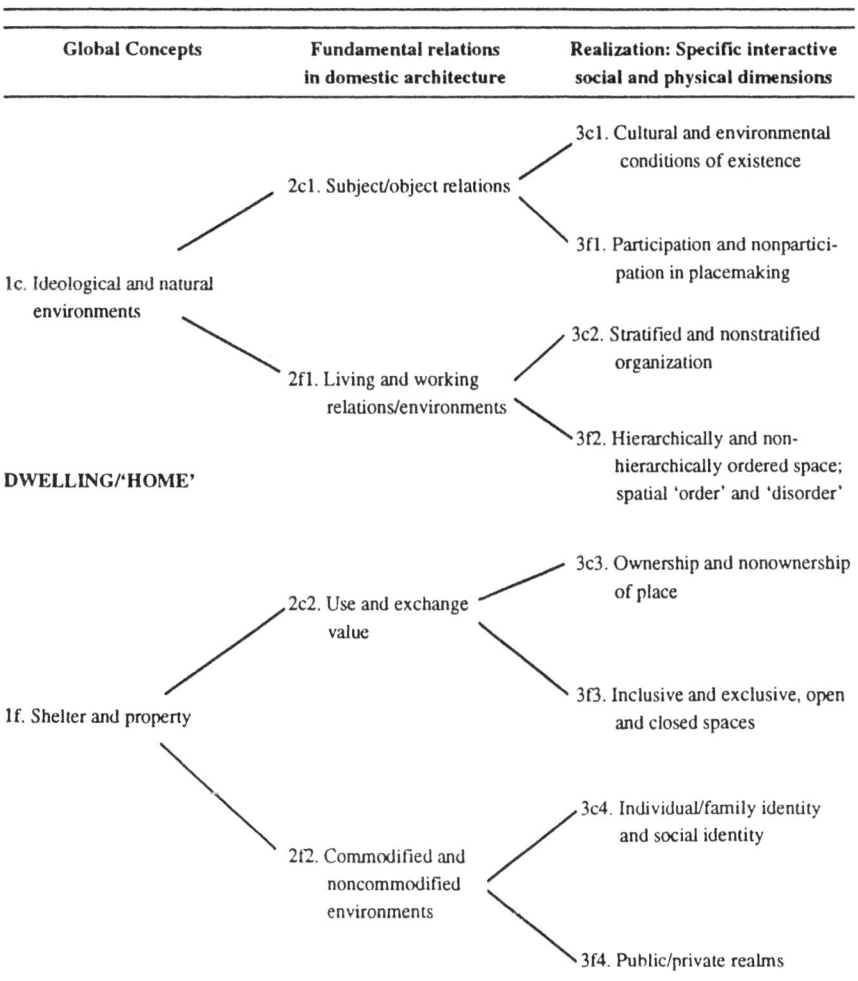

content contains form and form contains content, and going from the more general at the left, to the more specific at the right (Table 6.1). But we are more sure of the relational *elements* of this typology than of its "tree-like" nature; and an alternative diagram is also presented in Chapter Eight, (Figure 8.1), which is circular in form, using "polar coordinates." The latter also presents a progression, in this case from "core" (general) to "peripheral" (specific), but a more diffuse, global relationship is implied than in the tree diagram presented as Table 6.1.

Both Table 6.1 and Figure 8.1 depict a "working" typology of relationships in placemaking: this typology is dynamic, not static, and subject to revision over time. The dialectical relationships depicted are analytic categories—guides to the researcher in comparative vernacular architecture as to "what to look for" in the diachronic study of domestic places. They can structure inquiry and broaden it beyond the narrow constraints of environmental or cultural determinism. They are intended to provide a framework for understanding the incorporation of society into shelter and of shelter into society. The relationships proposed in the above extend in the two directions shown in Table 6.1, both horizontally and vertically, and within and between form/content pairs.

In what follows, we will attempt to elucidate the elements of this typology with examples.

A typology of relationships in placemaking

1c. *Ideological and natural environments.* In Chapter One, we made use of the concept of *ideological superstructure*, indicating that it relates to the technical and social aspects of the production process through the establishment of an explicit or implicit *rule system* that includes, among other aspects, specialized roles to be performed by certain members of a society. The specialized roles do not necessarily have equally specialized titles associated with them; thus, for example, among the Navajo Indians of the U.S., certain "singers" are specialized in house blessing ceremonies, which include the application of architectural, construction, and siting rules and expertise to the production of built environment.

Thus, contrary to the view put forth most notably by Rudofsky (1964) and Hakim (1986), among others, we contend that there is comparatively little "architecture without architects": what appears so is only because those who have, use, and transmit architectural wisdom do not bear the title "architect." The absence of a specialized title, however, cannot be taken to imply the absence of the function conventionally represented by the title. Further, the absence of

Beyond Impressions: Structuring an Explanation 263

easily recognizable building "codes" does not mean that the codification itself does not exist in one form or another (song or story, for example, in an oral society).

While ideological superstructure includes ideas, beliefs, sentiments, and types of thinking associated with particular ways of organizing production, it can also be described as the "mental" aspect of culture reflected in its "cognitive framework." As parts of the society to which they belong, architecture and the art of placemaking are the products of such a cognitive framework which organizes and structures practical aspects of human activity. In other words, the act of building is a purposive action wherein decision procedures for choosing among alternatives are developed. Where there are purposive decisions to be taken, someone or someones must take them; thus, *authority* is also involved. The exercise of this authority may be based in collective experience, traditional belief systems, secular power, or some combination. Since such authority is related to the cognitive framework of the culture in which it is operating, it takes on the function of expressing the ideology of the particular society. In the absence of the politico-juridical component of mode of production, this ideological base is much more pronounced; on the other hand, where the mechanisms for the appropriation of surplus labor are jointly maintained by the political and ideological components of mode of production, the act of building takes on the functions to exhibit and legitimize political authority. Hence, an architectural object or the product of placemaking assumes a concealed ideological role; stated differently, the built environment takes on and reinforces the ideology of its society. Thus, it happens that certain ritual reflecting, and necessary to the maintenance of, ideology can only take place in buildings of a certain form, shape, or location.

Conceptions of placemaking or acts of building restricted to instrumentalism, while revealing those aspects or relations among elements which are easily visible — functional, utilitarian, obvious causes and effects — conceal or misrepresent the ideological and political aspects of building activity. Unlike *ars est celare artem,* the instrumentalist conception of placemaking conceals the real nature of relations in the process and directs attention largely to architecture as mere product, independent of its culture's social contradictions.

When attention is focused on superficial relations rather than on the real conditions of existence that result from these contradictions, the ideological environment surrounding architectural activity disappears into the "natural" environment. This is a fundamental distortion which tends to reproduce itself, contributing to inadequate analysis as well as to inappropriate and false interpretation. The exclusion of the ideological environment in architectural analysis often results in a mechanistic interpretation, falsely representing a materialist point of view—or an idealist interpretation, emphasizing only subjective, metaphysical, ethical, or ahistorical *form*. Neither one brings an explanation sufficient to illuminate the relations and underlying interplay among built form, environment, and society.

While people are *part* of nature, the fulfillment of some of their needs requires action *against* nature. The natural environment is first affected by the social environment and later reshaped. The act of building is one of the major contributors to the reshaping of the natural environment. As a result of placemaking, among other activities, the natural environment becomes the product not only of itself, depending on its own laws and contradictions alone, but also the product of societal actions and the concomitant contradictions from which these actions emerge.

The natural environment, of course, provides the context within which (and with the help of which) placemaking occurs. It is both hazard and resource simultaneously producing the material *for* dwelling and the elements *from* which the dweller requires shelter. How the environment is perceived or understood by people is critical to how they construe the natural environment and placemaking (Kelley, 1955). Both this understanding of the natural environment and the traditional "codes and standards" regulating dwelling are part of a society's own *ethnoscientific tradition*. Ethnoscience, as a field of study, is largely a product of Western anthropology, but in the sense of Kelly's (1955) view (actually a product of psychology) that "every man's a scientist," ethnoscience is the property of each society that builds a theory of itself. In oral societies, the ethnoscientific view through which the society makes sense of the universe is incorporated into its ideology, its creation story, and its accompanying mythology, religious practices, natural history, and astronomy. The existence of "primitive" astronomies (Aveni, 1975, 1982) involves the recognition of recurrent variation (another important characteristic of natural environment) and an attempt to tie the society and its functions to a reliable predictive system that facilitates control over the society's relation to itself and to nature. This is true of highly predictable annual events such as observable celestial phenomena and the migration of animals; it is true of less predictable and longer-term events as well, such as climatic cycles. Astronomy requires at least a simple theory of relationship of one's location to heavenly bodies; thus, it is quite possible that the prehistoric Anasazi of America's arid Southwest had a theory of drought, as well.

1f. *Shelter and property*. Shelter has not always been based on the concept of private property held by isolated nuclear families. While the sheltering aspect of a dwelling is less difficult to define, relationships between production

Beyond Impressions: Structuring an Explanation 265

relations, property and family, and the dwelling itself are not so neatly and categorically spelled out. As the concepts of property and right of property developed from particular conditions of existence, the nature of dwelling was changed and broadened; in other words, the nature of shelter changed as private property was introduced. Since the right of private property is certainly neither self-evident nor axiomatic when viewed in historical perspective, the sheltering function and property function of dwelling can be separated if the natures of shelter and property are defined as clearly as possible.

Briefly, it can be said that shelter is a necessary precondition of life and social relations. It is one of the means to sustain, develop, and carry on life; it provides part of the necessary environmental conditions enabling people to conduct their life activities. In early times, the purely sheltering "house" belonged first to the public domain in a communal society, then to the private domain in a familial society. Here, "communal" and "familial" were viewed as different levels rather than opposites. A common feature of both cases, in early times was the absence of conflict between public and private. Shelter, whether in the public or private domain, was not in conflict with community and commonality. The commonality may have been of a temporary or permanent nature depending upon the particular historical conditions.

The introduction and emergence of private ownership leading to private property gradually shifts the above concept of "shelter" to "property." The principles on which shelter is then based come into conflict with community and commonality. This transition from shelter to property takes place when the shelter is no longer in the private or public domain but is absorbed by the *political* domain. At this stage, social organization is not limited to the family and dominated by kinship as when property is communal; relations of production and property become so firmly linked that dwelling as property inevitably becomes a tool for exploitation. While earlier, shelter as communal property was a *precondition* for life and social relations, now shelter as private property becomes the *aim* of life. As division of labor and surplus product increase, the nature of social relations changes, likewise, since "dwelling as property" contains within itself the seeds of latent exploitation; those gradually monopolizing the ownership of the means of production acquire the ability to control the production of dwellings.

A dwelling may be shelter and symbol, and the protector of property, as well as property itself; the dwellers may be occupants, owners, renters, producers. The earliest caves were for shelter and security only, keeping out the elements, animals, and unwanted people. All production was consumed by the producer; there was no surplus product, no distribution, no exchange. Dwelling was found rather than produced. With the investment of labor, dwelling eventually satisfied more than the need for shelter. It could be reoccupied, exchanged, and thereby acquire value: eventually it became property. During the recent past, the property function began to supersede the function of shelter; a dwelling became primarily — or, even in the more recent past, almost exclusively — something to be exchanged. The terms "use," "exchange," "commodity," and "value" apply to the built environment, and to the socio-cultural system of which that environment is a part; they apply to the *transitions* which have occurred from one mode of production to another.

2c1. *Subject/object relations.* Environment is both the physical source (or resource), the *subject* of labor (providing what is necessary to enable placemaking to occur), and the *object* of labor, i.e., the built environment that is eventually produced, the environmental product which emerges as the result of labor. This is the essentially *dialectical* nature of placemaking. Similarly, the cultural matrix provides both the social source of human labor (subject) and the reason for (object of) placemaking — the maintenance and enhancement of the culture.

2f1. *Living and working relations/environments.* At one time, "living" and "working" (separated as though work were no part of life) were intertwined, both spatially and temporally. People lived where they worked and produced, and stored their product at home. In early Anasazi settlements, the pithouse was space both for living and for storage of product; when pithouse became pueblo, storage and living spaces were further separated, but the relation between production and living were still preserved, actually as well as ceremonially. With further sedentarization, and the establishment of year-round settlement, specialization of labor undoubtedly emerged as a concomitant of necessary trade: craftsmen, masons, ceremonial leaders—perhaps even "traveling salesmen"—took their places alongside hunters and farmers. The spatial and temporal threads connecting "living" and "working" became frayed.

With the emergence of the nuclear family, division of labor, the growth of surplus labor and surplus product, and the development of private property, domestic life and work life became separated, especially in urban society; this separation has become mandated in Western societies through zoning. No longer does work serve the family; indeed, it has been argued that in the Capitalist West, the opposite is the case: people are no longer producers of their environment, but environment's product. With the emphasis on the exchange value of activities and products, including dwellings, the reduction of the human beings to a means in the economic process leads to alienation of people from their environment and from each other. The impersonal conditions of everyday life provide little basis for evaluation of one's own worth; under conditions of relative affluence, this leads to conspicuous consumption. Ownership and display of objects and dwellings of certain kinds becomes an end in itself; this reification results when the relationships between people and objects, and people and people, are dominated by market values.

The "dormitory community" of modern capitalist society, where the family/ work dialectic is played out in the entire urban space, is to be contrasted with traditional households where social production and reproduction, work and domestic activities, take place within the dwelling or dwelling compound, and in which the unity of the dialectic can be realized within a single structure.

2c2. Use value and exchange value. Production occurs in response to need; it yields artifacts which will be used, or consumed, and the need is satisfied by the consumption of the product. Consumption, in turn, creates the need or motive for additional production. Further, the product must be *distributed* or *exchanged* in some manner.

The product of placemaking activity, whether a simple shelter or a more elaborated dwelling, similarly satisfies a set of needs. The *use value* of a dwelling is a measure of its utility to the occupant as shelter and for other purposes apart from commodification. Housing may be redistributed or exchanged without commodification: appropriation and later utilization assign a use value to an architectural product. Use value is acquired first through need, then through utilization.

However, if the dwelling is constructed not just for occupancy by the builder or the built for, but for sale or rental, the dwelling acquires *exchange value*; it has been produced for the purpose of monetary exchange. But it must have use value before it acquires exchange value; indeed, as in urban "squatter" settlements in developing countries, the dweller often constructs a dwelling with only its use value in mind; exchange value emerges later.

Production for use takes place in all modes of production; production for exchange only in two. Exchange value is initially related (but not, in the long run, restricted) to the amount (time and monetary value) of labor required to produce a given product. Thus, vernacular housing attached to a piece of highly valued land is often exchanged at prices far above the value of labor incorporated in the house; but such exchange value is frequently more related to the commodified land (a nonproduct) than to the structure it supports. Further, exchange value may increase with no intervention of the owner or tenant, as when neighboring land increases greatly in exchange value.

It is important to note, finally, that what is "useless" at one point in history may become "useful" at another, and vice versa. Indian reservations are located where they are in the U.S. because the land was regarded as "useless" in the nineteenth century; it was only in the twentieth century that resources *under* the land acquired use and exchange values.

2f2. *Commodified and noncommodified environments.* When a dwelling acquires exchange value, it becomes a *commodity*. As indicated elsewhere (Turan, 1987), dwellings do not become commodities just because they are exchanged, but they may be exchanged because they are commodities. It is not the act of exchange but the fact of exchange *value* that commodifies environments. Thus, the form becomes commodified as the content comes to include exchange value.

The dwelling as a commodified environment, whose production is organized through exchange, differs *quantitatively* from other dwellings in its exchange value. On the other hand, the noncommodified dwelling, which has only use value, is *qualitatively* different from other dwellings. This qualitative difference relates to the specific character of the dwelling's use to the inhabitant (use value); and it cannot be *quantitatively* compared with the use values of other dwellings. The value of a dwelling as a commodified environment becomes *exchange value* when such an environment is compared with others in terms of potential for exchange. Furthermore, commodified dwelling makes individual labor social, since such environments are exchanged. This is true regardless of the levels of technology employed, social organization, construction methods, and cultural constraints. Dwellings as products of a particular form of labor, tend also to reduce social labor to individual labor in the process of exchange. The relation of people to people, and people to objects (in this case, the dwelling environment) in this process of production and exchange is one of the fundamental aspects of placemaking.

The tendency not to see these relations in the process of housing production may later lead to serious errors of interpretation, as in the understanding and interpretation of squatter settlements, for example (Turan, 1987). The underlying problem is the false dichotomy established between appearance and concealed reality. The housing environment or the dwelling itself, both products of a particular form of labor, start to appear independent of and divorced from the people who directly or indirectly took part in their creation. In other words, when the relations among people and their environments-as-products, as well as the process of production, are overlooked, the dwelling produced per se becomes the focus of attention, concealing the underlying social relations and thereby deceiving the observer.

3c1. *Cultural and environmental conditions of existence.* A society's material conditions and its cultural conditions, taken together, are its *conditions of existence*, a concept discussed earlier. The material conditions include climate,

Beyond Impressions: Structuring an Explanation 269

siting, and resources; the cultural conditions include kinship, and social and labor relations. Together, these are the prime movers of a society's mode of production. But societies are not static; hence, conditions of existence (or extant conditions) are complemented by conditions of change. Forces external to the society produce *conditions* of change while internal forces constitute the *basis* of change.

3f1. *Participation and nonparticipation in placemaking.* "Participation" is a term applied to the active dialectical relationship between people and the environment, and between people and other people concerned with shaping that environment. The most direct form of participation is represented by the labor invested in a self-built house, the result being the interaction between the builder's needs and his/her conditions of existence. In fact, participation as a generic term refers to the *manner* in which the house is built. Usually, it becomes an issue at the point where specialization, division of labor, and nonreciprocity enter the placemaking arena—and reaches crisis proportions only when one's labor is totally separated from production of one's own shelter, which inevitably occurs in advanced hierarchical societies. Participation is not measured by license; indeed, participation is often greatest in traditional societies whose building "rules" substantially restrict the latitude of permitted variation, and least in societies whose advanced technology allows a wide range of capricious variation. In the latter, the person has come full circle back to the situation of cave-dwelling ancestors: no longer a placemaker, he/she is a place-receiver once again.

Even more, the user/dweller becomes further and further separated from the *decision process* involving dwelling, especially when the architects involved are no longer local but governmental, quite unfamiliar with the physical and cultural context into which they are supposed to "fit" their design, as in both contemporary Cappadocia and the present American Southwest.

Thus, the "problem" does not inhere in any particular context or situation but is rather a function of *separation* among peoples (peoples whose cognitions of the environment are derived from different modes of production), and the privatization of *specialized* knowledge, exacerbated by cultural gaps. Specialization presents opportunities for professionalization and "mystification" of knowledge. Knowledge itself then becomes territory, to be privatized and defended, patented, even embargoed; such knowledge is not meant to be communicated to ordinary folk.

One early form of professionalization is associated with the emergence of religious hierarchy and the "house blessing" ceremonies that may accompany site selection, initiation of construction, the construction process, and occupancy of dwelling. The construction process itself is then professionalized and "mystified" (what could have been more mystical than the Society of Masons during the Middle Ages?). After a time, design and construction divide and the *Architect* emerges as a new professional, a new specialist.

Consideration of modern society allows us to consider, as well, a typology of participation and reintroduction of the lost dialectic:

(1) nonparticipation: the dweller is a passive recipient of a dwelling, as described in the paragraph above;

(2) symbolic participation: all aura, no actuality;

(3) token participation: only the few are chosen to participate;

(4) mass participation (nondialectical)

    a. indirect (Version 1): verbal questionnaire or survey;

    b. Indirect (Version 2): democratic decision making through limited verbal participation in community meetings; Note that both (a) and (b) above are hierarchically organized and professionally directed. Decisions are never jointly determined, nor reciprocal; the participant is allowed only to make inputs into the decision framework of the professionals;

(5) restored dialectical participation; here, the dweller (client/user) and environmental specialists share information nonhierarchically. Reciprocal communication is restored. This form of participation, also called "meaningful participation," is rare — but effective. It is a restoration as well of the subject/object dialectic.

3c2. *Stratified and nonstratified organizations.* Societies in the primitive communist (or kin-ordered) mode of production are characterized by *collective appropriation*; such societies are classless and unstratified. Stratification begins with the emergence of a protofeudal ruling class, often a "priesthood," or a class of ceremonial leaders. During an historical "transitional period" these ceremonial leaders may continue to labor; later they become an "upper stratum" of nonlaborers whose existence must be supported by a class of laborers. Sexual division of labor also results in stratification, with men usually occupying the upper stratum.

Stratification in a social organization emerges when the control of the means of production is vested (often concealed) in one group and establishes such indicators of social status as wealth, income, power, occupation, education, privileges, responsibilities, and cultural interests; along with these, *dwelling* takes on an important role as an expressive image of stratification. Social injustice results from societal stratification and concomitant private ownership of the means of production. Housing production is no exception; on the contrary, differentiation in residential space is very much an outcome of stratification in society (Castells, 1983; Harvey, 1973). Social and spatial relations are so tightly interwoven through class divisions, reproduction of social relations, and different modes of consumption, that patterns of spatial division and use manifested in the residential structure are not just temporary and passive expressions of broader social forces. Use of available land on one hand and the quality of dwelling conditions on the other represent residential differentiation and the degree of residential segregation, reinforcing certain types of spatial consumption, forms of tenure, and reproduction of social relations, all of which are essential to the class controlling the means of production. Hence, societal stratification, through the accumulation of property and authority, reinforces spatial differentiation based on ownership and tenure.

3f2. *Hierarchically and nonhierarchically ordered space; spatial "order" and "disorder."* Social stratification is associated both with social hierarchy and with spatial hierarchy. Within the realm of human settlement, an emerging hierarchy may be characterized by: (1) Differences in room or dwelling size; (2) Differentiated siting, with the more "favored" or more "favorable" sites occupied by the upper stratum; or (3) Proximity to central or important places; (4) Differentiation in room features, furnishing, or "amenities"; (5) Accumulated surplus product; (6) Paraphernalia (often ceremonial goods among societies in early protofeudal or prototributary stages).

Thus, in societies characterized by unspecialized labor, it is hypothesized that functional spaces dominate and that space is organized nonhierarchically. A change in mode of production to that characteristic of a more hierarchical society, with more specialized roles within the household, new public roles, and new social norms, results in changed space use and eventually in changed spaces. Glassie (1975; 1982) has recognized this in his studies of Virginian and Irish country houses.

When associated with the satisfaction of basic needs, functional organizations endure. But hierarchical arrangements differ: the precise nature of the hierarchy is not *given* by the mode of production. Both, however, are related through basic principles of spatial order. In traditional dwelling, spaces are ordered according to needs related to conditions of existence. Places for activities are related to the activities themselves, both sacred and mundane.

Spaces appear disordered for two reasons: (1) we do *not* understand the underlying rules of order (usually because we do not understand the conditions of existence of the society) and therefore impose, or judge, according to our own rule system or (2) we have *incorrect* understanding of that society's rule system. Thus, the apparent "messiness" surrounding a squatter dwelling, as in a *gecekondu* at an early stage of development, may actually be a "stockpiling" system for building materials, appliances, etc., to be used in future enlargement of the dwelling (Turan, 1987). People may construct and use outhouses or other outdoor spaces for bodily ablutions, not because they are ignorant of principles of sanitation or plumbing, but because it is culturally inappropriate (or otherwise inefficient, or economically unfeasible, to have a toilet inside a house).

A second important reason for apparent spatial "disorder" is an uncontrollable social or physical environment. This may result from a traumatic transition from one mode of production to another; the originally intended order may then give way to real disorder, disrupting or destroying the place/activity dialectic. If the space is flexible and therefore partially controllable, however, a new order emerges. (See below, *Inclusive and exclusive; open and closed spaces*).

With reference to the typology constructed at the beginning of the chapter, the top half is to some extent a set of "antecedents," the bottom a set of "consequences." If we depict each of the dialectical relations in the lower half as "polarities" (but *not* as opposites), the following relationships in domestic architecture emerge:

Dwelling/"Home"

Shelter	*Property*
use value	exchange value
noncommodified environment	commodified environment
nonowned place	owned place
inclusive space	exclusive space
open space	closed space
social identity	individual/family identity
public/private continuum	public/private separation

This may help to clarify the relevance of what follows to the overall structure outlined earlier.

3c3. *Ownership and nonownership of place.* A place may be "owned" informally, through accustomed use, or formally. Nonownership, or common use, is often associated with hunting and gathering societies in the early stages of the primitive communist (or kin-ordered) mode of production, whose need is primarily for temporary shelter, storage, and processing or butchering stations. Many cave dwellings, rock shelters, and open sites fall into this category. With adoption of sedentary living, it was possible to determine who could live in, pass through, or use a particular place; the last persists in some traditional societies in various forms, e.g., the "grazing permits" of certain North American Indian groups.

Formal ownership is associated with a place's acquisition of exchange value; the place, or part of it, can then be bought and sold. Eventually, ownership becomes more than just an economic state: it becomes a criterion for self-evaluation, for the establishment of individual/family identity *apart from* social identity— it becomes an expression of self-image. Hence, the dwelling as an environmental object acquires aspects of communication. Impersonal conditions of everyday life, growing with increased stratification of the society as exchange value gains precedence over use value, leave most people with no alternative but to make use of the dwelling and other material belongings as measures of their own worth in the society. In Wikse's words, "ownership is the authentic metaphor for identity" (1977; pp.33); certainly it goes as far back as ancestor worship in Catal Huyuk where the skulls of ancestors were buried under sleeping platforms to secure the family dwelling for future generations; here, establishment of *identity* was apparently tantamount to ownership.

3f3. *Inclusive and exclusive: open and closed spaces.* The subjective/objective (environmental/cultural) system of relations just described sets rules (norms and regulations) for the use of domestic spaces: what functions or persons are allowed, when and how the space may be used, etc. Some activities may be *proscribed.* In a Western house for example, bedrooms are typically not for entertaining, nor are dining rooms for making love. Grouping toilet, sink, and bath in a single room without partitions limits the number of persons who may use the room at once; also limited are compatible functions (the number of different activities that may take place simultaneously), and the relationship of the people (kinship, age, and sex) who may occupy the space at the same time. There are functional restrictions as well; one may read on the toilet but not pray.

Where separation of the sexes is rigidly enforced, there are spaces exclusively for men and others exclusively for women. But a space that *excludes* men may be meant to *include* more than one woman; it may be a sexually exclusive but socially inclusive space. If, for example, cooking is done by women and is culturally a social activity, a separated kitchen violates the inclusiveness of this activity. Some American Indian families demolish the wall separating the kitchen from the remainder of the dwelling in modern governmental housing.

In the latter example, the kitchen is "closed" relative to the rest of the dwelling. This is consonant with the Anglo American and Latin American values which spatially separate food production from food consumption (and other household functions) but nonconsonant with Native American values concerning open and closed spaces. The open/closed dimension relates both to the physical accessibility or inaccessibility of spaces, and to the individual/familial/social relations accommodated by these spaces. But openness/closedness is also *relative*: the courtyard is closed relative to the street, the balcony closed relative to the courtyard, and the room closed relative to the balcony.

Inclusive/open spaces tend also to be more *flexible* than exclusive/closed spaces. Flexibility, in turn, involves the potential changeability of an environment, its character as "flowing space," and the presence of architectural "loose parts"— uncommitted or only partially committed areas that allow the creation of "in between" spaces.

3c4. *Individual/family identity and social identity.* Many traditional societies in the primitive, communist (or kin-ordered) mode of production stressed commonality of interest and social identity; under conditions of existence characterized by a scarcity of tools, labor had to be pooled, and collective appropriation implied cooperative effort. Individual and family identity were therefore closely tied to social identity.

Western industrial capitalism, on the other hand, stresses the establishment of individual and familial identity, *apart* from social identity, through competition. The result is reflected even in the nature of the research we currently pursue, and the way we label phenomena, such as the emphasis upon crowding, territoriality, and privacy, in studies of environment and behavior (Maxwell, 1983).

Familial (nuclear family) identity gains special importance with the growth of surplus product. There is a dialectical relationship between the right to privacy, individuation, separation, etc., and social obligations: e.g., "Ancient Lights" in Britain, part of English common law, stresses traditional rights to sun, view, ventilation, etc. "A house of one's own" implies neither total autonomy nor, for that matter, self-sufficiency; the nuclear family is supported in part by the community with which it may or may not *identify*. Thus, vernacular symbolism is not of the house alone; the community, too, has its symbols of identity that, in part, limit the freedom of expression of its several households. There are mutually and dialectically related pressures toward stasis and change.

Most importantly, the house is the *locus* of many things. In the vernacular environment, it is the basic unit of social production, social relations, and social reproduction; of social praxis (in part) and personal autonomy (in later modes of production); of whatever links exist among individual, family, and social identity. New environmental demands — conditions of existence — may alter both the family's demands upon or social distance from the community and *vice-versa*.

3f4. *Private/public realms.* The desire for privacy, it has been said, is a socially created need; it is a form of "escape from the demands and burdens of social interaction" (Moore, 1984; p. 14), or a form of protection against the intrusive elements of the public realm. A wide sphere of social networks creates the public realm through division of labor, sharing of social product, kinship — nuclear family, lineage, band, tribe — relations, village/permanent settlement, occupational grouping, religious community, and political unit. This network of social relations also concerns property and authority (Moore, 1984; p.50). While property may be instrumental in creating spatial privacy as a protection from intrusion, authority may be double edged and may intrude as well as protecting against intrusion, depending upon specific circumstances, persons, or institutions. Whatever the source of desire for privacy — to escape from oppressive companionship or from a threatening obligation, individual possessiveness, modesty, cultural norms concerning human physiology, etc. — the private realm of a dwelling can only become meaningful and understandable when considered together with the public realm.

Private is not just "privacy." Altman and colleagues (Altman and Chemers, 1980; Altman and Gauvain, 1981) define privacy as "social regulation;" indeed the private/public dialectic, like the union/separation dialectic, is a nested hierarchy. The house is private relative to the community, the community private relative to the larger neighborhood, the larger neighborhood private relative to the city. There are no absolute "semiprivate" or "semipublic" spaces. In a dialectical sense, the relation of "public good" to "private property" in the economic domain insures this. In a social sense, admission of a group of strangers into a house may temporarily convert a part of the private household into a public zone. The "community-private" central plaza of the Indian pueblo becomes public during dances and festivals. Thus, it is spatially defined, but not impenetrably: there are openings at the corners.

The most important issue is not the definition of "public" or "private" alone, but that the definitions of "public" or "private" are:
(1) given only in the dialectical relation between the two, and
(2) inseparable from the degree of commodification of the space in question. The most "private" of all places is, in many ways, that which is termed private *property*.

In this chapter, we have attempted to construct a framework to improve our understanding of domestic architecture and settlement patterns — "vernacular" form — of traditional and transitional societies. We have emphasized the transitional aspect because it is so often assumed that vernacular building is only the unchanging product of static societies, which we termed "traditional." Such are the small minority, and most vernacular architecture is the product of an ever-changing process, incorporating older and newer elements, and both traditional and transitional values.

The framework introduced here has attempted to relate certain global concepts to fundamental relations derived from the theoretical position elucidated earlier; these in turn are further related to specific social and physical manifestations in built environment, some of which are reinterpretations of now-classic "environment-behavior interactions." The relationships are presented as part of an ecologically conceived whole and analyzed with reference to certain specific examples.

Chapter Seven

UNDERSTANDING PLACEMAKING:
THE ANATOLIANS AND THE ANASAZI

> How can space be "ideological"? ... The question has itself tended to be absorbed by naturalistic or anthropological perspectives, most often based on conceptions of the human body ... If the body is in reality a social body, if, therefore, there exists no pre-given human body as such, but rather the whole historical range of social experiences of the body, the whole variety of bodily norms projected by a series of distinct historical "modes of production" or social formations, then the "return" to some more "natural" vision of the body in space... comes to seem ideological ...
>
> F. Jameson, Architecture and critique of ideology.

Chapter Six presented a framework for analysis of observations made in the first five chapters, directed toward explanation and structured in terms of a form/content dialectic along one dimension, and successively embedded global concepts, fundamental relations in domestic architecture, and realization along the other. In Chapter Seven, we attempt to apply this analysis to an end of gaining greater understanding of our two case studies.

The chapter begins by recapitulating, in capsule form, the conclusions, tentative conclusions, suggestions, and indications drawn from material in Chapter Five and earlier chapters. Next, an attempt is made to reconstitute this material at three levels: transformational, relational and operational. The last of these is divided into the eight subcategories introduced under "specific, interactive social and physical dimensions" in Chapter Six, through which aspects of Anasazi and Anatolian placemaking are analyzed and, wherever possible, related.

Recapitulation

We have traced Anatolian prehistory through nearly twelve millennia from ancient Belbasi through Hacilar, to the Christian settlements of Cappadocia, from the beginnings of the primitive communist (PCMP) or kin-ordered mode of production (KOMP) to feudalism; and Anasazi prehistory from hunting-and-gathering Paleo-Indians through early pueblo periods, and the rise and fall of the great pueblos, to the Spanish conquest of what is now the American Southwest. To understand socioeconomic development in Anatolia through twelve millennia and its reflection in placemaking activity — the production of built environment — one must understand concomitant social changes that occurred in the long transition from communal cave dwelling to the individual family house. To recapitulate, a combination of economic base and ideology set conditions of existence in the PCMP or KOMP that affected placemaking activity throughout the period in question. From division of labor power by sex to division by families, from simple to complex labor, from collectively-produced and collectively-owned tools to specialized production and private ownership, forces of production shifted within the PCMP or KOMP as relations of production changed from pure egalitarianism to eventual social inequality. These changes resulted from increased surplus product and altered mechanisms for the extraction of surplus labor. Ideologically, parallel transitions occurred from matriarchal lineage systems primarily based on endogamy to exogamous patriarchies in Anatolia as isolated hordes gathered into tribes, with a concomitant change from magical to totemic ideology. Ideology of descent strengthened the family as the unit of production, and later strengthened the centralization of power, as reflected both in the architecture and settlement forms of the examples described.

The evidence for development and change in each of these areas inheres in the material culture of preliterate societies, and particularly in their architecture. To recapitulate further, we began with the personalization of caves in the cradles of both Anatolian and Anasazi civilizations, and discovered in communal storage pits and in preagricultural villages, the beginnings of surplus product and surplus labor. Circular structures gave way to rectangular structures, then to clusters of "row houses," presumably reflecting clan organization. Interior space became more differentiated and more detailed: rooms that had only hearths at one period boasted platforms and small ovens at a later time. Family living quarters even separated what had formerly been communal living space; positioning of ancestral skulls may have helped to define these new spaces in some Anatolian settlements, and at least a few burials among the Chacoan Anasazi may have been associated with the accumulation of luxury goods indicative of substantial surplus product. Religious functions were removed from house shrines to community shrines and, as the ratio of storage space to living space increased, the ratio of the number of shrines to living spaces decreased. As population increased, then, centralization of religious functions was apparently correlated with an increase in surplus product, an increase which

— because it was valuable — had to be protected or defended through the construction of walls—not just against human intruders, but against vermin and hostile climatic factors as well.

The analogies between Catal Huyuk and Chaco at equivalent stages of development are only approximate; while physical ecology was similar, conditions of existence were by no means identical. There had been no large game in the Chaco region during the past several millennia, and no pastoralism until the period of colonial expansion; hence, there was less reason for sexual division of labor or the consequent shift from matriarchal to patriarchal power. Even if such a shift were in the process of occurring at the beginning of the second millennium A.D., enthographic evidence suggests that it either never proceeded very far or reverted to a more egalitarian society at some time prior to the historic period.

In spite of these differences, however, other aspects of the Anatolian record just indicated appear to have had many developmental parallels among the Anasazi and in Anasazi architecture, as indicated in the foregoing section. Even in the area of religion, certain researchers have noted similarities between the two locations, e.g., "When I read the sizable comparative record compiled by the phenomenologist and historian of religions Mircea Eliade...[,] I get the distinct impression that by simply altering the terminology a bit for ancient Near Eastern religions, the statements could apply just as well to the pueblos" (Ortiz, 1972; p.141, quoted in Saile, 1985; p.164).

Cosmological orientation of Anasazi buildings (as well as Mesoamerican structures) has been noted by Doxtater (1990; 1991), among others. Whether early Anatolian parallels exist, and whether changes in modes of production in the latter are associated with decline in cosmic systems, as suggested by Doxtater, has not yet been determined.

Regarding Anasazi economic systems, the "long-distance trade" hypothesis, and the possible role of *pochteca* in bridging the "Chichimec Sea," Curtin (1984) notes:

> It may be surprising that the temple economy hypothesis regarding Mesopotamia could reach as far as the interpretation of Middle American history, but it happened. Anne Chapman (1957) took the Pochteca to be state servants on the model of the Mesopotamian temple servants who supposedly acted as trade agents. When the Pochteca went abroad to conduct cross-cultural trade, Chapman interpreted this as an administered trade...based...on the assumption that people at similar levels of development will have similar institutions. (Curtin, 1984; p.86).

It is now established that the structures of Chaco Canyon — such as the well-known Pueblo Bonito—played a central role in Anasazi society. Once supposed to be vast residential complexes, these are now believed to have had other, functions. Some contend that Chaco was a religious and ceremonial center, others that it was a nexus of commercial exchange (Lekson et al., 1988). Certainly, a major center need not have been exclusively religious, commercial, or residential, but could have performed *all* these functions.

The presence of specialized centers suggests the availability of much surplus labor. So, too, does the far-flung network of prehistoric roads connecting Chaco with its outliers (Powers, Gillespie, and Lekson, 1983) and with other centers. The existence of such roads, used only by travellers on foot, if more than ceremonial, implies extensive exchange, and most likely, considerable surplus product in at least certain locations; advanced pueblos apparently devoted a large amount of space to storage.

These results, when combined with others expressed earlier, suggest that more studies involving labor estimates, comparative populations, room sizes, household units, and public and ceremonial spaces may indicate whether the central canyon Chacoan settlements were approaching the tributary mode of production, characterizing a truly regional economic system and a nucleated settlement. An alternative sociopolitical model, introduced in Chapter Five, is dealt with further in Appendix Two.

As indicated in Chapter Five, Polgar (1975) has put forth a set of propositions concerning phenomena associated with the transition in mode of production from primitive communism (or the kin-ordered mode of production) to feudalism (or the tributary mode of production). Among these are more specialized architecture, more sophisticated defense systems, and more provision for storage and exchange activity. Our findings suggest that while Polgar's criteria may characterize both areas under consideration here, they constitute necessary but not sufficient conditions for the kin-ordered to tributary transition.

Reconstitution

Among the Anasazi and prehistoric Anatolians, indications are that these societies, whose appearance was widely separated in time, went through similar, early stages of development, moving from early hunting and gathering stages through socially unstratified small semi-sedentary villages to larger sedentary villages, eventually producing truly urban places. Our tentative conclusion is that stratified societies developed in both locations; however, for reasons not yet certain but later to be explored, the evolution of such stratifica-

Understanding Placemaking 281

tion, if it ever began, may have ceased (and may have possibly reversed) in the case of the Anasazi, while continuing, at least in part, among the societies of central Anatolia.

In the last chapter, we outlined a scheme for the reconstitution of the evolution of placemaking and settlement, a scheme based upon a dialectical relationship between form and content, between the natural and human-made environment and associated human action. In this chapter, we apply this scheme more explicitly to the Anasazi of North America and to central Anatolia.

Transformational level

Global concepts constitute the transformational level which indicates a change either in external form or inner nature, i.e., the content of the architectural program, purpose, function, need, aspirations. It is in this transformation that the broadly conceived purposive activity of placemaking is realized.

Natural environment, per se, may not offer shelter beyond large tree trunks, cavities, or caves in rocks. However, in its broader meaning, natural environment is an all-encompassing setting, providing not only places for habitation and for all that is necessary to sustain, develop, and reproduce life but also a surrounding landscape, a material source (resource). People use this natural environment as wealth, in the sense of both subsistence and instruments of labor. In other words, human labor makes natural environment the subject of such labor: "Nature becomes one of the organs of his activity, one that he annexes to his own bodily organs, adding stature to himself ... " (Marx, 1967; I, p.179).

By acting with and against nature, people change and, in fact, transform both the environment and themselves, thus generating the idea of nature existing apart from human beings (Glacken, 1967). "Nature," as Williams succinctly puts it, "has to be thought of... as separate from man, before any question of intervention or command, and the method and ethics of either, can arise" (1980; p.75). Thus do different ideas of nature—metaphysical, religious, secular, or rational—develop and become part of a culture's thought system. Reciprocity between the sensuous and the intellectual, between the natural and the cultural, between form and content, plays an important role in human perception and cognition of the natural environment. Domination or appropriation of nature thus becomes an important dimension of a society's art and culture, of which placemaking is a subcategory.

Further, a society's art and culture, its expressive and symbolic forms, its magical and totemic aspects, are closely entwined with its ideology. In other words, ideology is more than just political or religious; it is more than economic, too, including the work of the artisan and the craftsperson. Artistic works, such as the "decorative" aspects of placemaking and its changes, are expressions of the ideology of both the artist and the society (and its subgroups): art is therefore a representation of the artist's cognition of skills, of means of expression, of society's values. In the KOMP (PCMP) ideology is strongly totemic and magical; early temples differed in scale and decoration from dwellings. In the TMP (FMP), dwellings of the wealthy are qualitatively as well as quantitatively different from those of ordinary citizens, expressing divergent relations of production.

Techne (from which the word "technology" is derived) employed in architectural activity includes ideologies of societies, in addition to materials, tools, and skills. Within the framework of these ideologies, the designer's/builder's art and interpretation(s) of symbolic meaning are expressed. The degree to which artistic expression is individual or collective is determined by the nature of social relations—*techne* is art, a combination in placemaking of expressive ability and construction skill; the building *process* is an inseparable part of built form. Knowledge and wisdom concerning environment and expressive power are neither independent nor autonomous: they are both part of what constitutes *techne*. In the framework of production relations, *techne* thus expresses societal ideology through built form.

Along with other aesthetic forms, commodities, law, and logic, societies create, perpetuate, and develop architectural forms. The content of these forms is determined by the society's environmental and cultural conditions of existence. Subjectivity and objectivity of content, that is, levels of *perceived* experience and what *is* experienced respectively, coexist in a state of dialectical interaction. Dwelling/home, regardless of its form, its content, its scope, and its degree of subjectivity or objectivity, is socially conditioned and therefore a societal category. In the course of formation of this societal category, the dwelling becomes much more than mere shelter in both its form and content. The dwelling is associated with domesticity, intimacy, privacy, convenience, efficiency, leisure, pleasure, coziness, restfulness, and expressiveness.

In the historical process that brought placemaking from caves to cities, placemaking itself changed in fundamental ways, including a shift in the very basis of rationality. The spatial interests of dominant groups, always among the constituents of architectural form, became determinants. While the forces that shape architectural forms start with present reality, or with the results of stages in the historic past, such reality is only fragmentary, disconnected and partial. Dwelling resulting from placemaking activity emerges from natural environment, and is transformed into ideological environment. In the transformation from natural to ideological environment the use of abstract categories of

Understanding Placemaking 283

cognition and perception become increasingly prevalent. Extrapolating reality in accordance with that which is selected and accepted by the dominant groups, architectural specialists mistake the part for the whole, and fail to comprehend their own presuppositions.

Viewed from the outside, ideological environments seem self-contained, rational, all-embracing, collective representations. This facilitates confusing ideological with natural environment, strongly reflected in environmental and cultural deterministic points of view, which attempt to establish links between environment or culture and people's architectural activity. Ideological environments serve as instruments in the conflicts among classes and among different interest groups. On one hand, their form reflects partial reality; on the other, it masks the true needs, interests and aspirations of all the groups involved, as well as concealing the structural characteristics of social relations that give rise to such forms. When mistaking the part for the whole, environmental and cultural determinists support architectural mythmaking through intellectual legitimation of ideological environments.

Images that ideological environments create serve three primary functions (Lefebvre, 1968; p.76):

(1) to create an identity for and to proclaim the preponderance of the dominant class itself (e.g., priesthood);

(2) to exalt the position of the class struggling for dominance among other classes; and,

(3) to subdue subordinate groups and devalue the positions of "inferior" classes.

Form becomes content through image-creation. In other words, "content" contains the ideological aspects of the society which give shape to a specific architectural form, and to the image desired. However, images do not transform themselves into deep-rooted structures since they are not independent of production relations.

As ideology becomes subsumed in and more rigorously absorbed into the cultural system, natural environment becomes form and ideological environment content. On the other hand, at the transformational level, while the natural and ideological environments constitute content, shelter and property make up form. Within the form aspect of the transformational category, the relation of shelter to property also bifurcates into form and content. The concept of property in spatial organization gives rise to ideological environment, making property the content, and shelter the form. The reciprocity of form and content at the transformational level articulates the different levels of placemaking as a societal category. The two interacting and intersecting dimensions of the dialectic that shapes the dwelling/home (first, the natural/ideological environment and shelter/property; second, the interrelationships within each) exist at this transformational level determining the evaluation of existing order and, hence, of the decision process in placemaking. However, the dialectical reciprocity of form and content does not stop here; it is also inherent in the relational and operational levels.

Relational level

As indicated in Chapter Six, environment is both the subject and object of labor. Subject and object coexist dialectically. The architect as the producer and the building as the product are part of the same moments of history. The user or inhabitant and the environment used or inhabited are the products of the same forces. The nonparticipating user (subject) becomes external to the built environment (object). In other words, the nonbuilt environment is a resource (subject) converted by users and builders (other subjects) into built environment (object). The built environment, *once realized and occupied*, becomes subject relative to other factors. The resulting contradiction between subject and object alienates both producer and user from the reified architectural product.

A similar dialectical unity on the form side of this relationship exists in living and working relations/environments: both also have a "need" dimension. The dialectic between living needs and work needs establishes a relationship determined by the positions of these needs at a given moment of history. As labor becomes detached from the laborer, the separation between living and working becomes more pronounced. Parallel to it is the separation between city and countryside. Separation between living needs and work needs further enhances passivity: people behave as if the world outside their very own were shaped entirely by "others." Further, certain "shapers" acquire more power than their colleagues:

> Specialization of function also introduces another aspect of social organization. While it does not force it, it opens potentiality for differential status and power within a human community. Some functions might, from time to time, have seemed more indispensable than others and opportunities to acquire status and power would have existed (Festinger, 1983; p.109).

Beyond the satisfaction of needs to cope with various social and environmental forces, dwelling/home directly or indirectly, also gratifies people's *wants*—desires and wishes to possess and enjoy an intimate environment providing comfort and other conditions necessary to sustain life and to carry on daily activities. Within this scope, the dwelling/home is useful to the inhabitant. Whether or not this, the immediate environment, is produced by the inhabitants themselves or by others specializing in construction, if the dwelling is *consumed by an inhabitant without passing through a market*, the production of the dwelling is for use rather than exchange. Thus, *the use value of a dwelling is its capacity to satisfy the needs and wants of the user.* The individuals' labor, involved in the production of the dwelling for use, is thus expended within the bounds of personal social relations.

Dwelling/home may also be produced for exchange. For its production to acquire an exchange value (apart from actual exchange), a dwelling must acquire qualitative equality with other commodities and differ only quantitatively in the amount of exchange value possessed by each. This implies commodification of the dwelling. A commodified environment must possess exchangeability independent of its use value.

Dwellings are shelters/houses/homes and have use value as long as they are inhabited and used. Dwellings are also products of human labor. But a dwelling, even with these properties, does not become a commodity until something is added to its use value. "To become a commodity," a dwelling as a product "must be transferred to another, whom it will serve as a use-value, by means of an exchange" (Marx, 1967; I, p.41). The exchange value is attached to the substance, i.e., the use value, of the dwelling. "The commodity" Marx draws attention to is also

> ... the direct *unity* of use-value and exchange-value, and at the same time it is a commodity only in relation to other commodities. The *exchange process* of commodities is the *real* relation that exists between them. This is a social process which is carried on by individuals independently of one another, but they take part in it only as commodity-owners; they exist for one another only in so far as their commodities exist, they thus appear to be in fact the conscious representatives of the exchange process (1970b; p.41).

Obviously, commodity exchange, in one form or another, took place in pre-capitalist societies. The central question here is: when does an environment become commodified, and to what extent does this commodification have an effect on the shaping of the environment? To summarize the argument: an environment becomes commodified after it acquires use value for someone other than the producer, by means of an exchange, and only after an exchange value is attached to the particular environment, which makes it exchangeable against other commodities. These conditions include a dwelling being produced by and/or with the help of persons specialized in construction. However, this surplus physical production is qualitatively different in different modes of production and under different conditions of existence. "The qualitative difference between the commodity as one form among many regulating the metabolism of human society and the commodity as the universal structuring principle has effects over and above the fact that the commodity relation as an isolated phenomenon exerts a negative influence at best on the structure and organization of society" (Lukacs, 1971; p.85). Therefore, determination of the extent to which an exchange process is the prevailing form of change in the dwelling per se cannot be based on quantitative or functional attributes alone.

Changes occurring in domestic architecture are primarily the result of changing values of a society. The social relations of production are the dominant factors contributing to the shaping of the dwelling. With reference to pre-capitalist societies, as Marx observes, "[t]he social relations between individuals in the performance of their labour, appear at all events as their own mutual personal relations, and are not disguised under the shape of social relations between the products of labour" (Marx, 1967; I, p.77). However, as the producer is separated from his means of production, as all personal relations involved in the construction process dissolve, as commodification of the environment proceeds, and as exchange value overpowers use value, all other social and economic conditions necessary to enter the capitalist mode of production develop, as do the forces shaping the environment in general and the dwelling in particular. While the placemaking process may exhibit some quantitative similarities in different modes of production, placemaking is qualitatively transformed with the social relations that belong to different modes of production. As these qualitative differences build up, they manifest themselves quite distinctively in the placemaking process. Aesthetic and conceptual boundaries, for instance, between vernacular and institutionalized architecture, between handicrafts and art, and in the division of labor involved in each, require restructuring and re-organization, both quantitative and qualitative.

Operational level

Cultural and environmental conditions of existence. Buildings in general and dwellings in particular are cultural and environmental terrains. No architecture emerges and survives in an environmental and/or cultural vacuum. Buildings produced also create their own environment and culture as well as their own variations, primarily dependent on cultural and environmental conditions of existence specific to certain modes of production prevailing in the society. Social formation, the purpose of production, and the mechanisms that appropriate surplus labor all affect the shaping of the built environment. The intervention of determinate social relations between individuals takes place first only at economic and ideological levels, then, with the emergence of the state apparatus, on the political level as well. However, it should be noted that it is "[t]he

Understanding Placemaking

mode of production of material life" that "conditions the general process of social, political and intellectual life" (Marx, 1970 b; pp.20-21). Variations at the level of material conditions — productive forces and environmental conditions — do not exclude variations at the cultural level. On the contrary, it is primarily the cultural conditions of existence that intervene at the economic level.

One of the most important contributions of cultural conditions of existence to the evolution of the dwelling in Anatolia was the emergence of the family following the germination of the concept of property. Shelters previously accommodating non-family labor units developed into "homes" for families. Ancestor worship as a claim upon property developed so as to be instrumental in the intervention of cultural conditions in the shaping of the dwelling. With its more definite spatial boundaries, the emerging, "family dwelling" was a major breakthrough from collective living quarters or temporary shelters accommodating labor units, whether caves/cavates or huts. However, while the family dwelling represented substantial alteration in habitation, it did not introduce notable changes in the collective significance of placemaking throughout the PCMP.

Another outstanding cultural contribution to the formation of the dwelling in Anatolia, and perhaps among the Anasazi as well, was the centralization of religious authority. This separation between sacred and mundane brought about relative secularization of everyday life and the formalization of the priesthood. It also secularized dwelling architecture and sanctified the architecture of worship. As long as people had beliefs of any sort prior to the formalization and centralization of religious authority, house and shrine were the same. Following the differentiation of religious functions, the shrine developed as a separate architectural space. Emergence of this new cultural condition and of societal stratification was antecedent to both secularization of the dwelling and the elaboration of religious space.

This separation also led to new architectural forms and spatial developments. While the house/shrine was under a single roof, the union formed the locus for surplus control. With the separation of the above two functions, the locus shifted to the shrine. The dwelling lost both cultural and economic power. Although the development of property and the nuclear family allowed some individual control over the dwelling and led to new developments in the spatial organization of the dwelling itself, transfer of power to the shrine not only prepared conditions for a "higher" mode of production—protofeudal—through the development of property, but also created new architectural forms. After 4000 B.C. the locus of surplus control in Anatolia shifted to the higher level of settlement, by now under the total control of a central religious authority. Separation and differentiation of functions continued to give individual significance to some selected buildings, such as houses of special persons, temples, and later, defensive structures.

In the Anasazi area after the tenth century A.D., the "Chaco Phenomenon" and Chacoan system were qualitatively and quantitatively different from developments elsewhere in their region of North America because the Chacoans apparently overcame the economy and ideology of scarcity by "distributing the load" of scarcity in such a way that the system thrived. Whether it was actually characterized by a partially redistributive economy (as discussed in Chapter Five), and whether the system involved "exploitation" in any form, is still in some dispute (Mathien and McGuire, 1986).

A major issue regarding the Anasazi is: did the ideological system change? At its earliest stages of development, Anasazi society was characterized by kin-ordered ideology. However, changes in *placemaking* behavior — from cave to pithouse to above-ground dwelling — are indicative, in the absence of a written record, not simply of "progress" in the ability to manipulate built form, but of other qualitative *and* quantitative changes.

Two primary "revolutions" — the extinction of large game and the introduction of maize — occurred long before the appearance of the first pithouse. Later changes appear to have stemmed from alterations involving increases in quantities of game harvested, and improvements in maize types and in cultivation of other crops. This enabled both greater reliance on sedentary agriculture and an increase in the quantity of surplus product, requiring permanent and secure storage facilities. Changes in agricultural production were accompanied by changes in building technology supporting and facilitating nuclear family formation and reducing reliance upon the fully communal society appropriate to hunting and gathering. Thus, while ideology of kinship remained, the spatial distribution of the unit comprising the kinship system changed. The evolution from "found shelter" to pithouses facilitated the greater choice of location necessary for cultivation in a highly variable semi-arid environment and allowed horticulture to emerge more easily. Hence, change in dwelling permanence, as well as in form and location, paralleled changes from the pursuit of large game through the pursuit of smaller game to the "cultivation" of still smaller game, and from plant gathering to plant cultivation.

The relation between culture and environment is also reflected in the dialectical relationship between natural and supernatural forces. That the human agents involved in this dialectic had not been separated from spiritual forces in the early stages of puebloan development is indicated by the absence, when compared with later stages, of specialized ceremonial/religious structures; presumably, major collective rituals took place at natural sites (Doxtater, 1990).

Understanding Placemaking 289

Participation and nonparticipation. Nonparticipation is the separation of those who "do" from those who are "done for." Nonparticipation in built environment is a function of the degree of specialization. Where specialization is highly structured, one "does" only in the realm of one's speciality; one is "done for" in all other realms. This is related, as well, to subject/object relations: the greater the degree of specialization, the greater the separation between "subject" and "object" aspects of the environment.

Unfortunately, without the support of a written record, Anasazi and pre-Hittite Anatolian built environments allow us to draw no firm conclusions concerning degree of specialization in placemaking activity. Prior to Lekson's (1984a) assertions that extraordinary amounts of ordinary labor may *not* have been required for Chacoan great house construction, it seemed reasonable to picture a large undifferentiated mass of workers laboring mightily under the direction of relatively few planners/architects/urban designers. Lekson's thesis leaves open the possibility, if prodigious amounts of labor were *not* required for construction, of both "worker" and "professional" specialization: the former through a division between agriculture and construction, the latter a division among planners, master builders, and artisans.

During the PCMP, communal labor not only allowed but also required direct participation of individuals in every facet of daily activities, including placemaking, in spite of the genesis of specialization and separation of living and working environments. The social character of labor, as Marx points out "is evidently not effected by the labour of the individual assuming the abstract form of universal labour or his product assuming the form of a universal equivalent. The communal system on which this mode of production is based prevents the labour of an individual from becoming private labour and his product the private product of a separate individual; it causes individual labour to appear rather as the direct function of a member of the social organisation" (Marx, 1970 b; pp. 33-34).

We have stated earlier that environment is both the *subject* and the *object* of labor. Lekson's (1984a) observations on the forces of production (labor) indicate, without minimizing the extraordinary accomplishments of Anasazi architects, planners, and urban designers, that their monumental accomplishments were by no means miraculous. Nonetheless, they achieved what they did in the absence of means of production — draft animals and metal tools — taken for granted in Middle Eastern building at the same stage of development. Because of this scarcity of resources, the Anasazi must have understood and conserved their environment to a remarkable degree. Their accomplishments seem to have required an ideology of human relationship to the environment that recognized scarcity and the necessity of interrelationships requiring cooperative living patterns, and — at least at early stages of development — the need for some rudimentary defense of scare surplus product.

Nonstratified and stratified organization. As the shrine assumed the fundamental role in surplus control and redistribution, reciprocal systems of exchange gave way to a major reliance on redistribution. Power and wealth were accumulated in the hands of a small minority of religious leaders. Centralization of control over the allocation and use of land, while motivating the producers to create more surplus (especially with the intensification of agricultural production), initiated development of power differentials between kin groups. On one hand, this change in the economic system and the rise of the political system prepared the necessary conditions for the formation of states and urbanization, driving wedges between settlements and between town and country; on the other, the new developments led to social stratification.

With the rise of the powerful Hittite Empire, stratification of Anatolian society developed into a rigid system. Differentiation in dwellings and the beginnings of the megaron form as distinct units of property are observed as early as the sixth millennium B.C. at Hacilar. Construction of grandiose palaces, monumental temple complexes, and heavy fortification systems was as much for defense from insiders and for image creation as for protection from outsiders and control of wealth, surplus, and power.

The question of whether Anasazi society at its apex of development was stratified or non-stratified is at the center of our argument. At least some of the available evidence points, if not to a highly stratified society, at least to the substantial improbability that a *simple* unstratified society could have accomplished what the Anasazi did in their attempt to cope with a hostile environment in a flexible manner. If stratification did in fact exist (and there is at least one plausible alternative, as indicated in Chapter Five), it seems likely that it was "introduced" or "appeared" as part of the pueblo to great pueblo transition which occurred at Chaco at the end of the first millennium A.D. and in other locations somewhat later.

Societal change, to the extent that there was any, may have occurred because of the existence of hostile neighbors or external threats (although there is little evidence of fortification or mass burning, for warfare or defense, on any scale); or may have been, in part, a response to a manifest need for a tightly organized, complex economic system devised to "even out" the effects of a climatically unpredictable environment; or it may have evolved together with a system of trade that included not just exchange *within* the Chaco system, but directly or indirectly with Mesoamerica as well.

Understanding Placemaking 291

The change in spatial order, which occurred at the end of the first millennium A.D., suggests some adjustment in mode of production. Part of this is treated in the following section concerning the hierarchical organization of space. Other evidence suggests that Chacoan structures were more than just larger pueblos. Such evidence stems from a consideration of at least ten factors, most of them — in the absence of a written record, once again — gleaned from manifest architecture and planning:

(1) quality of construction;
(2) elaboration of architectural details;
(3) road system;
(4) sizes and internal diversity of megastructures;
(5) room sizes;
(6) storage areas;
(7) *possible* defensive elements such as the absence of ground-level entrances;
(8) burials;
(9) sizes and multiplicity of kivas;
(10) evidences of advanced, comprehensive planning and urban design.

However, it should be stressed that *Chacoan* great houses and small houses were similar in all the above *except* 9 and 10.

Such differentiating factors are said to have characterized the development of built environment in stratified societies. While the major argument usually cited for total nonstratification is the ethnographic record of the American Southwest Ellis (1979) has indicated in the case of the "town chief" or *cacique* of present-day Isleta, that even contemporary pueblos are not completely egalitarian:

> Because all his time was spent in his ceremonial house "working" for his people, [the cacique] and his family were publicly supported. The field set aside for him was planted and harvested under direction of the war priest, and one or more great jars buried in front of his fireplace kept filled with seed corn for which the poor could apply (Ellis, 1979; p.361).

Hierarchically and nonhierarchically ordered space; spatial "order" and "disorder." Development of productive forces and social formation have not always been smooth and progressive on the Anatolian peninsula. Economic and political fluctuation, combined with ideological persistence of the different in-migrants and what they brought with them (e.g., different kinds of experience, knowledge, and technological innovation), led to upheavals which caused either traumatic transitions or unstable conditions for extended periods of time. These sociopolitical convulsions, which caused temporary discontinuities in otherwise fairly steady developments or which may have led to periods of retrogression, deviating considerably from the process of forward-moving development, obviously took its toll on the built environment as well. Lloyd and Mellaart observed such spatial disorder in the late Chalcolithic (ca. 4000 B.C.) architecture of Beycesultan:

> After the prodigies of creative invention among peoples of the Neolithic period...and their prolongation into the early Chalcolithic at Hacilar, some ethnical change of great significance must have taken place, which temporarily eclipsed the ascending star of civilized aspiration. For, in the deepest levels of the Beycesultan sounding, which represent the beginnings of a later Chalcolithic phase, there are conspicuous signs of cultural regression and a return to the primitive living conditions of much earlier times. It is as though all the urbane attributes achieved by humanity in the two previous millennia had been suddenly eradicated and a fresh start made with the meager resources of a village mentality (1965; II, p.60).

Metzger points to a similar regressive phenomenon during the Hellenistic period, approximately four thousand years later, in the dwelling houses of Priene (1969; p.185). Far from an improvement on earlier types, rooms opening onto a small courtyard adjacent to the street represented a backward step to a much earlier form. Carved dwellings of Cappadocia, at least in view of their antecedents and progressive standards of efficiency and change maintained evenly from earliest times onward, may also be considered architectural products of a stagnant or even retrogressive period.

None of these "relapses," however, hindered the development of the Anatolian megaron (with a central hearth and vestibule), or the courtyard (atrium) house, or the carved and built-out houses with *eyvan* in Cappadocia. These developments partially involve a hierarchical ordering of spaces. Previously undifferentiated spaces went through diversification and differentiation as a result of change in specific function both within and outside the dwelling. What is at issue here is not the actual form but the architectural content that is significant in such gradual evolution.

As space in the Anasazi pithouse became separated into "living" and "working" environments, so exterior space became specialized as well. Amorphous collections of pithouses evolved into planned pueblo communities, whose outdoor spaces were often elevated above surrounding fields, and further subdivided with low walls, as in Chacoan great houses. Production originated in the irrigated and cultivated fields, while processing took place in the open spaces defined by pueblo compounds and later-emerging megastructures. Complementary to spaces that may have served as threshing floors or communal areas for grinding maize with *mano* and *metate* were kivas, great and small, and plazas for ceremonial dances. Thus, associated with what may have been an increasingly specialized society were more specialized spaces.

During the initial stages of sedentary dwelling, living, working, storage, and ritual were accommodated in propinquitous spaces. With the development of economic exchange and more centralized religious functions, working and ceremonial activities required spaces of their own. Spatial separation possibly reached its apex during the height of the Chacoan system when, according to some theorists, Chacoan structures may have ceased to function as egalitarian residences (if ever they did so) becoming, instead: (1) ceremonial centers; (2) market centers; (3) elite residences; or (4) some combination of these. Perhaps, at this point in prehistory, whatever residents there were served primarily as caretakers.

Separation of storage spaces from other spaces is less clear. There is the suggestion of a separation of storage from dwelling at Mesa House among the Moapa Valley Anasazi in the work of Lyneis (1986), who notes that between 950 and 1150, small rooms became smaller and large rooms larger:

> By analogy with ethnographic societies, large rooms are considered to be habitation rooms and small rooms storage, although that is no doubt an oversimplification.... [Another] trend is an increase in the ratio of storage space per habitation unit (Lyneis, 1986, p. 72).

But Mesa House also contains attached rooms that have no associated smaller (presumably storage) rooms. For these, all storage space appears to have been

> ...in formally arranged chains of storerooms attached to very large habitation rooms. This interpretation of Mesa House suggests the emergence of lineages with communal storage facilities and a recognized individual or family as the head of the lineage (Lyneis, 1986, p.72).

The shift to communal storage that is thus suggested seems to be associated with the emergence of, in Lyneis's words, "multifamily corporate groups" — perhaps precursors, on this western fringe of Anasazi habitation, to the development of clans.

While spatial hierarchy may have existed in the Anasazi world prior to the emergence of the "Chaco Phenomenon," hierarchically ordered space emerged most prominently in the Chacoan great houses. Indices of hierarchy summarized in the last chapter characterized Chacoan building: there are evidences of hierarchies within structures, among structures within the central canyon, between the central canyon and those towns referred to as outliers, and within the outlier towns themselves.

Evidence for nonhierarchically organized space might involve the demonstration that Anasazi megastructures were no more than collections of relatively undifferentiated dwelling units. The search for such dwelling units, once assumed to be the "building blocks" of Chacoan great houses, has been frustrated by several factors:
- marked discrepancies in room sizes;
- problematic association of hearths or exterior location with dwelling;
- the strong possibility that Chacoan great houses were not dwellings at all, or began as dwellings and became market/ceremonial centers, and/ or reverted to dwelling use during the presumed later occupation (so-called "McElmo period") by Mesa Verdeans.

Here, as elsewhere, the number of questions exceeds the number of answers. Was there dwelling stratification in the central canyon? Were some of the small structures (presumably dwellings) south of Casa Rinconada, in contrast to Vivian's (1990) contention, actually a "poor" ("working class") district and, if so, does this imply the existence of a "managerial class?" Did this managerial class actually exist? If so, did its members also participate in the building process?

Ownership and nonownership of place. One of the factors through which the development of productive forces affects the nature of dwelling is the transition from communal to individual ownership, along with shifts from matrilineal to patrilineal social organization and from larger clan units to family units. Dwelling/home is one of the first means of production to be claimed as property, extracted from communal ownership by the family. Ideology of descent or ancestor worship can be traced back to Catal Huyuk (seventh millennium B.C.), the recorded beginning of a long tradition of intramural burial of adults that became a common practice in Anatolia in the third and second millennia B.C. and continued as late as the Bronze Age — ca. 2000 B.C. — (Mellink, 1956; pp.45-50).

Ownership that emerges with the concept of property develops partly due to scarcity of housing and natural resources, and partly due to the desire to keep these in the family; "the product of labour bore the specific social imprint of the family relationship with its naturally evolved division of labour" (Marx 1970b; p.33) under the rural patriarchal system. Commencement of competition, exploitation, and social inequality are also the results of scarcity or lack of productive forces (Polgar, 1975) — means of production and labor power. Coupled with increase in productivity (Thomson, 1978; p.297), scarcity of housing germinated individual property and in the past, the family. Also contributing to this development were certain physical characteristics of the dwelling, among which were a fixed location, and, to serve varied uses, relatively complexity (Harvey, 1973; pp. 157-160). The immobility of the house restricted simple exchange but provided wealth in a different form: its relative long life, providing "social security," and its ability to respond to diversified use made the dwelling more attractive as family property and added powerful impetus to the growth of private ownership. Furthermore, on one hand, rising central authority in control of surplus product, and, on the other, the penetration of simple exchange mechanisms from the "borders" to "the interior of the community, exerting disintegrating influence upon" (Marx, 1970b; p.50) communal property in favor of individual property, contributed to family ownership of the dwelling.

The shaping of the megaron house, the courtyard house, and the house with *eyvans* paralleled the development of the family as a social unit. Their articulated individual forms (in contrast with the communal nature of the previous collectives) were essential to the sustenance and development of a new social unit: the family and its ownership of the dwelling.

Paralleling changes in content — the purposes of shelter — were changes in form. In the evolution of Anasazi shelter/building, six stages of development can be distinguished:

(1) "found" shelter/temporary camps/butchering stations: communal shelter;
(2) simple constructed shelter/pithouses; extended/nuclear family, limited surplus product sheltered with family;
(3) constructed shelter; groupings of pithouses according to presumed kin (clan) relations; surplus product shelter attached to dwelling apart from family;
(4) mixtures of pithouses and puebloan structures: property stored in separate buildings; nonpithouse kivas;
(5) extended pueblos, mixing dwellings and storage;
(6) megastructures: great kivas and multistoried units.

As Gilman's (1983) seminal thesis indicates, the transition from pit storage to above-ground storage has climatic advantages and may even reduce required construction labor; pueblo rooms protect property at least as well against human theft, and better against vermin.

There is no evidence that either land or structures ever acquired exchange value. However, there is indication of substantial, even widespread trade in goods among the Anasazi, perhaps extending as far as central Mexico; of short- and intermediate-distance trade with neighboring Anasazi in basic subsistence goods and over longer distances, in luxury goods of substantially greater exchange value, such as turquoise (Harbottle and Weigand, 1992). With increased surplus product, substantial and even extensive trade was undoubtedly possible, and the possession of luxury goods, along with status burials and larger quarters, *may* have contributed to the creation of an elite element in Chacoan society.

Anasazi housing and settlement was apparently never individually "owned" in the narrow sense of the word. From a broader perspective, however, while *individual* Anasazi may not have "owned" dwelling space and surrounding areas, Anasazi *groups* or *collectives* clearly "owned" the buildings they constructed and the land they occupied. The widespread Chaco system, in sum, was undoubtedly not just a religious symbol, nor an economic necessity, nor merely a facilitator of economic exchange, but a political statement, an indication of a sense of stability, of collective "ownership" of a wide area over which the Anasazi exercised control.

Inclusive and exclusive; open and closed spaces. Ownership introduces the concept of restricted use of some space by certain persons. This goes beyond functional differentiation and personal comfort. Exclusive use of space is related to segregative and seclusive values. Acar (1978), in his brief essay, correlates these values with the evolution of a slave society and of the courtyard (or atrium) house. The inwardly-oriented Anatolian courtyard house with its almost blank outside walls, in addition to responding favorably to environmental conditions, also accommodated slaves, segregated them, provided a pleasant and comfortable indoor/outdoor space for the master and his family, and protected both from noise, dust and dirt, and from the intrusive presence of other people and their slaves. The development of self-contained, individual family dwellings, with their courtyard and two-story organizations during the Hittite period strongly parallels the introduction of *nam.ras* into the life of affluent people. In spite of the absence of private ownership of land among the Hittites, ownership of dwelling, among other means of production, existed. Elite individuals, apart from the aristocracy, were allowed ownership. Such widespread individual or family ownership of property in Hittite society, together with its use of war captives as slaves, was manifested in the provision of inclusive and exclusive use of space in the courtyard house.

Even in the Cappadocian dwellings which combined masonry building and carved-out spaces, inclusive and exclusive uses of spaces are very apparent. For reasons other than the accommodation of slaves, hierarchical spatial organization of the dwelling allowed for exclusive use of certain spaces, especially in houses of wealthy merchants. The development of houses with *eyvans* is also related to "exclusivity," spatially expressed.

The functional specialization of Anasazi places, which probably antedated the pithouse, continued as pithouses evolved into pueblos, and pueblos into

Understanding Placemaking

great pueblos. What started in the pithouse as sleeping and storage areas later proliferated and became further divided into such interior and exterior spaces as:
- dwelling rooms;
- storage rooms;
- open plazas (for communal labor);
- open ceremonial spaces;
- small kivas;
- great kivas;
- *ramadas*, or outdoor shade houses.

There are other divisions as well. Dwelling rooms differed greatly in size as did storage rooms and there is the indication, in Chacoan great houses, of a hierarchy of spaces which suggests that, with centralization and possible stratification, there was a need *both* for larger storage rooms and for elite sleeping areas. It is in these large rooms, too, at upper levels, that the "corner windows" presumably associated with astronomical observation are located in Pueblo Bonito.

At least three forms of "exclusivity" must be considered: group size, sex, and age. Who can occupy what spaces and when is, in the ethnographic present, determined by whether one is male or female; a child, adult, or senior; and represented as an individual, or a member of a family, a clan, or another group/society. Kivas, for example, are primarily restricted to adult males in present-day pueblos, but we know less about the nature of the exclusivity represented by the great kiva-small kiva distinction in Anasazi times. Lekson (1984a), as indicated earlier, has suggested that small kivas may be just "small rooms" (an outgrowth of the round pithouse) rather than an indication of the "privatization of religion." Predecessors to Lekson interpreted the small kivas as "family" ceremonial centers; these interpreters have failed, however, to associate specific "family" kivas with specific "family" living or storage areas; in fact, the number of small kivas is less than the smallest estimate of the number of families purported to have been resident in the Chacoan great houses. This points to a number of possible explanations, varying in the degree of exclusivity they suggest:

   a. the small kivas are simply "round rooms";

   b. some or all of the small kivas were each used by several families, possibly sequentially. Perhaps the sequent occupants of a particular kiva later became a clan of sorts; this would imply that the construction of great kivas may have *preceded* the evolution of clans and that the "groups" served by great kivas were *other* than clan-based;

   c. some or all of the small kivas may *not* have been accessible to everyone or at all times, but only to certain families (functioning as something analogous to "private chapels") or on special occasions. If — as seems less likely than before given Vivian's (1990) argument — a relatively permanent class structure existed, there may have been class divisions among kiva users in terms of who used them as well as when and how they were used.

Similarly, one can also ask, with regard to the Chacoan road system: were certain roads for the exclusive use of certain groups, for the sole purpose of certain ceremonial processions, or for multiple use, facilitating the transport of goods and building materials (Obenauf, 1980), and therefore "open" to a wider group of potential users?

Individual/family identity and social identity. From communal cave dwelling to the development of the individual family house in cities, placemaking is a manifestation of the invention and use of instruments of production, of which buildings are a part. Also, buildings represent a concretization of labor as a social process, as well as constituents of productive forces. "The labour-time materialised in the use-values of commodities is both the substance that turns them into exchange-values and therefore into commodities, and the standard by which the precise magnitude of their value is measured.... Regarded as exchange-values all commodities are merely definite quantities of congealed *labour-time*" (Marx, 1970b; p.30). An abstract and subjective dimension of a building's value, in this "congealed labour-time," is revealed by exchange and corresponding subjective and objective commodity relations: the image created by its appearance. This is particularly true when the dwelling becomes a means of exchange; the image a dwelling creates is also its identity, closely related to but qualitatively different from the image of ideological environments, for the inhabitants, at least within the norms of the society. The social character of labor, in image-creating or identity-assigning, appears to be objectively manifested in the physical dwelling. In the course of this manifestation, not only is the labor of the producer alienated, but the owner also identifies with an image, detached from the dwelling's real value.

As environments become commodified, the social identity that a dwelling environment may provide for all is transformed into individual identity for some. In the commodified form of the dwelling, individual identity for such people becomes the content of the architectural program constraining the appearance of social identity only as part of the form. Individual identity thrives dialectically on social identity, yet contradicts the latter. Reciprocity between identities enables dwelling, among other products of social labor, to indicate social distinction. However, for individual identity to be meaningful there must also be social identity, which itself comes into existence with division of labor. The universality of social identity is responsible, both objectively and subjectively, for the abstraction of individual identity in commodified environments.

Understanding Placemaking

While environments serving public functions — temples, market places, fortifications, etc. — still maintained a social identity in prehistory, their ideological images notwithstanding, dwellings of the wealthy or powerful, or of individuals personifying public functions, had to be different in appearance to exhibit the opulence and power of the owner or inhabitant. Such individual identity is obviously distinct from the identity required by certain groups for economic and social reasons, as was the case with artisans and their guilds in most feudal societies, or with the Assyrian merchant colonies in the Hittite cities. Dwelling as an instrument of individual identity became increasingly important with heightened commodification of the environment, even in the carved dwellings of Cappadocia.

Land and structures possessed no exchange value among the Anasazi during the pre-conquest epoch. Thus, habitation was not commodified in the sense of the acquisition of exchange value, but there are many examples of *quantitative* differences among spaces *within* a structure, and *qualitative* differences among structures in different locations (e.g., Chaco vs. Mesa Verde, assuming they were part of the same "system," etc.). The quantitative differences may have reflected differential occupant status, authority, and power.

The family/community dialectic which characterized early Anasazi society undoubtedly shifted with expansion and evolution of the Anasazi world. The communal hunting-and-gathering groups of the Paleo-Indian period evolved into the egalitarian and cooperative family groups inhabiting pithouses. A major issue at the height of the great pueblos is whether families, as such, were ever permanent residents of the megastructures. If the great houses were in fact residences/"hotels" for the elite, most ordinary people *may* have been relegated to outliers, increasing the range but decreasing the intensity of social interaction and social identity. We know that conditions of existence in Chaco and elsewhere within the Anasazi realm — the need to maintain agricultural productivity in a semi-arid environment under conditions of uncertain precipitation and increasing population — necessitated an expansion of the resource base. The diffusion and dilution of social identity that this entailed, over the immense range (for foot travel) that the Chaco system represented, may have been more than could be sustained over considerable time. Other alliances (e.g., that among the historic pueblos during the 1680 to 1692 period of the revolt) have crumbled under similar stresses of geographic separation and infrequent contact.

Public and private realms. In the course of the development of productive forces, one dialectical relation affected spatial organization, the practice of architecture, and the shaping of architectural theory: the private/public dialectic. One aspect of the dialectic does not exist without the other; they contradict each other; both are derivatives of the property concept. Space used collectively gets broken up with the division of labor and the rise of private property, as does function; the separation between private and public grows with increasing division of labor and the development of individual ownership. In the course of this process, private and public realms exercise considerable control over means of production.

Both realms represent a form of control over space. However, the qualitative difference lies in the fact that the public realm usurps the managing functions of redistribution, from material content to social form of a community, from physical to intellectual work, from economic to ideological and political activities. The private realm protects individual property against "others" and against the public, blocking out intrusive elements of the outside world. While social relations necessitate a public realm, such a public realm comes into conflict not only with the private realm but with itself. It serves to consolidate and to dissolve power; it is inclusive and exclusive space for both ruling and subordinate classes; it is collective and individual; it is essential in a spatial context for social relations (yet, from the point of view of individual ownership, totally dispensable); it is diversified and specialized. Objectively, a public realm is where objects, and relations between commodities and activities, are launched and reified; subjectively, it is estranged from the individual's own domain and it becomes detached from the individual.

With the emergence of public/private realms in spatial context, additional and special places for the rising elite were provided primarily to meet their needs of security and comfort, and to enable them to exercise control. The majority of the population was only of secondary importance. As spatial entities, both realms came into being as a result of the emergence of surplus product and the division of labor. In one sense, the "public" spaces were "private" to some members of the community. Shrines — later temples and palaces during the PCMP, the protofeudal, and the FMP — served as private realms of the ruling groups. Yet they purported to be public, public because they fulfilled not only religious and royal domestic functions per se, but also provided workshops, storage houses, and "offices" where some production, redistribution of products, and commercial activities were organized, directed and managed. On the other hand, the individually private space of the ordinary citizen was only a sleeping platform or, at most, a family house as a distinct unit of property.

We suspect that the Anasazi "house" became more secularized with time, and that (if the evolution of small and great kivas is an index) as religion became more centralized, more people visited Chaco from other locations. We do not know whether these visitors paid tribute, nor whether — if the Chacoan great houses served partly as "hotels" for people engaged in commerce or ceremonial observances — transient residents paid "rent," which certainly would have been a form of commodification. We also do not know whether the roles of site planner, master builder, and "priest" were tied together in a single individual (as among today's Navajo) or separated among specialists.

In many places, walls define private spaces. The presence of some walls characterized Chacoan, Kayenta, and Pajaritan settlements: low walls appear to have divided functionally separated community spaces — spaces for communal labor from ceremonial spaces, or ceremonial spaces from each other — while high walls separated spaces within each megastructure — dwellings from storage and from other dwelling spaces. There is little indication, however, of the division of productive, agricultural spaces from each other.

How privacy was accomplished, in the sense of "regulation of social interaction" (e.g., Altman and Chemers, 1980), is still an issue. The ethnographic record does not provide an answer. Hospitality is clearly an important value among contemporary pueblo societies, yet such people regulate interaction with non-pueblo societies very closely. This problem of outside intrusion may or may not have existed among the Anasazi. While not confronted with the threat of active interference by Hispanic or Anglo-American forces, such as has characterized the past 400 years, they may have had to contend with the influence of "foreign" traders.

From the perspective of Anasazi prehistory, private spaces emerged as individual sleeping areas in early cave dwellings. Extended family dwellings gave way to pithouses, probably representing the establishment of privacy at the nuclear family level, with private storage pits and an undefined public realm. With the appearance of small pueblos, what may have been private ceremonial spaces became kivas, perhaps serving several families; the undifferentiated public realm became a central plaza, while family spaces retained their private but egalitarian nature.

If the evolution of great pueblos represented a change in mode of production, it may also have involved the evolution not just of spaces for additional societal functions but for an emerging elite as well. If so, these elite spaces may have been even "more private." The "public" realms may have become more specialized in terms of who attended, who participated, and in what functions. "Group private" spaces perhaps represented more specialization regarding elite or non-elite participants, or were related to the evolution of clans. Finally, such "group private" spaces may have been opened to an as yet undefined "public" on certain occasions.

Chapter Eight
RECONSTRUCTION: TOWARD NEW FOUNDATIONS

> Solutions are not found in history. But one can always diagnose that the only possible way is the exasperation of the antitheses, the frontal clash of the positions, and the accentuation of contradictions.
>
> M. Tafuri, *Theories and history of architecture.*

In this final chapter, we start by summarizing, in different words, some aspects of an argument earlier presented technically.

Culture has its genesis, at the earliest stages of a society's development, in the "management" of survival. Survival within a given set of circumstances, also termed "conditions of existence," is dependent upon the production of certain basic necessities, the primary school trilogy of "food, clothing, and shelter." In the process of evolving ethnoscience, humans also invest the production process with additional meaning, resulting in ritual and ceremony, and elaboration of both domestic and public architecture. As the complexity of ceremonies and rituals increases, their management often becomes professionalized and vested in a new social class, the priesthood, and an associated specialized built form, the temple. Increased surplus product frequently results in the need to defend that surplus; a warrior class thus emerges with its associated palace architecture.

A combination of a "tourist view" of traditional societies and a desire to endow the producers of vernacular products with a value system more spiritual than that of the contemporary West often leads architectural historians, researchers, and theoreticians to cultural determinisms. Our negation of this is in no way to deny the important role of culture, but rather to question its primacy *in vacuo*, and, separated from its economic and political components, as a generator of built form.

The basic point, then, is that complex cultural systems emerge as the process of production begins to transcend mere subsistence. Thus, ritual, ceremonial, and architectural meaning are not generated spontaneously: their genesis is material rather than abstractly spiritual or

Reconstruction: Toward New Foundations

aesthetic. The marriage ceremony, however magnificent its manifestation, is the ritualized conclusion of property relationships between husband and wife, or of an economic and political union between one family or nation and another; thus, it is "wealth and marriage" rather than "love and marriage" that "go together like a horse and carriage." Rain dances are spectacular, but they are fundamentally intended to be economically productive; harvest dances are aesthetically expressive, but they are also ritualized communications often associated with the disposition and distribution of crops. Similarly, the Navajo (Dineh) house-blessing ceremony relates the practical necessities of domestic building — siting, orientation, etc. — to the world view represented in the Dineh creation story.

Thus, domestic architectural form is not abstractly expressive; rather, its expressiveness is derived from and representative of systems of production and reproduction, of socioeconomic relationships within and among socioeconomic units, whether these be individuals, nuclear families, extended families, or other entities. Alexander (1964) was careful to point out that the most aesthetically satisfying architecture did not emerge from rarefied "intuition;" it was, in his view, an outgrowth of satisfactory resolution of architectural subproblems, of potential "misfits," through the process of "hierarchical decomposition" (and subsequent recomposition).

As the social and production relations of a society change, the built form changes, or people adapt older forms to new uses. In Mexican cities of the 1960s, for example, most middle class families had resident servants; the economic crisis of the 1980s rendered this no longer possible. Some new architectural forms reflected this change in class relations, but older forms had to be adapted — in interesting ways — to changed social circumstances. It is important to emphasize that this critique of cultural determinism, and of the fragmentation of the concept of culture in its relation to built form, is in no way uniquely Marxist. Lawrence (1987), for example, talks about "context-dependency" (similar to the "conditions of existence" to which we have referred). He criticizes Rapoport's (1969) denial of the pertinence of a chronological perspective (although Rapoport does argue for the study of adaptation and transformation), and the specific way in which the latter divides influences over house form into primary determinants (sociocultural determinants) and modifying factors (political, economic, material resources, etc.); Lawrence also reminds us that Rapoport, in the preface of his 1969 book, "wrote that his contribution was an exploratory analysis, being a personal interpretation rather than a definitive and accepted body of thought" (Lawrence, 1987, p.77).

Unfortunately, as in so many cases, this caveat seems to have been ignored by readers. A similar point is made in Alexander's "pattern language" (Alexander, Ishikawa, and Silverstein, 1977), which was originally intended as a methodology for generating and integrating what might turn out to be culturally-specific patterns. Ignoring this intention, many users have simply taken the illustrative patterns as universal "givens," reproducing them in wholly inappropriate situations.

Therefore, we reiterate our own caveat here: we claim no final word on our subject — what we have done is to follow a line of reasoning to see where it leads, to indicate a new, and (to us) interesting interpretation of inquiry. Our hope, once more, is that readers of this book will take careful note of this intent.

We have attempted to demonstrate that placemaking is a part of social production, a sociospatial action connecting the behavioral and cognitive aspects, environmental factors and use values of space, institutionalized in "architectural practice" of one form or another. It is neither primarily "technical," "formal," "conceptual," nor "culturally expressive": it is a process to which the producers (builders, architects) contribute, containing social relations that affect all parties involved. Therefore, through production relations, placemaking is simultaneously economic, cultural, and political—and an integral part of one or more modes of production.

The gradual transformation from one mode of production to another inevitably carries some of the social, cultural, and economic forms of the previous mode of production to the successor at varying degrees, in different enclaves of the society. Therefore both the meaning of "tradition" (Chapter One) and traditional means of production need to be reevaluated. Societies or those enclaves of societies in which not "all the productive forces [are] sufficient" for the "new superior relations of production" to exist and, in which not all the necessary "material conditions for their existence have matured within the framework of the old society" (Marx, 1970 b; p.21), have not completed the transformation and continue with their "traditional" means of placemaking. A long-established custom or practice of placemaking may be replaced both conceptually and materially by a new one wherever and whenever conditions of existence allow such deployment, creating new contradictions between the older and more recent practices. The new practice, while establishing its own structure, leads to contradictions between itself and the earlier "traditional," as long as the latter continues to exist in certain segments of society. The new practice also develops contradictions within itself just as the older "traditional" did throughout its existence. Eventually, the new practice is bound to become "traditional" itself as changing conditions of existence require new forms of placemaking.

Another contradiction between the existence of communal property and the growth of individual property leads to formative relationships among class structure, political institutions, and property. The outcome of placemaking activity as a physical, built form acquires use value, accommodating certain functions of everyday experience. At the same time placemaking is used to acquire wealth and control over social relations. Hierarchically ordered space is related to property relations; therefore, placemaking is not only *part* of productive forces and production relations but itself a *product* of these relations, becoming a political implement in the control over space and spatial relations. The scope of class stratification and societal segregation that leads to spatial isolation of underprivileged groups is manifested in placemaking. Disintegration and hierarchical ordering of spatial organization caused by societal stratification provides the ruling elite a powerful tool for easier and more effective social control of institutional mechanisms and their agents, eventually producing disparate standards of living.

A critique of inquiry concerning placemaking

The effectiveness of the influence of productive forces on placemaking is contingent on relationships at the "operational level" (as defined in Chapter Seven). The realization of placemaking specific to the interactive social and physical dimensions at the operational level involve interdependencies among possible developments in the realm of productive forces. While the development of productive forces extends and changes the scope and constituents of placemaking, this extension is not manifested only in objective conditions but also in the subjective interaction among the builder/architect and other agents involved in the placemaking process. Both objective and subjective relations of environmental and cultural conditions of existence play an important role in the placemaking process, as the natural environment external to the human is appropriated and transformed into something useful (i.e., acquires *use value*).

Ranges of transformational changes in ideological environments and in the property relations incorporated into the built form of the dwelling can be reconstructed only within the framework of *the specific features of placemaking*. This implies, first of all, that the universal, *absolute* validity claimed by "mainstream" approaches to architecture (usually confined to mere appearance and form) are highly questionable. The true identity of placemaking is blurred, if not obscured, when its changing boundary conditions and its internal structural transformations are not taken into account in the understanding and evaluation of built form. Not only are the "facts" distorted, since the totality is broken into selected fragments, but the values that are intrinsic to the facts are also separated from them, establishing an artificial dichotomy. Hence, what could have been an insightful evaluation often degenerates into banal description. The purported universal characteristics result from treating architectural activity in general and placemaking in particular as independent phenomena.

Thus, many empirical, aesthetic studies turn out on close examination to be distortions. In addition, claims of validity turn out under close scrutiny to be false since they lead nowhere toward explaining the true structure of placemaking activity. This "helpless, formless relativism," to use Harvey's term, (1973; p.17), stands on a surface that is slippery and without foundations.

This situation poses a predicament for the student of placemaking. It is an irreconcilable dilemma deforming the structure of placemaking, rendering norms invalid when faced with demands for discursive justification, producing results against which standards of rationality may not be measured.

As long as researchers in the "mainstream" are concerned primarily with architectural form per se, values pertaining specifically to use and exchange, commodification of environments and property relations of placemaking are overlooked, by omission or commission. The "mainstream" approach, by ignoring the powerful forces of socioeconomic, political, and cultural organization at work in placemaking, ascribe mystical properties to ill-understood aspects of dwelling environments, often merely reifying characteristics of the location itself. Production, sustenance, and reproduction of architectural forms do not occur by themselves nor do they take place in a space devoid of environmental and cultural conditions of existence. Discussion of the evolution of placemaking without reference to social relations is as fruitless as arguing for instance, that architectural form exists without content.

The sharp distinction between fact and value, between description and evaluation articulated in the empiricist tradition, leads inevitably to treating placemaking as an isolated phenomenon, detached from all the relational aspects that constitute the totality of the building and dwelling process. Also, internal development of a mode of production does not only create both cultural and environmental objective conditions of existence but subjective conditions as well. Thus, questions regarding placemaking need to be formulated in such a way as to include relational characteristics and subjective conditions so as to overcome the distortions of a perspective informed by mere "architectural facts."

Rather than dealing with a purely ontological question in the abstract, such as "what is placemaking?" and trying to set up simplistic cause-and-effect relationships, or to create a totality independent of its parts, the nature of placemaking requires an inquiry which focuses on the broader environment and social formation, asking how all the constituents of a society are related specifically to placemaking. The ontological status of placemaking can be more realistically determined by knowing its parts and the true nature of their connections. Then, "what constitutes placemaking?" and "how is placemaking materialized?" become the questions that will reveal the "whatness" of placemaking: its ontological status.

"Facts" themselves are conditional: they must be related to specific times and locations in order to establish correctly the antecedents of existing environmental and cultural conditions. It is inadequate simply to connect architectural form to a set of facts existing independently of historical changes. Since the historical process assigns values to the act of placemaking from its inception to its completion, as well as to the builder, architect, and inhabitants, the premise of autonomy or even neutrality cannot lead to explanation. Hypostatizing ahistorical, incorporeal characteristics of placemaking and claiming both impartiality and absolute validity for these provides neither a theoretical framework that resolves the ontological status of placemaking nor a truly "neutral" methodology.

The positivist claim to objectivity on one hand, and the impressionistic exaltation of aestheticism on the other, do not address the question of what constitutes the architectural object that is produced, perceived, cognized, and experienced simultaneously. The "fact fetish" of empiricism does not address the relational aspects of placemaking, and therefore ignores that facts are products of theories, as well as of social relations. Traditional aesthetic theory does not usually set the ground for evaluating forms of placemaking with regard to essential human characteristics. Much of it is mere idealist essentialism, and asserts that built form is only a reflection of pictorial form.

Behaviorist and other empiricist mainstream approaches often distort architectural reality. Synthesis and conclusions arrived via isolated pieces of information are legitimized under the guise of neutrality or scientific objectivity. Architecture and placemaking are reduced to a set of behavioral patterns, to combinations of environmental forces, or to technological dimensions by means of which the form is examined with no reference to the social relevance of architectural activity. Therefore, the social construction of architectural reality is excluded even from studies "researching" placemaking (which itself is socially conditioned, produced, distributed, consumed, and experienced). Approaches emphasizing mainly aesthetics or idealist treatments of architecture/placemaking as art have two principal characteristics. First, they assign to the relation between the architectural object as art and as spatial organization an epiphenomenal status which overrules any aspect of production and consumption of place (and, therefore, its true social relevance). Materialization and realization of an architectural object becomes a metaphorical localization in which the artistically independent architect creates forms, artistically beautiful (and fictive in nature), for pure enjoyment and pleasure. Architectural objects are produced to fulfill the requirements of aesthetic merit. Thus, the symbolic functions and intrinsic features become the center of focus.

Second, possessive and individualistic, modern, Western lifestyles are related in this type of analyses to the more fundamental question of constitution only if the artist/architect or artist/builder is remote from social and historical circumstances. Often other agents and forces involved in the process are negated in order to emphasize the realization of artistic or aesthetic values.

Obviously, these values are representative of the dominant ideology of the time. This fragments both thought and experience. While subjectivity is supposedly eliminated from empiricist studies, which pretend to be value-neutral, such subjectivity is apparently present in numerous artistic approaches. Further *collective* subjectivity has no necessarily greater significance in the culture of a society.

There appears to be a common line of reasoning in these two dominant yet qualitatively different mainstream approaches: an environmental object (built form) can be (and often is) analyzed and evaluated on the merits of its present existence with reference neither to its historical antecedents nor to its relation with the rest of the forces that shape it. No attempt is made to bridge the gap between appearance and social reality. This split between contemplative thought and everyday experience is often forced to its extreme as if the two were dichotomous and independent of each other.

What constitutes placemaking is only part of the subject under consideration. It is not only the elements or constituents of placemaking that matter but their relation and connection to each other under different circumstances. It is the level of articulation that imparts a broader and more powerful explanatory capacity to inquiry. The contextual evidence, i.e., the material conditions, the nexus of their interconnectedness, and their inherently conditional nature, illuminate an architectural reality increasing our knowledge of the object. Hence, by dehistoricizing and desocializing the act of inquiry, placemaking appears to be a transcendental and unconditioned activity. This tendency prevents us from comprehending the inner structure of placemaking. It is further deficient in its lack of connection to praxis.

A theoretical explanation of placemaking requires consideration of the interrelationship between internal and external structure, and an understanding of the transformation of this relationship into sociospatial development. In other words, theoretical *explanation* (apart from simple description) requires that we not only establish the *constituents* of placemaking, but also the influence of specific *conditions of existence* and *praxis* on them and on their interrelationship. This interrelationship is a combination of three elements: possible hierarchies, internal structure, and structural elements, usually considered "external" to placemaking, including economic, social, and cultural factors.

A consideration of *constituents* leads us to inquire into the meaning of "constitution:"

> ...one could say that the historical-materialist grounding of the "constitution problem" [was] what constituted the objects of our perception, judgement and action.... [*Conditions*] of knowing [are] not only...regulative ideas and categorical forms through which...we per-

ceive sense data as particular objects or events.... In principle, we never see or know objects as they really are, but only as they are "constituted" through these filtering and ordering forms (Gebhardt, 1978; p.380).

A critique of inquiry is also essentially a critique of the *method* of inquiry, and as Gebhardt indicates, "a method is simply a question" (1978, p. 379). In preceding chapters we have developed a set of issues to which questions may be related, and the most exhaustive of these are those represented in our "typology of placemaking relationships" in Chapter Six. As promised therein, we present here the same set of relationships in a circular diagram, i.e., in "polar" form. (Figure 8.1). In Chapter Seven we referred back to the three columns of Table 6.1 in Chapter Six—global concepts, fundamental relations in domestic architecture, and realization (going from the most general to the most particular) as "transformational," "relational," and "operational" respectively. Questions related to these categories can be classified as ontological, transformational, and epistemological. These may be further related to the journalistic "who, what, when, where, why, and how" in the following way: ontological questions deal with what exists: primarily with the "what" and "where." Transformational questions deal with change: primarily with the "when" and "why." Epistemological questions "seek to uncover the procedures and conditions that make knowledge possible" (Harvey, 1973; p.296); these deal primarily with the "how." "Who"—the human agents, actors, participants, and recipients of placemaking activity—is relevant to all of the above.

Now, returning to our circular diagram, and working from the inside out, the "core" is of course the product of domestic placemaking—the dwelling, or home—the innermost ring is the transformational level, the next ring the relational level, and the outermost ring the operational level of questioning. The second and third are related most closely to the ontological and epistemological classes of question, as described above.

Let us now take the most general question—"what constitutes placemaking?" — and break it down into some constituent sub-questions under the "operational," "relational," and "transformational" headings:

operational
- how is placemaking materialized or realized?
- what are the constituents of placemaking?
- what is the structural composition (in the material sense) of placemaking constituents?

relational
- how is placemaking related to human action?
- what are the dynamics of placemaking?
- how are the constituents of placemaking related?

relational and transformational
- how do structural transformations in placemaking correspond to changes in social relations?

transformational
- how are the dynamics of placemaking related to changing historical periods?
- what are the ideological and political contexts of placemaking?
- what is the structural composition (in a philosophical sense) of placemaking constituents?

This list is meant to be suggestive, rather than exhaustive, of the questions which arose during the course of our research (rather than prior to its initiation), and to which, for the most part, we have provided only partial answers. The list is "biased" in the sense that it is more representative of our view, our window on reality, than that of researchers concerned primarily with symbolic meaning and aesthetic expression. These are in sum, and from the perspective of this book, "directions for future research."

Recapitulation

(1) We have presented the case that, as part of an ecological/dialectical/ materialist concept of the relation of culture to built environment, principles of *production* and *exchange* are essential to the understanding of the evolution of placemaking:

Trade, barter, exchange of goods for other goods or for services rendered must be an inherent feature of all cultures from earliest times onward.... Human contacts, exchange of information at all levels, whether accompanied by gifts, trade goods, thefts or raids, marriage contracts or slavery, are the essential basis for cultural development. All else stems from this (Mellaart, 1975; p.277).

According to this view, intra-societal trade is all important. However, neither an advanced traditional economy nor its architecture are self-sufficient, and building materials and techniques used in one society's placemaking activity are often exchanged—at least in part—with the members of other societies as well.

(2) Placemaking is part of a scalar view of designed space, extending from the smallest physically demarcated area to the entire region. The interrelation of the various scales cannot be explained by appealing to architectural, anthropological, or archaeological theories alone; nor is adequate description or explanation possible without considerations of cultural, physical, and economic *context*. The nature of settlement in the pre-conquest American Southwest, for example, cannot be understood fully without considering the interrelated system which extended at very least from Casas Grandes (Paquime) in Chihuahua to Mesa Verde in Colorado, encompassing the Anasazi and their neighbors in a system of exchange which may have included the Toltecs of central Mexico (e.g., Hers, 1989). To risk a pun, architecture cannot stand alone, and vernacular architecture cannot conceptually be separated from the nature of the settlement and region in which it is embedded: all are part of placemaking.

(3) The utility of placemaking as a study tool is dependent upon a most obvious characteristic: its durability. Thus, we know much more about the civic and ceremonial architecture of certain societies than about their domestic architecture, not just because the former has traditionally been of more interest, but also because civic and ceremonial buildings are more likely to have been constructed of durable materials. In the same way, we know more about pots than about baskets: the former are less subject to selective survival. Our conclusions about prehistoric societies, such as the abandoned dwelling systems of preliterate people, are therefore both based on and biased by the artifactual evidence which has endured.

(4) In an earlier section, we stated that our purpose was to transcend cultural relativism, to uncover, through comparative study, not just the peculiarities of placemaking in particular regions but also certain general relations between built form and culture:

... comparative cultural studies should interest themselves in recurrent phenomena as well as in unique phenomena, and... anthropology [should recognize] that a legitimate and ultimate objective is to see through the differences of cultures to the similarities to ascertain processes that are duplicated independently in cultural sequences (Steward, 1955; p.180).

Such cultural sequences, embedded in modes of production, are presumably reflected in the architectural products of a society.

(5) Comparative, longitudinal (diachronic) studies such as this make clear that the important comparisons are *not* between societies, societal achievements, or architectural production at the same point in world history—i.e. the same position in global time—but at the same *stage of historical development*.

Thus, it would be no more appropriate to compare the American Southwest with Anatolia at 5500 B.C., the apex of Catal Huyuk, than to compare Anatolia with the American Southwest at A.D. 1000, the ascension of the Chacoan system. Rather, we have been comparing Anatolian and Anasazi phenomena and achievements at similar *stages* in the developmental sequence which characterizes the evolution of modes of production. It is this sequence, rather than dates, which reveals, in a comparative sense, what was actually occurring in the two cultures.

Reconstruction

This book was intended as more than mere research, mere reinterpretation of existing, raw, undigested data; rather, it was to be a combination of a story, even an odyssey, complemented with a radically new interpretation. It began with an outline of an interpretive methodology and continued with a comparative prehistoric progression of two cultures—those of central Anatolia and the Anasazi region of the U.S..

We found, early on, that the only explanatory framework with which we were comfortable, and which seemed to handle the millennia of data confronting us, was dialectical. Dialectical thinking, fortunately, is more acceptable today than it was some three decades ago:

> Today, this dialectical mode of thought is alien to the whole established universe of discourse and action. It seems to belong to the past and to be rebutted by the achievements of technological civilization. The established reality seems promising and productive enough to repel or absorb all alternatives (Marcuse, 1978; p.445; reprinted from *Reason and Revolution,* 1960).

We began to realize that one of the most pressing obligations of serious placemaking studies was to *incorporate* specific conditions of existence—the experience and its evaluation—associated with the *act* of placemaking, into the explanatory framework. We examined the question of *constitution*—the constituents of built environment—in an attempt to bridge the gap between "fact" and "value," the cleavage between "empirical" and "normative," and finally between "theory" and "praxis." Our positivist education had taught us that theory must precede praxis, but our experience in composing this book indicated the opposite: it was only through immersion in the contradictions and problematics of prehistoric Anasazi and Anatolian society that the necessary theoretical framework emerged.

Reconstruction: Toward New Foundations

We examined the historical progression of settlement in two widely separated but geologically identical areas in an attempt to discover, beyond simplistic environmental or cultural determinisms, what was actually going on. Raw "facts," slices through time, were misleading because they were abstracted from the historical progression, changing conditions of existence, production relations, and so forth; the most satisfactory interpretation, therefore, seemed to lie within the realm of dialectical materialism. We claim only a start—but a good start, we hope—in this direction.

To abuse an old cliche, we found both continuity and change in the prehistoric Anatolian and Anasazi regions. Given the environmental similarities of the two areas, we were led to reject simplistic environmental and cultural determinisms, and to adopt a position that was both ecological and dialectical. Ours was by no means the first attempt at an explanation, but only the first attempt at explanation from a *comparative* viewpoint. Certainly, physical environment played a role, as did "culture" in its narrow sense, but there seemed to be much more. Earlier explanations, it appeared, fell short because they relied on undigested "facts," dealt with purely aesthetic aspects of built environment, made wrong assumptions, reasoned fallaciously, assumed that ill-understood aspects of these prehistoric cultures were *solely* "ceremonial" or "religious" in nature, and/or relied on other simplistic determinisms. They were partial or even misleading because they lacked explanatory power, logic of structure, or critical coherence (Parekh, 1982; pp.186-210).

Further work in this realm of study needs to consider several factors in more detail: just how quantitative changes *within* a mode of production and qualitative changes *between* modes of production may be read from settlement form and derived human activity; whether *core* elements of a placemaking process change only with qualitative changes in mode of production; and the relation of the ethnographic present to the prehistoric past. More general methodological questions include further inquiry into the place of built form as a research tool, the possible future of dialectical/ecological theory, and the place of comparative study in this form of inquiry.

In summary, then, we feel that a unified, truly ecological view of the fascinating historical transitions evidenced by these two geographical areas — among others — requires a union of theory with praxis, and of fact with value. We hope that we have contributed some new bases for future efforts in the study of placemaking.

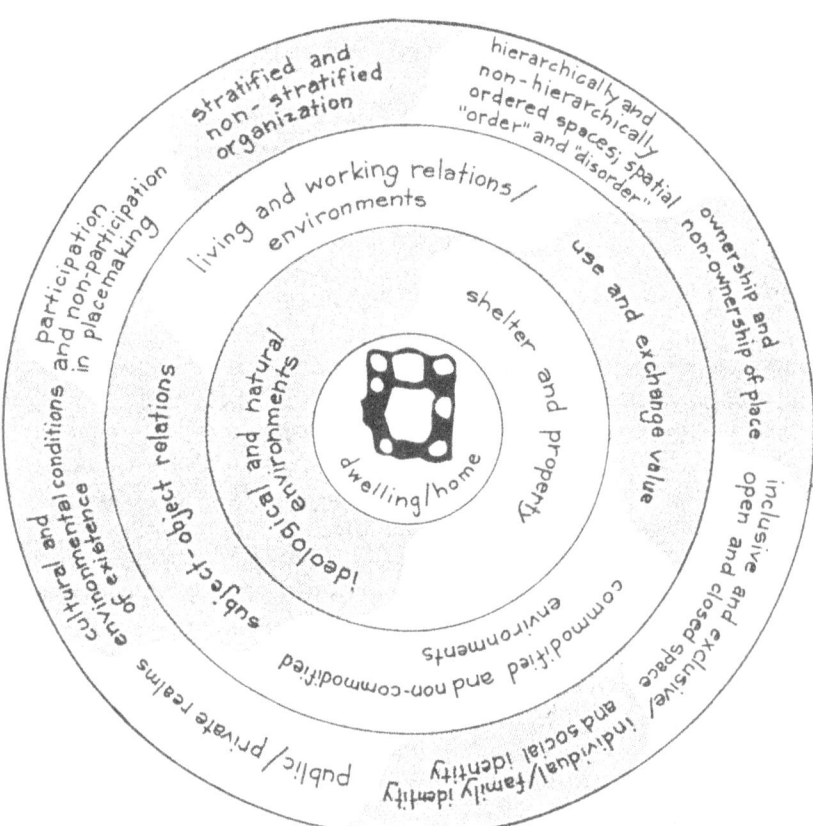

Figure 8.1 Typology of placemaking relationships. Dialectically related pairs are separated by shading.

Appendix One

ANASAZI ABANDONMENTS AND THE "MESOAMERICAN CONNECTION"

> The Chacoan collapse did not seem to have a major effect on subsequent affairs in its area. Life continued much as it had before. The Casas [Grandes] collapse, however, left a southern Mogollon area largely devoid of ceremonial architecture. Kivas were gone for all practical purposes and precious little else remained. This suggests that an area influenced by Casas had undergone a fundamental transformation of social relations that speaks of equally fundamental differences between the effects of egalitarianism and elitist social systems (Johnson, 1989; p.386).

It is usually supposed that, upon abandonment of the great pueblos, the inhabitants engaged in a stepwise migration first to such intermediate locations as Bandelier; then to sites, abandoned in historic times, east of the Sangre de Cristo, Sandia, and Manzano Mountains; and, finally to the still-extant settlements that constitute the Rio Grande, western New Mexico, and Hopi pueblos of today. This explanation for migration assumes the operation only of "push" factors, postulating that both the abandonment of the pueblos and the nature of the subsequent migration were simply reactions to stress.

The Anasazi clearly migrated—but where (and why) did they go? Explanations based purely on "push," on cultural and environmental stress (and, hence, on cultural and environmental determinisms), seem inadequate. We have referred earlier to the probability of prolonged contact between the Anasazi and Mesoamerica, and to the likelihood that the Anasazi not only engaged in commercial exchange with the people of pre-Columbian Mexico, but in the exchange of information as well. That the Toltecan or post-Toltecan society with which they were interacting was a technologically well-advanced prototributary society was likely clear to them and may have contributed a potential "pull."

Suppose that a division existed in Anasazi society in transition from a kin-ordered to a tributary mode of production (Wolf, 1982) similar to that in today's transitional pueblo communities (between "traditionals" and "moderns," or "progressives" and "conservatives"). We then have the basis for an hypothesis: two migratory streams emerged from collapsing Anasazi settlements. One, motivated primarily by "push" factors, moved to the sites of modern pueblos; the other, motivated by "pulls," moved southward.

There is little discussion in the literature about the possibility of such a southward movement into Mesoamerica. But it is not entirely a new idea. More than a half century ago, Hewett (1930) made the radical suggestion that the unexplained origin of a group of immigrants who mysteriously appeared in the valley of Mexico in the early fourteenth century, later called "Aztecs," was to be found among the Anasazi. The evidence, at present, is indeed scanty and circumstantial, yet the less radical possibility that at least some Anasazi moved *southward* during, or subsequent to, the "great drought" must be entertained. There is a bit of support for this, in the architectural record, to be found in relationships between architectural forms in Chaco, and those in Paquime (Casas Grandes) and La Quemada, in the Mexican states of Chihuahua and Zacatecas, respectively. A logical assumption had been that these relationships represented innovations moving from the more technologically-advanced south to the less technologically-advanced north.

Later studies, however, point to the possibility of movement and influence also in the *opposite* direction: DiPeso (1974), for example, suggests that the culminating stage of development at Casas Grandes in Mexico occurred *after* the abandonment of Chaco. More recent evidence (reported, for example, by Associated Press, 1984) indicates extensive movement in the present El Paso area between Chaco and Casas Grandes in the thirteenth and fourteenth centuries, as indexed by the presence of ephemeral pit houses (used for short periods).

The case for a southward Anasazi migration would, of course, be much stronger if there were clear evidences of Anasazi architectural influences along the presumed route(s) of travel, or Anasazi-style modifications to existing or abandoned sites. But placemaking requires time-in-residence, and if the migration were relatively rapid (or the Anasazi merged entirely with the migrating Chichimeca) such artifactual indications would be unavailable. In that case, the only habitational evidence might be the remains of temporary camps, such as those at La Quemada (Hers, 1989).

That at least some people moved southward, we are reasonably sure; we are quite unsure of whether or not this migratory stream included more than Chichimeca. In other words, how far north the migration began has yet to be determined, and in the context of hypothesized Mesoamerican "spheres of influences," it has been a subject of considerable conjecture. Adams (1966), for one, speculates on the extent of Toltec influence:

> Under the conditions of territorial expansion and from political control that seemingly obtained at the time of the Toltec "empire"...there is evidence that the zone of settlement not only reached its outermost continuous limits but jumped beyond them to form a series of isolated enclaves of local irrigation extending northward for hundreds of miles....[W]ith the internal collapse of Toltec political control...most of these marginal groups would have had little choice but to drift *southward* into the heart of the former Toltec realm...(p. 62; emphasis added).

Palerm and Wolf (1957) had also written on the relations between the Toltecs and such advanced marginal groups as the Chichimecs of Xolotl, and of the latter's migration toward (and through) the Toltec capital at Tula. The question of "who moved where, and when," is thus far from settled, leaving a significant gap in the research literature.

There is one more possible source of information: the Aztec's own story of their origin. The legend of the Mixtecan (Aztec) migration into the Valley of Mexico has been variously interpreted. The most frequently hypothesized geographical location for their (perhaps mythical) Aztlan ("place of the Aztecs," in Nahuatl) is Mexcaltitan; but other sites, including New Mexico, have also been mentioned in both the Tovar Manuscript and the Codex Ramirex (Duverger, 1983). Recently, El Museo del Templo Mayor, Mexico, has highlighted another site of prime importance in Mixteca legend: "the seven caves," or Chicomostoc, where the Mixteca, according to their own legend, met with seven other migrating tribes, all presumably heading for the Valley of Mexico. Chicomostoc is the name of the contemporary village at the site of La Quemada.

Placemaking, production, and migration

What evidence would tend to support the hypothesis that elite (if there were elite) Anasazi migrated southward after "abandonment?" Clearly, there are two aspects to be demonstrated: (1) that a southward migration into present-day Mexico, in fact, occurred; and (2) that it was the elite members of a prototributary society that migrated. In the demonstration of each of these, placemaking plays a role.

Unfortunately, available evidence is sparse in some cases and virtually nonexistent in others. Support for the preceding migration hypothesis would involve a demonstration of architectural similarities between sites, architectural disparities within sites, and class differentiations in artifacts and evidence of trade goods. We have already demonstrated this in the case of the relationship between Chacoan and Casas Grandes placemaking; architecture and the time relationship between the ascendance of the two offer some support for the hypothesis of a southward migration. Unfortunately, placemaking evidence markedly declines south of Casas Grandes. There is some evidence of a Chacoan/Mesoamerican mixture at La Quemada, but that is all. The rest of the sites mentioned earlier were certainly major settlements, major examples of placemaking, but consist largely of unexcavated mounds at present.

So the hypothesis remains unsupported, the question unanswered. Mexican architects and archaeologists are just beginning to demonstrate interest in northern Mexican placemaking prior to 1400, and North American architects and archaeologists (apart from a few, including the late Charles DiPeso and Philip Weigand) have yet to become involved. We assert that placemaking evidence is critical to the substantiation or refutation of the hypothesis stated above—but that such evidence is scanty at best and perhaps, in critical circumstances, presently unavailable.

The story presented in earlier chapters, read into the Anasazi ruins, is not yet a popular one. Still prevalent is a picture based almost entirely upon ethnographic analogy and apparent strong architectural resemblance between Anasazi buildings and present-day pueblos. That ethnographic analogy may frequently be, at least in part, "ethnographic fallacy," has already been indicated.

The view recently popular among archaeologists, was that Chaco was primarily (if not exclusively) a ritual and ceremonial center, and that its elements — great houses, rooms, kivas, roads, and the location of the complex itself — were ritually determined and ceremonial in purpose. Exchange of both luxury and essential trade goods was limited and overwhelmingly local. Interactions with other peoples were confined primarily to the Anasazi region, and if interaction with Mesoamerica existed at all, it was very limited, and, in terms of information transfer, almost incidental. Anasazi society was much like today's pueblos: egalitarian, or, in our terms, confined within the KOMP (i.e., no changes in mode of production have occurred). In this view, while ancient Anatolian society may have been characterized by *inter*regional dynamics, economically and politically determined, Anasazi society was primarily ritualistic, an indigenous religious phenomenon characterized by limited *intra*regional exchange and negligible interregional economics.

Appendix One 319

Architecturally, the great house sites, constructed at different dates, in different forms, and with different construction techniques, were autonomous, according to this position, and subordinated to Chaco Canyon's great kiva, Casa Rinconada, while other aspects of placemaking relating to built environment, e.g., irrigation, did not exert a major societal influence. In other words, the so-called "Chaco Phenomenon," far from representing or accommodating movements toward major social, political, or economic changes, was an ephemeral "flash in the pan," an architecturally (and, presumably, ceremonially) impressive experiment which, for whatever reason, eventually failed. Supporting this point of view, the ethnographic analogy is supplemented by the *absence* of evidence which would support the position presented in this book; for example, the absence of evidence (e.g., extensive burials) of large or permanent population, of large-scale movements of goods, of definitively "elite" housing. Fairly recent calculations indicate that enormous labor inputs were not required for building, and that constructions in Chaco Canyon proper did not necessarily predate the construction of all of the more than 80 outliers.

To this we respond that the evidence is irrefutable in *neither* direction and there seems to be at least as much for a polynucleated, multiregional, economic trade network — however fragile — centered on Chaco and connected to Mesoamerica, as for a relatively isolated group of ceremonial great houses coupled to a far-flung network of ceremonial roads; and for a centrally planned, incipiently hierarchical society as for an unequivocally egalitarian one.

The argument boils down to a denial of "either/ors," to the existence, once again, of contradictions that are dialectical rather than dichotomous. In the pre-Columbian cities of lower Mesoamerica, market and ceremonial activities were architecturally integrated; in contemporary Latin American villages and towns, they still are. Too, moderately hierarchical societies have their egalitarian cooperative segments as well. Further support for our perspective may await expanded research on the "Chichimec Sea."

Two other issues require clarification: increase in production, and trade. First, increase in crop production has been accomplished throughout Mesoamerica through irrigation; indeed, the lowland Maya of the otherwise unproductive Yucatan probably depended upon it to feed their apparently dense population. The Hohokam, neighbors of the Anasazi, practiced an extensive and sophisticated form of irrigation. While the remains of Chacoan irrigation works are certainly less impressive, there is no indication that they were markedly less important to the survival of Chaco society (especially since recent research has vastly reduced the estimated number of Chaco inhabitants requiring sustenance).

Second, trade is often accomplished through the well-known medium of market exchange, and through reciprocity and redistribution (Polanyi, 1957).

Simple reciprocity, characteristic of KOMP, is in fact found in all modes of production, while market production seems to have appeared in Anatolia several millennia before Mesoamerica, and whether it was ever achieved by the Anasazi is questionable. However, and most germane to the "Chaco Phenomenon":

> Redistributive systems...require bureaucratic governments to be effective.... [I]t appears that redistribution was comparatively late in time, because elaborate bureaucracies developed comparatively late. (Curtin, 1984; p.88).

This creates something of a dilemma. Individual Chacoan great houses exhibit, in their physical growth patterns, indications of planning — such is possible in the KOMP at an advanced stage. Hypothesized Mesoamerican trade also required some coordination, but this might have been provided by pochteca and could have thrived at the level of reciprocity. But the real problem lies with the far-flung Chacoan system itself. If this system, as proposed by some "Chichimec Sea" researchers, existed for the purpose of redistributing surplus product in a region of highly variable microclimates, from areas of high production to areas of low production (during a given year), then, according to Curtin (1984), a centralized bureaucracy would have had to exist. Thus, while local planning and even long-distance trade are conceivable, the existence of a full-fledged redistributional system seems, in this light, highly problematic — this point *may* have to be conceded to the opposition. On the other hand, a "weak" redistributive economy could have existed with even a primitive bureaucracy, and it may have been the failure of such a bureaucracy to coordinate redistribution effectively, which led to the "collapse" of the "Chaco system."

Appendix Two

TRANSITIONS IN MODES OF PRODUCTION: ALTERNATIVE MODELS OF SOCIAL CHANGE

In Chapter Five, the question was introduced of whether climax Chacoan society was primarily characterized by a kin-ordered (egalitarian) or tributary (hierarchical) mode of production. An alternative proposed by Vivian (1990), similar to that of Johnson (1989), was also presented: that of "rotating sequential hierarchy," a model of complex egalitarianism which introduces periodically shifting hierarchy over an egalitarian base.

The purpose of this Appendix is to suggest how the "rotating sequential hierarchy" model—which, as indicated in Chapter Five, *may* apply both to the Chaco system and to Catal Huyuk (Johnson, 1989)—can be incorporated into or reconciled with modes of production. We have chosen to do so with a series of small schematic diagrams.

Figure AII-1 shows a gradual shift from one mode of production to another (a) under a "static" assumption of no change within a mode of production; and (b) assuming that slow changes occur *within* a mode of production (probably giving impetus to a shift in modes). We consider (b) more likely to represent the true state of affairs under Model 1.

Model 2, (Figure AII-2), depicting a stepwise or "quantum" change (Von Neuman, 1958; Penrose, 1989) in mode of production, analogous to certain "one-element" or "all-or-none" mathematical models of learning (e.g., Bower and Theios, 1964; Atkinson and Estes 1965) is shown diagrammatically in (a)

An alternative, analogous to genetic changes in mutation (Schroedinger, 1967), shown in (b).

The probable existence of at least some "rotating sequential hierarchies" (RSH) can be incorporated in several ways, assuming that they (i) are a stage along a "mediated transition" between simple KOMP and TMP; (ii) are unstable and either become TMP or revert to KOMP; or (iii) represent a stable end point to a path alternative to that which has capitalism as its eventual and inevitable end point. These are shown in Figure AII-3.

If Catal Huyuk and Chaco are, as suggested above, representative of RSH's, Catal Huyuk is depicted in (i) and Chaco in (ii) or (iii) —probably (iii) if both Ortiz (1965, 1969) and Johnson (1989) are correct, for the assertions of the two taken together is that an RSH can be stable and persistent over time. Why? The answer, presumably, is the great degree of adaptive flexibility, or adaptive mobility, that RSH affords. "The key to this sequential structure, as well as to the absence of convincing evidence of political elites and hierarchies in the traditional sense, must certainly have been...adaptive mobility..." (Johnson, 1989; p. 381).

The question of Anasazi societal structure remains open. However, risking an ethnographic fallacy in reverse, what is evidently true of the ethnographic Tewa and may have been true of the Chacoans, may also in one form or another characterize all of the modern pueblos that claim descent from the Anasazi; far from being anything like "primitive," they may incorporate a level of adaptive, sustainable complexity that has sustained them through half a millennium of contact and conquest, complexity far greater than that with which they have been credited.

Appendix Two 323

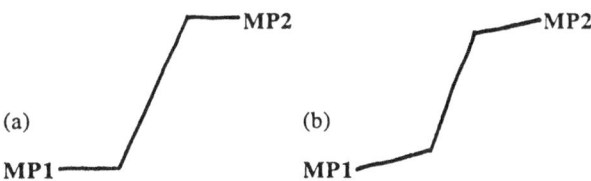

1. Gradual shifts in mode of production (MP).

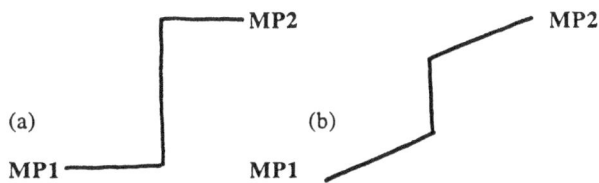

2. Stepwise or "quantum" changes in mode of production.

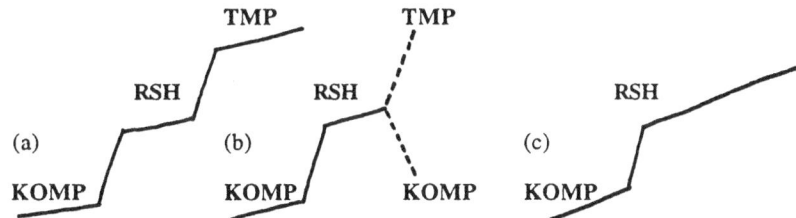

3. Three models for incorporation of rotating sequential hierarchies (RSH) into modes of production.

Figure AII Models of transition in modes of production (see text for elaboration).

Bibliography

Acar, E. (1978), A brief history of housing as a social product: The Anatolian case. (Limited circulation). Faculty of Architecture, M.E.T.U., Ankara.

Adam, M. (1975), Design and production of architectural and other products. *M.E.T.U. Journal of the Faculty of Architecture*, v. 1, no. 1, pp. 31-44.

Adams, E. C. (1983), "The appearance, evolution, and meaning of the Katsina Cult to the Pre-Hispanic Pueblo World of the Southwestern United States." A paper presented at the Symposium entitled, *Models of Pueblo prehistory* at the XI International Congress of Anthropological and Ethnological Sciences.

Adams, R. M. (1966), *The evolution of urban society*. Chicago: Aldine Publishing Co.

Adams, R. M. (1968), The natural history of urbanism. *The fitness of man's environment* (Smithsonian Annual II). Washington, D.C.: Smithsonian Institute.

Adams, R. M. (1972), The origin of cities. *Old world archaeology*, (Readings from *Scientific American*). San Francisco: W. H. Freeman, pp. 137-143.

Adorno, T. W. (1978), Subject and object. A. Arato and E. Gebhardt (eds.), *The essential Frankfurt School reader*. New York: Urizen Books, pp. 497-511.

Agnew, J. (1982), Home ownership and identity in capitalist societies. J.S.

Duncan (ed.), *Housing and identity: Cross-cultural perspectives.* New York: Holmes and Meier Pub., pp. 60-97.
Akins, N. J., (1984), Evidence for organizational complexity as seen from the mortuary practices at Chaco Canyon. W. J. Judge and J. D. Schelberg (eds.), *Recent research on Chaco prehistory.* Albuquerque: U.S. Dept. of the Interior, NPS, Division of Cultural Research.
Aksoy, E. (1963), Ortamekan: Turk sivil mimarisinde temel kurulus prensibi. *Mimarlik ve Sanat,* no. 7-8, pp. 39-92.
Aksoy, O. (1974), *Uyum surecinin 'mimarlik sistemi' icinde orneklenmesi.* Trabzon: K.T.U. (Genel Yayin no. 66).
Akurgal, E. (1971), The great civilizations of Anatolia. L. Giovannini (ed.), *Arts of Cappadocia.* London: Berrie and Jenkins, pp. 17-27.
Alexander, C. (1964), *Notes on the synthesis of form.* Cambridge: Harvard University Press.
Alexander, C., Ishikawa, S., and Silverstein, M. (1977), *A pattern language.* New York: Oxford University Press.
Alexander, C. and Chermayeff, S.I. (1963), *Community and privacy.* Garden City, NY: Doubleday.
Alkim, U. B. (1968), *Anatolia I: From the beginnings to the end of the 2nd millennium B.C.* Trans. by J. Hogarth. Cleveland: The World Publishing Co.
Alp, S. (1949), Hititlerde sosyal sinif 'Nam.ra'lar ve ideogramin Hititce karsiligi. *T.T.K. Belleten,* v. 13, no. 50, pp. 245- 270.
Altman, I. and Chemers, M.M. (1980), *Culture and environment.* Monterey: Brooks/Cole.
Altman, I. and Gauvain, M. (1981), A cross-cultural and dialectic analysis of homes. L.S. Liben, A.H. Patterson, and N. Newcombe (eds.), *Spatial representation and behavior: Application and theory across the life span.* New York: Academic Press, pp. 283-320.
Altman, I., Vinsel, A., and Brown, B.B. (1981), Dialectical conception in social psychology: An application to social penetration and privacy regulation. *Advances in Experimental Social Psychology,* 14. New York: Academic Press.
Altschul, J.H. (1978), The development of the Chacoan interaction sphere. *Journal of Anthropological Research.* v. 34, n.1, pp. 109-46.
Amin, S. (1977), *Unequal development: An essay on the social formations of peripheral capitalism.* Trans. by B. Pearce. New York: Monthly Review. (1973).

Anati, E. (1968), Anatolia's earliest art. *Archaeology*, v. 21, no. 1, pp. 22-35.

Anderson, D.B. (1982), "Through the looking glass: Or does site structure accurately reflect behavior and organization?" Unpublished Ph.D. dissertation proposal, University of New Mexico, Department of Anthropology, Albuquerque, NM.

Andolfato, U. and Zucchi, F. (1971), The physical setting. L.Giovannini (ed.), *Arts of Cappadocia*. London: Barrie and Jenkins, pp. 51-61.

Angel, J.L. (1971), Early Neolithic skeletons from Catal Huyuk: Demography and pathology. *Anatolian Studies*, v. XXI, pp. 77-98.

Anyon, R. and LeBlanc, S.A. (1984), *The Galaz Ruin: A prehistoric Mimbres village in Southwestern New Mexico*. Albuquerque: University of New Mexico Press.

Arato, A. and Gebhardt, E., (eds.), (1978), *The essential Frankfurt School reader*. Oxford: Basil Blackwell.

Ardrey, R. (1961), *African genesis*. London: Atheneum.

Ardrey, R. (1966), *The territorial imperative*. New York: Atheneum.

Arel, A. (1982), *Osmanli konut geleneginde tarihsel sorunlar*. Izmir: Ege Universitesi, G.S.F. Yayinlari.

Associated Press. (1984), Archaeological find indicates border Indians were nomadic. *Denver Post*, 4B, (April 22).

Atkinson, R.C. and Estes, W.K. (1965), Stimulus sampling theory. R.D. Luce, R.R. Bush and E. Galanter (eds.), *Handbook of mathematical psychology*. v. 2; Ch. 10; New York: Wiley.

Aveni, A.F. (ed.), (1975), *Archaeoastronomy in pre-Columbian America*. Austin: University of Texas Press.

Aveni, A.F. (ed.), (1982), *Archaeoastronomy in the New World*. Cambridge: Cambridge University Press.

Baars, D.L. (1983), *The Colorado Plateau: A geologic history*. Albuquerque: University of New Mexico Press.

Bandelier, A.F. (1890), Final report of investigations among the Indians of the Southwestern United States (Part 1). *Papers of the Archaeological Institute of America, American Series 3*.

Bandelier, A.F. (1892), Final report of investigations among the Indians of the Southwestern United States (Part 2). *Papers of the Archaeological Institute of America, American Series 3*.

Bandelier, A.F. (1971), *The delight makers*. New York: Harcourt Brace Jovanovich. (1890).

Banham, R. (1976), *Megastructure*. London: Thames and Hudson.

Beals, R.L. (1932), The comparative ethnology of Northern Mexico before 1750. *Ibero-Americana*, v.2.
Beekmann, P.H. (1966), *The Pliocene and Quaternary volcanism in the Hasan Dag-Melendiz Dag region.* Ankara.
Benedict, R. (1934), *Patterns of culture.* New York: Houghton-Mifflin.
Berktay, H. (1983), *Kabileden feodalizme.* Istanbul: Kaynak Yayinlari.
Bernal, J.D. (1965), *Science in history.* 3rd ed. New York: Hawthorn Books. (1954).
Berry, M.S. (1982), *Time, space and transition to Anasazi prehistory.* Salt Lake City: University of Utah Press.
Bilgic, E. (1946), Anadolu'nun ilk yazili kaynaklarindaki yer adlari ve yerlerinin tayini uzerine incelemeler. *T.T.K. Belleten*, v. X, no. 39, pp. 381-423.
Bittel, K. (1956), Kappadokya'da bulunan bir ates sunagi. *Turk Arkeoloji Dergisi*, v. 6/2, pp. 35-42.
Bittel, K. (1970), *Hattusha: The Capital of the Hittites.* New York: Oxford University Press.
Blanton, R. and Feinman. G. (1984), The Mesoamerican world system. *American Anthropologist*, v. 86, pp. 673-682.
Blau, P.M. (1977), *Inequality and heterogeneity: A primitive theory of social structure.* New York: The Free House.
Blegen, C.W. (1971), The identification of Troy. *The Cambridge Ancient History* (3rd ed.); v. 1, part 2. Cambridge: Cambridge University Press, pp. 411-416.
Blegen, C.W. (1973), Troy VI. *The Cambridge Ancient History* (3rd ed.); v. 2, part 1. Cambridge: Cambridge University Press, pp. 683-685.
Borhegyi, S.F. (1971), Pre-Columbian contacts - the dryland approach: The impact and influence of Teotihuacan culture on the pre-Columbian civilizations of Mesoamerica. C.L. Riley et al. (eds.), *Man across the sea.* Austin: University of Texas Press.
Bostanci, E.Y. (1962), A new Upper Palaeolithic and Mesolithic facies at Belbasi rock shelter. *Turk Tarih Kurumu Belleten*, v. 26, pp. 252-292.
Bostanci, E.Y. (1965), The Mesolithic of Beldibi and Belbasi. *Antropoloji*, v. 3, pp. 91-134.
Bower, G.H. and Theios, J.A. (1964), Learning model for discrete performance levels. R.C. Atkinson (ed.), *Studies in mathematical psychology.* Stanford: Stanford University Press.
Boyer, L.L. and Grondzik, W.T. (1987), *Earth shelter technology.* College Station: Texas A & M University Press.

Braidwood, L.S. and Braidwood, R.J. (eds.), (1982), *Prehistoric village archaeology in southeastern Turkey: The eighth millennium B.C. site at Cayonu — its chipped and ground stone industries and faunal remains.* Oxford: BAR International Series 138.

Braidwood, L.S. and Braidwood, R.J. (1986), Prelude to the appearance of village-farming communities in southwestern Asia. J.V. Canby et al. (eds.), *Ancient Anatolia.* Madison, WI: The University of Wisconsin Press, pp.3-11.

Braidwood, R.J. and Cambel, H. (1982), The Cayonu excavations. L.S. Braidwood and R.J. Braidwood, (eds.), *Prehistoric village archaeology in southeastern Turkey.* Oxford: BAR International Series 138, pp.1-15.

Braidwood, R.J. and Howe, B. (1962), Southwestern Asia beyond the lands of the Mediterranean littoral. R.J. Braidwood and G.R. Willey (eds.). *Courses toward urban life: Archaeological considerations of some cultural alternates.* Chicago: Aldine Publishing Co., pp. 132-146.

Braidwood, R.J. and Willey, G.R. (eds.), (1962), *Courses toward urban life: Archaeological considerations of some cultural alternates.* Chicago: Aldine Publishing Co.

Braniff, C.B. (1990), The identification of possible elites in prehispanic Sonora. P.E. Minnis and C.L. Redman (eds.), *Perspectives on Southwestern prehistory.* Boulder, CO: Westview Press.

Braudel, F. (1981), *Civilization and capitalism, 15th-18th Century.* 3 vols; *The structure of everyday life:The limits of the possible,* v.1; Trans: S. Reynolds; New York: Harper and Row, (1979).

Breternitz, C.D. (1982), "Identifying prehistoric activity areas: Analysis of temporal and functional variability among Dolores Area structures, A.D. 575-900." Unpublished Masters Thesis, Department of Anthropology, Washington State University, Pullman.

Brew, J.O. (1943), On the Pueblo IV and the katchina - tlaloc relations. *El Norte de Mexico y el sur de Estados Unidos:Tercera reunion de Mesa Redonda Sobre Problemas Antropologicos de Mexico y Centro America.* Mexico, D.F.: Sociedad Mexicana de Antropologia, pp. 241-245.

Brodia, J. (1986), Arqueoastronomia y desarrollo de la sciencias en el Mexico prehispanico. M.A. Moreno Corral (ed.), *Historia de la astronomia en Mexico.* Mexico, D.F.: Fondo de Cultura Economica.

Brody, J.J. (1979), Pueblo fine arts. A. Ortiz (ed.), *Handbook of North American Indians: Southwest.* Washington, D.C.: Smithsonian Institute, v. 9, pp. 603-608.

Brown, D.N. (1979), Picuris Pueblo. A. Ortiz (ed.), *Handbook of North American*

Indians: Southwest.Washington, D.C.: Smithsonian Institute, v. 9, pp. 268-277.
Brunskill, R.W. (1971), *Illustrated handbook of vernacular architecture*. New York: Universe Books.
Bryan, K. (1925), Date of channel trenching (arroyo cutting) in the arid southwest. *Science*, v. 62, pp. 338-344.
Bryan, K. (1941), Precolumbian agriculture in the Southwest as conditioned by periods of alluviation. *Annals of the American Association of Geography*, v. 31, no. 4, pp. 219-242.
Bryan, K. (1954), The geology of Chaco Canyon, New Mexico, in relation to the life and remains of the prehistoric peoples of Pueblo Bonito. *Smithsonian Miscellaneous Collections*, v. 122, no. 7.
Cabrero, G.M.T. (1989), *Civilizacion en el norte de Mexico*. Mexico, D.F.: Universidad Nacional Autonoma de Mexico.
Cambel, H. (1964), Anadolu'nun tarih oncesinde bazi ana sorunlar. *Turk Tarih Kurumu yillik konferanslari*. Ankara: TTK, pp. 253-265.
Cambel, H. and Braidwood, R.J. (1972), An early farming village in Turkey. *Old world archaeology*, (Readings from *Scientific American*). San Francisco: W.H. Freeman, pp. 113-119.
Cameron, C.M. (1984), A regional view of chipped stone raw material use in Chaco Canyon. W.J. Judge and J.D. Schelberg (eds.), *Recent research on Chaco prehistory*. Albuquerque: U.S. Department of the Interior, NPS, Division of Cultural Research.
Cameron, K.N. (1973), *Humanity and society: A world history*. Bloomington: Indiana University Press.
Camilli, E.L. and Cordell, L.S. (1983), Applications to cultural resources in Southwestern North America. *Remote Sensing* (Supplement No.8), Cultural Resources Management, NPS, U.S. Department of the Interior, Washington, D.C.
Canby, J.V., Porada, E., Ridgeway, B.S. and Stech, T. (eds.), (1986), *Ancient Anatolia: Aspects of change and cultural development*. Madison, WI: The University of Wisconsin Press.
Castells, M. (1977), *The urban question. A Marxist approach*. Trans. by A. Sheridan. Cambridge, MA: The MIT Press. (1972).
Castells, M. (1983), *The city and the grassroots: A cross-cultural theory of urban social movements*. Berkeley: University of California Press.
Chapman, A. (1957), Port of trade enclaves in Aztec and Maya civilizations. K. Polanyi et al. (eds.), *Trade and market in the early empires*. Glencoe, IL: The Free Press, pp. 114-153.

Chapman, R.C. and Biella, J.V. (1980), 4000 Years on the Southern Pajarito. *Bandelier National Monument*. Santa Fe: School of American Research.

Childe, V.G. (1951), *Man makes himself*. New York: New American Library, Mentor Books. (1936).

Childe, V.G. (1952), *New light on the ancient Near East*. London: Routledge and Kegan Paul.

Childe, V.G. (1964), *What happened in history*. London: Penguin Books. (1942).

Clavijero, F.J. (1979), *Historia antiqua de Mexico*. Mexico, D.F.: Porrua.

Coe, M.D. (1984), *Mexico*. London: Thames and Hudson.

Cohen, M.N. (1975), Population pressure and the origins of agriculture: An archaeological example from the coast of Peru. S. Polgar (ed.), *Population, ecology, and social evolution*. The Hague: Mouton Publishers.

Cole, S. (1965), *The Neolithic revolution* (3rd edition). London: British Museum. (1959).

Contreras Sanchez, E. (1982), *La zona arqueologica de Casas Grandes, Chih.: Paquime*. Mexico, D.F.: Instituto Nacional de Antropologia y Historia.

Cooke, R.U. and Reeves, R.W. (1976), *Arroyos and environmental change in the American South-West*. Oxford: Clarendon Press.

Cordell, L.S. (1982), The Pueblo period in the San Juan Basin: An overview and some research problems. F. Ploy and W. Wait (eds.), *The San Juan tomorrow*. Santa Fe: National Park Service, Southwest Region, and School of American Research.

Cordell, L.S. (1984), *Prehistory of the Southwest*. Orlando, FA: Academic Press.

Cordell, L.S. and Gumerman, G.J. (1989), Cultural interaction in the prehistoric Southwest. L.S. Cordell and G.J. Gumerman (eds.), *Dynamics of Southwest prehistory*. Washington, D.C.: Smithsonian Institution Press.

Cosgrove, C.B. (1947), Caves of the Upper Gila and Hueco Areas in New Mexico and Texas. *Papers of the Peabody Museum of American Archaeology and Ethnology*, Harvard University. v. 24, no. 2.

Cowgill, G.L. (1974), 'Comment' on models of cultural process; testing hypotheses: Suggestions from Southwestern archaeology by W.A. Longacre. C.B. Moore (ed.), *Reconstructing complex societies*; Supplement to the *Bulletin of the American Schools of Oriental Research*, v. 20, pp. 29-40.

Crown, P.L. and Judge, W.J. (eds.), (1991), *Chaco and Hohokam: Prehistoric regional systems in the American Southwest*. Santa Fe: School of American Research Press.

Curtin, P.D. (1984), *Cross-cultural trade in world history*. New York: Cambridge University Press.

Davies, N. (1982), *The ancient kingdoms of Mexico.* London: Allen Lane.

Davis, E.L. (1965), Small pressures and cultural drift as explanations for abandonment of the San Juan area, New Mexico. *American Antiquity,* v. 30, no. 3, pp. 353-355.

Dean, J.S. (1969), Chronological analysis of Tsegi phase sites in northeastern Arizona. *Papers of the Laboratory of Tree-Ring Research,* v. 3. Tucson.

Dean, J.S. (1970), Aspects of Tsegi phase social organization: A trial reconstruction. W. Longacre (ed.), *Reconstructing prehistoric pueblo societies.* Albuquerque and Santa Fe: University of New Mexico Press and School of American Research.

Dean, J.S. (1988), A model of Anasazi behavioral adaptation. G.J. Gumerman (ed.), *The Anasazi in a changing environment..* New York: Cambridge University Press.

Devalle, S.B.C. (1990), Tribe in India: The fallacy of a colonial category. D.N. Lorenzen (ed.), *Studies on Asia and Africa from Latin America.* Mexico, D.F.: El Colegio de Mexico.

Dick, H.W. (1965), *Bat Cave.* Santa Fe, NM: School of American Research (Monograph #27).

Di Peso, C.C. (1956), The Upper Pima of San Cayetano del Tumacacori: An archaeo-historical reconstruction of the Ootam of Pimeria Alta. *The Amerind Foundation,* No. 7 (Dragoon, Arizona).

Di Peso, C.C. (1966), Archaeology and ethnohistory of the Northern Sierra. G.F. Ekholm and G.R. Willey (eds.), *Archaeological frontiers and external connections*; vol. 4; (R. Wauchope [gen. ed.], *Handbook of Middle American Indians).* Austin: University of Texas Press.

Di Peso, C.C. (1968a), Casas Grandes and the Gran Chichimeca. *El Palacio,* v. 75, pp. 47-61.

Di Peso, C.C. (1968b), Casas Grandes, a fallen trading center of the Chichimeca. *The Masterkey,* v. 42, pp. 20-37.

Di Peso, C.C. (1974), Medio Period architecture. C.C. Di Peso, J.B. Rinaldo, and G.H. Fenner (eds.), *Casas Grandes 4.* Dragoon, AZ: The Amerind Foundation.

Di Peso, C.C. (1979a), Prehistory: Southern periphery. A. Ortiz (ed.), *Handbook of North American Indians: Southwest.* Washington, D.C.: Smithsonian Institute, v. 9.

Di Peso, C.C. (1979b), Prehistory: O'otam. A. Ortiz (ed.), *Handbook of North American Indians: Southwest.* Washington D.C.: Smithsonian Institute, v. 9.

Di Peso, C.C., Rinaldo, J.B., and Fenner, G. (1974), *Casas Grandes, a fallen trading center of the Gran Chichimeca.* Dragoon and Flagstaff, AZ: Amerind Foundation and Northland Press.

Dixon, J.E., Cann, J.R., and Renfrew, C. (1972), Obsidian and the origins of trade. *Old world archaeology*, (Readings from *Scientific American*). San Francisco: W.H. Freeman, pp. 80-88.

Doolittle, W.E. (1984a), Settlements and the development of "statelets" in Sonora, Mexico. *Journal of Field Archaeology,* v.11, pp.13-24.

Doolittle, W.E. (1984b), Cabeza de Vaca's land of maize: An assessment of its agriculture. *Journal of Historical Geography,* v.10, n.3, pp.246-262.

Doolittle, W.E. (1991a), *Canal irrigation in prehistoric Mexico: The sequence of technological change.* Austin: University of Texas Press.

Doolittle, W.E. (1991b), *Pre-Hispanic occupance in the valley of Sonora, Mexico.* Tucson: University of Arizona Press; (Anthropological Papers of the University of Arizona, no. 48).

Dove, D.E. (1982), "Prehistoric subsistence and population change along the lower Aqua Fria River, Arizona: A model simulation." Unpublished M.S. Thesis, Arizona State University, Department of Anthropology.

Doxtater, D. (1990), Architecture as medium in the history of human space: The cosmic, architectonic and semiotic. H. Pamir, V. Imamoglu and N. Teymur (eds.), *Culture, space, history;* v. 2. Ankara: M.E.T.U. , Faculty of Architecture.

Doxtater, D. (1991), Reflections on the Anasazi cosmos, E. Engelstad and I. Lindblom (eds.) *Social Space: Human spatial behavior in dwellings and settlements.* Odense: Odense University Press.

Doyel, D.E. (1979), The prehistoric Hohokam of the Arizona Desert. *American Scientist,* v. 67, no. 5, pp. 544-554.

Doyel, D.E. (1980), Hohokam social organization and the Sedentary to Classic transition. D.E. Doyel (ed.), *Proceedings of a Symposium.* Tempe: Arizona State University. *Anthropological Research Papers*, no. 23.

Doyel, D.E., Breternitz, C.D., and Marshall, M.P. (1984), Chacoan Community structure: Bis Sa'ani Pueblo and the Chaco-Halo. W.J. Judge and J.D. Schelberg (eds.), *Recent research on Chaco prehistory.* Albuquerque, NM: U.S. Department of the Interior, Division of Cultural Research.

Dozier, E.P. (1960), The pueblos of the south-western United States. *Journal of the Royal Anthropological Institute of Great Britain and Ireland,* v. 90, nos. 1-2, pp. 146-160.

Drager, D.L. (1976), Anasazi population estimates with the aid of data derived from photogrammetric maps. T.R. Lyons (ed.), *Remote sensing experiments in cultural resource studies.* Albuquerque: University of New Mexico and

National Park Service, (Report of the Chaco Center No. 1).
Duverger, C. (1983), *L'origine des Azteques.* Paris: Editions du Seuil.
Ebert, J.I and Lyons, T.R. (1980), Prehistoric irrigation canals identified from Skylab III and Landset imaging in Phoenix, Arizona. T.R. Lyons and F.J. Mathien (eds.), *Cultural resources remote sensing.* Albuquerque: University of New Mexico and U.S. National Park Service.
Eddy, F.W. (1966), *Prehistory in the Navajo Reservoir district,* Northwestern New Mexico. Santa Fe: Museum of New Mexico Press.
Elbert, J.I. and Hitchcock, R.K. (1973), "Spatial inference and the archaeology of complex societies." Unpublished paper, Mathematics in Social Sciences Board Conference on Formal Methods for the Analysis of Regional Social Structure, Santa Fe, New Mexico.
Eldem, S.H. (1955), *Turk evi plan tipleri.* Istanbul: Istanbul Teknik Universitesi, Mimarlik Fakultesi.
Eliade, M. (1957), *The sacred and the profane.* New York: Harper and Row.
Ellis, F.H. (1951), Patterns of aggression and the war cult in Southwestern pueblos. *Southwestern Journal of Anthropology,* v. 7, no. 2, pp. 177-201.
Ellis, F.H. (1978), Small structures used by historic pueblo peoples and their immediate ancestors. A.E. Ward (ed.), *Limited activity and occupation sites.* Albuquerque: Center for Anthropological Studies, pp. 59-68.
Ellis, F.H. (1979), Isleta Pueblo. A. Ortiz (ed.), *Handbook of North American Indians: Southwest.* Washington, D.C.: Smithsonian Institute, v. 9.
Engels, F. (1942), *The origin of the family, private property and the state.* New York: International Publishers. (1884).
Erencin, A. (1979), *Kapadokya yerel konutlarinda turizme yonelik yenileme calismalarina bir yaklasim.* Doctoral Dissertation. Istanbul: I.T.U., Faculty of Architecture.
Esin, U. and Benedict, P. (1963), Recent developments in the prehistory of Anatolia. *Current Anthropology,* v. 4, no. 4, pp. 339-346.
Estes, W.K. (ed.), (1975-78), *Handbook of learning and cognitive processes.* Hillsdale, NJ: Erlbaum.
Faris, J.C. (1975), Social evolution, population, and production. S. Polgar (ed.), *Population, ecology, and social evolution.* The Hague: Mouton Publishers.
Farrington, I.S. (1980), The archaeology irrigation canals, with special reference to Peru. *World archaeology,* v. 11, pp. 287-305.
Ferdon, E.N., Jr. (1955), A trial survey of Mexican-Southwestern architectural parallels. *School of American Research, Museum of New Mexico,* Monograph 21.

Fergusson, E. (1973), *New Mexico*. Albuquerque: UNM Press.
Festinger, L. (1983), *The human legacy*. New York: Columbia University Press.
Fewkes, J.W. (1909), *Antiquities of the Mesa Verde National Park - Spruce Tree House*. Washington, D.C.: Smithsonian Institution, Bureau of American Ethnology Bulletin 41.
Fewkes, J.W. (1911a), *Preliminary report on a visit to the Navajo National Monument, Arizona*. Washington, D.C.: Smithsonian Institution (Bureau of American Ethnology Bulletin 50).
Fewkes, J.W. (1911b), *Antiquities of the Mesa Verde National Park - Cliff Palace*. Washington, D.C.: Smithsonian Institution (Bureau of American Ethnology Bulletin 51).
Fewkes, J.W. (1916), *The excavation and repair of Sun Temple, Mesa Verde National Park*. Washington, D.C.: U.S. Department of the Interior.
Fewkes, J.W. (1917), A prehistoric Mesa Verde pueblo and its people. *Annual Report of the Smithsonian Institution for 1916*, pp. 461-488.
Firth, R. (1965), *Primitive Polynesian economy*. New York: W.W. Norton.
Fitch, J.M. (1961), *Architecture and the esthetics of plenty*. New York: Columbia University Press.
Flannery, K.V. (1972), The Origins of the villages as a settlement type in Mesoamerica and the Near East: A comparative study. P.J. Ucko, R. Tringham, and G.W. Dimbleby (eds.), *Man, settlement and urbanism*. London: Duckworth, pp. 23-53.
Ford, R.I. (1968), "An ecological analysis involving the population of San Juan Pueblo, New Mexico." Unpublished Ph.D. dissertation, Department of Anthropology, University of Michigan, Ann Arbor.
Ford, R.I. (1972a), An ecological perspective on the Eastern Pueblos. A. Ortiz (ed.), *New perspectives on the Pueblos*. Albuquerque: University of New Mexico Press, pp. 1-17.
Ford, R.I. (1972b), Barter, gift, or violence: An analysis of Teuva intertribal exchange. E. Wilmsen (ed.), *Social exchange and interaction*. Ann Arbor, MI: University of Michigan Museum Memoirs No. 46, pp. 21-45.
Ford, R.I. (1977), The technology of irrigation in a New Mexico Pueblo. H. Lechtman and R. Merrill (eds.), *Material culture: Styles, organization and dynamics of technology*. Proceedings of the American Ethnological Society, pp. 139-154.
Foster, M.S. (1986), An overview of the greater Southwest in the protohistoric period. F.J. Mathien and R.H. McGuire (eds.), *Ripples in the Chichimec Sea: New considerations of Southwestern - Mesoamerican interactions*.

Carbondale, IL: Southern Illinois University Press.
Frazer, J.G. (1963), *The golden bough: A study in magic and religion*. New York: Macmillan, (1922).
Frazier, K. (1986), *People of Chaco: A canyon and its culture*. New York: W. Norton.
French, D.H. (1962-1968), Excavations at Can Hasan (First-Seventh Preliminary Report). *Anatolian Studies*, v.s XII-XVIII, pp. 27-40 ('62), pp. 29-42 ('63), pp. 125-137 ('64), pp. 87-94 ('65), pp. 113-123 ('66), pp. 165-178 ('67), pp. 45-53 ('68).
Fried, M.H. (1967), *The evolution of political society*. New York: Random House.
Fried, M.H. (1975), *The notion of tribe*. Menlo Park, CA: Cummings.
Frisbie, T.R. (1978), High status burials in the greater Southwest: An interpretive synthesis. C.L. Riley and B.C. Hedrick (eds.), *Across the Chichimec Sea; Papers in Honor of J. Charles Kelley*. Carbondale and Edwardsville: Southern Illinois University Press, pp. 220-227.
Frisbie, T.R. (1980), Social ranking in Chaco Canyon, New Mexico: A Mesoamerican reconstruction. *Transactions of the Illinois State Academy of Science*, v. 72, pp.60-64.
Fry, R.E. (1979), The economics of pottery at Tikal, Guatemala: Models of exchange for serving vessels. *American Antiquity*, v. 44, pp. 494-512.
Gaxiola, G.M. and Clark, J.D. (1989), *La obsidiana en Mexico*. Mexico, D.F.: Institute Nacional de Antropologia y Historia.
Gebhardt, E. (1978), A critique of methodology. A. Arato and E. Gebhardt (eds.), *The essential Frankfurt School reader*. Oxford: Basil Blackwell, pp. 371-406.
Gelb, I.J. (1955), Old Akkadian inscriptions in Chicago Natural History Museum: Texts of legal and business interest. *Fieldiana: Anthropology*, v. 44, no. 2, pp. 161-338.
George, R.D. (1927), *Geology and natural resources of Colorado*. Boulder: University of Colorado.
Gilman, P.A. (1983), "Changing architectural forms in the prehistoric Southwest." Unpublished Ph.D. Dissertation, Department of Anthropology, University of New Mexico, Albuquerque.
Giovannini, L. (1971), The rock settlements. L. Giovannini (ed.), *Arts of Cappadocia*. London: Barrie and Jenkins, pp. 67-80.
Giovannini, L. (ed.), (1971), *Arts of Cappadocia*. London: Barrie and Jenkins.
Glacken, C.J. (1967), *Traces on the Rhodian shore*. Berkeley: University of

California Press.
Gladwin, H.S. (1957), *A history of the ancient Southwest.* Portland, ME: The Bond Wheelwright Co.
Gladwin, H.S., Haury, E.W., Sayles, E.B., and Gladwin, N. (1938), Excavations at Snaketown I: Material culture. *Medallion Papers.* Gila Pueblo, Globe, AZ, v. 25.
Glassie, H. (1975), *Folk housing in middle Virginia.* Knoxville, TN: The University of Tennessee Press.
Glassie, H. (1982), *Passing the time in Ballymenone: Culture and history of an Ulster community.* Philadelphia: University of Pennsylvania Press.
Godelier, M. (1978a), The concept of the 'Asiatic Mode of production' and Marxist models of social evolution. D. Seddon (ed.), *Relations of production: Marxist approaches to economic anthropology.* Trans. by H. Lackner. London: Frank Cass, pp. 209-257.
Godelier, M. (1978b), The object and method of economic anthropology. D. Seddon (ed.), *Relations of production: Marxist approaches to economic anthropology.* Trans. by H. Lackner; London: Frank Cass.
Godelier, M. (1982), The ideal in the real. R. Samuel and G.S. Jones (eds.), *Culture, ideology and politics.* London: Routledge and Kegan Paul, pp. 12-38.
Goetze, A. (1953), Two cultures of Anatolia. *Proceedings of the American Philosophical Society*, v. 97, no. 2, pp. 214-221.
Goetze, A. (1975), The Hittites and Syria (1300-1200 B.C.). *The Cambridge Ancient History*, 3rd ed.. Cambridge: Cambridge University Press, v. 2, part 2, pp. 252-273.
Golany, G.S. (1983), *Earth-sheltered habitat: History, architecture and urban design.* New York: Van Nostrand Reinhold.
Grady, M.A. (1976), "Aboriginal agrarian adaptation to the Sonoran Desert: A regional synthesis and research design." Ph.D. dissertation, Department of Anthropology, University of Arizona, Tucson.
Grant, C. (1978), *Canyon de Chelly: Its people and rock art.* Tucson: University of Arizona Press.
Grebinger, P. (1973), Prehistoric social organization in Chaco Canyon, New Mexico: An alternative reconstruction. *The Kiva*, v. 39, no. 1, pp. 3-24.
Guevara Sanchez, A. (1984), *Las Curarenta Casas: Un Sitio arqueologico del Estado de Chihuahua.* Mexico, D.F.: Instituto Nacional de Antropologia y Historia.
Guevara Sanchez, A. (1988), *Arcaeologia del Valle de las Cuevas, Chihuahua.*

Mexico, D.F.: Instituto Nacional de Antropologia y Historia.
Gumerman, G.J. (1988), A historical perspective on environment and culture in Anasazi country. G.J. Gumerman (ed.), *The Anasazi in a changing environment.* New York: Cambridge University Press.
Gumerman, G.J. and Dean, J.S. (1989), Prehistoric cooperation and competition in the Western Anasazi area. L.S. Cordell and G.J. Gumerman (eds.), *Dynamics of Southwest prehistory.* Washington, D.C.: Smithsonian Institution Press.
Gumerman, G.J. and Euler, R.C. (1976), Black Mesa: Retrospect. G.J. Gumerman and R.C. Euler (eds.), *Papers on the archaeology of Black Mesa, Arizona.* Carbondale, IL: Southern Illinois University Press.
Gurcay, H. (1973), Yeralti sehirleri. *Kultur ve Sanat,* no. 5, pp. 160-168.
Gurcay, H. and Akok, M. (1965), Yeralti sehirlerinde bir inceleme ve Yesilhisar ilcesinin Soganlidere koyunde bulunan kaya anitlari. *Turk Arkeoloji Dergisi,* v. 14, pp. 35-68.
Gurney, O.R. (1961), *The Hittites.* Baltimore: Penguin Books. (1952).
Gurney, O.R. (1973a), Anatolia, ca. 1750-1600 B.C. *The Cambridge Ancient History.* (3rd ed.). Cambridge: Cambridge University Press, pp. 228-255 (Ch. VI).
Gurney, O.R. (1973b), Anatolia, ca. 1600-1380 B.C. *The Cambridge Ancient History.* (3rd ed.). Cambridge: Cambridge University Press, v. 2, part 1, pp. 659-685 (Ch. XV).
Haas, J. (1988), Foreword. G.J. Gumerman (ed.), *The Anasazi in a changing environment.* New York: Cambridge University Press.
Habermas, J. (1975), *Legitimation crisis.* Trans. by T. McCarthy. Boston: Beacon Press. (1973).
Hakim, B.S. (1986), *Arab-Islamic cities: Building and planning principles.* New York: KPI.
Hall, S.A. (1977), Late Quarternary sedimentation and paleoecological history of Chaco Canyon, New Mexico. *Geological Society of American Bulletin,* v. 88, pp. 1593-1618.
Hammond, G.P. and Rey, A. (eds. and trans.), (1928), *Obregon's history of 16th century exploration in western America, 1584.* Los Angeles: Wetzel Publishing Co.
Hammond, M. (1972), *The city in the ancient world.* Cambridge, MA: Harvard University Press.
Hanlon, D. (in press), The Spanish mission church in the upper Rio Grande Valley: A study in architectural morphology. *American Indian Culture and Research Journal.*

Hantman, J.L. (1983), "Social networks and stylistic distributions in the prehistoric plateau Southwest." Unpublished Ph.D. dissertation. Department of Anthropology, Arizona State University, Tempe.

Harner, M.J. (1970), Population pressure and the social evolution of agriculturalists. *Southwestern Journal of Anthropology*, v. 26, no. 1, pp. 67-86.

Harner, M.J. (1975), Scarcity, the factors of production, and social evolution. S. Polgar (ed.), *Population, ecology, and social evolution*. The Hague: Mouton Publishers.

Harbottle, G., and Weigand, P.C. Turquoise in Pre-Columbian America. *Scientific American*, 1992(Feb.), 266(2), 78-85.

Harvey, D. (1973), *Social justice and the city*. Baltimore: The Johns Hopkins University Press.

Haury, E.W. (1945), The problem of contacts between the Southwestern United States and Mexico. *Southwestern Journal of Anthropology*, v. 1, pp. 55-74.

Haury, E.W. (1950a), *The stratigraphy and archaeology of Ventana Cave, Arizona*. Tucson: University of Arizona Press.

Haury, E.W. (1950b), A sequence of great kivas in the Forestdale Valley, Arizona. E.K. Reed and D.S. King (eds.), *For the Dean: Essays in anthropology in Honor of Byron Cummings on his eighty-ninth birthday*. Santa Fe : Southwestern Monuments Association.

Haury, E.W. (1976), *The Hohokam, desert farmers and craftsmen: Excavations at Snaketown, 1964-65*. Tucson: University of Arizona Press.

Hayes, A.C. (1981), A survey of Chaco Canyon archaeology. A.C. Hayes, D.M. Brugge, and W.J. Judge (eds.), *Archaeological surveys of Chaco Canyon, New Mexico*. Publications in Archaeology 184, Chaco Canyon Studies. Washington, D.C.: U.S. National Park Service.

Hayes, A.C., Brugge, D.M., and Judge, W.J. (eds.), (1981), *Archaeological surveys of Chaco Canyon, New Mexico*. Publications in Archaeology 184, Chaco Canyon Studies. Washington, D.C.: U.S. National Park Service.

Hayes, A.C. and Lancaster, J.A. (1975), *Badger House community*. Washington, D.C.: National Park Service (Publications in Archaeology 7E, Wetherill Mesa Studies).

Hazer, F. (1976), Cultural-ecological interpretation of the historic underground cities of Goreme, Turkey. F.L. Moreland (ed.), *Alternatives in energy conservation: The use of the earth covered buildings*. Washington, D.C.: National Science Foundation, pp. 21-36. (Proceedings and notes of a conference held in Ft. Worth, Texas, July 9-12, 1975).

Heiken, G. (1980), Volcanoes: Bandelier's turbulent geologic past. D.G. Noble, J. Kepp, and B. James (eds.), *Bandelier National Monument*. Santa Fe: School of American Research.

Helbaek, H. (1964), First impressions of the Catal Huyuk plant husbandry. *Anatolian Studies*, v. XIV, pp. 121-123.

Heller, M.M. (1976), "Zoo-archaeology of Tularosa Cave, Catron County, New Mexico." M.A. thesis, Department of Biology, University of Texas, El Paso.

Hers, M. (1989), *Los Toltecas en Tierras Chichimecas*. Mexico, D.F.: Universidad Nacional Autonoma de Mexico.

Hewett, E.L. (1913), The physiography of the Rio Grande Valley, New Mexico, in relation to Pueblo culture. *Bureau of American Ethnology Bulletin 54*. Washington, D.C.: Bureau of American Ethnology.

Hewett, E.L. (1930), *Ancient life in the American Southwest*. Indianapolis: Bobbs-Merrill.

Hewett, E.L. (1938), *Pajarito Plateau and its ancient people*. Albuquerque: University of New Mexico.

Hibben, F.C. (1955), Specimens from Sandia Cave and their possible significance. *Science*, v. 122, pp. 688-689.

Hibben, F.C. (1975), *Kiva Art of the Anasazi at Pottery Mound*. Las Vegas, NV: K.C. Publications.

Higuchi, T. (1983), *The visual and spatial structure of landscapes*. Trans. by C.S. Terry. Cambridge: The MIT Press. (1975).

Hill, J.N. (1970), Broken K Pueblo: Prehistoric social organization in the American Southwest. *Anthropological Papers of the University of Arizona*, Tucson, v. 18.

Hindess, B. and Hirst, P. (1975), *Pre-captialist modes of production*. London: Routledge & Kegan Paul.

Hirth, K.G. (1978), Interregional trade and the formation of prehistoric Gateway Communities. *American Antiquity*, v. 43, no. 1, pp. 35-45.

Historic American Building Survey (1934), *Pueblo of Acoma*. Washington, D.C.: U.S. Department of the Interior, Office of National Parks, Buildings, and Reservations, Branch of Plans and Design (HABS NM-6).

Hopkins, D.M. (1967), Quaternary marine transgressions in Alaska. D.M. Hopkins (ed.), *The Bering land bridge*. Stanford: Stanford University Press, pp. 47-90.

Horgan, J. Early arrivals. *Scientific American*, 1992(Feb.), 266(2), 17, 20.

Hough, W. (1914), Culture of the ancient pueblos of the Upper Gila River

Region, New Mexico and Arizona. *United States National Museum*, Bulletin 87.
Huet, O. (1982), Troglodyte habitations in France. *Underground space*, v. 6, pp. 343-354.
Huntington, E. (1912), The physical environment of the Southwest in pre-Columbian days. *Records of the Past*, v. 11, no. 3, pp. 128-141.
Huntington, E. (1914), The climatic factor as illustrated in arid America. *Publications of the Carnegie Institution of Washington*, No. 192.
Huo, Y. (1986), Cave dwelling and human health. *Report on the International Symposium on Earth Architecture*, pp. 108-117.
Instituto Nacional de Antropologia y Historia, Mexico (1982), *La zona arquelogica de Casas Grandes, Chihuahua: Paquime*. Mexico: INAH.
Irwin-Williams, C. (1977), Black boxes and multiple working hypotheses: Reconstructing the economy of early Southwest hunters. *The Kiva*, v. 42, nos. 3-4, pp. 285-299.
Irwin-Williams, C. (1980), Investigations at Salmon Ruin: Methodology and overview. C. Irwin-Williams and P.H. Shelley (eds.), *Investigations at the Salmon site: The structure of Chacoan society in the Northern Southwest*. Portales, NM: Eastern New Mexico University Press.
Irwin-Williams, C. and Shelley, P.H. (eds.), (1980), *Investigations at the Salmon site: The structure of Chacoan society in the Northern Southwest*. Portales, NM: Eastern New Mexico University Press.
Jackson, J.B. (1984), *Discovering the vernacular landscape*. New Haven: Yale University Press.
Jacobs, J. (1970), *The economy of cities*. New York: Vintage Books.
Jameson, F. (1985), Architecture and critique of ideology. J. Ockman (ed.), *Architecture, criticism, ideology*. Princeton, NJ: Princeton Architectural Press.
Jaroff, Leon, Nature's time capsules. *Time*, 1992 (Apr. 6), 139(14), 61.
Jennings, J.D. (1966), Glen Canyon: A summary. *Anthropological Papers of the University of Utah 81*. Salt Lake City: University of Utah, Glen Canyon Series 31.
Johnson, A. E. (1966), Archaeology of Sonora, Mexico. G.F. Ekholm and G.R. Willey (eds.), *Archaeological frontiers and external connections*; v. 4; (R. Wauchope (gen. ed.), *Handbook of Middle American Indians)*. Austin: University of Texas Press.
Johnson, G.A. (1982), Organizational structure and scalar stress. C. Renfrew et al. (eds.), *Theory and explanation in archaeology : The Southhampton*

Conference. New York: Academic Press.
Johnson, G.A. (1989), Dynamics of Southwestern prehistory: Far outside — looking in. L.S. Cordell and G.J. Gumerman (eds.), *Dynamics of Southwestern prehistory.* Washington, DC: Smithsonian Institution Press.
Jones, D. and Cordell, L.S. (1985), *Anasazi world.* Portland, OR: Graphic Arts Center Publishing Co.
Jorde, L.B. (1977), Precipitation cycles and cultural buffering in the prehistoric Southwest. L.R. Binford (ed.), *For theory building in archaeology: Essays on faunal remains, aquatic resources, and systemic modeling.* New York: Academic Press, pp. 385-396.
Judd, N.M. (1954), *The material culture of Pueblo Bonito.* Washington, D.C.: Smithsonian Miscellaneous Collections 124.
Judd, N.M. (1959), *Pueblo del Arroyo, Chaco Canyon, New Mexico.* Washington, D.C.: Smithsonian Miscellaneous Collections 138(1).
Judd, N.M. (1964), *The architecture of Pueblo Bonito.* Washington, D.C.: Smithsonian Miscellaneous Collections 147 (1).
Judge, W.J. (1979), The development of a complex cultural ecosystem in The Chaco Basin, New Mexico. R.M. Linn (ed.), *Proceedings of the First Conference on Scientific Research in the National Parks.* Washington, D.C.: U.S. Government Printing Office.
Judge, W.J. (1989), Chaco Canyon: San Juan Basin. L.S. Cordell and G.J. Gumerman (eds.), *Dynamics of Southwestern prehistory.* Washington, DC: Smithsonian Institution Press.
Judge, W.J., Gillespie, W.B., Lekson, S.H., and Toll, H.W. (1981), *Tenth century developments in Chaco Canyon.* Albuquerque: Archaeological Society of New Mexico Anthropological Papers.
Judge, W.J. and Schelberg, J.D. (eds.), (1984), *Recent research on Chaco prehistory.* Albuquerque: U.S. Department of the Interior, National Park Service, Division of Cultural Research.
Kehoe, A.B. (1962), A hypothesis on the origin of Northeastern American pottery. *Southwestern Journal of Anthropology,* v. 18, pp. 20-29.
Kehoe, A.B. (1971), Small boats upon the North Atlantic. C.L. Riley et al. (eds.), *Man across the sea.* Austin. University of Texas Press.
Kelley, J.C. (1956), Settlement patterns in North-Central Mexico. G.R. Willey (ed.), *Settlement patterns of the New World.* Viking Fund Publication in Anthropology, no.23.
Kelley, J.C. (1966), Mesoamerica and the Southwestern United States. G.F. Ekholm and G.R. Willey (eds.), *Archaeological frontiers and external*

connections. v. 4; (R. Wauchope (gen ed.), *Handbook of Middle American Indians)*. Austin: University of Texas Press.

Kelley, J.C. (1971), Archaeology of the Northern Frontier: Zacatecas and Durango. G.F. Ekholm and I. Bernal (eds.), *Archaeology of Northern Mesoamerica*. Austin: University of Texas Press.

Kelley, J.C. (1986), The mobile merchants of Molino. F. J. Mathien and R.H. McGuire (eds.), *Ripples in the Chichimec Sea: New considerations of Southwestern - Mesoamerican interactions*. Carbondale, IL: Southern Illinois University Press.

Kelley, J.C. (1991), The early Post-classic in Northern Zacatecas and Durango. F. Sodi Miranda (ed.), *Mesoamerica y Norte de Mexico: Siglo IX - XII*. (Seminario de Arqueologia "Wigberto Jiminez Moreno"); Mexico, D.F.: Museo de Antropologia y Historia, pp. 487-519.

Kelley, J.C. and Kelley, E.A. (1975), An alternative explanation of Anasazi culture history. T.R. Frisbie (ed.), *Collected Papers in Honor of Florence Hawley Ellis. Papers of the Archaeological Society of New Mexico*, v. 2, Santa Fe, pp. 178-223.

Kelley, G.A. (1955), *The psychology of personal constructs*. 2 vols.; New York: Norton.

Kempe, D. (1988), *Living underground: A history of cave and cliff dwelling*. London: The Herbert Press.

Kennedy, R.A. (1971), A transatlantic stimulus hypothesis for Mesoamerica and the Caribbean, ca 3500 to 2000 B.C. C.L. Riley et al. (eds.), *Man across the sea*. Austin: University of Texas Press.

Kent, S. (1984), *Analyzing activity areas*. Albuquerque: University of New Mexico Press.

Kidder, A.V. (1927), Southwestern Archaeological Conference. *Science*, v. 68, pp. 489-491.

Kidder, A.V. (1936), Discussion. A.V. Kidder and A.O. Shepard (eds.), *The pottery of Pecos*. New Haven : Yale University Press, v.2, pp. 589-628.

Kidder, A.V. (1958), Pecos, New Mexico: Archaeological notes. *Papers of the Robert S. Peabody Foundation for Archaeology 5*. Andover, Massachusetts.

Kidder, A.V. (1962), *An introduction to the study of Southwestern archaeology with a preliminary account of the excavations at Pecos, and a summary of Southwestern archaeology today*. (ed.: I. Rouse); New Haven: Yale University Press.

King, A.D. (1984), *The bungalow: The production of a global culture*. London: Routledge.

King, A.D. (1990), Theorising difference: Culture, globalisation and space. H. Pamir, V. Imamoglu and N. Teymur (eds.), *Culture, space, history;* (vol.5). Ankara: M.E.T.U. , Faculty of Architecture.
King, P. (1975), *Pueblo Indian religious architecture.* Salt Lake City: Publisher's Press.
Klima, B. (1962), The first ground-plan of an Upper Paleolithic loess settlement in Middle Europe and its meaning. R.J. Braidwood and G.R. Willey (eds.), *Courses toward urban life: Archaeological considerations of some cultural alternates.* Chicago: Aldine Publishing Co., pp. 193-210.
Knowles, R. (1974), *Energy and form: An ecological approach to urban growth.* Cambridge, MA: The MIT Press.
Kokten, I.K. (1949), Anadolu'da prehistorik adamlarin kullandiklari malzeme ve ele gecen bazi maddi kultur belgelerinin etnografya yolu ile izahi. *Turk Tarih Kurumu Belleten,* v. 13, no. 50, pp. 331-337.
Kokten, I.K. (1952), Anadolu'da prehistorik yerlesme yerlerinin dagilisi uzerine bir arastirma. *A.U. Dil ve Tarih-Cografya Fakultesi Dergisi,* v. 10, pp. 167-207.
Kokten, I.K. (1963), Die Stellung von Karain innerhalb der turkischen Vorgeschichte. *Anatolia,* v. 7, pp. 59-86.
Konishi, T. and Aoki, S. (1986), Research on underground dwelling in the loess land of China: Part 1 - Types and locations of earth construction. *Report on the International Symposium on Earth Architecture,* pp. 44-46.
Kostof, S. (1972), *Caves of God: The monastic environment of Byzantine Cappadocia.* Cambridge, MA: The MIT Press.
La Barre, W. (1971), Materials for a history of studies of crisis cults: A bibliographic essay. *Current Anthropology,* v. 12, pp. 3-27.
Labs, K. (1976a), The use of earth covered buildings through history. F.L. Moreland (ed.), *Alternatives in energy conservation: The use of the earth covered buildings.* Washington, D.C.: National Science Foundation, pp. 7-19. (Proceedings and notes of a conference held in Ft. Worth, TX, July 9-12, 1975).
Labs, K. (1976b), The architectural underground. *Underground Space,* v. 1, pp. 1-8.
Lagasse, P.F., Gillespie, W.B., and Eggert, K.G. (1984), Hydraulic engineering analysis of prehistoric water- controlled systems at Chaco Canyon. W.J. Judge and J.D. Schelberg, (eds.), *Recent research on Chaco prehistory.* Albuquerque: U.S. Department of the Interior, NPS, Division of Cultural Research.

Lawrence, R.J. (1987), *Houses, dwellings, and homes.* New York: Wiley.
Landmann, M. (1974), *Philosophical anthropology.* Trans. by D.J. Parent. Philadelphia: The Westminster Press. (1955).
Le Blanc, S.A. (1983), *The Mimbres People.* London: Thames and Hudson.
Le Blanc, S.A. (1986), Aspects of Southwestern prehistory: AD 900-1450. J.F. Mathien and R.H. McGuire (eds.), *Ripples in the Chichimec Sea: New considerations of Southwestern - Mesoamerican Interactions.* Carbondale, IL: Southern Illinois University Press.
Le Blanc, S.A. (1989a), Cibola: Shifting cultural boundaries. L.S. Cordell and G.J. Gumerman (eds.), *Dynamics of Southwestern prehistory.* Washington, DC: Smithsonian Institution Press.
Le Blanc, S.A. (1989b), Cultural dynamics in the Southern Mogollon area. L.S. Cordell and G.J. Gumerman (eds.), *Dynamics of Southwestern prehistory.* Washington, DC: Smithsonian Institution Press.
Lee, R.B and DeVore, I. (eds.), (1968), *Man the hunter.* Chicago: Aldine/ Atherton.
Lefebvre, H. (1968), *The sociology of Marx.* Trans. by N. Guterman. New York: Pantheon Books. (1966).
Leiss, W. (1972), *The domination of nature.* New York: George Braziller.
Lekson, S.H. (1978), *Bonito Phase architecture.* Albuquerque, NM: U.S. National Park Service Division of Cultural Research.
Lekson, S.H. (1982a), Chacoan architecture in continental context. (Paper presented at the Anasazi Symposium, Mesa Verde, CO; October 3, 1981; revised: January 18, 1982; contribution No. 35, Chaco Center.)
Lekson, S.H. (1982b), Architecture and settlement plan in the Redrock Valley of the Gila River, Southwestern New Mexico. P.H. Beckett and K. Silverbird (eds.), *Mogollon archaeology: Proceedings of the 1980 Mogollon Conference.* Ramona, CA: Acoma Books.
Lekson, S.H. (ed.), (1983), *The architecture and dendochronology of Chetro Ketl, Chaco Canyon, New Mexico.* Albuquerque: U.S. National Park Service (Chaco Center).
Lekson, S.H. (1984a), Standing architecture at Chaco Canyon and the interpretation of local and regional organization. W.J. Judge and J.D. Schelberg (eds.), *Recent research on Chaco prehistory.* Albuquerque: U.S. Department of the Interior, NPS, Division of Cultural Research.
Lekson, S.H. (1984b), *Great Pueblo architecture of Chaco Canyon, New Mexico.* Albuquerque: U.S. Department of the Intertior, NPS.
Lekson, S.H. (1990), Sedentism and aggregation in Anasazi archaeology. P.E.

Minnis and C.L. Redman (eds.), *Perspectives on Southwestern prehistory.* Boulder, CO: Westview Press.

Lekson, S.H., Windes, T.C., Stein, J.R., and Judge, J.W. (1988), The Chaco Canyon community. *Scientific American*, (July), v. 259, no. 1, pp. 100-109.

Leon-Portilla, M. (1986), Astronomia y cultura en Mesoamerica. M.A. Moreno Corral (ed.), *Historia de la astronomia en Mexico.* Mexico, D.F.: Fondo de Cultura Economica.

Levi-Bruhl, L. (1978), *La mitologia primitiva.* Barcelona: Ediciones Peninsula.

Lightfoot, K.G. and Feinman, G.M. (1982), Social differentiation and leadership development in early pithouse villages in the Mogollon region of the American Southwest. *American Antiquity*, v. 47, no. 1, pp. 64-86.

Linton, R. (1944), Nomadic raids and fortified pueblos. *American Antiquity*, v. 10, no. 1, pp. 28-32.

Lister, R.H. (1958), *Archaeological excavations in the Northern Sierra Madre Occidental, Chihuahua and Sonora, Mexico.* Boulder, CO: University of Colorado Series in Anthropology, v. 7.

Lister, R.H. and Lister, F.C. (1981), *Chaco Canyon.* Albuquerque: University of New Mexico Press.

Lister, R.H. and Lister, F.C. (1987), *Aztec ruins on the Animas.* Albuquerque: University of New Mexico.

Lloyd, S. and Mellaart, J. (1965), *Beycesultan.* 2 vols.; London: The British Institute of Archaeology at Ankara.

Lopez Luhan, L. (1989), *Nomadas y sedentarios: El Pasado prehispanico de Zacatecas.* Mexico, D. F.: Instituto Nacional de Antropologia y Historia.

Love, D.W. (1977), Dynamics of sedimentation and geomorphic history of Chaco Canyon National Monument, New Mexico. *New Mexico Geological Society Guidebook, 28th Field Conference.* Socorro, NM: New Mexico Bureau of Mines and Mineral Resources.

Love, D.W. (1980), "Quaternary geology of Chaco Canyon, Northwestern New Mexico." Unpublished Ph.D. Dissertation, Department of Geology, University of New Mexico, Albuquerque.

Luce, R.D. Bush, R.R. and Galanter, E. (eds.), (1965), *Handbook of mathematical psychology.* New York: Wiley.

Lukacs, G. (1971), *History and class consciousness: Studies in Marxist dialectics.* Trans. by R. Livingstone. Cambridge: The MIT press. (1922).

Lumholtz, C. (1972), *El Mexico Desconcido.* Mexico: Editora Nacional.

Lyneis, M.M. (1986), A spatial analysis of Anasazi architecture, A.D. 950-1150, Moapa Valley, Nevada. *The Kiva*, v. 52, no. 1, pp. 53-74.

MacNeish, R.S. (1964), Ancient Mesoamerican civilization. *Science*, v. 143, no. 3606, pp. 531-537.

MacQueen, J.G. (1975), *The Hittites and their contemporaries in Asia Minor*. London: Thames and Hudson.

Marcuse, H. (1978), A note on dialectic. A. Arato and E. Gebhardt (eds.), *The essential Frankfurt School reader*. Oxford: Basil Blackwell, pp. 444-451.

Marshall, M.P. and Doyel, D.E. (1981), "An interim report on Bi sa'ani Pueblo, with notes on the Chacoan regional system." Unpublished ms. Window Rock, Arizona: Navajo Nation Cultural Resource Management Program.

Marshall, M.P., Stein, J.R., Loose, R.W., and Novotny, J.E. (1979), *Anasazi communities of the San Juan Basin*. Albuquerque: U.S. Department of the Interior.

Martin, P.S. (1979), Prehistory: Mogollon. A. Ortiz (ed.), *Handbook of North American Indians: Southwest*. Washington, D.C.: Smithsonian Institute, v. 9.

Martin, P.S., Rinaldo, J.B., and Anteys, E. (1949), Cochise and Mogollon Sites in Pine Lawn Valley, Western New Mexico. *Fieldiana: Anthropology*, v. 38, no. 1.

Martin, P.S., Rinaldo, J.B., Bluhm, E., Cutler, H.C., and Grange, R.(Jr.) (1952), Mogollon cultural continuity and change: The stratigraphic analysis of Tularosa and Cordova Caves. *Fieldiana: Anthropology*, v. 40.

Martin, P.S., Roys, L., and Von Bunin, G. (1936), Lowry Ruin in Southwestern Colorado. *Anthropological Series*, v. 23, no. 1. Chicago: Field Museum of Natural History.

Marx, K. (1964), *Pre-capitalist economic formations*. Trans. by J. Cohen (edited and with an Introduction by E.J. Hobsbawm). London: Lawrence & Wishart. (1857-1858).

Marx, K. (1967), *Capital*. 3 vols.; Trans. by S. Moore and E. Aveling. New York: International Publishers, v. 1/1867, v. 2/1885, v. 3/1894.

Marx, K. (1970a), *Critique of Hegel's 'Philosophy of Right'*. Trans. by A. Jolin and J. O'Malley. J. O'Malley (ed.). Cambridge: Cambridge University Press. (1843; 1927).

Marx, K. (1970b), *A contribution to the critique of political economy*. Trans. by S.W. Ryazanskaya. M. Dobb (ed.). New York: International Publishers. (1859).

Marx, K. (1973), *Grundrisse: Foundations of the critique of political economy*. Trans. by M. Nicolaus. New York: Random House. (1939, 1857-1858).

Marx, K. and Engels, F. (1942), *Selected correpsondence 1846 - 1895*. Trans.

by D. Torr. New York: International Publishers.
Marx, K. and Engels, F. (1947), *The German ideology*. Parts I & II. R. Pascal (ed.). New York: International Publishers. (1846).
Maslow, A.H. (1954), *Motivation and personality*. New York: Harper.
Mathien, F.J. (1981), "Economic exchange systems in the San Juan Basin." Unpublished Ph.D. Dissertation, Department of Anthropology, University of New Mexico, Albuquerque.
Mathien, F.J. (1984), Social and economic implications of jewelry items of the Chaco Anasazi. W.J. Judge and J.D. Schelberg (eds.), *Recent research on Chaco prehistory*. Albuquerque: U.S. Department of the Interior, NPS, Division of Cultural Research.
Mathien, F.J. and McGuire, R.H. (1986), Adrift in the Chichimec Sea. F.J. Mathien and R.H. McGuire (eds.), *Ripples in the Chichimec Sea: New considerations of Southwestern - Mesoamerican interactions*. Carbondale, IL: Southern Illinois University Press.
Mathien, F.J. and McGuire, R.H. (eds.), (1986), *Ripples in the Chichimec Sea: New considerations of Southwestern-Mesoamerican interactions*. Carbondale, IL: Southern Illinois University Press.
Matson, R.G. and Lipe, W.D. (1978), Settlement patterns on Cedar Mesa: Boom and bust on the northern periphery. R.C. Euler and G.J. Gumerman (eds.), *Investigations of the Southwestern Anthropological Research Group: Proceedings of the 1976 conference*. Flagstaff: Museum of Northern Arizona.
Maxwell, R.J. (1983), *Contexts of behavior: Anthropological dimensions*. Chicago: Nelson-Hall.
McGregor, J.C. (1941), *Southwestern archaeology*. New York: John Wiley.
McGuire, R.H. (1986), Prestige economics in the prehistoric Southwestern periphery. F.J. Mathien and R.H. McGuire (eds.), *Ripples in the Chichimec Sea: New considerations of Southwestern - Mesoamerican interactions*. Carbondale, IL: Southern Illinois University Press.
McGuire, R.H. (1990), Elites and regional systems. P.E. Minnis and C.L. Redman (eds.), *Perspectives on Southwestern prehistory*. Boulder, CO: Westview Press.
McKenna, P.J. (1982), *A Chacoan primer: Village excavations in Chaco Canyon, 1973-78*. Albuquerque, NM: Chaco Center, NPS.
McKern, W.C. (1937), An hypothesis for the Asiatic origin of the Woodland pattern. *American Antiquity*, v. 3, pp. 138-143.
Mellaart, J. (1965), *Earliest civilizations of the Near East*. New York: McGraw-

Hill Book Co.
Mellaart, J. (1967), *Catal Huyuk: A Neolithic town in Anatolia.* New York: McGraw-Hill.
Mellaart, J. (1970), *Excavations at Hacilar.* 2 vols; Edinburgh: Edinburgh University Press.
Mellaart, J. (1971), Anatolia, ca. 4000-2300 B.C. *The Cambridge Ancient History.* (3rd ed.). Cambridge: Cambridge University Press, v. 1, part 2, pp. 363-416.
Mellaart, J. (1972a), Anatolian Neolithic settlement patterns. P.J. Ucko, R. Tringham, and G.W. Dimbleby (eds.), *Man, settlement and urbanism.* London: Duckworth, pp. 279-284.
Mellaart, J. (1972b), A Neolithic city in Turkey. *Old world archaeology,* (Readings from *Scientific American*). San Francisco: W.H. Freeman, pp. 120-129.
Mellaart, J. (1975), *The Neolithic of the Near East.* London: Thames and Hudson.
Mellaart, J. (1978), *The archaeology of ancient Turkey.* London: The Bodley Head.
Mellink, M.J. (1956), *A Hittite cemetery at Gordion.* Philadelphia: The University Museum (University of PA).
Mellink, M.J. (1966), Anatolia: Old and new perspectives. *Proceedings of the American Philosophical Society,* v. 110, no. 2, pp. 111-129.
Mera, H.P. (1935), Ceramic clues to the prehistory of North Central New Mexico. *Technical Series Bulletin 8.* Santa Fe, NM: Laboratory of Anthropology.
Mera, H.P. (1938), Some aspects of the Largo Culture Phase, Northern New Mexico. *American Antiquity,* v. 3, no. 3.
Metzger, H. (1969), *Anatolia II: First Millenium B.C. to the end of the Roman Period.* Trans. by J. Hogarth. London: Berrie & Jenkins.
Mindeleff, V. (1891), A study of pueblo architecture: Tusayan and Cibola. *Eighth Annual Report of the Bureaus of Ethnology for the Years 1886-87.* Washington, D.C.: Bureau of Ethnology, pp. 13-228.
Minnis, P.E. and Redman, C.L. (eds.), (1990), *Perspectives on Southwestern prehistory.* Boulder, CO: Westview Press.
Morgan, J.R. (1977), Were Chaco's great kivas ancient computers of astronomy? *El Palacio,* v. 83, no. 1, pp. 28-41.
Morgan, L.H. (1964), *Ancient Society.* New York: Henry Holt. (1877).
Moore, B., Jr. (1984), *Privacy: Studies in social and cultural history.* Armonk,

NY: M.E. Sharpe, Inc.
Mulligan, H. (1983), Environmental characteristics of the vernacular underground dwelling. *Proceedings of the 2nd International Conference on Passive and Low Energy Architecture.* Rethymnon, Crete.
Nabakov, P. (1986), *Architecture of Acoma Pueblo: The 1934 Historic American Buildings Survey Project.* Santa Fe, NM: Ancient City Press.
Narez, J. (1991a), *Casas Grandes.* Mexico, D.F.: Instituto Nacional de Antropologia y Historia.
Narez, J. (1991b), *Oasis America.* Mexico, D.F.: Instituto Nacional de Antropologia y Historia.
Naumann, R. (1975), *Eski Anadolu mimarligi.* Trans. by B. Madra. Ankara: Turk Tarih Kurumu. (1955).
Nelson, B.A. (1991), Observaciones acerca la prensencia tolteca en La Quemada, Zacatecas en Mesoamerica y Norte de Mexico. F. Sodi Miranda (ed.), *Mesoamerica y Norte de Mexico: Siglo IX - XII.* (Seminario de Arqueologia "Wigberto Jimenez Moreno"). Mexico, D.F.: Museo de Antropologia y Historia.
Nelson, R.S. (1986), Pochtecas and prestige: Mesoamerican artifacts in Hohokam sites. F.J. Mathien and R.H. McGuire (eds.), *Ripples in the Chichimec Sea: New considerations of Southwestern - Mesoamerican interactions.* Carbondale, IL: Southern Illinois University Press.
Nicholas, L.M. (1981), "Irrigation and sociopolitical development - The Salt River Valley, Arizona: An exmaination of three prehistoric canal systems." M.A. Thesis, Department of Anthropology, Arizona State University, Tempe.
Noble, D.G. (ed.), (1984), *New light on Chaco Canyon.* Santa Fe: School of American Research.
Obenauf, M. (1980), "The Chacoan roadway system." Unpublished M.A. Thesis, Department of Anthropology, University of New Mexico, Albuquerque.
Odum, E.P. (1969), The strategy of ecosystem development. *Science*, v. 164, no. 3877, pp. 262-270.
O'Laughlin, T.C. (1980), *The Keystone Dam Site and other archaic and formative sites in Northwest El Paso, Texas.* El Paso: University of Texas El Paso Centennial Museum (Publication No. 8).
Old world archaeology; Foundations of civilization. (Readings from *Scientific American*). San Francisco. W.H. Freeman. 1972.
Oliver, P. (ed.), (1969), *Shelter and society.* New York: Praeger.

Orcutt, J.D., Blinman, E. and Kohler, T.A. (1990), Explanations of population aggregation in the Mesa Verde region prior to A.D. 900. P.E. Minnis and C.L. Redman (eds.), *Perpectives on Southwestern prehistory*. Boulder, CO: Westview Press.

Orlin, L.L. (1970), *Assyrian colonies in Cappadocia*. The Hague: Mouton.

"Ortahisar: Arastirma - degerlendirme ve genel koruma projesi." Asama 1/ Rapor 1. Ankara: T.C. Kultur Bakanligi, Eski Eserler ve Muzeler Genel Md. 1975.

Ortiz, A. (1965), Dual organization as an operational concept in the Pueblo Southwest. *Ethnology*, v. 4, no. 4, pp. 389-396.

Ortiz, A. (1969), *The Tewa world: Space, time, being, and becoming in a pueblo society* Chicago: University of Chicago Press.

Ortiz, A. (1972), Ritual drama and the pueblo world view. A. Ortiz (ed.), *New perspectives on the pueblos*. Albuquerque: School of American Research, University of New Mexico.

Ortiz, A. (1979), *Handbook of North American Indians: Southwest*. Washington, D.C.: Smithsonian Institute.

Ozguc, T. (1963), Early Anatolian archaeology in the light of recent research. *Anatolia*, v. 7, pp. 1-21.

Ozguc, T. (1964), The art and architecture of ancient Kanish. *Anatolia*, v. 8, pp. 27-48.

Ozguc, T. (1972), An Assyrian trading post. *Old world archaeology: Foundations of civilization*. (Readings from *Scientific American*.) San Francisco: W.H. Freeman and Co., pp. 243-249.

Ozguner, O. (1970), *Koyde mimari: Dogu Karadeniz*. Ankara: ODTU, Mimarlik Fak.

Ozkan, S. and Onur, S. (1975), Another thick wall pattern: Cappadocia. P. Oliver (ed.), *Shelter, sign and symbol*. London: Barrie and Jenkins, pp. 95-106.

Ozkan, S., Turan, M., and Ustunkok (1979), Institutionalised architecture, vernacular architecture and vernacularism in historical perspective. *M.E.T.U. Journal of the Faculty of Architecture*, v. 5, no. 2, pp. 127-156.

Pailes, R.A. (1980), The upper Rio Sonora Valley in prehistoric trade. C.L. Riley and B.C. Hedrick (eds.), New Frontiers in the archaeology and ethnohistory of the Greater Southwest, *Transactions of the Illinois State Academy of Science*, v. 72, no. 4, pp. 20-39.

Pailes, R.A. (1990), Elite formation and interregional exchange in peripheries. P.E. Minnis and C.L. Redman (eds.), *Perspectives on Southwestern*

prehistory. Boulder, CO: Westview Press.
Palerm, A. and Wolf, E.R. (1957), Ecological potential and cultural development in Mesoamerica. *Studies in Human Ecology.* Washington, D.C.: Panamerican Chion (Social Science Monographs No. 3).
Palkovich, A.M. (1984), Disease and mortality patterns in the burial rooms of Pueblo Bonito: Preliminary considerations. W.J. Judge and J.D. Schelberg (eds.), *Recent research on Chaco prehistory.* Albuquerque: U.S. Department of the Interior, NPS, Division of Cultural Research.
Parekh, B. (1982), *Marx's theory of ideology.* Baltimore: The Johns Hopkins University Press.
Parsons, E.C. (1925), *The Pueblo of Jemez.* New Haven: Yale University Press.
Parsons, E.C. (1939), *Pueblo Indian religion.* Chicago: University of Chicago Press.
Pasquare, G. (1968), *Geology of the Cenozoic volcanic area of Central Anatolia.* Rome.
Peckham, S. (1979), When is a Rio Grande Kiva? A.H. Schroeder (ed.), *Collected papers in Honor of Bertha Pauline Dutton.* Albuquerque: Archaeological Society of New Mexico, pp. 55-86.
Peckham, S. (1984), The Anasazi culture of the northern Rio Grande rift. *New Mexico Geological Society Guidebook.* Rio Grande Rift: Northern New Mexico, pp. 275-281.
Penrose, R. (1989), *The Emperor's new mind.* New York: Penguin.
Perkins, D., Jr. (1969), Fauna of Catal Huyuk: Evidence for early cattle domestication in Anatolia. *Science,* v. 164, no. 3876, pp. 177-179.
Perkins, D., Jr. and Daly, P. (1972), A hunters' village in Neolithic Turkey. *Old world archaeology.* (Readings from *Scientific American.*) San Francisco: W.H. Freeman, pp. 105-112.
Piaget, J. (1954), *The construction of reality in the child.* New York: Basic Books.
Pierson, L.M. (1949), "The prehistoric population of Chaco Canyon, New Mexico: A study in methods and techniques of prehistoric population estimation." Unpublished Master's Thesis, Department of Anthropology, University of New Mexico, Albuquerque.
Pilles, P.J., Jr. (1979), Sunset Crater and the Sinagua: A new interpretation. C. Renfrew and K.I. Cooke (eds.), *Volcanic activity and human ecology.* New York: Academic Press.
Pinxten, H. (1980), *Anthropology of space.* Ghent: Rijksuniversiteit te Ghent.
Plog, F., Gumerman, G.J., Euler, R.C. Dean, J.S. Hevly, R.H. and Karlstrom,

N.V. (1988), Anasazi adaptive strategies: The model, predictions, and results. G.J. Gumerman (ed.), *The Anasazi in a changing environment.* New York: Cambridge University Press.

Plog, F., Upham, S. and Weigand, P.C. (1982), A perspective on Mogollon-Mesoamerican interaction. P.H. Beckett and K. Silverbird (eds.), *Mogollon archaeology: Proceedings of the 1980 Mogollon Conference.* Ramona, CA: Acoma Books.

Plog, S. (1976), Measurement of prehistoric interaction between communities. K.V. Flannery (ed.), *The early Mesoamerican village.* New York: Academic Press.

Polanyi, K., Arensberg, C.M. and Pearson, H.W. (eds.), (1957), *Trade and market in the early empires.* Glencoe, IL : The Free Press.

Polgar, S. (1975), Population, evolution, and theoretical paradigms. S. Polgar (ed.), *Population, ecology, and social evolution.* The Hague: Mouton.

Polgar, S. (ed.), (1975), *Population, ecology, and social evolution.* The Hague: Mouton Publishers.

Powell, G.E. (1967), *Latest Aztec discoveries.* San Antonio, TX: The Naylor Company.

Powell S. (1983), *Mobility and adaptation: The Anasazi of Black Mesa, Arizona.* Carbondale, IL: Southern Illinois University Press.

Powell, S. (1990), Sedentism or mobility: What does the data say? What did the Anasazi do? P.E. Minnis and C.L. Redman (eds.), *Perspectives on Southwestern prehistory.* Boulder, CO: Westview Press.

Powers, R.P. (1984a), Outliers and roads in the Chaco System. D.G. Noble (ed.), *New light on Chaco Canyon.* Santa Fe: School of American Research Press.

Powers, R.P. (1984b), Regional interaction in the San Juan Basin: The Chacoan Outlier System. W.J. Judge and J.D. Schelberg (eds.), *Recent research on Chaco prehistory.* Albuquerque: U.S. Department of the Interior, NPS, Division of Cultural Research.

Powers, R.P., Gillespie, W.B., and Lekson, S.H. (1983), *The Outlier survey.* Albuquerque, NM: U.S. Department of the Interior (Chaco Center).

Purtymun, W.D. and Kennedy, W.R. (1971), Geology and hydrology of Mesita del Buey. Los Alamos: Los Alamos Scientific Laboratories Report LA-4460.

Quilter, J.B., Ojeda, E., Pearsall, D.M., Sandweiss, D.H., Jones, J.G. and Wing, E.S.(1991), Subsistence economy of El Paraiso, an early Peruvian site. *Science,* no. 251. pp. 277-283.

Ramsay, Sir W.M. (1972), *The historical geography of Asia Minor*. New York: Cooper Square Publishers. (1890).
Ransom, W.H. (1960), *Buildings for the storage of crops in warm climates*. London: Department of Scientific and Industrial Research, Building Research Station (Tropical Building Studies #2), Her Majesty's Stationery Office.
Raphael, M. (1968), *The demands of art*. Trans. by N. Guterman. Princeton: Princeton University Press. (1947).
Rapoport, A. (1969), *House form and culture*. Englewood Cliffs, NJ: Prentice-Hall.
Rapoport, A. (1982), *The meaning of the built environment: A nonverbal communication approach*. Beverley Hills, CA: Sage Publications.
Rapoport, A. (1983a), Environmental quality, metropolitan areas, and traditional settlements. *Habitat International*, v. 7, no. 3/4, pp. 37-63.
Rapoport, A. (1983b), Development, culture change and supportive design. *Habitat International*, v. 7, no. 5/6, pp. 249-268.
Ravesloot, J.C. (1988), *Mortuary practices and social differentiation at Casas Grandes, Chihuahua, Mexico*. Tucson: University of Arizona Press.
Redman, C.L.(1978), *The rise of civilization: From early farmers to urban society in the ancient Near East*. San Francisco: W.H. Freeman.
Reed, E.K. (1971), Commentary: Section I. C.L. Riley et al. (ed.), *Man across the sea*. Austin: University of Texas Press.
Reid, J.J. (1989), A grasshopper perspective on the Mogollon of the Arizona mountains. L.S. Cordell and G.J. Gumerman (eds), *Dynamics of Southwestern prehistory*. Washington, DC: Smithsonian Institution Press.
Reid, J.J. and Whittlesey, S.M. (1990), The complicated and the complex: Observations on the archaeological record of large pueblos. P.E. Minnis and C.L. Redman (eds.), *Perspectives on Southwestern prehistory*. Boulder, CO: Westview Press.
Renfrew, C., Dixon, J.E., and Cann, J.R. (1966), Obsidian and early cultural contact in the Near East. *Proceedings of the Prehistoric Society for 1966*, New Series, v. 32, no. 2, pp. 30-72.
Report on the International Symposium on Earth Architecture. Architectural Institute of Japan. 1986.
Reyman, J.E. (1976), Astronomy, architecture, and adaptation at Pueblo Bonito. *Science*, v. 193, pp. 957-962.
Reyman, J.E. (1977), Solstice misalignment at Sun Temple: Correcting Fewkes. *The Kiva*, v. 42, no. 3-4, pp. 281-284.

Reyman, J.E. (1978), Pochteca burials at Anasazi sites? L. R. Carroll and C.H. Basil (eds.), *Across the Chichimec Sea. Papers in Honor of J. Charles Kelley*. Carbondale and Edwardsville: Southern Illinois University Press, pp. 242-259.

Reyman, J.E. (1980), An Anasazi solar master? *Science*, v. 209, pp. 858-859.

Reyman, J.E. (1985), A reevaluation of bi-wall-and tri-wall structures in the Anasazi Area. W.J. Folan (ed.), *Contributions to the archaeology and ethnohistory of greater Mesoamerica*. Carbondale: South Illinois University Press.

Riley, C.L. (1982), *The frontier people: The greater Southwest in the protohistoric period*. Carbondale: Southern Illinois Center for Archaeological Investigation, Occasional Paper 1.

Riley, C.L. (1986), An overview of the greater Southwest in the protohistoric period. F.J. Mathien and R.H. McGuire (eds.), *Ripples in the Chichimec Sea: New considerations of Southwestern - Mesoamerican interactions*. Carbondale, IL: Southern Illinois University Press.

Riley, C.L. and Kelley, J.C., Pennington, C.W., and Rands, R.L. (eds.), (1971), *Man across the sea: Problems of pre- Columbian contacts*. Austin: University of Texas Press.

Rodley, L. (1985), *Cave monasteries of Byzantine Cappadocia*. Cambridge: Cambridge University Press.

Rogers, E.M. (1983), *Diffusion of innovations*. New York: Free Press.

Rohn, A.H. (1971), *Mug House, Mesa Verde National Park, Colorado*. Washington, D.C.: National Park Service Archaeological Research Series #7-D.

Rohn, A.H. (1977), *Cultural change and continuity on Chapin Mesa*. Lawrence, KS: Regent Press of Kansas.

Rohn, A.H. (1985), Prehistoric developments in the Mesa Verde Region. D.B. Noble, M. Elliott, and D. Flynn (eds.), *Understanding the Anasazi of Mesa Verde and Hovenweep*. Santa Fe: School of American Research.

Rohn, A.H. (1989), Northern San Juan prehistory. L.S. Cordell and G.J. Gumerman (eds.), *Dynamics of Southwestern prehistory*. Washington, DC: Smithsonian Institution Press.

Rudofsky, B. (1964), *Architecture without architects*. Garden City, NY: Doubleday and Co.

Rudofsky, B. (1977), *The prodigious builders*. New York: Harcourt Brace Jovanovich.

Ruppe, R.J., Jr. (1953), "The Acoma culture province: An archaeological concept." Unpublished Ph.D. Dissertation, Department of Anthropology, Harvard University, Cambridge.

Ruppe, R.J., Jr. (1966), The archaeological survey: A defense. *American Antiquity*, v. 31, pp. 313-333.

Sadalla, E.R., Snyder, P.Z., and Stea, D. (1976), House form and culture revisited. *Proceedings, Environmental Design Research Association* . Vancouver, B.C. : University of British Columbia.

Sahlins, M. (1972), *Stone age economics*. Chicago: Aldine-Atherton.

Sahlins, M. and E. R.Service, *Evolution and Culture*, Ann Arbor: Univ. of Michigan Press, 1960.

Saile, D. (1977), Architecture in prehispanic pueblo archaeology: Examples from Chaco Canyon, New Mexico. *World Archaeology*, v. 9, no. 2, pp. 157-173.

Saile, D. (1985), Many dwellings: Views of a Pueblo World. D. Seaman and R. Mugerauer (eds.), *Dwelling, place, and environment*. Dordrecht, Holland: Nijhoff, pp. 159-181.

Samuels, M.L., and Betancourt, J.L. (1982), Modeling the long-term effects of fuelwood harvests on piñon-juniper woodlands. *Environmental Management*, v. 6, no. 6, pp. 505-515.

Sando, J.S. (1976), *The Pueblo Indians*. San Francisco: The Indian Historian Press.

Sando, J.S. (1982), *NeeHemish: A history of Jemez Pueblo*. Albuquerque: Univeristy of New Mexico Press.

Sauer, C. (1932), The road to Cibola. *Ibero-Americana*, v. 3.

Sauer, C. and Brand, D. (1932), Aztatlan: Prehistoric Mexican Frontier on the Pacific Coast. *Ibero-Americana*, v. 1.

Sayles, E.B. (1936), An archaeological survey of Chihuahua, Mexico. *Medallion Papers*. Globe Arizona, no. 22.

Schaafsma, C.F. (1976), *Archaeological survey of maximum pool and Navajo excavations at Abiquiu Reservoir, Rio Arriba County, New Mexico*. Santa Fe: School of American Research.

Schaafsma, P. (1972), *Rock art in New Mexico*. Santa Fe, NM: State Planning Office.

Schaafsma, P. and Schaafsma, C.F. (1974), Evidence for the origins of Pueblo kachina cult as suggested by Southwestern rock art. *American Antiquity*, v. 39, no. 4, pp. 535-545.

Schelberg, J.D. (1982), "Economic and social development as an adaptation to a marginal environment in Chaco Canyon, New Mexico." Ph.D. Dissertation,

Department of Anthropology, Northwestern University, Evanston.
Schelberg, J.D. (1984), Analogy, complexity, and regionally-based perspectives. W.J. Judge and J.D. Schelberg (eds.), *Recent research on Chaco prehistory.* Albuquerque: U.S. Department of the Interior, NPS, Division of Cultural Research.
Schroeder, A.H. (1957), The Hakataya cultural tradition. *American Antiquity*, v. 23, no. 2, pp. 176-178.
Schroeder, A.H. (1960), The Hohokam, Sinagua, and the Hakataya. *Archives of Archaeology.* Madison, WI, No. 5.
Schroeder, A.H. (1979), Prehistory: Hakataya. A. Ortiz (ed.), *Handbook of North American Indians: Southwest.* Washington, D.C.: Smithsonian Institute, v. 9.
Schroeder, A.H. (1981), How far can a *Pochteca* leap without leaving footprints? A.H. Schroeder (ed.), *Collected papers in honor of Erik Kellerman Reed. Papers of the Archaeological Society of New Mexico*, v. 6, pp. 43-64.
Schroeder, A.H. and Wendorf, F. (1954), Excavations near Aragon, New Mexico. F. Wendorf (ed.), *Highway salvage archaeology.* (Vol. 1.) Santa Fe: New Mexico State Highway Department and Museum of New Mexico, pp. 53-105.
Schroedinger, E. (1967), *What is life?* New York: Cambridge University Press.
Schwartz, D.W. (1984), Foreword. D.G. Noble (ed.), *New light on Chaco Canyon.* Santa Fe: School of American Research Press.
Seddon, D. (ed.), (1978), *Relations of production: Marxist approaches to economic anthropology.* Trans. by H. Lackner. London: Frank Cass & Co.
Senyurek, M.S. (1956), The excavation of a cave near the village of Magaracik in the vilayet of the Hatay: Preliminary notice. *Anatolia*, v. 1, pp. 81-83.
Senyurek, M.S. (1958), Test excavation made in a cave in the vicinity of Samandag. *Anatolia*, v. 3, pp. 64-70.
Senyurek, M.S. and Bostanci, E. (1958), Prehistoric research in the Hatay province. *Turk Tarih Kurumu Belleten*, v. 22, pp. 157-166.
Service, E. (1962), *Primitive social organization.* New York: Random House.
Siemers, C.T. and King, N.R. (1974), Macroinvertebrate paleoecology of a transgressive marine sandstone, Cliff House, sandstone (upper cretaceous), Chaco Canyon, Northwest New Mexico. C.T. Siemers (ed.), *New Mexico Geological Society Guidebooks, 25th Field Conference, Central-Northern New Mexico.* Ghost Ranch, Central-Northern New Mexico, pp. 267-286.
Slatter, E.D. (1973), "Climate in pueblo abandonment of the Chevelon drainage, Arizona." Unpublished paper, 38th Annual Meeting, American Anthropological Association.

Smith, R.L., Barley, R.A., and Russell, S.A. (1978), The volcanic evolution of the Jemez Mountains and its relation to the Rio Grande Rift. K.H. Olsen and C.E. Chapin (eds.), *1978 International Symposium on the Rio Grande Rift*. Los Alamos: Los Alamos Scientific Laboratory.

Smith, W. (1952), Excavations in the Big Hawk Valley, Wupatki National Monument, Arizona. *Museum of Northern Arizona Bulletin*, No. 24.

Snow, C.T. (1977), "Some proposals concerning the possiblity of an early exchange network in the San Juan Basin." Unpublished ms.

Snyder, P.Z., Stea, D., and Sadalla, E.K. (1976), Socio-cultural modification and user needs in Navajo housing. *Journal of Architectural Research*, v. 5, no. 3, pp 4-9.

Sofar, A., Zinser, V., and Sinclair, R.M. (1979), A unique solar marking construct. *Science*, v. 206, pp. 283-291.

Sorenson, J.L. (1971), The significance of an apparent relationship between the Near East and Mesoamerica. C.L. Riley et al. (eds.), *Man Across the Sea*. Austin: University of Texas Press.

Soygenis, M.D. (1985), Pueblo settlements: A structural study. *The Chesopiean: A Journal of North American Archaeology*, v. 23, no. 2, pp. 9-19.

Stalker, A. Mac S. (1980), The geology of the ice-free corridor: The Southern Half. *Canadian Journal of Anthropology*, v. 1, no. 1, pp. 11-14.

Stark, B.L. (1986), Perspectives on the peripheries of Mesoamerica. F.J. Mathien and R.H. McGuire (eds.), *Ripples in the Chichimec Sea: New considerations of Southwestern - Mesoamerican interactions*. Carbondale, IL: Southern Illinois University Press.

Stea, D. (1981), Waahi Marae: Cultural adjustments to new patterns of settlement among the Maori. N.J. Ericksen (ed.), *Environmental perception and planning in New Zealand*. Hamilton, New Zealand: Univeristy of Waikato.

Stea, D. (1983), Critical elements in culturally-adaptive housing and settlement. J.B. Calhoun (ed.), *Environment and population: Problems of adaptation*. New York: Praeger.

Stea, D. (1990), The twelve 'smudge pots' of vernacular building: Notes on explorations into architectural mythology. M. Turan (ed.), *Vernacular architecture: Paradigms of environmental response*. Aldershot, U.K.: Gower Press.

Stea, D. and Turan, M. (1986), Placemaking and production in prehistory: A comparative study in dialectical perspective. D.G. Saile (ed.), *Architecture in cultural change: Essays in built form and culture research*. Lawrence,

KA: Built Form and Culture Studies, School of Architecture and Urban Design, The University of Kansas, pp. 91-107.

Steen, C.R. (1971), An archaeologist's summary of adobe. *El Palacio*, v. 77, no. 4, pp 29-38.

Steen, C.R. (1977), Pajarito Plateau: Archeological survey and excavations. Los Alamos: Los Alamos Scientific Laboratory Report LASL-77-4.

Steen, C.R. (1980), Prehistory of the Northern Plateau. D.G. Noble, J. Kepp, and B. James (eds.), *Bandelier National Monument*. Santa Fe: School of American Research.

Sterrett, J.R.S. (1888), *An epigraphical journey in Asia Minor*. Boston: Damrell and Upham.

Sterrett, J.R.S. (1919), The cone-dwellers of Asia Minor. *The National Geographic Magazine*, v. 35, no. 4, pp. 281-331.

Steward, J.H. (1955), *Theory of culture change: The methodology of multilinear evolution*. Urbana: University of Illinois Press.

Strabo (1854), *The geography of Strabo*. Trans. by H.C. Hamilton and W. Falconer. 3 vols.; London: Henry G. Bohn.

Stuart, D.E. and Farwell, R.E. (1983), Out of phase: Late pithouse occupations in the highlands of New Mexico. J.C. Winter (ed.), High altitude adaptations in the Southwest. *Cultural Resources Management Report 2*. Albuquerque: U.S.D.A. Forest Service, Southwestern Region, pp. 115-158.

Swedlund, A.C. and Sessions, S.E. (1976), A developmental model of prehistoric population growth on Black Mesa, Northeastern Arizona. G.J. Gumerman and R.C. Euler (eds.), *Papers on the archaeology of Black Mesa, Arizona*. Carbondale: Southern Illinois University Press, pp. 136-148.

Tafuri, M. (1980), *Theories and history of architecture*. Trans. by G. Varrecchia; New York: Harper and Roe, (1976).

Thomson, G. (1966), *Aeschylus and Athens: A study in the social origins of drama*. London: Lawrence and Wishart. (1941).

Thomson, G. (1978), *The prehistoric Aegean*. London: Lawrence and Wishart. (1949).

Thurnwald, R. (1965), *Economics in primitive communities*. Oosterhout N.B., The Netherlands: Anthropological Pub. - Oxford University Press. (1932).

Todd, I.A. (1965), The obsidian industry of Avla Dag. *Anatolian Studies*, v. 15, pp. 95 ff.

Todd, I.A. (1966), Asikli Huyuk, a Protoneolithic site in Anatolia. *Anatolian Studies*, v. 16, pp. 139-163.

Todd, I.A. (1976), *Catal Huyuk in perspective*. Menlo Park, CA: Cummings.

Todd, I.A. (1980), *The prehistory of Central Anatolia I:The Neolithic period.* (Studies in Mediterranean Archaeology, v. LX). Goteburg: Paul Astroms Forlag.
Toll, H.W. (1984), Trends in ceramic import and distribution in Chaco Canyon. W.J. Judge and J.D. Schelberg, (eds.), *Recent research on Chaco prehistory.* Albuquerque: U.S. Department of the Interior, NPS, Division of Cultural Research.
Toll, H.W., Windes, T.C., and McKenna, P.J. (1980), Late ceramic patterns in Chaco Canyon: The pragmatics of modelling ceramic exchange. R.E. Fry (ed.), *Models and methods in regional exchange.* SAA Papers 1, pp. 95-117.
Trigger, Bruce G. Settlement archaeology: Its goals and promises. *American Anthropologist*, 1967, 32(2), 149-159.
Tringham, R.E. (1991a), Men and women in prehistoric architecture. *Traditional Dwellings and Settlements Review*, v.3, no.1, pp. 9-28.
Tringham, R.E. (1991b), Households with faces: The challenge of gender in prehistoric architectural remains, J.M. Gero and M.W. Conkey (eds.) *Engendering Archaeology: Women and Prehistory*, London: Basil Blackwell.
Turan, M. (1980), Insan-cevre iliskisine elestirel bir bakis. *M.E.T.U. Journal of the Faculty of Architecture*, v. 6, no. 1, pp. 31-54.
Turan, M. (1987), Poverty, prudence, and place-making: Strolling through *gecekondus. Habitat International*, v. 11, no. 3, pp. 77-102.
Ucko, P.J., Tringham, P. and Dimbleby, G.W. (eds.), (1972), *Man, settlement and urbanism.* London: Duckworth.
Upham, S. (1982), *Politics and power: An economic and political history of the Western Pueblo.* New York: Academic Press.
Upham, S. (1986), Imperialists, isolationists, world systems and political realities: Perspectives on Mesoamerican-Southwestern interaction. F.J. Mathien and R.H. McGuire (eds.), *Ripples in the Chichimec Sea: New considerations of Southwestern - Mesoamerican interactions.* Carbondale, IL: Southern Illinios University Press.
Upham, S., Lightfoot, K.G. and Jewett, R.A. (1989), *The sociopolitical structure of prehistoric Southwestern societies.* Boulder, CO: Westview Press.
Upham, S., and Rice, G. (1980), Up the canal without a pattern: Modelling Hohokam interaction and exchange. D. Doyel and F. Ploz, (eds.), *Current issues in Hohokam Prehistory: Proceedings of a Symposium.* Tempe, AZ: Arizona State University (Anthropological Research Paper 23).
Urban, M. (1969), *Yeralti schechri:* Die unterirdischen Siedlungen

Sudostanatoliens. Allenschwand: (published by the author).
Urban, M. (1973), Das Ratsel der unterirdischen Stadte Sudostanatoliens. Zweiter Teil: Geschichtlicher Rahmen und Deutungen, *Vorland*, v. 1, pp. 174-181. Dritter Teil: Maginotlinie der Fruhgeschichte, *Vorland*, v. 1, pp. 205-212.
Van Loon, M. (1968), The Oriental Institute excavations at Mureybit, Syria: Preliminary report on the 1965 campaign. *Journal of Near Eastern Studies*, v. 27, no. 4, pp. 265-290.
Vivian, G. (1959), *The Hibbard Site and other tri-wall structures in New Mexico and Colorado*. Washington, D.C.: National Park Service (Archaeological Research Series 5).
Vivian, G. and Reiter, P. (1960), *The Great Kivas of Chaco Canyon and their relationships*. Santa Fe: Monographs of the School of American Research and the Museum of New Mexico, No. 22.
Vivian, G. and Reiter, P. (1965), *The Great Kivas of Chaco Canyon*. Albuquerque: University of New Mexico Press.
Vivian, R.G. (1970a), "Aspects of prehistoric society in Chaco Canyon, New Mexico." Unpublished Ph.D. Dissertation, Department of Anthropology, University of Arizona, Tucson.
Vivian, R.G. (1970b), An inquiry into prehistoric social organization in Chaco Canyon, New Mexico. W.A. Longacre (ed.), *Reconstructing prehistoric pueblo societies*. Albuquerque: University of New Mexico Press.
Vivian, R.G. (1972), *Prehistoric water conservation in Chaco Canyon*. (Technical report to National Science Foundation.) Washington, D.C.: National Science Foundation.
Vivian, R.G. (1974), Conservation and diversion: Water control systems in the Anasazi Southwest. T.E. Downing and G. McGuire (eds.), *University of Arizona Anthropological Papers*, No. 25. Tucson: University of Arizona.
Vivian, R.G. (1983), The Chacoan phenomenon: Cultural growth in the San Juan Basin. Paper presented at the Second Anasazi Symposium, Salmon Ruin, New Mexico.
Vivian, R.G. (1990), *The Chacoan prehistory of the San Juan Basin*. New York: Academic Press.
Vivian, R.G. and Mathews, T.W. (1965), *Kin Kletso, a Pueblo III community in Chaco Canyon*. Southwest Parks and Monuments Technical Series 6 (1).
Von Neuman, J. (1958), *The computer and the brain*. New Haven: Yale University Press.
Wallerstein, I. (1974), The rise and future demise of the world capitalist system:

Concepts for comparative analysis. *Comparative Studies in Society and History*, v. 16, pp. 387-415.
Wallerstein, I. (1979), *The modern world system*. New York: Academic Press.
Wallerstein, I. (1982), *The capitalist world economy*. New York: Academic Press.
Washburn, D.K. (1978), "A reanalysis of the grave goods from Pueblo Bonito: Some Mexican affiliations." Unpublished paper presented at the Annual Meeting, Society for American Archaeology, Tucson.
Washburn, D.K. (1980), The Mexican connection: Cylinder jars from the Valley of Oaxaca. *Transactions of the Illinois Academy of Science*, v. 72, no. 4, pp. 70-82.
Weber, Max. *Grundriss der Sozialeökonomik*, III Abteilung: *Wirtschaft und Gesellschaft*, 2 Halbband [J. C. B. Mohr (Paul Siebeck), Tübingen, 1925]
Weigand, P.C. (1978), La Prehistoria del Estado de Zacatecas: Una Interpretacion. E. Sanchez (ed.), *Zacatecas: Anuario de Historia*. Zacatecas: Universidad Antonoma de Zacatecas, pp. 203-248.
Weisberg, L. (1985), From the heights. *Journal North*, pp. 8-9.
Wendorf, F. and Reed, E. (1955), An alternative reconstruction of northern Rio Grande prehistory. *El Palacio*, v.62, nos. 5-6, pp. 131-173.
Werner, H. (1948), *Comparative psychology of mental development*. New York: International University Press.
Westerveld, J. (1957), *Phases of Neogene and Quaternary volcanism in Asia Minor*. Mexico City.
Wheatley, P. *The Pivot of the Four Quarters*. Chicago: Aldine Publishing Co, 1971.
Whitecotton, J.W. and Pailes, R.A. (1986), New World Precolumbian world systems. F.J. Mathien and R.H. McGuire (eds.), *Ripples in the Chichimec Sea: New considerations of Southwestern - Mesoamerican interactions*. Carbondale IL: Southern Illinois University Press.
Wikse, J.R. (1977), *About possession: The self as private property*. University Park: Pennsylvania State University.
Wilcox, D.R. (1986a), An historical analysis of the problem of Southwest-Mesoamerican connections. F.J. Mathien and R.H. McGuire (eds.), *Ripples in the Chichimec Sea: New considerations of Southwestern - Mesoamerican interactions*. Carbondale, IL: Southern Illinois University Press.
Wilcox, D.R. (1986b), The Tepiman connection: A model of Mexican-Southwestern interaction. F.J. Mathien and R.H. McGuire (eds.), *Ripples in the Chichimec Sea: New considerations of Southwestern - Mesoamerican*

interactions. Carbondale, IL: Southern Illinois University Press.

Wilczynski, J. (1981), *An encyclopedic dictionary of Marxism, socialism and communism*. Berlin: De gruyter.

Wilford, J.N. (1985), Excavation in Turkey reveals signs of formal architecture and culture. *The New York Times*, p. 10, Sunday, June 2.

Williams, J.L. (ed.), (1986), *New Mexico in maps*. Albuquerque: University of New Mexico Press.

Williams, R. (1980), *Problems in materialism and culture*. London: NLB.

Williamson, R.A., Fisher, J., and O'Flynn, D. (1977), Anasazi solar observations. A. Aveni (ed.), *Native American Astronomy*. Austin: University of Texas Press.

Windes, T. (1984), A New Look at Population in Chaco Canyon. W.J. Judge and J.D. Schelberg (eds.), *Recent research on Chaco prehistory*. Albuquerque: U.S. Department of the Interior, NPS, Division of Cultural Research.

Winter, J.C. (1985), Hovenweep through time. D.G. Noble, M.Elliott, and D. Flynn (eds.), *Understanding the Anasazi of Mesa Verde and Hovenweep*. Santa Fe: School of American Research.

Wolf, E.R. (1982), *Europe and the people without history*. Berkeley: University of California Press.

Wormington, H.M. (1978), *Prehistoric Indians of the Southwest*. Denver: Denver Museum of Natural History. (1947).

Wynne-Edwards, V.C. (1962), *Animal dispersion in relation to social behavior*. New York: Hafmer.

Xenophon (1867), *The Anabasis or Expedition of Cyrus and the Memorabilia of Socrates*. Trans. by Rev. J.S. Watson London: Bell & Daldy.

Zeilik, M. (1985), Sun Watching. *New Mexico*, v. 63, no. 3, pp. 48-55.

Index

abandonment 37, 38, 50, 102, 127, 140, 141, 165, 180, 197, 203, 204, 206, 214, 219
  regional abandonments 205
  sequential occupants 204
Acar 296
Acem Huyuk 135
Aceramic Can Hasan 87, 88, 104, 113, 130, 134
Aceramic Hacilar 70, 85, 112, 127
Acheulean 39
Acigol 76, 166
Acoma 197, 199
Adams 11, 29, 44, 69, 102, 103, 198
Adiyaman 74
administration 28, 30, 31, 117
adytum 137
Aegean immigration 45
aesthetics 9, 195, 196, 307
Africa 22, 75, 142
age 109, 273, 297
Ages
  Bronze Age 43, 294
  Stone Age 125
Agora 46
agricultural settlements
  farming village 82
agriculture 22, 23, 29, 30, 33, 37, 42, 44, 69, 71, 86, 91, 95, 101, 112, 132, 136, 166, 170, 189, 289

agricultural technology 91
  dry farming 85
  garden tillage 82, 85
  incipient cultivation 82
  intensified agriculture 91, 95
  irrigated agriculture 101, 103
  irrigation 95, 103, 114, 142, 180
  manos 293
  metates 293
  sedentary 29, 51, 288
Ain Mallaha 80
Akok 175
Aksaray 34, 83
Aksoy 11
Akurgal 44
Alaca Huyuk 135
Albuquerque, New Mexico 46
Aleppo 80
Alexander 17, 303
Alexander the Great 168
alienation 266
Alisar, city of 135, 136
Alkali Ridge Village 90
Alkim 42, 74, 129
Alp 138
Alta Vista 180, 209, 210
Altai mountains 46

Altman 275, 301
Altschul 117
American Indians
  Indian reservations. *See* Native Americans: Indian reservations
American Southwest 25, 28, 29, 33, 37, 46, 50, 69, 70, 72, 77, 92, 101, 110, 114, 164, 165, 187, 203, 208, 211, 214, 259, 269, 278, 291, 311
Amin 11
Amisos 176
Anabasis 168
Anasazi 1, 4, 5, 8, 22, 28, 29, 33, 35, 38, 46, 47, 48, 50, 69, 70, 72, 76, 85, 94, 96, 102, 114, 116, 118, 124, 125, 127, 141, 164, 179, 180, 182, 183, 188, 199, 200, 201, 202, 203, 205, 207, 210, 213, 214, 215, 219, 264, 277, 278, 280, 281, 288, 289, 295, 311, 312
  Kayenta Anasazi 179, 183
  Moapa Valley Anasazi 293
Anati 75
Anatolia
  Anatolian peninsula 34, 35, 39, 40, 136, 291
  central Anatolian plateau 34, 75, 85, 87, 103, 112, 166
  Greco-Anatolian 45
  southern Anatolia 74
ancestor worship 84, 113, 273, 287, 294
Ancient Lights 274
Anderson 93
Andolfato 34
Angel 104
Anglo American forces 301
Anglo American values 273
Ankara 75
Antalya, city of 74
  Antalya caves 76
Antelope House 184
anthropology 1, 9, 22, 200, 215, 264, 311
anthropomorphic shapes 129
Aoki 173
Apaches 46
Aphrodisias 46
appropriation
  collective 33, 71, 113, 270, 274
  inter-tribal mode of 72
  nature of 24
  social 14, 33, 86
Arabs 176
Archaeological Periods
  Aceramic period 83
  Basketmaker 77, 89, 90, 120
  Basketmaker III 120
  Chaco Periods 294
  McElmo Period 182
  Classic period 115
  Classic Pueblo 48, 93
  Colonial period 115
  Mesa Verde Pueblo I period 179
  Pecos 77
  Pueblo I 71, 89, 92, 95, 126, 179, 183
  Pueblo II 71, 92, 93, 126, 179
  Pueblo III 77, 140, 179, 180, 198, 199, 208
  Pueblo IV 197, 198
  Pueblo V 198, 214
  Sedentary period 115
archaeology 1, 9, 22, 199, 201
architect 20, 193, 262, 270, 284, 307
  builder/architect 22, 305
architectural product 19, 267, 284
architecture
  apartment houses 190
  architectonics 39, 83, 132
  architectural codes 20
  architectural detailing 83
  architectural techniques 82
  architecture without architects 20, 203, 262
  ceremonial architecture 69, 82, 121, 311
  construction technology 82
  institutionalized architecture 286
  military 43, 135
  Ottoman domestic architecture 260
  selfconscious 17
  specialized architecture 121, 213, 280
  terrazzo floor 83
  unselfconscious 17
  vernacular architecture 3, 7, 13, 28, 192, 198, 202, 262, 275, 311
architecture, Anasazi
  pecked rock 182
  site-unit intrusions 182
architecture, Pueblo
  pueblo to great pueblo transition 290
architecture/construction
  adobe (construction materials) 70, 89, 125, 130, 179, 180, 198
  Anatolian building features
    box walls 135
    casemate-walls 135
    compartmented ramparts 135
    corbeled technique 135
    gates 135
    posterns 135
    subterranean passages 135
  architectural aesthetics
    aesthetic forms 282
    minimalist aesthetic 195
  architectural content 195, 292

Index

architectural features 82, 85, 87, 111, 187, 209
  decorative details 169
  facade decoration 195
architectural form 27, 48, 130, 195, 196, 282, 287, 303
architectural loose parts 274
atrium 292, 296
beams 87, 106, 186, 189
beaten clay (construction materials) 134
ceremonial/religious structures 288
circulation 88, 110, 171, 191
citadels 44, 133, 136
communal areas 292
cross walls 135
doorways 85, 111, 130, 142, 180, 185, 218
duration of construction 106
fire chambers 111
flooring systems 84
foundations 80, 82, 89, 107
foundations, stone 82, 85, 130, 134, 135
houses, attached 132
interior architecture
  antechambers 89, 179
  benches 89, 94, 109, 134, 169, 179
  decorative flourishes 82, 83, 89, 109, 111
  deflectors 89, 181
  fireplace design 89, 185
  fireplaces 185
  furniture 109, 177
  platforms 105, 109, 111, 114, 135, 177, 273, 278
  sleeping ridges 185
  ventilation shaft 89, 172, 178
  wall niches 89, 90, 125
jacales 90, 93
market centers 50, 293
masonry deflectors 181
  corbeled technique 181
megaron 130, 135, 290, 292, 295
mud plaster 85
mud-brick 84, 85, 106, 109, 135
packed earth 86
passageways 88, 131
pilasters 181
plaster floors 84, 86
pole-wall construction 90
porches 186
post holes 85
puddled adobe (construction materials) 125, 142
ramadas 90, 297
retaining walls 186
rock shelter architecture 180
roof entrance 110
roof timbers 86
roofing systems 84
roofs 86, 88, 94, 110, 132, 179, 181, 202
roofs, flat 132, 195
scarcity of materials 170
space, architectural
  public/private realms 16, 260, 300
  spatial hierarchy 271, 293
  spatial ordering 260
stairways 186
stairways with traps 132
standardized bricks (construction materials) 107
standards 264
stones (construction materials) 46, 70, 80, 83, 90, 106, 135, 137, 186, 189, 195
storage bins 70, 90, 185
threshing floors 292
timber 70, 85, 111, 130, 134, 166, 170, 189, 206
turrets 132
unit of construction 105, 106, 107
white clay (construction materials) 134
windows 87, 110, 192
wood (construction materials) 31, 115, 122, 180, 202
architecture/planning
  platform mounds 115
Arel 260
Arizona 4, 47, 48, 76, 77, 90, 93, 94, 114, 178, 179, 183, 184, 185, 188, 199, 210, 212
arroyos 95
art 23, 43, 44, 46, 75, 102, 109, 207, 214, 263, 282, 286, 307
  art objects 74, 75, 109
  artistic creativity 89
  kiva ceremonial art 214
  kiva murals 207
  statuettes 109
  wall painting 74, 75, 104
arts/crafts
  ceremonial weaving 186
Asikli Huyuk 69, 83, 85, 166
Aspendus 46
Assyrians 42, 43, 45
astronomy 264
  astronomical alignments 49, 210
  celestial phenomena 264
  primitive astronomies 264
astronomy, Anasazi
  astronomical observation 125
  calendrical measurement 125
  corner windows 125
  equinoctial sunrises 125

equinoctial sunsets 182
Fajada Butte 125, 182
solstice 125, 182
sun dagger 125
Sun Temple 182, 188
Athabascans 46, 188, 197
atlatls 47
authority 263, 271, 275
centralization of power and authority 42
Aveni 264
Avla Dag 75
Aztec Ruin 179, 183

Babylon 43, 168
Babylonian state 43
baking. *See* ovens: baking
Balkans 43
ball courts 115
ball game implements 185
Bandelier 186, 188
Bandelier National Monument 35, 187, 201
bands
macrobands 70
roaming bands 42, 70, 73, 75
Banham 119
base state 204
bases
economic base 18, 101, 278
basic needs 31, 195, 271
Basketmaker 47, 48, 90
modified Basketmaker 89
Bat Cave 77
Beekman 34
Beidha 40
Belbasi cave 74
Beldibi, city of 74, 82
belief systems 30, 106, 112, 128, 165, 263
natural and supernatural forces 288
traditional belief systems 263
Benedict 75
Bering Straits 46
Berktay 33, 42, 71, 113, 136, 138
Bernal 113
Berry 89
Betancourt 122, 206
Betatakin 179, 180, 183
Beycesultan 43, 292
Bittel 136, 137, 165
Black Mesa 93
Black Sea 168, 176
Bogazkoy, city of 135, 136, 138
Bonito phase 49, 120, 179

Bonito phase architecture 116, 119
Bostanci 74, 75
Boyer 166
Braidwood 39, 70, 79, 81
Braudel 101
Brew 214
Britain 274
Ancient Lights 274
Brody 207, 210
Bronze Age. *See* Ages: Bronze Age
Brown 205
Bryan 37
builder 19, 192, 193, 194, 195, 267, 307
builder/architect 22, 305
builder/designer 193
master builders 289, 301
vernacular builder 17, 192, 193, 195
buildings
above-ground structures 89, 90
communal buildings 82
courtyards 69, 82, 85, 87, 92, 110, 113, 181
domestic buildings 82, 109
hotels 299
institutionalized building 13
masonry 48, 70, 90, 94, 106, 115, 117, 179, 184, 189, 190, 193, 296
monumental buildings 136, 137
nondomestic buildings 82, 109
public buildings 83
built form 2, 3, 4, 6, 9, 11, 14, 19, 24, 28, 29, 126, 142, 199, 259, 282, 288, 302, 303, 304, 305, 307, 308, 311, 313
Burdur 85
burials 49, 84, 85, 112, 113, 115, 119, 181, 182, 200, 202, 213, 278, 291, 296
burial customs 109, 129
high status burials 119
high-status burials 213
intramural burial 294
tombs 136
underground burial 181
butchering stations 33, 73, 80, 272, 295
Byzantines 46, 176
Byzantine art 46

Caesarea 171, 176
calendrical dating 201
Cambel 39, 70, 71, 81
Cameron 12, 34, 213
Camino Real de Chihuahua 209
camps 4, 33, 69, 73, 295
Can Hasan 90, 101, 114, 130, 134

Index

Cann 40, 76
Canyon de Chelly 184
capitalist mode of production (CMP) 23, 286
Cappadocia 2, 21, 28, 33, 34, 35, 85, 112, 164, 165, 166, 167, 168, 170, 171, 175, 176, 189, 192, 204, 269, 277, 292, 299
Cappadocia, towns of
  Avanos 194
  Avcilar 192, 194
  Derinkuyu 174, 177
  Goreme 174, 175, 176
  Goztezin 175
  Gulsehir 174, 175
  Hasakoy 174
  Ihlara 174, 176
  Kaymakli 174, 177
  Kayseri 176
  Mustafapasa 174, 194
  Nevsehir 175
  Ortahisar 175, 192, 194
  Selime 175
  Soganli 174, 176
  Taskinpasakoy 174
  Uchisar 175, 194
  Urgup 194
  Zelve 174
caretakers 123, 293
Cark In 74, 76
carrying capacity 38, 93, 181
carving 21, 77, 165, 166, 168, 173
Casas Grandes 114, 125, 140, 141, 180, 185, 198, 200, 208, 209, 211
  Paquime phase 114
Castells 103, 270
Catal Huyuk 10, 84, 86, 87, 90, 101, 102, 103, 104, 105, 107, 108, 112, 113, 120, 127, 132, 134, 135, 137, 142, 164, 219, 273, 279, 294, 312
cave dwelling 72, 77, 80, 165, 178, 179, 188, 189, 272, 278, 298
caves 2, 25, 33, 36, 40, 69, 72, 77, 80, 92, 127, 164, 171, 178, 180, 187, 188, 265, 278, 281, 287
  Antalya caves 76
  cavate towns 164, 180
  cavates 40, 72, 81, 178, 287
  cave dwellers 77
  cave kivas 186
  caverns 166
  cities in caves 127, 178, 183
  Cordova Caves 77
  marauding bands 127
  rock shelter architecture 180
  rock villages 169, 190

troglodyte settlements and communities 167, 168, 171, 178
Cayonu 69, 81, 83, 84, 85
Cebolleta Mesa 197
Central Asia 46
ceramics 47, 115, 209, 213
ceremonial leaders 18, 266, 270
  singers 262
  war priest 291
ceremonies 19, 43, 72, 262, 269, 302
  house blessing ceremonies 262
Chaco architecture
  Casa Chiquita 120, 179, 182
  Casa Rinconada 121, 124, 125, 200, 294
  Chacoan core-veneer masonry 120
  Chetro Ketl 95
  circular rooms 94, 123
  cribbed log roofs 94
  Hungo Pavi 95, 120
  Kin Bineola 95
  Kin Kletso 115, 121, 179
  masonry-lined roads 125
  Penasco Blanco 95
  plazas 123, 124, 142, 293
  Pueblo Alto 115, 121, 182, 218
  Pueblo Del Arroyo 121, 182, 218
  smokehole entryways 94
  specialized architecture 121
  Una Vida 95
  wall niches 125
  Wijiji 120
Chaco Canyon 37, 48, 94, 101, 123, 179, 180, 199, 279
Chacoan megastructures 50, 102, 115, 164. *See also* megastructures
Chaco Phenomenon 95, 102, 114, 115, 117, 120, 127, 164, 182, 203, 288, 293
  ancestral communities 119
  center-periphery relation 120
  central canyon 120, 121, 124, 280, 293
  Chaco Halo 119, 120, 123
  community storage facilities 121
  multinucleated settlements 121
  outliers 119. *See also* outliers
  public ceremonial architecture 121
  regional economic system 124
  road features 121
  satellites 49, 119
  scion communities 119
  suburbs 121
Chaco River 37
Chaco Wash 95, 120
Chacoan outliers. *See* outliers: Chacoan outlier
Chacoan regional system 117

Chacoan roads. *See* roads
Chacoan societies, theories of
  imperialist   208
  interactionist   208
  isolationist   208
Chalchihuites   140, 209, 212
Chapin Mesa   180
Chapman   279
Chemers   275, 301
Chetro Ketl   95, 115, 121, 207, 218
Chichimec Sea   5, 76, 140, 208, 209, 212, 279
Chichimeca   140, 208, 209
Chihuahua   47, 76, 125, 140, 180, 184, 185, 201, 209, 210, 311
Childe   22, 103
China, People's Republic of   197
  Gansu   173
  Henan   173
  Huang Tu Plateau   173
  Ningxia Huizu   173
  Qinghai   173
  Shaanxi   173
  Shanxi   173
  Xinjiang Uygur   173
Christian Greeks   165
Christianity   165, 169
  Christian art   46
  Christian community   171
  Christian settlements   277
  Christian theology, center of   171
Christians   165, 176
Cibola   94, 140, 218
Cifllik   76, 83, 166
cities in caves. *See* caves
city   28, 29, 30, 31, 33, 42, 102, 124, 133, 139, 275, 284. *See also* settlement
  economy   41
  fortification   24, 134, 136
civilization
  civilized societies   17
  primitive societies   17
civilizations
  Aramaean   45
  Assyrian   45
  Carian   45
  Greco-Anatolian   45
  Lycian   45
  Lydian   45
  Phoenician   45
  Phrygian   45
clans   71, 72, 106, 113, 293, 298
  clan size   105
  clan-based organization   91
  moieties   72, 181

classes   18, 20, 24, 167, 283, 300
  priestly class   29, 41, 101, 133
Cliff Canyon   181
cliff dwelling   166, 178, 183, 186, 187
cliffs   36, 37, 172, 184, 191
climate   12, 38, 92, 106, 110, 166, 170, 189, 268
  climatic cycle   264
  drought. *See also* drought
    amplitude   206
    frequency   206
    periodicity   206
  droughts, cyclical nature of   206
  erosion   34, 35, 165, 172, 185, 189, 206
  microclimatic variations   92
  rainfall   37, 91, 117, 206
  seasonal temperature fluctuations   110
  temperature variation   50, 91
  variable rainfall   117
climatic control   91
Clovis complex   47
Cochise   77
Cochiti Lake   36
codification   20, 263
cognitive framework   20, 263
Cole   22
collecting   23, 30, 72, 73, 74, 79, 85, 101, 103, 106, 113, 136
collective experience   263
Colorado   47, 48, 93, 119, 178, 188, 311
Colorado Plateau   38, 206, 207
Colorado River   48
commerce   23, 42, 125, 301
  barter   42, 101, 310
commodity   23, 133, 139, 195, 266, 268, 285
  commodification   19, 267, 285, 299, 301, 306
  commodified   15, 25, 267, 268, 285, 298
commonality   265, 274
communal
  communal storage   293
communication
  Chacoan towers   125
  communications nodes   125
  communications technology   125
  exchange of information   208
  inter-regional   211
  intra-regional   211
  reciprocal communication   270
  signaling stations   120
  visual communication   115, 120, 205
communism
  primitive communism   17, 280
community   10, 14, 31, 40, 49, 81, 87, 102, 133, 134, 265, 274, 275, 284, 300
  cenobitic communities   174

Index

communal buildings 82
  hermetic communities 174
  monastic communities 174
  religious communities 169
  secular communities 169, 194
complexity 117, 118, 200, 215
compounds 70, 73, 80, 136, 292
conditions of existence 8, 11, 22, 23, 26, 32, 39, 40, 51, 71, 79, 91, 95, 103, 104, 114, 171, 196, 208, 263, 265, 269, 271, 274, 278, 279, 299, 302, 303, 304, 308, 312, 313
  cultural 21, 282, 287, 305, 306
  environmental 22, 282, 305, 306
conflict 16, 32, 265
conquistadores 201, 209
construction 7, 9, 11, 19, 21, 25, 46, 48, 70, 73, 80, 82, 83, 84, 87, 88, 89, 95, 101, 105, 107, 111, 116, 122, 123, 169, 172, 178, 179, 181, 182, 183, 187, 189, 190, 192, 193, 196, 198, 262, 268, 269, 270, 282, 285, 289, 291, 297, 307. *See also* architecture: construction technology
  system of 107, 130
consumption 3, 10, 14, 19, 33, 40, 79, 86, 267, 271, 273, 307
  conspicuous consumption 267
content 15, 24, 32, 138, 139, 168, 195, 196, 260, 277, 281, 282, 283, 292, 295, 298, 300, 306
context 9, 11, 12, 13, 29, 50, 102, 196, 200, 216, 259, 269, 303, 311
context of placemaking 9, 259
continuity of habitation 202
contradictions 4, 11, 14, 15, 16, 22, 139, 260, 263, 264, 284, 302, 304, 312
Cooke 37
cooperation
  cooperative co-existence 72
copper 41, 43, 44, 69, 83, 115, 135, 209
  copper artifacts 83
  copper bells as luxury items 115
Cordell 37, 47, 77, 79, 89, 93, 118, 120, 178, 184, 187, 188, 198, 201, 204
Coronado 197
Cosgrove 77
courtyards 104
craftsmen 128, 193, 266
  artisan 137, 193, 282, 289, 299
  weavers 44, 128
critical view 16
  inclusive/exclusive 16
  open/closed 16, 273
  stratified/nonstratified 16
crossroads 38, 50, 96, 176
crowding 11, 274

cults
  cult centers 126
  cult symbols 109, 111
  cult-related objects 109
cultural heterogeneity 11
culture
  American Indian 201
  cultural identity 106
  cultural inappropriateness 272
  cultural matrix 266
  cultural regression 292
  cultural relativism 259, 311
  second "revolution" in human culture 103
Cumra 103
Cuneiform 44
Curtin 279
custom 39, 41, 42, 109, 129
Cyprus 40
Cyrus 168

Daly 71, 86
Dardanelles 43
Davis 188
Dean 38, 92, 124, 183, 198, 215, 216
decision process 269
  democratic 270
defense 44, 87, 88, 105, 107, 126, 131, 132, 140, 164, 186, 188, 205, 213, 280, 290
  boundary walls 121
  citadel. *See also* architecture/construction: citadels
  enemies 72, 104, 107, 110, 127, 133, 164, 190
  fire damage 104, 108
  fortified settlement 127, 133
  invaders 111
  ladders 110
  massacres 128
  merlons 132
  round stone slab 177
  stairways with traps 132
  turrets 132
dendochronology 201
  tree-ring data 50
design 14, 17, 126, 130, 138, 173, 187, 193, 195, 269, 270. *See also* urban design
determinism
  cultural 3, 18, 39, 262, 302, 313
  environmental 2, 28, 38, 39, 167, 259
Develi Dag 34
development
  stages of 33, 112, 279, 280, 288, 290, 295
DeVore 73
Di Peso 118, 125, 201, 207, 208

diachronic perspective 17
diachronic study 262
dialectics 16, 260
   dialectical contradictions 16
   family/community dialectic 299
   private/public dialectic 300
dichotomies 17, 206, 216, 260, 268
Dick 77
diet 79, 101, 104
   fats 104
   protein 51, 104
disease
   epidemic disease 205
   smallpox 214
distribution 18, 20, 72, 199, 216, 265, 303
   redistributional system 117
Dixon 40, 76
Dolni Vestonice 73
domestic functions 14, 83, 89, 123, 300
domestic life 266
domestication
   animal domestication 71, 82, 85
   animal husbandry 70, 103
   corrals 111
   plant domestication 82, 85
dormitory community 267
Dove 114
Doxtater 20, 279, 288
Doyel 114, 116, 118, 119, 123
Drager 122
drought 38, 50, 183, 198, 205, 206, 264. *See also* climate
   cyclical nature of 206
   the great drought 38, 184, 197, 206
dwelling 8, 10, 21, 36, 39, 70, 72, 166, 169, 170, 171, 173, 174, 175, 189, 192, 193, 207, 261, 264, 265, 268, 269, 270, 272, 282, 285, 287, 288, 290, 293, 299, 305
   as shelter
      hazard 264
      resource 264
   dwelling units 82, 106, 134, 175, 294
   dwelling/shrine 41
   excavated dwellings 185
   individual dwellings 82, 84, 87, 134, 172, 174
   open-front dwellings 185
   semi-subterranean dwelling 89
   traditional and underground 173
   underground and traditional
      troglodyte settlements and communities 167, 168, 171, 178

early Christian period 174
Eastern Orthodox Church 177
ecological perspective 6, 11, 13, 14
ecology
   ecological theory 259, 313
economics 8, 12, 41
economy 6, 8, 12, 13, 18, 30, 31, 43, 77, 88, 103, 108, 129, 170, 173, 194, 195, 213, 214, 288, 310. *See* Cities: city economy
   domestic 106
   economic activity 259
   economy of scarcity 173, 195
   reciprocal exchange relations 113
   redistributive exchange relations 113
   regional interaction 178
egalitarianism 201
Egypt 43, 142
Egyptian state 10, 43
Elbert 50
Eldem 196
Eliade, Mircea 114, 279
elites 44, 119, 123, 213, 214
   elite residences 119
Ellis 188, 291
empiricism
   naive 18
endogamy 71, 278
energy, conservation of
   heat gain 92
   heat loss 92, 110, 172
   solar energy 115
   thermal disadvantage 91
   thermal mass 166
   thermally advantageous pithouses 91
   ventilation, natural 172
Engels 31, 135, 139, 259
environment
   built environment 1, 6, 11, 12, 33, 113, 194, 262, 278, 286, 310, 312
   commodified environments 16, 268, 272, 285, 299
   environmental adequacy 13
   environmental control 113
   environmental management 26, 28
   ideological environment 16, 24, 262, 263, 282, 283, 305
   living and working relations/environments 24, 266, 284
   natural environment 12, 24, 167, 262, 264, 281, 282, 283, 305
   noncommodified environments 15, 16, 25, 268, 272
   residential 10
environment and behavior 274

environment/behavior studies 8
Ephesus 46
Epipaleolithic 73, 74, 75
Erciyes Dagi 34
Erencin 192
Ergani, town of 82
erosion. *See* climate: erosion
Esin 75
Estancia Basin 197
Ethnographic Atlas 91
ethnography 3, 117, 123, 201, 202, 218, 291, 293, 301, 313
  ethnographic present analogy 202, 206
ethnoscience 20, 260, 264, 302
Euler 183
Euphrates River 80
Europe 2, 22, 43, 73, 74, 75
  Central Europe 73
evolution, unilineal 201
exchange 102, 106, 118, 129, 139, 165, 194, 210, 212, 265, 268, 280, 285
  monetary exchange 19, 267
exogamous patriarchies 278
exogamy 71, 72
experiential value 13
experiment
  controlled experiment. 11
exploitation 31, 42, 43, 103, 126, 138, 139, 265, 288, 294
eyvan 191, 192, 292, 295, 296

fact 312
Fajada Arroyo 37
families 80, 106, 107, 112, 128, 273, 278, 298, 299, 303
  family ownership 113, 295, 296
  monogamous family 130, 135
  polygamy 135
  traditional households 267
family
  extended 19, 128, 217, 301, 303
  nuclear 19, 91, 217, 218, 264, 266, 274, 287, 288, 301, 303
  structure
    monogamous nucleated family 90
    polygamously extended household 90
famine 118
Faris 138
Fertile Crescent 40, 51, 70, 90, 91, 126
Festinger 284
feudal mode of production (FMP)
  bureaucrats 137

  centralized authority 112, 167
  dignitaries 137
  kings 137, 138
  noblemen 137
  ordinary citizens 137
  princes 44, 138
feudalism 22, 194, 278, 280
  protofeudalism 45, 135, 139
Fewkes 182
Fewkes Canyon 124, 181
firepits 89, 122
fish 104
  fish bones 74, 104
Fisher 115
fishing 74, 104, 129
Fitch 11
flexibility 13, 274
flooding 37, 106
  flood water 95
  water runoff 95
Folsom 77
foodstuffs
  cereals 101, 104
  corn 79, 291
  grain 70, 75, 80, 135
  maize 288
forces
  productive forces 287
Ford 122
form 15, 24, 28, 32, 139, 168, 179, 195, 196, 260, 264, 277, 281, 282, 283, 284, 295, 303, 306
  built form 288
form/content
  tree diagram 261
form/content dialectic 260, 277
formal 3, 11, 27, 260, 304
fortification 24, 44, 95, 126, 132, 133, 134, 135, 136, 140, 141, 164, 199, 290, 299
fortress 44, 130, 134, 164
Foster 211
Four Corners 24, 48
France 197
  Blois 173
  Cher 173
  Haute Isle 173
  La Roche Guyon 173
  Langeais 173
  Loir 173
  Loire 173
  Longue 173
  Rhone 173
  Seine 173
  Vouvray 173
France, early settlements

Barry 173
Bouches-du-Rhone 173
Bourre 173
Brissac 173
Cadenet 173
Cales 173
Correze 173
Cotignac 173
Cumeray 173
Dordogne 173
Doue 173
Gennes 173
Jonas 173
La Madeleine 173
La Roque-Saint-Christophe 173
Lamouroux 173
Le Baux 173
Le Roches 173
LesBeaumettes 173
Maine et Loire 173
Montreuil 173
Perriers 173
Puy de Dome 173
Rochemenier 173
Tourettes 173
Troo 173
Vaucluse 173
Villaines 173
Villercroze 173
Frazer 1
French 87, 113, 134
Frijoles Canyon 35, 36, 164, 186
Frisbie 113, 213
fuel 123
   firewood 93, 188, 206
   wood 31, 115, 122, 189
function 9, 11, 28, 42, 43, 49, 92, 105, 119, 123, 133, 197, 212, 216, 260, 265, 266, 281, 284, 292, 300
Gadsden Purchase 212
Gaspar Perez De Villagra 214
gateway communities 49
Gauvain 275
Gebhardt 15, 16, 309
gecekondu 271
Gelb 45
gender/sex 33, 80, 106, 109, 273, 278, 297
   fertility 109
   phallic symbols 109
geologic periods
   Cenozoic 35
   Holocene 35
   Miocene 34
   Oligocene 34

Pleistocene 35
Pliocene 35
Quaternary 35
Tertiary 34, 35
geology
   pumice stone 189, 196
   talus 37, 186
   tuff 35, 36, 178, 184
   tuffaceous rock 35, 168, 190
   volcanic eruptions 184
   volcanic tuff 184
Gila River 77, 207
Gillespie 280
Gilman 91, 93, 295
Giovannini 166, 167, 170, 174
Gladwin 188, 205
Glassie 271
global concepts 24, 260, 276, 277, 281, 309
Godelier 28, 133, 138, 139
Goetze 44, 167
Golany 166, 173
Grant 184
grazing permits 273
great houses 37, 106, 115, 124, 213, 217, 289, 291, 293, 297, 299, 301
great pueblos 115
Greece 43, 45, 168
   Greco-Anatolian 45
   Greek 46, 165, 168
   Hellenistic 45
   Hellenistic period 292
grinding rooms 92
Grondzik 166
grottoes 166, 173
Guasave 210
Guevara Sanchez 180
Gumerman 77, 93, 183, 198, 201, 215
Gurcay 174, 176
Gurney 43, 45, 137, 167

Haas 205
Habermas 16
Hacilar 45, 90, 101, 113, 127, 128, 129, 132, 134, 137, 164, 194, 277, 290, 292
   Aceramic Hacilar 127
Hacilar I 130, 131, 132, 133
Hacilar II 130
Hakataya 114
Halys 176
Hammond 139
hans 171
Hantman 205
Harvey 270, 295, 305, 309
Hasan Dagi 34

Index

Hatay, city of 74
Hatti 44
Hattians 43, 134
Hattus, city of 135, 136, 138
Haury 77, 114, 211
hautezziyas 137
Hayes 48, 115, 118, 122, 179, 181
hazards, natural 106, 107
Hazer 166, 175
hearths 80, 87, 88, 92, 111, 121, 130, 134, 179, 278, 294
Heiken 36
Helbaek 103
Herodotus 168
Hewett 36, 185, 188, 205
Hibben 47, 207
Hierapolis 46
hierarchies 30, 31, 109, 114, 215, 216, 219, 269, 271, 293, 308
 hierarchical order 105, 108, 196, 305
 nested hierarchy 275
 social hierarchy 167, 181, 271
 spatial hierarchy 271, 293
 status differentiation 113
 status relations
  egalitarian 113
Hindess 18
hinterland 30, 42, 69, 126, 133, 194
Hirst 18
Hirth 49
Hispanic influence 301
historical materialism 4, 8
Hitchcock 50
Hittites 42, 43, 45, 136, 138, 167, 296
 Hittite cities 135, 136, 138, 299
 Neo-Hittite 45
Hohokam 47, 114, 116, 185, 207, 209, 210
home 10, 37, 70, 165, 169, 170, 184, 272, 282, 283, 285, 287, 309. *See also* houses
home ranges 73
Homo Sapiens 72
 Homo Neanderthalensis 72
Hopi 48, 197
Hosta Butte 116, 119
house decorations 19
houses 10, 34, 79, 80, 84, 85, 86, 90, 94, 101, 104, 105, 110, 111, 112, 127, 129, 130, 137, 168, 185, 186, 191, 265, 269, 274, 275, 285, 287, 298, 300, 301, 303
houses and homes
 attached dwelling units 134
 domestic units 123
 individualization of the dwelling 137
 Irish country houses 271

Ottoman domestic architecture 260
Ottoman house types 260
outhouses 272
rectangular houses 90
room blocks 90
row houses 85, 130, 278
traditional households 267
Virginian country houses 271
Howe 73, 79
hunting 19, 23, 30, 40, 47, 69, 70, 71, 72, 73, 74, 75, 81, 82, 86, 95, 101, 103, 129, 164, 272, 278, 280, 288
hunting and gathering 19, 23, 40, 47, 70, 72, 91, 95, 280, 288
 food collecting 23, 72, 74, 79, 103
 mammoth killers 73
hunting and gathering societies
 hunter's village 86
Huo 178
Hurrians 45
huts. *See* shelter
 circular huts 90, 91

Ice Age 25, 28, 33
iconoclasts 177
identity 13, 272, 273, 283, 298
 individual/family 25, 193, 272, 274, 298
 social 25, 106, 193, 272, 274, 298, 299
ideological base 71, 263
ideology 12, 15, 26, 32, 41, 113, 195, 263, 278, 282, 283, 308
 ideological structure 72, 201
 ideology of descent 278
 ideology of magic 72
 totemic ideology 72, 113, 278
Igdeli Cesme 76, 166
industry
 industrial production 44
 metal industry 43
 metallurgy 43, 83, 136
 metalworking 44
information, transmission of 92
 food information network 92
insulae 137
intensive collecting 82
internal strife 205
Ionia 45
irrigation 95, 103, 114, 142, 180
 canals 95
 check dams 95
 ditches 95
 irrigated agriculture 101, 103

Irwin-Williams   124, 183
Islam   46, 194
  Muslims   195
Isleta pueblo   291
Israel   80
Italy
  Avola Vecchia Huet   173
  Italian hill town   119
  Sicily   173

Jacobs   30, 42
Jemez mountains   35
Jennings   183
Jericho   40
Jews   195
Jones   179
Jorde   50, 206
journalism   15
Judd   116, 122
Judge   49, 115, 117, 216

kabuti   137
kachina cult   214
Kanes   43, 44
Kanesh, city of   136
Kara In   74, 75, 76
Karaman   87
Katpatouka   168
Katpatuka   168
Katpatukya   168
Kayenta   48, 164, 179, 180, 183, 197, 204, 301
Kayenta Anasazi   179, 183
Keciboydoran Dagi   34
Kelley   118, 140, 201, 207, 208, 209, 211, 214, 264
Kiatuthlanna   90
Kidder   77, 213
Kiet Siel   179, 180, 183, 205
kin-ordered mode of production (KOMP)   5, 102, 214, 215, 277, 280
King   11
Kinishba   48
kinship lineage   71
kivas   70, 94, 123, 124, 179, 183, 218, 291, 293
  cave kivas   186
  great kivas   49, 94, 115, 211, 295
  keyhole kivas   180, 181
  kiva murals   207
  towers/great kivas   115
Kizilirmak   34, 176
Klima   73

Knowles   11, 49, 115, 181, 189
Kokten   74
Konishi   173
Konya plain, the   87, 101, 103
Kostof   165, 171
Kultepe, city of   136

La Quemada   125, 140, 209, 210, 212, 213
labor   8, 13, 19, 33, 71, 106, 133, 173, 178, 189, 193, 266, 267, 268, 269, 271, 274, 280, 281, 289, 298
  building time   107
  divisions of labor   33, 71, 86
  duration of construction   106
  forced labor   135, 138, 167
  labor intensive methods   84
  labor investment   122
  labor power   14, 21, 22, 31, 32, 71, 113, 176, 278, 294
  labor schedule   122
  labor units   71, 287
  laborers   24, 113, 137, 270, 284
  maintenance   18, 122
  necessary labor   18
  object of labor   21
  person-hours   106
  preconstruction preparation sequence   107
  production system   107
  reproduction of   18
  social labor   13
  unit of construction   105, 106, 107
  unstratified labor   91
  work life   266
Labs   166, 175
Lake Huleh   80
Lake Sugla   86
Lake Van   168
land   18, 21, 30, 31, 135, 138, 171, 173, 189, 202, 267, 271, 290, 295, 296, 299
landlords   171, 194
languages
  Akkadian   45
  Hurrian   45
  Indo-Aryan   39
  Luwian   45
  Palaic   45
  Semitic   39
  Ural-Altaic   39
Las Cuaranta Casas   180
Las Ventanas   184
Latin American values   273
law   42, 43, 274, 282

Index

English common law 274
Lee 73
Lefebvre 283
Lekson 11, 106, 115, 120, 121
Levant 75, 76, 166
Levant coast 75, 166
Linton 188, 205
Lipe 183, 205
Lister 122, 183
lithospace 175
Little Colorado valley 182
livestock 41, 171
Llano Estacado 197
Lloyd 292
logic 282, 313
Loma San Gabriel 211
Loose 49
Love 37
Lukacs 286
Lyneis 293

MacNeish 33
MacQueen 43, 44, 136, 137, 138
macrobands. See bands: macrobands
Macun Cay River 75
Magaracik 74
maize 47, 50, 89, 197, 288, 293
malachite 83
mammals 47, 51, 71
 animal husbandry 70, 103
 aurochs 104, 109
 cattle 41, 74, 85, 104, 168
 deer 74, 75, 85, 86
 dogs 86, 104
 mammal remains 74
 migration of animals 264
man-environment relations 8
management 26, 28, 30, 117, 302
Marcuse 312
markets 3, 41, 46, 50, 120, 164, 212, 294, 299
Marmara Sea 43
Marshall 49, 50, 116, 118
Martin 77
Marx 2, 4, 6, 11, 14, 16, 23, 31, 32, 259, 281, 285, 287, 289, 294, 295, 298, 303, 304
Marxist 2, 4, 7, 8, 303
masonry
 core-veneer masonry 125, 142, 181, 183
masons 269
material life 31, 101, 287
materialism
 dialectical 12, 313
 historical 4, 8

materials
 raw materials 21, 28, 31
 scarcity of 170. See also architecture/construction
Mathews 182
Mathien 76, 118, 208, 213, 288
Matmata Plateau 173
matriarchy 71
 matriarchal lineage systems 278
Matson 183, 205
Mavrucan 34
Maxwell 274
Maya 125, 141
McElmo Phase 182
McGuire 76, 118, 208, 212, 213, 214, 288
McKenna 89, 90, 182
meaning
 intended meaning 13
medicine men 18
Mediterranean littoral 72, 75, 80
Mediterranean Sea 176
megastructures 50, 101, 102, 115, 119, 164, 291, 295
Melendiz 34
Melendiz Cay 83
Melendiz Daglari 34
Mellink 44, 136, 294
Mendeleff 92
merlons 132
Mersin, town of 134, 135, 143
Mesa Verde 48, 118, 119, 164, 178, 179, 180, 200, 299, 311
Mesa Verde architecture
 Cliff Palace 119, 179, 181
mesa-top dwellers 184
Mesoamerica 1, 5, 33, 70, 76, 89, 96, 114, 118, 125, 142, 185, 200, 201, 203, 207, 208, 209, 210, 211, 213, 214, 219, 279, 290
 Mesoamerican connection 1, 115, 118, 126, 201, 207
 Mesoamerican frontier 76, 140, 203, 209
 Toltecs 140, 207, 208, 210, 311
Mesopotamia 43, 142, 279
 Mesopotamian villages 40
metals. See industry
Metzger 45, 292
Mexico 1, 33, 47, 50, 72, 114, 125, 140, 180, 189, 200, 208, 209, 210, 211, 212, 213, 295, 311
 Durango 76, 89, 141, 180, 201, 209
 northern Mexico 33, 114, 189, 203, 208, 211
 Sonora 76, 180, 201, 209, 210, 211
 Valley of 207, 211
 Zacatecas 180, 201, 209
migration 29, 38, 46, 50, 81, 92, 174, 176, 182,

203
emigration 29, 104, 108, 210
in-migrants 184, 188, 291
migratory life pattern 79
of animals 264
Mimbres 47, 198
mines 138, 182
Mississippi River 208
mode of appropriation
  inter-tribal 72
modes of production
  capitalist 23, 286
  feudal 22, 23, 135, 170, 171, 173
  kin-ordered 5, 22, 23, 102, 213, 270, 272, 274, 277, 280
  primitive communism 17, 22, 23, 270, 272, 277, 280
  prototributary 219, 271
  tributary 5, 22, 23, 124, 213, 215, 280
Mogollon 47, 77, 116, 140, 178, 210
Mogollon Mountains 182
Montezuma Valley 178
Moore 275
Moravia 73
Morgan 115, 125
Mug House 181
Mulligan 173
Mummy Lake 181
Mureybet 80
mythology 264
  creation story 264

nam.ra 138, 296. *See also* slavery
Native Americans. *See also* Pueblo Indians
  Indian reservations 267
Natufian parallels 75
natural history 264
nature 12, 26, 30, 32, 165, 166, 173, 190, 264, 281
Naumann 132, 134, 136, 137
Navajo, the 46, 49, 117, 262, 301, 303
  Navajo language 46
  singers 262
Near East 40, 41, 42, 43, 73, 75, 103
need 12, 19, 23, 30, 33, 40, 50, 80, 87, 95, 108, 140, 141, 166, 173, 189, 193, 266, 267, 272, 275, 281, 284, 290, 297, 299, 302, 304, 306
  basic needs 9
neighborhood 105, 275
Neolithic 30, 39, 40, 42, 44, 76, 85, 93, 129, 135, 292
  early Neolithic 42, 72, 134
  Protoneolithic villages 83, 108, 166

New Alto 179, 182
New Empire 45
New Mexico 1, 2, 4, 35, 47, 48, 51, 76, 77, 79, 90, 93, 94, 95, 102, 115, 116, 178, 184, 187, 188, 198, 210
  Albuquerque 47
  Santa Fe 182, 209
  Tularosa 77
Nice, France 34
Nicholas 114
nomadism
  nomadic 71, 82, 199, 204, 209
  semi-nomadic 71, 91, 205, 208
  semi-nomadism 93
nondomestic functions 89
normative behavior 20
North America 22, 24, 29, 33, 51, 91, 207, 210, 281, 288
Novotny 49

Oasis America 76, 180, 210
Obenauf 298
object of labor 33, 266, 284, 289
objective 15, 27, 273, 298, 299, 300, 305, 306
obsidian 31, 40, 41, 74, 76, 83, 166
  obsidian trade 41, 96, 133
O'Flynn 115
Okuzlu In 74, 76
O'Laughlin 79
Olmec 211
Onur 190
open sites 14, 79, 272
open-air sites 69, 73, 75, 80
Orlin 40, 45, 136
Ortiz 179, 217, 279
Otowi 36
Ottoman Turks 46
outhouses 272
outliers 49, 50, 115, 119, 120, 142, 179, 183, 280
  Chacoan outlier 117
ovens 85, 87, 110, 111, 191, 278
  baking 110, 111
  bread ovens 111
  domed baking area 111
owner 194, 265, 267, 285, 299
ownership 15, 25, 29, 31, 84, 193, 260, 267, 272, 294, 295, 296
  collective 113, 193
  private 41
Ozguc 41, 43, 44, 45, 136, 137
Ozkan 13, 190

Pailes 51, 96, 118, 200, 209, 212, 213, 215
Pajarito Plateau 2, 26, 36, 180, 184, 185, 197, 204
palaces 10, 19, 41, 42, 44, 136, 139, 171, 290, 300, 302
palaeontology 259
Palanli, city of 74
Paleo-Indians 46, 77, 278
Paleolithic 39, 42, 71, 74
  late Paleolithic 40, 72
Palestine 74
Paquime 114, 180, 311
Parekh 16, 313
Parsons 205
participation 13, 260, 269, 270, 289
  dialectical participation 270
  meaningful participation 270
  nonparticipation 25, 289
Pasquare 34
pastoralism 23, 71, 86, 113, 279
patriarchy 71, 72
Pecos River 48, 197
Pecos village 197
Penasco Blanco 95, 117, 120
perception 11, 12, 30, 281, 283, 308
Perge 46
periphery 17, 126, 129, 212
Perkins 71, 86, 104
Perrot, Jean 80
Persians 45, 165, 168, 176
  Persian throne 168
person-hours (PH) 106
person/environment relations 8, 17, 259
Peter 171
petroglyphs 74
photography, aerial 49, 114, 117, 181
Piaget 4
Pierson 122
Pine Lawn Valley 79
pithouses 70, 79, 89, 90, 93, 94, 179, 288, 292, 295, 299, 301
  pithouse-to-pueblo transition 91, 93
placemaking 1, 6, 7, 9, 10, 11, 16, 17, 21, 29, 70, 73, 81, 102, 110, 138, 192, 194, 199, 215, 259, 263, 269, 277, 281, 304, 305, 311
  composite placemaking 196
  definition of 1
  instrumentalist conception of 263
  traditional means of 304
placemaking activity 8, 9, 11, 15, 18, 19, 23, 27, 38, 39, 40, 74, 82, 84, 171, 175, 259, 267, 278, 282, 289, 304, 305, 309, 310
planning 1, 7, 9, 14, 88, 105, 107, 115, 129, 131, 134, 137, 172, 173, 181, 183, 213, 217, 291
  master plan 49, 107, 108

site planner 301
urban planning 115
plazas 123, 124, 142, 198, 275, 293
pochteca 200, 208, 211, 212, 279
Polanyi 164
polar coordinates 262
Polgar 113, 213, 280, 294
political organization/systems 12
  cacique 291
  political domain 265
  town chief 291
Pontic Steppe 43
population 38, 101, 102, 104, 105, 106, 108, 113, 117, 121, 124, 127, 138, 176, 179, 187, 194, 197, 217, 278
  composition of
    elderly 18, 107, 109
  decline 204
  density 91, 121
  shift 204
potreros 36
pottery 48, 74, 75, 111, 115, 129, 132, 135, 198
pottery kilns 111
Powell 51, 184, 202
power
  centralization of power and authority 42
  secular 263
Powers 117, 118, 119, 124, 280
praxis 10, 274, 308, 312, 313
pre-capitalist societies 285, 286
pre-Columbian contact 208
preliterate societies 3, 6, 8, 22, 26, 203, 278
Priene 292
priests 18, 112, 113, 114, 124, 138, 209
primitive communist mode of production (PCMP) 23, 33, 130, 277, 282, 287, 300
privacy
  private spaces 88, 301
private ownership 134, 138, 193, 194, 265, 270, 278, 295, 296
production
  agricultural production 30, 50, 93, 95, 288, 290
  collective labor production 20
  forces of 43, 71, 278, 289
  industrial production 44
  instruments of production 21, 28, 298
  means of 7, 14, 18, 21, 31, 32, 136, 194, 265, 270, 286, 289, 294, 300, 304
  production group 106
  relations 9, 14, 18, 20, 21, 31, 32, 86, 135, 264, 265, 278, 282, 283, 303, 304, 313
  rural production 30, 32
  unit of 18, 90, 278
productive forces 9, 11, 14, 18, 21, 28, 29, 31, 32,

139, 193, 287, 291, 294, 298, 300, 304, 305
property   29, 90, 105, 113, 137, 193, 264, 265, 272, 275, 283, 287, 300
  collective   15
  private property   264, 266, 275, 300
property relations   11, 303, 304, 305, 306
protofeudal   23, 136, 271, 287, 300
psychology   1, 200, 264
public good   275
public/private continuum   272
public/private separation   272
Pueblo Alto   115, 121, 182, 218
Pueblo Del Arroyo   121, 182, 218
Pueblo Indian land claims   202
Pueblo Indians   117, 184
pueblos   48, 77, 89, 91, 94, 119, 199, 205, 266, 290
  architecture
    pueblo to great pueblo transition   290
  architecture and regional planning
    towers/great kivas   115
  astronomy
    astronomical observation   115
  great pueblos   48, 50, 93, 113, 202, 203, 214, 278, 301
  periods of. *See* archaeological periods
  pithouse-to-pueblo transition   91, 93
  Pueblo Bonito   10, 48, 49, 95, 117, 121, 125, 218, 279, 297
  sedentary pueblos   206
Puye Pueblo   185, 188
pyraitheia   165

querns   86, 111
Quetzalcoatl   208, 214

rabuti   137
Ramsey   176
Raphael   196
Rapoport   17
reconstruction   24, 27, 302, 312
Redman   11
Reed   47, 212
Reeves   37
refuse mounds   70, 90
regional organization   95, 118, 181
relations
  living and working relations/environments   24, 266, 284
  socio-economic   23
  subject/object. *See* subject/object relations

religion
  clergy   137
  natural and supernatural forces   288
  religious centers   174
  religious practices   88, 264
  spiritual center   112, 132
  spiritual life   129
Renfrew   40, 76
"rent"   301
research, methods of
  faunal analysis   86
residential differentiation   271
residential segregation   271
resource base   8, 47, 51, 299
resource pooling   117
resources   12, 33, 39, 73, 82, 83, 112, 120, 122, 167, 213, 215, 268, 269, 289, 292, 294, 303
Reyman   113, 115, 119, 125, 182
Riley   208, 211
Rio Grande   36, 47, 48, 184, 187, 198, 199, 210
Rio Grande Pueblos   185, 187, 198
Road to Cibola   209
roads   49, 50, 102, 115, 117, 120, 125, 141, 209, 280, 298
  prehistoric roads   49, 280
roadway related isolated structures   120
Rocky Mountains   47, 182, 197
Rodley   167, 170, 171
Rohn   93, 124, 180, 181, 216
Romans   46, 138, 165, 168
Royal Road   176, 209
Rudofsky   11, 20, 262
rule system   20, 262, 271
Ruppe   197
Saile   116, 279
Salado   48
Salmon Ruin   183
Salt Lake   34
Salt River   48
Samandag   74
Samsun   176
Samuels   122
San Francisco River   77
San Ildefonso Pueblo   185, 187
San Juan Basin   37, 49, 95, 116, 120, 180, 187, 197, 214
San Juan Pueblo   122, 182, 185, 204
San Juan range   182
San Juan River   37, 179
Sandia Man   77
Sandia Man-Cave   46
Sando   46
Santa Clara Pueblo   185, 187, 204
Sardis   46, 168

Index

Sauer 209
Schaafsma 188, 205, 214
Schelberg 116, 119, 124, 201, 213
schlepping 86
Schroeder 114, 118, 211, 212
science 3, 14, 125, 200, 201
seasonal stations 73
sedentarism 22, 47, 70, 71, 80, 89, 187, 202, 204, 206, 207, 216, 272, 293
  sedentarization 29, 33, 71, 266
  sedentary agriculture 29, 51, 288
  sedentary pueblos 206
selective collecting 79, 81, 88
selective hunting 79, 80, 82
selfconscious architecture. *See* architecture
Seljuks 46
Senyurek 74
servants 138, 279, 303
settlement patterns
  aggregated 118, 178, 183, 206
  dispersed 118, 143, 164
  nucleated 71, 118, 124, 183, 206, 280
settlements
  cellar villages 174
  food-producing settlement 43, 85
  fortified settlement 127, 133
  hunter's village 86
  loess settlement 73
  neolithic towns 42
  preagricultural villages 278
  proto-urban 25
  squatter settlement 19, 268
  town and country 30, 31, 32, 167, 171, 290
  towns 4, 28, 29, 33, 70, 102, 115, 116, 164
  troglodyte settlements and communities 167, 168, 171, 178
  underground and traditional
    cellar villages 174
    burrows 174
  villages 4, 23, 29, 31, 33, 70, 71, 81, 90, 102, 115, 121, 133, 164, 167
settlements, Anasazi
  Abo 197
  Gran Quivira 197
  Quarai 197
Seven Cities of Cibola 209
Shabik' Eschee 90
Shalako 49
shell fish 74
Shelley 183
shelter 7, 12, 25, 26, 33, 40, 69, 72, 80, 81, 177, 262, 264, 267, 272, 281, 282, 283, 285, 287, 295, 302
  found shelter 25, 69, 72, 79, 288

huts 69, 73, 80, 90, 287
huts/shelters 80
rock shelters 40, 73, 75, 79, 179, 272
shade houses 297
Side 46
Sinagua 47
Sinclair 115
Sinop 176
sipapu 89, 179
skills 12, 13, 82, 282
skulls 84, 112, 273, 278
Slatter 206
slavery 45, 138, 167, 173, 310
  enslavement 214
  Graeco-Roman slavery 138
  master/slave relationship 138
  slaves 138, 167, 296
  war captives 138, 296
Snaketown 114
Snow 49
social injustice 270
social labor 268, 299
social organization 14, 41, 42, 79, 80, 81, 87, 88, 91, 108, 132, 137, 140, 174, 200, 265, 268, 270, 284, 294
  clan-based organization 91
  social complexity 83, 84
  socioeconomic organization 208
social praxis 274
social relations 8, 10, 31, 43, 103, 126, 131, 167, 171, 193, 195, 265, 274, 282, 286, 300, 304
  reproduction of 271
social reproduction 14, 108
social strata 167
societies
  hunting and gathering societies 164, 272
    free-wandering hunters 39, 73, 76
  transitional societies 260, 275
society
  complex society 206, 216
  oral society 263
  proto-urban 29
  social hierarchy 167, 181, 271
  social injustice 270
  social organization 102
  social reproduction 274
  social stratification 114, 135, 137, 167, 212, 271, 290
    aristocracy 43, 136, 137, 296
    bureaucrats 137
    centralized authority 112, 167
    chiefdom 116, 200
    dignitaries 137
    high status burials 119

kings 137, 138
noblemen 137
ordinary citizens 137
prestige goods 213
priestly minority 133
priests 301
princes 44, 136, 138, 171
ranked society 117
secular aristocracy 137
slavery. *See* slavery
specialization of function 119, 284
stratified level 116
town chief 291
working class 294
state-level societies 201
Society of Masons 269
sociocultural milieu 260
sociocultural systems 117
socioeconomic classes
managerial class 294
multifamily corporate groups 293
sociology 9
sociopolitical ideas 214
sociopolitical organization 5, 117
sociospatial organization 21
Sofar 115, 125, 182
solar energy 12, 115, 181, 189
Southwest. *See* American Southwest
Soygenis 89, 90
space
closed space 16, 272, 273, 296
domestic/nondomestic 108
exclusive spaces 16, 25, 273, 296, 300
hierarchically ordered space 25, 196, 271, 291, 293, 304
inclusive spaces 16, 25, 105, 272, 296, 300
nonhierarchically ordered space 271, 291, 294
open space 272, 273, 296
secular/sacred 108
social
spatial privacy 275
spatial consumption 271
spatial differentiation 93
spatial disorder 271, 292
spatial hierarchy 271, 293
spatial markers 110
spatial morphology 21
spatial organization 14, 26, 28, 32, 81, 83, 84, 87, 106, 108, 112, 127, 129, 130, 171, 172, 192, 196, 217, 283, 287, 296, 300, 305, 307
spatial complexity 172
Spain 201
specialization 32, 42, 43, 93, 106, 269, 284, 289, 297

degree of specialization 19, 289
St. Basil 171
Stalker 46
state 18, 20, 135, 200, 279, 286
statehood 42
Stea 17, 203
Stein 49, 115
Sterrett 165, 170, 190
Steward 13, 17, 311
stimulation 11
stone pavements 137
stone, slabs of 137
chipped stone 213
storage 23, 36, 69, 80, 86, 92, 95, 103, 106, 117, 134, 174, 188, 197, 266, 272, 280, 293, 297
communal storage 278
communal storage spaces 69, 90
granaries 92
basket granaries 92
bins 92
cribs 92
mealing bins 90
storage bulk 92
storage facilities 69, 80, 121, 288, 293
storage pits 80, 90, 179, 278, 301
storerooms 111, 293
Strabo 165
stress 206
structure
structural transformations 21, 305, 310
Suberde, village of 86
subject/object relations 266, 289
subject/object relationships 24
subjective 15, 27, 264, 273, 298, 299, 305, 306
subsistence 13, 18, 33, 69, 70, 188, 209, 210, 213, 281, 295, 302
subterranean
semi-subterranean 70, 80, 89
subterranean buildings 70
subterranean structures 89, 95, 135, 167, 175
Sun Temple 182, 188
Sunset Crater 48
superstructures
ideological 18, 19, 114, 262
politico-juridical 18, 20
surplus labor 18, 20, 23, 26, 31, 32, 33, 42, 82, 83, 139, 213, 263, 266, 278, 280, 286. *See also* Labor
surplus product 23, 33, 69, 70, 71, 89, 95, 113, 114, 127, 188, 265, 266, 271, 274, 278, 280, 295, 300, 302
survival 38, 47, 108, 166, 302, 311
symbolic 2, 11, 270, 281, 282, 307, 310

Index

symbols
  cult symbols 111
  vernacular symbolism 274
Syria 43, 80, 81
  Syrian steppe 73
systems
  adaptive systems 118
  redistributional system 117
  regional economic system 124
  sociocultural systems 117

Tafuri 302
tandir 191
tandir evi 191
Tarascan society 201
Taurus Mountains 72, 74, 75, 76, 86, 134
Tauruses 34
technology 6, 9, 43, 82, 83, 85, 91, 92, 103, 106, 125, 268, 269, 282, 288
  agricultural technology 91
  metallurgy 83
  pyrotechnology 83
  subsistence technology 92
  techne 282
temples 10, 19, 41, 42, 44, 136, 139, 142, 182, 188, 279, 282, 288, 290, 299, 300, 302
  Greek temples 10
  Sun Temple 182, 188
tenant 267
tent rocks 35, 36
tenure 271
Teotihuacan 211
Termessu 46
terraspace 175
territorial 11, 30, 31, 44, 76, 81, 127, 166
territoriality 11, 26, 33, 80, 274
  extended territory 92
  family ownership 113, 295, 296
  territorial domination 166
Tewa 187, 217
Texas 79, 210
  El Paso 79, 198
theft 91, 295, 310
theoretical framework 4, 24, 26, 201, 307, 312
Thomson 41, 72, 136, 294
Tigris River 82
Todd 75, 84, 138, 139, 166
Toledo-Valles caldera 36
Toll 182, 213
tools 13, 21, 28, 31, 32, 40, 72, 74, 75, 83, 103, 111, 125, 133, 135, 274, 278, 282, 289. *See also* weapons

axes 84, 86, 111, 135, 169
blade-tool 79
bone awls 84
bone tools 75
draft animals, lack of 125, 289
flakes 84
grindstones 75, 135
mano 293
metal tools 125
metates 293
pickaxes 169
sickle blades 75
stone tools 39, 72, 111
surveying instruments, absence of 125
tool making 76
wheeled vehicles, absence of 125
totems 19, 106
town and country. *See* settlements
towns 22, 29, 87, 88, 102, 164, 171, 194, 293. *See also* settlements
trade
  commercial exchange 208
  foreign traders 301
  inter-regional 211
  intra-regional 211
  obsidian trade 41, 133
  prestige goods 213
  trading node 125
trade goods
  crafts 23, 42, 102, 194, 286
  jewelry 41, 115
  luxury items 41, 115
  parrot feathers 115
  turquoise 96, 115, 182, 210, 213, 295
tradition 138, 169, 195, 260, 304
  placemaking, traditional means of 304
  traditional 304
transformations 12, 22, 39, 45, 103, 133, 138, 143, 190, 194, 214, 282, 303, 304, 308
trash middens 202
tribal organization 72
  clans 72
  moieties 72
tribal systems 105, 106
Tribalism 200
tributary mode of production (TMP). *See also* modes of production
  bureaucrats 44, 137
  centralized authority 112, 167
  dignitaries 137
  king 137, 138
  noblemen 137
  ordinary citizens 137
  princes 138

Troy 43
Tsankawi 186
Tsin Kletsin 182
Tula 201, 207, 210, 212, 213
Tunisia 173, 197
Turan 13, 268, 272
Turkey 1, 24, 259
 peoples of
  Seljuk Turks 176
 Turkish Cappadocia 26, 28
 Turkish house 192, 196
 Turkish sofa 109
 Turks 194
Tyuonyi 185, 188

U.S. Southwest 46, 180, 188, 197. *See also* American Southwest
Una Vida 95, 117
underground settlements 174. *See also* settlements: underground and traditional
 Derinkuyu 174
 traditional
  inverse megastructures 175
  underground city 177
unselfconscious architecture. *See* architecture
unstratified society 24, 102, 290
Upham 198, 200, 212, 213, 215
Ural Mountains 46
Urartians 45
Urban 175
urban design 6, 7, 28, 119, 183, 289, 291
urban environment 139
 urbanization 121
urban geography 119
urban revolution 164
 abortive cities 139
 urban life 164
 urban phenomenon 139
urbanization 11, 24, 25, 29, 101, 121, 132, 290
Ustunkok 13
Utah 48, 90, 93
 Alkali Ridge Village 90

value 312
 exchange value 7, 19, 194, 266, 267, 285, 295
 use value 10, 19, 267, 268, 272, 285, 304, 305
van Loon 80
Ventana Cave 77
ventilation 76, 87, 89, 110, 172, 178, 274
 air shafts 178
 ventilator systems 179
vernacular architecture 3, 7, 13, 28, 192, 198, 202, 262, 275, 286, 311
vernacular building 3, 13, 17, 275

villages 42, 116. *See also* settlements
 cellar villages 174
 farming village 82
 hunting villages 30
 peripheral villages 133
 preagricultural villages 278
 rock villages 169, 190
 underground burrows 174
 village aggregation 180
Vivian 77, 94, 115, 117, 120, 124, 141, 181, 182, 197, 215, 217, 218, 294, 298
volcanoes 34, 102

Wadi Fallah 75
wars 71
Washburn 118
washes. *See* specific washes
wealth 32, 41, 43, 44, 126, 128, 135, 136, 194, 196, 270, 281, 290, 295, 303, 304
weapons
 harpoons 74
 microlithic points 74
 triangles 74
 truncated blades 74
Weisberg 205
Wendorf 47
Western Pueblos 184, 197, 198
Westerveld 34
Wetherill Mesa 180
Wheatley 142
White House 184
Whitecotton 118, 212, 213
Wikse 273
Wilczynski 16
Wilford 81
Williams 36, 124, 183, 281
Williamson 115, 125
Windes 49, 115, 122, 182, 197
Wolf 11, 13, 22, 124, 200, 207
work life 266
Wormington 47, 179

Xenophon 168

yao dong 173

Zawi Chemi 82
Zeilik 48
Zelve valley 171
Zinser 115
Zucchi 34
Zuni 48, 180, 197

For Product Safety Concerns and Information please contact our EU
representative GPSR@taylorandfrancis.com
Taylor & Francis Verlag GmbH, Kaufingerstraße 24, 80331 München, Germany

www.ingramcontent.com/pod-product-compliance
Lightning Source LLC
Chambersburg PA
CBHW071229290426
44108CB00013B/1351